THE MEANING AND PURPOSE OF LIFE

The Big Jigsaw Puzzle

Brian Sadler

First published in 2011 by Mowbray Books
www.mowbraybooks.co.uk

All Biblical quotations are from the King James version.

A CIP catalogue record for this book
is available from the British Library

ISBN 978-0-9569969-5-4

Printed and bound in Great Britain by Direct POD.
(Part of Lonsdale Print Solutions Ltd.) Denington Estate, Wellingborough,
Northamptonshire, NN8 2RA
01933 233011 www.direct-pod.com

Cover design and illustrations by Richard Chetland
www.rdigital-illustration.co.uk
Indexing by Linda Haylock, BA (Hons), MSc

Dedication

This book is dedicated to all the struggling souls of humanity who are seriously looking for answers to life's meaning and purpose in this mad, mad world. Also to all the persecuted Seers, Sages, Spiritual Masters, Prophets, Mystics and Philosophers who, since the dawn of time, have tried to turn a planet of ignorance into enlightenment with noble acts of love and compassion – thus teaching Truth.

'Hear me my brother,' he said. 'There are three truths which are absolute, and which cannot be lost, but yet may remain silent for lack of speech.

The soul of man is immortal, and its future is the future of a thing whose growth and splendour has no limit.

The principle which gives life dwells in us and without us, is undying and eternally beneficent, is not heard or seen or smelt, but is perceived by the man who desires perception.

Each man is his own absolute lawgiver, the dispenser of glory or gloom to himself, the decreer of his life, his reward, his punishment.

These truths, which are as great as is life itself, are as simple as the simplest mind of man. Feed the hungry with them.'

From 'The Idyll of the White Lotus'

Contents

Illustration Contents

Acknowledgements

This book could never have been written without the cooperation of many people; therefore I would like to acknowledge the following with heartfelt thanks and the deepest gratitude.

First and foremost, I would like to thank my wife and best friend, Patricia, for her love, encouragement, support, constructive comments and enduring patience throughout the inception and incubation period of the manuscript. I would also like to take this opportunity to thank her for being such a wonderful companion on the most amazing 'journey' that I could ever have dreamed of. And my grateful thanks to *all* my family – sons, daughters-in-law and grandchildren – for their undying love, support, help and encouragement during this project. I am also indebted to all those who contributed their personal experiences in order that others may take comfort from and try to understand and cope with life's enigmas and traumas, as well as to those who offered constructive comments and encouragement; namely:

Valerie Aldridge, Ken, Deb and Fern Alexander, Anne Barrett, Veronica Bennett, Betty Bolton, Janet Bowers, Linda Bridges, Mandy Chetland, Lorna Coleman, Mike Collins, Eric Davis, Sue Dawson, Andrew and Liane Dodd, Joan Double, David Fahn, Audrey Fletcher, Ray Gaines, Bertha Gill, Bill Gill, Wendy Glen, Keith Hagar, Idetha Harvey, Virginia Harvey (U.S.A.), Doreen Hunter, June Ives, Maureen and Phil Kay, Mark Lathwell, Veronica and Stan Mather (Australia), Lin McCloughlin, James McQuitty, Brian and Sheila Meeling, Clive and Devinder McMellon, Geoff Meredith, Carolyn Mutter, Mary Norris, Sue Norton, Rosie Nutting, Eve O'Sullivan, Bill and Maureen Palmer, Ron Powell, Margaret Prentice, Margaret Pyle, Catherine Radclyffe, Syed Rahman, Jean Raza, Margaret Robinson, Natalie Sadler, Roger Sadler, Angela and Charlie Savage, Dawn Shwalbe, Betty Spencer (U.S.A), Carol and Philip Swann, David Walsh, Jan Walsh, Jeff Watts, Peggy Weber, Norman and Jean White, Beryl Whiting, Janet Whitmore, Margaret Withers, Gary Wright and Kevin and Mary Wright.

I would also like to gratefully thank Andrew Cursons, Mark Sadler, Neil Sadler (U.S.A.), Gordon Perham, Adam Fahn and David White who, at periodic intervals, gave invaluable IT support and advice – especially when computer glitches occurred! Also, my thanks to Clare Lill, Toby Lane and Clair Keenan of Direct-POD whose help and support in turning the manuscript into book form was amazing – and where nothing was too much trouble. And a big thank you to Dorothy Gregory and copywriter Nikki Zalewski who did preliminary editing and to journalist Sarah Holmes who did the final editing. My gratitude also, to Linda Haylock for her Indexing skills and to Richard Chetland for his artwork.

Over the years, it has been a great privilege and honour to have met many kind and compassionate people from all walks of life, but I would like to say a special thank you to some who no longer tread this Earth but who changed and enriched my life. They are: Alan Chantrey and Derek Markwell, who taught me the discipline and necessity of accurate mediumship; Michael Gardner-Jones (Mike) for his friendship, kindness, sense of humour and teaching the art of meditation and spiritual healing; to Vera Gardner-Jones for her love and compassion to all who needed comforting and healing, be they human or animal; to Idetha Harvey who gave selflessly to those who had lost hope, and to Fred G, for being the perfect role model in humility as well as an endearing companion on the 'Pathway'.

My eternal gratitude to our wonderful Chinese friend, mentor and spiritual guide – known to us as 'Laughing Boy' – for his spiritual strength, love, support and guidance over the past 30 years, and not forgetting his infectious and uplifting laughter. Also, to our other spiritual guides who have given so much love, support, encouragement and protection to Patricia and I over the years. I will also be forever indebted to the late Dr Paul Brunton whose profound writings on spiritual philosophy have been a source of inspiration and encouragement for nearly four decades.

So many of you gave advice and support during the writing of this book, and should I have inadvertently forgotten anybody, please forgive me. You know who you are, so please accept my grateful thanks.

Finally, I would like to acknowledge and thank the following for their permission to quote from copyrighted material:

The Human Givens Institute for excerpts from *How to Lift Depression Fast* by Joe Griffin & Ivan Tyrrell (www.hgi.org.uk)
James McQuitty for excerpts from *Religion: Man's Insult to God.*
Veronica Bennett for excerpts from *Practical Palmistry* by David Brandon-Jones.
Gwen and Alf Byrne for permission to include the materialisation story of their son Russell.
Richard Wilkins for permission to quote: *'Death is merely a more advanced form of living.'* (The Ministry of Inspiration Ltd. www.theministryofinspiration.com).
Mark Macy (U.S.A.) for excerpts from *Miracles in the Storm* (www.worlditc.org).
Credence Publications for excerpts from *Health Wars* by Philip Day.
The Paul Brunton Philosophical Foundation (U.S.A.) for excerpts from *Discover Yourself* and *The Secret Path* by Paul Brunton (www.paulbrunton.org).
Martin Nathanael for excerpts from *LIFE beyond DEATH.*
Willis Meek (U.S.A.) for permission to include George Meek's personal message.
'The Seeker' Publications for the quotation: *'We are all seekers in the quest for truth'.* (www.directeddaydreams.co.uk).
Peter Wakeham for excerpts from his letter in *The Seeker* (Vol. 3, No. 2).

From the book *Living with the Himalayan Masters* by Swami Rama. Copyright 1978 by The Himalayan International Institute of Yoga Science and Philosophy of the U.S.A. Reprinted with permission of Himalayan Institute Press (1-800-822-4547, www.himalayaninstitute.org)
Buddha Maitreya (Koji Takeuchi) for excerpts from the *'Pureland'* Meditation Centre literature (www.buddhamaitreya.co.uk)
Hay House (UK) for excerpts from *Spirit Messenger* by Gordon Smith (www.hayhouse.co.uk).

Foreword

As a child, like most children, I was naturally curious. Always wanting to know, why? What? Where? When? How? Natural curiosity was one of the driving motives that drew me towards mathematics and science, and hence a fledgling career in engineering. Engineering, by default, leads one to become inquisitive to seek solutions to complex problems. Thus, as a professional engineer, it seemed only right and proper that I should seek scientific answers and explanations to the somewhat less obvious questions that life seemed to pose.

Even from an early age it was difficult for me to accept what I was told unless it had foundation in fact and was provable to my satisfaction. Perhaps it was just stubbornness on my part, but as I grew up it struck me how dogmatic organised religion seemed to be, and that as a freethinking person, to accept the imposition of dogma as fact could not be right.

Thus my quest began as a deep and impenetrable yearning to know the meaning to life. Why were we born? Why did we die? What happened after we died? Why did we need religion? And a thousand other such questions.

In 1984, at the age of 23, I left home to find my pathway and savour the freedom of decision of mind, body and spirit that I yearned for. Within days of starting in the design office of a company in Bedfordshire, I met the most curious and enigmatic man. Charming, affable and happy, and willing to talk about the strange book he was reading during his lunch break.

With so many questions to ask, and seeking so many answers, might this man be able to assist me in my quest? In short, the answer was a resounding yes. Like all great teachers he showed boundless enthusiasm and patience, but most importantly, he taught me to investigate, research, and think for myself and, in so doing, he freed the shackles of my mind!

And the mysterious man in question? Need you ask? Many of us are lucky enough to meet one person during a lifetime that has the vision and wisdom to change the way we think forever, and hence change our lives for the better. For me, that person, a fellow engineer and freethinker, is the author of this book.

As complex as our lives may appear, the answer to the question, 'What is the meaning and purpose of life?' is not as overwhelming as it might seem. The knowledge this book will provide is based on a lifetime of learning by the author. It covers the reality of material life, and the experiences, good, bad and indifferent of a multitude of people from all walks of life. The common denominator that unites these individuals is a desire, often through great personal hardship and adversity, to seek answers to life's seemingly unfathomable questions.

I put it to you that this book offers no finer place to start that journey yourself. Whether you are a novice, or ardent seeker of truth, you will experience the full gambit of emotions. But above all, it is offered to you in the spirit of love and humility so that you can take the first steps on the pathway to understanding The Meaning and Purpose of Life.

Andrew Dodd – Sandy Hills beach, Galloway – June 2011

Introduction

Never utter these words: 'I do not know this therefore it is false.'
One must study to know; know to understand; understand to judge.
Apothegm of Narada

What you are about to read is the result of countless requests for acceptable answers from people that have, for many different reasons, cried buckets of tears when their lives were suddenly turned upside down and changed forever, causing them to question the futility of life.

It is a truism that when everything is 'hunky-dory' and we are having a good time, most of us never care to think too deeply about life. But when tragedy strikes, taking the ground from under our feet and plunging us into the depths of grief and despair, we are shaken out of our complacency. 'Why me?' or 'Why has this happened to us?' have been voiced numerous times whilst witnessing the sense of hopelessness and tears in their eyes. All I can say is, their tears have not been in vain, for they have driven me even harder to find the answers, not just for myself, but for all who cry tears of grief.

Those who have gone through such traumas are, without doubt, changed people. Some think life is cruel, godless and pointless. Fortunately, after the initial shock, the majority are often left with a refined humility, a higher standard of integrity, a deeper thinking frame of mind and a greater love and respect for life and all living things. But equally important, they are now ready to *listen*! We may feel that life takes from us at times, but it always leaves something in return if we have the courage to recognise it.

In honouring the many requests for answers, this book is part of that promise. It is also my endeavour to help others who find life hard going or are having a rough time, as well as encouraging those that have already ventured onto the pathway of unlocking some of life's 'mysteries'. I will, therefore, put into a no-nonsense layman's language the story of my search to see if life is merely a '*cosmic accident*' or whether it has any intelligent ***meaning and purpose.***

In so doing, let me say that it is not my wish or intention to change or convert anyone from their existing pathway or religion – whatever it may be – particularly if they are happy with their lot. But, during my search for life's deeper meaning, I have found very few who admit to being happy with their lot. Mouths may lie but the eyes never do! Neither am I in the convincing game. I have no desire whatsoever to convince anyone about anything. If people have to be converted or convinced about something then it is not Truth – it is dogma and brainwashing. There are so many sincere people who *want* to investigate and understand the philosophy of life, and they are the ones to whom I devote time and energy.

You will find the word Truth mentioned in many chapters, and in searching for life's answers I became what is known as a 'Seeker of Truth'. I wanted the truth, the whole truth and nothing *but* the Truth, as you will see in the chapters that follow. I was not interested in opinions, faith, beliefs, myths, legends, lies, hearsay, frauds or debunkers – just knowledge based on experience and provable facts.

Experience has taught me that Truth doesn't have to be learned like other subjects. People find that it either makes sense or it doesn't, according to their degree of open-mindedness. There are many who have an in-depth understanding of such subjects, and when asked how they came upon this knowledge, nearly all replied that they had instinctively known these things, and that reading books and attending lectures had merely confirmed what they inwardly knew. Those who have eyes and ears for Truth will *always* recognise it, be it written or spoken.

There is another word that you will see time and again running through this book, rather like a theme tune in a good movie. That word is **LOVE**, and it is vital to any student of life that they fully understand this word and all its implications if life is going to make any sense at all. I know that you are a sensitive person, and that you have the ability to give and receive love in one way or another, because you would not have chosen or been given this book had it not been so.

Life, for most of us, is a roller coaster ride, with highs of happiness and lows of despair. We will be analysing some of the highs – which can be easy to cope with – but also delving into the lows that cause us so much grief, because that is when we find it hard to cope with life in a seemingly alien world. In doing so, I would warn my readers to expect a bumpy ride from time to time as we look at life in the raw – warts and all! You will also become aware that I am not one for mincing my words and prefer to call a spade a spade. If something needs to be said, then I will say it.

In various chapters you will read the personal experiences of people much like yourself. Their stories relate to the unexpected highs and lows of everyday life, some of which I am sure you will identify with. Despite my initial hesitation, I have, in some chapters, included personal details of my own life, as those who read the early manuscript felt that it would relate more to you, the reader, particularly if life has given you a hard time. Thankfully, I started on life's philosophical quest before some of destiny's arrows struck home. The little knowledge and experience I had at the time helped to soften the blows and heal some of the wounds.

Once we start to seriously question life, we realise that we have left the mainstream monotony of existence and started on an exiting journey, a quest if you like, and something inside us will not let us rest until we get satisfactory answers. All the myriad of brave souls in the past that made this journey, and the thousands today who are still making it would tell the same story and give you the same advice – namely that it is not an easy journey. Disappointment and heartache can often be companions on our pathway since there are many 'minefields', booby traps, false trails, cults, sects, superstitions, blind alleys and false prophets en route for even the most intrepid traveller to overcome. In that respect, I humbly offer my experience, advice and guidance for would-be seekers.

We should also be wary of the gullibility of believing everything that we read and hear without checking the information, because we *want* to believe it – whether it is truth, myth or lies. This can cause many to get lost in a fog of confusion and contradiction and fall by the wayside. Conversely, we can also observe the closed minds of highly sceptical materialists that dismiss everything as rubbish and, as a consequence, throw the baby out with the bath water! It's very easy to ridicule or scoff at something that we don't understand, but, as I will repeat as often as necessary, ***criticism without investigation is the highest form of ignorance***. And, as we will see, the truth about life and death is there for investigation.

As a Design Engineer for much of my working life, it was initially with an engineering and scientific logic that I approached my quest for life's answers. So on a need to know basis with an open mind and a mild degree of scepticism, I started to investigate life – just like a piece of machinery – to see how it worked. I then made *myself* a promise, that if what I found made sense and gave plausible answers to my questions, I would devote the rest of my life to the quest. If, on the other hand, I couldn't come to any definite conclusions, then I would pack it all in and call it a day. I was not the sort of person to waste a life chasing a dream or living a lie – I had better things to do. That was 40 years ago!

Over those years, I travelled thousands of miles, talked to thousands of people from all over the world whilst attending or giving lectures on metaphysical and esoteric subjects, and read countless books on all related topics. But most important of all, at periodic intervals on my journey, I have been fortunate enough to have had many psychic and mystical experiences, both subjective and objective in nature, to give me personal evidence and proof. It is from the latter that most of this book is based.

There is another quality that sincere seekers are advised to have, and that is a good sense of humour. I appreciate that there may be times when you feel more like crying than laughing, but life has taught me that a sense of humour in this crazy world is essential if we are to maintain any form of sanity and resemblance of happiness. One of the philosophical 'tricks of the trade' is not to take this world of false values too seriously, which I trust you will appreciate as our quest unfolds.

What is *not* advisable 'baggage' on our quest is egotistical arrogance and the harbouring of preconceived ideas and prejudices about people and things, or life will always remain a mystery and appear to be against us every step of the way. Nature can be very patient, but she will eventually, sooner or later, tame our egos and make us earn humility the hard way. Few of us are immune – even the high and mighty eventually fall. I have seen the most hardened amongst us break down and cry with grief when personal tragedy struck. The choice is always ours of course, but the moral of the story is, that if we are not prepared to investigate the philosophy of life and learn its laws, then we shouldn't complain when it hits us hard!

Incidentally, I cannot think of a better subject to study, as it is certainly one of the most rewarding. When you become a student of life and understand the philosophy behind it, you will find that the Truth really *can* set you free. Free from the suffocating complacency and trivia that continually clog the minds of the masses that the media often refers to as 'Mr and Mrs Average'.

I have often thought of life as a gigantic jigsaw puzzle where the completed picture has been shrouded from our physical senses. If we examine any single piece of a jigsaw it won't make much sense or give us any idea of the whole picture. But if we find and clip interlocking pieces together, then the whole scenario gets more interesting and certainly a lot clearer. That is my advice to those who see life's comedies and tragedies as seemingly unrelated and pointless incidents. So at the end of each chapter I will offer you a piece of life's jigsaw and eventually you will see an emerging picture.

With this philosophy in mind, come with me, and we will critically examine some of these pieces and put a sensible amount of the puzzle together. Hopefully, it will encourage you to look at life from a different perspective, be more enlightened, deeper thinking, happier, healthier and have a greater understanding of life's meaning and purpose.

The truth which makes men free is for the most
part the truth which men prefer not to hear.
Herbert Agar 1897 – 1980 (American author and poet)

If any man can convince me that I do not think aright,
gladly will I change, for I search after truth,
by which man never was harmed.
Marcus Aurelius 121 – 180 AD (Roman emperor and philosopher)

1 *Life* – *The Continuing Drama*

To live is the rarest thing in the world.
Most people exist, that is all.
Oscar Wilde 1854-1900 (Irish playwright and poet)

Many years ago a wise and learned elderly gentleman advised me to be an impartial observer of life. 'Look and listen,' he said very softly, 'look at what people do, and listen to what people say.' He paused awhile before continuing in the same gentle voice. 'After a few years of observation you will understand the reasons for human misery and suffering.' I took his advice seriously, not just because I respected him as a person, but because I sincerely wanted to know the reasons for human misery and suffering.

So, over the following years I did just that, and observed people and life everywhere I went – In the supermarkets and the offices, on committees and at parties, in the trains and on planes, on the roads and the high streets, and at home and abroad. And do you know what? He was right, and I would like to thank all the thousands of men, women and children who unwittingly showed me the reasons why. Today, I am still an observer – and the reasons are still the same!

If you have ever wondered why there is so much turmoil and suffering on this planet, I will reveal the reasons to you as the quest unfolds because it is a very important piece of the jigsaw. To help you find the answers *before* my revelations, I would like to set you a little task and remind you of it in a later chapter. Let yourself be an impartial observer of people and life say, just for one month, be it at work or play. Have *no* opinions or prejudices – just *observe*! If it helps, you could always imagine you are a visitor from another planet that has come to observe and report on the human race and life here on Earth.

Everyone, be they young or old, wise or foolish, has something to teach us, and I have always remembered the old sayings: 'Those who stand before me are my teachers', and 'The wise man always learns from the fool, but the fool never learns from the wise man'.

Now, here comes the crunch. Whilst you are being an observer of life, may I ask that you also be an observer of *yourself?* Observe your own *thoughts* and *actions* for a while. They may well surprise you, and you may even learn something about yourself and life's enigmas in the process!

The unexamined life is not worth living.
Socrates 469 – 399BC (Greek philosopher)

Life in the Raw

There are 7 billion of us – increasing at the rate of 100 million every year – all living on a tiny dying ball of rock called Earth, which according to the latest, scientific, geological and astronomical studies is at least 4,500 million years old. It is hurtling through space at 67,000 miles an hour, and spinning on its inclined axis at 1,000 miles an hour on an elliptical orbit that takes approximately 25,920 years to complete. All this is taking place in our little Galaxy we call the Milky Way, which in itself is billions of miles across, this in turn is also revolving within the Cosmos which houses billions of other galaxies, that are billions of light years apart!

This is the setting in which we play out the drama of everyday life, and I have often wondered how many of us are aware of our galactic heritage. Have you ever stared into a night sky full of glistening stars and wondered whether we are the only life forms in such a vast and indescribable void? Many have stated that it sure puts earthly problems into perspective!

So, let us stand back and scrutinise our predicament down here – warts and all. Let us be brave enough, just for a moment, to see our world for what it is. Not what we would necessarily *like* it to be – what it actually *is* – whether we *like* what we see or whether we *don't*.

The study of history shows us that for thousands of years we have lived on a violent planet torn asunder by the ravages of Nature and the atrocities of war. The last 100 years alone has seen horrendous global carnage inflicted on a very war-weary populace. Technology doesn't appear to have made us more civilised; we have merely substituted the gun for the sword and the missile for the bow and arrow. And with our atomic and chemical weapons, we now have the ability to wipe ourselves off the face of the Earth. This alone should tell us that we are far from being mature as a race and an eternity away from being civilised.

I am reminded of the time when Mahatma Gandhi, the instigator of Indian independence, visited London in 1947. A British government official showed him around and asked him what he thought of Western civilisation. With a wonderful sense of humour Gandhi replied: 'I think it's a good idea, let me know when you achieve it.' Over six decades later, many might say that we are still trying to achieve it! The mark of any civilisation (the act of being civilised) should be the way a society has compassion for, and cares for, the sick, the disabled, the old, the poor, the homeless and the hungry.

As the historian Arthur Findlay pointed out in his banned masterpiece *The*

Curse of Ignorance, the human race has, for centuries, been manipulated and controlled by governments, religions and banking establishments for clandestine vested interests. We expect such institutions to create a civilised utopia, but as we know, history abounds with bureaucratic greed, corruption and incompetence that has caused monumental disasters and created more problems than has been solved. This leaves two-thirds of the Earth's population (4.7 billion people) being classified at poverty level struggling from cradle to grave merely to survive!

I sincerely believe that banking establishments
are more dangerous than standing armies.
Thomas Jefferson 1743 – 1826 (3rd President of the USA)

Anyone who's been round the block a few times and seen a bit of life, will know the harsh lessons of a world that seems to be starved of happiness, love and peace of mind for many of its inhabitants, be they rich or poor, king or peasant. The pain and anguish of such lessons cause many to see life as pointless and want to stop the world and get off – they have genuinely had enough of life's rough games.

Any politician or businessman will tell you that our world operates on Nature's policy of 'survival of the fittest' – both mentally and physically. It is a world where the strong prey upon the weak, either as individuals, companies or countries. For like it or not, the human race is still 'animal' by nature. An 'animal' that segregates itself by nationality, colour, class, caste, wealth, politics and religion – and one that kills and tortures both its own kind and animals for gratification and gain.

With dozens of wars, skirmishes and terrorist activities going on somewhere on our tiny planet, and thousands of people the world over incarcerated and tortured every day for one reason or another, an observer would probably liken us to children squabbling and fighting in a school playground – complete with school bullies. Whilst we are engaged in such stupidity, the international project, The Square Kilometre Array (SKA) of 3,000 radio telescopes, scans the Universe seeking far flung galaxies for habitable planets. And the SETI project (Search for Extra-Terrestrial Intelligence) transmits signals and send probes into the furthest reaches of space also to search for intelligent life! Perhaps it will encourage us to cultivate more intelligence on our own planet – or perhaps I should say wisdom!

A lamp can break a 1,000 years of darkness.
Wisdom can break ten thousand years of stupidity.
Buddhist saying

Would you like to know where 'hell' is? Ask a civilian during wartime bombing raids, a soldier in the midst of a bloody conflict or, perhaps, someone who is searching the rubble for their lost loved ones after an earthquake. I'm pretty sure that survivors of wartime concentration camps would also tell you, in no uncertain terms, where 'hell' is. Would you like to know where 'heaven' is? Ask a loving couple on their wedding day, a holidaymaker on a paradise island or a young couple having their much longed for baby. It takes little imagination to realise that we are making our own 'heaven' and 'hell' here on Earth, which can make life seem like a lottery – an unpredictable game of chance with winners and losers. Some seem to have the Midas touch and everything they do brings success, whilst others seem fated with bad luck and go from one disaster to another. Which all goes to make our jigsaw puzzle of life very interesting!

We would have to walk around with our eyes shut or wear blinkers to be unaware of our planet's problems, but some may find the truth uncomfortable and adopt the 'ignorance is bliss' or the 'I don't want to get involved' stance. It will be difficult to improve our lot here – or understand life's true purpose – unless we become aware of our faults and failures and try to eradicate them.

The vast majority of the human race seems to know nothing about who they really are or why they are here and what the purpose of life is. Many never think of questioning, and go to their graves as ignorant about life as the day they were born. Could you imagine yourself doing a menial task without questioning as to why you are doing it or what the end product was for? How many of us *really* know and understand ourselves? And if we don't understand ourselves, then how will we ever understand others? And if we don't understand others we will never be at peace with them or within ourselves – and most certainly we will never understand life.

> It is admiral to consider how many millions of people come into and go out of the world, ignorant of themselves and the world they have lived in.
> *William Penn 1644 – 1718 (English Quaker)*

The psychoanalyst's couches are full of lost souls trying to find their own identity, and establish where they fit into this 'fruit cake' world, with many wondering what drug, sexual deviation or alcoholic drink will give them the next temporary thrill to divert their minds from worldly problems.

One has only to be an observer of life for a very brief while to see how many of us have peace of mind. I can tell you that very few are in possession of this luxury. The minds of our Mr and Mrs Average are continually restless and full of negative emotions, thereby spoiling today with the worries, fears and anxieties of yesterday or tomorrow.

None of this is helped by the confusing array of religions, sects, cults and gurus that claim to have the answers to humanities problems and promise us salvation and everlasting life. Amidst all this confusion many are left wondering whether there is a god or a devil, whether there is an after-life or oblivion, whether they are saints or sinners or whether life is just a big cosmic joke!

Our immature, selfish and greedy behaviour on this beautiful planet would probably make an 'alien' observer laugh hysterically in disbelief. So perhaps our essential sense of humour should teach us to laugh at ourselves and look at life as an endless soap drama – a drama that can make us both laugh and cry. And, with humility, let us not forget that Nature *always* has the last laugh!

Death smiles on us all. All we can do is smile back!
Marcus Aurelius 121 – 180AD (Roman emperor and philosopher)

Respect for Nature

As a backdrop to our drama of life we have the splendour of the natural world, with its mountains, hills, forests, lakes and rivers, all entwined with an incredible array of flora and fauna in magnificent variety. Added to these we have the beauty of indescribable sunrises, sunsets and starry nights, with music supplied by courtesy of a myriad of birdsongs, whistling winds, rustling leaves, babbling brooks, mountain streams and the breaking of ocean waves.

For centuries, Nature has been trying to give us the answers to life's questions. She whispers in our ears and puts proof before our very eyes and under our noses. But in our blind materialistic haste to achieve success, power and wealth, we have failed to 'see' and 'hear' her sublime message. Many of the problems that beset the human race have been the same for thousands of years, and unless we learn the lessons that life is trying to teach us we will be plagued with them for decades to come.

We have held Nature with the same contempt that we have had for our own kind and all the other poor unfortunate creatures that share our planet and have had to suffer our intolerance and lack of respect. Even now, in our so-called 'civilised' and more 'enlightened' world, we continue to tear our earthly home apart and are literally wrecking the 'spaceship' we live on. With our atomic waste, pesticides, nitrates, fossil fuels, plastics and a host of other toxic chemicals, we are polluting the soil, the rivers, the sea and the air that we breathe. We are decimating the rain forests (the lungs of the planet), making hundreds of animal species extinct and using the Earth's natural resources at an alarming rate. We are literally cosmic vandals!

Perhaps we came here from Mars after we wrecked it – now we are wrecking this place and *seriously* thinking of going back to Mars! Astrobiologists are already planning to terraform its surface using a series of huge biospheres.

Nature can fight back in unpredictable and terrifying ways, frequently reminding us that she is definitely the boss, so provoking her with pollution and other malpractices is surely asking for trouble – hell hath no fury like Nature scorned! We will only survive by working *with* Nature and not battling *against* it. The Earth is a living cell; it had a birth and will, like all living things, eventually have a death. In the past, many indigenous tribes affectionately called her Mother Earth. She was treated with great respect and anything taken from her was, in one way or another, always replaced. Races that understood this simple truth survived for thousands of years, whereas we will be lucky to survive the next 100 unless we mend our ways.

True wisdom consists in not departing from nature but in
moulding our conduct according to her laws and model.
Lucius Annaeus Seneca 4BC – 65AD (Roman philosopher and statesman)

Many of us have an aversion to change and tend to be creatures of habit. Feeling comfortable with the status quo, we go through the same routines every day and complain when life forces us to do something different or puts us outside our comfort zones. Nature is *continually* changing, that's why everything is in a constant state of decay and renewal. Metal rusts, wood rots, stone and bricks crumble and all living things grow old and die, ready to be recycled in the great cosmic scenario. Change drives the evolution of the Universe.

Nothing on this planet stays the same forever and we should treasure each moment because, when it's gone, it's gone! That is why we should never waste our lives, as so many do, arguing, whinging and bickering over pointless things, or fighting over a piece of land or country that 'belongs' to someone else. How can we be so petty or find life boring when there is so much *good* to be done, so many people to help and so little time? Life is brief – it is but the striking of a match in cosmic terms; and perhaps we should continually remind ourselves that *none of us has a promise of a tomorrow*!

Why do we make such hard work of life? To most of us, being born is relatively easy; dying is inevitable and as easy as falling off a log, but it's that bit in between called *living* that many of us seem to have a problem with. You wouldn't think it could be so difficult, but living a happy, loving and peaceful life seems to elude many of us. Why do we find it easier to be nasty rather than nice, and why do we find it so difficult to communicate with each other and express love?

We like to think that we are the most intelligent creatures on the planet, so why *can't* we all pull together as one race of humans, irrespective of cultural differences, colour of skin, politics or religion? After all, we are all Earthlings, aren't we? Only when we understand and put into practice the simple truths of life can we hope for a better world. And we can only have a better world when we have better people in it. And better people begin with us!

The world has enough for everyone's need, but not enough for everyone's greed.
Mahatma Gandhi 1869 – 1948 (Indian Leader)

Summary

So, amidst this continuing 'Drama of Life', are we destined for a better world? Although a relative newcomer on the evolutionary scale, the human race – in various guises – is much older than most people realise. In the cyclic rise and fall of nations, advanced civilisations have come and gone, leaving behind archaeological glimpses of their once greatness. From time to time down the centuries, as with other life forms, they have been partially wiped out by climate changes and global catastrophes with survivors starting again from first principles with garbled memories of a past heritage. 'Modern' humanity is once more like a 'rebellious teenager' at this stage of its evolution, slowly but surely waking up to its adult responsibilities and hopefully turning away from such conflicts that demean us lower than the beasts – premeditated and planned violence.

As we will see, when we look at the *Good and Evil* piece of our jigsaw, we are, at last, seeing the signs of more caring and deeper thinking people – people who *really* care about people, the welfare of animals and the state of the environment. They express concern for future generations when, due to ignorance, selfishness, corruption and greed, we leave them a legacy of mega-problems to solve.

There *is* a lot of good being achieved 'behind the scenes', and much of it never makes media headlines. Good news doesn't sell newspapers – fear does! With satellite communication, television, computers, mobile phones and air travel, the world is a much smaller and rapidly changing place. Problems occurring within countries thousands of miles away instantly become the world's problems. Hence we are now seeing millions of unsung heroes who, with a love for humanity and the natural world, volunteer to help the global unfortunates who suffer hardship and deprivation through many diverse causes, be they by the ravage of Nature or our own ignorance.

Hopefully, with a new-found wisdom, courage and compassion, nationality and racial barriers will eventually dissolve. People are people wherever they live on this planet, and most struggle to look after their families and come to terms with the everyday problems of living and dying. We can now see that all human suffering and pain is the same – we just have different ways of showing it.

As a race, we have reached one of the most exciting periods in our planet's history. We are now at major crossroads in our scientific technology and spiritual awareness, and should study the signposts very carefully before deciding which direction to take. With hindsight, we should learn from history and past mistakes or we will pay a great price for taking the wrong road. It is the choice between 'Armageddon' and 'Utopia', and those who have eyes to 'see' will notice that one signpost points to *'Ignorance, confrontation, greed, violence and disaster'*, and the other to *'Wisdom, cooperation, love, peace and happiness'*.

So, let me present you with the first piece of life's jigsaw puzzle – it is *hope*. Hope that the human race will choose the right road. Perhaps we should listen to Mother Nature now before it is too late, for she seems to be saying to the human race, 'WAKE UP!'

In the chapters that follow we will be analysing many of the above enigmas that form part of life's puzzle, but first, we will put some of our lifestyles up for scrutiny.

Only after the last tree has been cut down,
Only after the last river has been poisoned,
Only after the last fish has been caught,
Only then will you find that money cannot be eaten.
Native American prophesy

There is no hope without fear, and no fear without hope.
Baruch Spinoza 1632 – 1677 (Dutch philosopher)

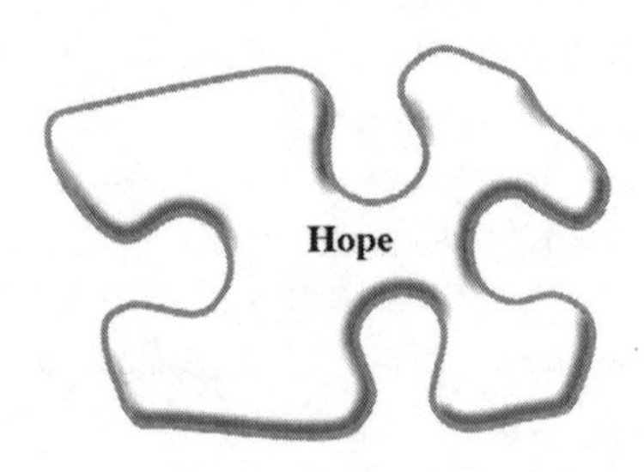

2 Health – *A Precious Gem*

With Health, everything is a source of pleasure; without
it, nothing else, whatever it may be, is enjoyable.
Arthur Schopenhauer 1788 – 1860 (German philosopher)

Watching their child undergo chemotherapy for leukaemia or other forms of cancer, is probably one of the most traumatic and emotional experiences that any parent can go through. They invariably ask such questions as, 'Why? What has our child done to deserve this?' Or, 'How can God allow this to happen?' Seeing a loved one trying to cope with any serious disease or sickness is heart wrenching. And those who have contracted one and have to live with it also ask, 'Why me? How did I get it?' – And other meaningful questions.

Forty years ago I became interested in Spiritual Healing. This eventually brought me into contact with very sick people, many of them terminally ill. This affected me emotionally and prompted many soul-searching questions, as it was the first time I had encountered those who had been given potential 'death sentences'. From then on I took a serious interest in health and wellbeing as it saddened me to observe so many sick people in our society. With full hospitals, long waiting lists and crowded doctors' surgeries, it was an indication that something was dreadfully wrong with our lifestyles. Understanding where sickness and disease fitted into Nature's plan proved vital if I was ever going to make sense of life's puzzle.

At the time, I was in my early thirties, healthy and, like most people of that age and younger, thought I was physically immortal and could eat and drink anything and get away with it. The story is different now and, being that much older and wiser, I am very particular what substances go on my body and what food and liquids go into my mouth.

When we buy a motor vehicle we read the maintenance handbook to make sure that it is serviced properly, and that we use the correct fuels and oils so that it will give us years of reliable motoring without breaking down. When it comes to looking after our own bodies it is a very different story. Our Mr and Mrs Average are inclined to put a fair degree of 'junk' into their mouths – particularly if it's called 'Chocolate Temptation' or other mouth-watering names. Being laden with sugar, salt or fat seems to be ignored. That is, until the wake-up call, when the necessity to visit the doctor's surgery informs them that their complaint is serious and requires a hospital visit for X-rays and further tests – a never ending scenario!

Many are now beginning to realise that if they wish to enjoy a long and healthy life free of prescription drugs and hospital food, then taking personal responsibility for their own health and scrutinising what they eat and drink is a necessity. Processed foods, fizzy (carbonated) drinks, excess sugar and salt, for example, become off limits – or heavily restricted. This, if coupled with being physically and mentally active – particularly as the years advance – helps to keep rigor mortis at bay for as long as possible!

If you are fit and well and come into the health conscious category, then what I have to say will be common sense, so please bear with me. Unfortunately, as health statistics prove, it is not common sense to the vast majority of us!

Where Have We Gone Wrong?

As a design engineer, I have long admired the logistics of the human body and how it has evolved and adapted to its environment over the centuries. It's an amazing and complex organism capable of living up to 120 years of useful life – as evidenced by the Hunza people in Pakistan. It has an in-built, self-repairing immune system, programmed to attack and repel thousands of viruses that invade our bodies as well as all the internal and external repair jobs it is required to do when we get injured. Our body needs the correct maintenance schedule to run efficiently and give reliable and lengthy service. The basic requirements being:

- Nutritious food and drink (for energy, cell growth, immune system and DNA and gene protection).
- A positive attitude of mind (motivational body intelligence for cells and immune system).
- The right environment (clean air to breathe).
- Regular moderate exercise (strengthens bones, muscles, heart and immune system).

If any of these factors are wrong then we invite potential health problems and a possible early demise. This means that the organism breaks down, becomes unreliable and is possibly scrapped – a condition we call 'death'.

For centuries, those who lived close to Nature and worked in harmony with it knew that certain herbs and plants brought relief or cure for every known sickness and disease. Nature's healers, such as Aloe Vera, ginger, ginseng and garlic, for example, are known to aid the immune system.

In theory, if our immune system was 100 per cent efficient we would be in peak health. Unfortunately, due to lifestyle ignorance, many of us are ticking over with a system that, at *best,* is only about 50 per cent efficient. That's why so many of us, particularly in later life, have health problems. If we *permanently* lose our health, we lose the most valuable asset we have, and our quality of life *and* that of our nearest and dearest is then seriously challenged.

Would you give up your health in exchange for a large sum of money? You would be foolish if you did. But many of us are naïvely prepared to give up our health by wrecking our immune system with the following negative traits and habits. Let me touch briefly on them and you will see what I mean.

Eating Habits: We are what we eat and drink, and if we consume the wrong food then we are playing with our mental and physical health. As a nation, we are rapidly becoming addicted to processed (manufactured) junk food, which has very little goodness in it because it has been lost during the processing. That's why it's called junk and that's why it's cheap! Much of it contains toxic chemicals (artificial flavours, colours and preservatives) that are *known* to cause asthma, eczema and hyper-activity amongst children. Surveys reveal that 33 per cent of parents are not interested in their children's nutrition, and ignorance of the damage these chemical additives can do will leave their offspring vulnerable to future health problems.

Many are artificial colourings (azo dyes) such as tartrazine (E102), quinoline yellow (E104), sunset yellow (E110), carmoisine (E122), amaranth (E123), ponceau 4R (E124), allura red (E129), which can be found in several packaged 'convenience' foods, sweets, cakes, biscuits, ice cream, jellies and even some prescription medicines!

Also suspect, are flavour enhancer monosodium glutamate (E621), preservative sodium benzoate (E211), and the artificial sweetener aspartame (E95) that is in most fizzy drinks – drinks that are known to health nutritionists as '*osteoporosis in a can*' (or bottle) as they leach calcium from our bones. *SWEET POISON: How the World's Most Popular Artificial Sweetener is Harming Us* by Janet Starr Hull will both alarm and enlighten you! Plus we have the added danger of hydrogenated vegetable oils – artificial fats known as trans-fats. These substances are *known* to have serious affects on health with many being termed *carcinogenic* (cancer and tumour forming)!

To prove a point, many schools have conducted experiments where parents were asked to cut out all foods containing the additives listed above from their children's diet. After a few weeks, teachers noticed that the children concentrated better and were more alert, and parents reported that their children slept better and had no more disruptive temper tantrums. Time and again, parents – and university scientists – are finding that when children are given good wholesome food instead of 'chemical cocktail' junk, behavioural and hyperactive problems cease, including many assessed with attention deficit hyperactivity disorder (ADHD). Such results have been described as 'miraculous'.

> It is estimated that there are about a thousand chemical substances in regular use as additives for food, only a fraction of which have been exhaustively tested for harmful effects. For the sake of what manufactures call "a longer shelf life", these poisons – as many of them unquestionably are – are pumped into our food.
> *Michael Hennessey in 'Tit Bits'*

This should cause us to question why manufacturers are allowed to put 'permitted' chemicals in their products, knowing the harm they can do – particularly to children's health – when many of them have been banned in other countries. Some of the more enlightened companies that are now putting health *before* profit, *are* aware of the harmful effects of these artificial toxic substances and gradually phasing them out of their products. For those who are *not*, perhaps sending them copies of *E for Additives* by Maurice Hanssen, listing the dangerous E-number additives in our processed foods and drinks, and *We Want Real Food* by Graham Harvey will prod their consciences! Reading the 'ingredients' list on packets and bottles – to make sure that they contain no artificial flavours, colours and preservatives – may sound like a chore, but visiting a doctor's surgery is an even bigger one!

University nutrition studies investigating the health costs of poor diets conclude that the high fat, salt and sugar content in processed foods are linked with heart disease, obesity, high blood pressure, diabetes and other degenerative diseases. Nutritionists are now aware that many serious diseases *are* diet related, and emphasise the '*eat now, pay later*' slogan. On a global scale, fast foods certainly live up to their name – they get us to the cemetery *quicker,* thus prompting many nutritionists to describe them as *'the only truly effective weapons of mass destruction'*.

Paying a little more for healthy, energy-giving foods can be the least expensive in the long run. Money saved purchasing cheap junk food will more than likely be spent later on prescription charges, as those who eat and drink junk today will probably fill the doctors' surgeries and hospital beds of tomorrow – which can only be good news for the pharmaceutical companies. They just *love* sick people, because sick people mean *big* profits!

Whilst visiting a local Residential Home, the manager confided that, unlike her elderly residents that had grown up with organic fruit and vegetables and led active lives, she feared that many of today's youngsters would never make old bones. She cited lack of exercise due to watching too much television and playing endless computer games. But her most worrying aspect was their diet of chemically laden junk food and drinks and their aversion to healthy eating.

'When the parents eat and drink junk, then what hope is there for their kids?' she remarked.

Continual over-eating can play havoc with the digestive system, damage the liver and send dangerous cell destroying free radicals (scavenger cells) on the rampage. Scientific health studies show that overeating is a major cause of obesity, degenerative diseases and premature ageing. After studying groups of centenarians, scientists concluded that it is better to eat smaller meals if we wish to live long and healthy lives. How often do we hear someone say: 'I couldn't eat another thing, I'm absolutely stuffed?' In the Western world it seems we are literally eating ourselves to death!

Alcohol: We are also drinking ourselves to death according to medical research. Apparently, we are consuming too much alcohol which, in large doses, affects the brain, destroys the liver and addiction to it kills over 22,000 people every year in the UK. Growing numbers of young people face serious health problems and early death because of heavy binge drinking which has been linked to boredom or stress caused by career pressures or family problems.

Alcoholism is a disease and a major social problem with 1 in 13 people in the UK alcohol dependant. This can be the start of a downward spiral that can split families, cause accidents, crime, domestic abuse, depression and even lead to suicide. The police and hospital Accident and Emergency departments, particularly in large cities on Friday and Saturday nights, have to deal with the badly beaten, bloodied and bruised victims and assailants involved in drunken fights and brawls. Others consume vast quantities of alcohol and stagger around the streets swearing whilst in a drunken stupor, often ending up semi-conscious laying in their own vomit – and that's called having a good time!

So, beware of saying 'I need a drink. I've had one of those days'. It can be the start of a *very* slippery slope! Maybe water is a better and safer option since our body is made up of at least 70 per cent of the stuff. Drinking water is good health therapy according to *Your Body's Many Cries for Water* by Dr F Batmangheldidj, and *Water – Pure Therapy* by Alice Kavounas.

Smoking: Common sense tells us that inhaling cigarette smoke into the lungs is neither natural nor healthy, particularly when scientists state that it contains 69 cancer causing chemicals. And yet 70 per cent of the UK's 13 million smokers are seriously trying to give up the craving for financial as well as health benefits but find themselves addicted to the nicotine. Nicotine is a proven *carcinogenic drug* that enters the blood stream via the lungs. And since blood passes through every organ in the body we can understand why, statistically, one in every two smokers will die of a smoking related disease.

And, despite the warning '**Smoking kills**' on the packets, it's estimated that, globally, cigarettes cause over five million deaths a year – including 83,000 Britons!

Scientific research has also found evidence that pregnant women who smoke, transmit a powerful cancer forming chemical to the foetus in the womb. The chemical, called NNK is a by-product of nicotine. This was found in lethal doses in the blood stream, vital organs and bone marrow of developing foetuses. It was even found in the urine of smokers' babies after birth! Researchers are convinced this evidence shows why these babies tend to develop serious illnesses as they grow up.

Passive smoking (breathing second-hand smoke) is a medically recognised health hazard, particularly for babies and children. The Royal College of Physicians found that children who are regularly exposed to cigarette smoke are more at risk of cancer, asthma, bronchitis, meningitis and cot death. Perhaps it should be classified as child abuse if they have no other choice! Only when we take the dangers of smoking and its addiction seriously, will the carnage in the name of a 'pleasure pursuit' cease.

Every year, tobacco companies need thousands of new customers for their products – the younger the better – to compensate for their lost customers who die prematurely through smoking related diseases. Because of public smoking bans, negative publicity and the attendant reduction in smokers in the UK, the likes of China and third world countries are now seen as lucrative sales targets.

Smokers who seriously want to quit and not be one of the 47 per cent who never live long enough to draw their pension, should consider reading *Stop Smoking in One Hour* by Valerie Austin, or *Easy Ways to Stop Smoking* by Alan Carr. Breathing the smoke from a bonfire or garden Chimenea has also been described as a health hazard!

Emotions: Here we have a major player in the health stakes. University studies show that our bodies become weaker or stronger according to our mental state. They emphasise that prolonged negative emotions can deplete the immune system, cause heart attacks and trigger certain cancers and tumours, suggesting that *dis-ease* in the mind can cause *disease* in the body.

It's easy to observe the health-destroying and ageing effects of harbouring long-term negativity, such as fear, stress, anxiety, worry, frustration, anger, hatred, sadness, resentment and guilt. This often leads to depression, with feelings of hopelessness and worthlessness in the form of low self-esteem. Top of the 'worry list' for most of us would appear to be money, work, health, relationship and family problems.

Billions of cells in our body take their orders from our mind, so if this is in a depressed or stressed mode then imagine the confusion they receive. Little wonder that law and order within our body breaks down. Negative emotions can also turn saliva to acid which upsets the digestive system. This in turn poisons the bloodstream, once again inviting serious health problems.

We all know that life can be frustrating, stressful and extremely difficult at times, but if we truly value our health, the evidence overwhelmingly tells us that we need to calm down and adopt a positive attitude of mind to distressing situations. Quite often, one person's problem can be another's challenge. Therefore, it's not necessarily the *problem* that causes our fear, anxiety or stress, but our *attitude* to it.

Happiness and contentment are known to boost the immune system by creating feelings of mental and physical wellbeing. This, as we will see in later chapters, is the natural state of inner peace and harmony that we should cultivate if we wish to remain healthy. Can anyone tell me what worry ever solved?

Hygiene: One would expect hygiene, particularly where kitchens and toilets are concerned, to be a matter of common sense, but it appears that even in our more 'enlightened' times, ignorance of the subject abounds. A hygiene survey by the Food and Drink Federation found that 25 per cent of people didn't wash their hands after using a toilet, 42 per cent didn't wash their hands after handling pets, 21 per cent didn't wash their hands before *preparing* food and 69 per cent didn't wash their hands before *eating* it!

If that isn't frightening enough, a Foods Standards Agency survey found that 39 per cent of kitchen staff in the catering industry failed to wash their hands after using the toilet! Perhaps that's another reason why nearly one million of us suffer from food poisoning every year after eating out, with over 500 cases being fatal! Super-bugs must think they are living in paradise!

When surveys uncover such ignorance of basic hygiene, is it any wonder that deadly bacteria like MRSA, E. Coli, C difficile, salmonella and campylobacter are still infecting us? Particularly through self-infection when we stick contaminated fingers in mouths, up noses and in our ears! In food poisoning or flu outbreaks it's usually the very young and the elderly who are the most vulnerable. Once again, it's those with strong immune systems who would probably survive such an attack. The virus seems to be Nature's way of culling on a 'survival of the fittest' policy. Perhaps we should learn the rules of the game by respecting hygiene and make sure that we are fit!

Sleep: Sleep is a rest, repair, and detoxification time for our bodies and a vital element in life if we are to remain healthy. The immune system functions best when left alone to do its job without the hindrance of negative emotions or physical effort. That's why sick people need a lot of sleep so that healing can take place.

It's not necessarily the number of hours we sleep that is important, but the *quality* of sleep that matters. Some people can make do on very few hours and still be bright and breezy the next day. 'Burning the candle at both ends' for long periods might sound great when we are young, but health abuse always has a payback time!

Insomnia is a national problem and, although it can be caused by medical conditions, 40 per cent of us have sleepless nights worrying about work, home life and dozens of other personal problems that always seem to be magnified ten-fold in our minds at three o'clock in the morning! Cutting out caffeine drinks, taking a bath, reading and listening to soft music before bedtime can often help. Many years ago work issues frequently kept me awake, but meditation became a tremendous help – a discipline that we will be looking at later on.

There are many do's and don'ts about getting a refreshing nights sleep, so if you suffer from this problem and find yourself wide awake in the early hours, you could always read *The Insomniac's Best Friend: How to Get a Better Night's Sleep* by Lynda Brown.

Exercise: Did you know that only 20 per cent of us get enough exercise to keep our bodies healthy? That probably means the 80 per cent of us who don't are in *deep* trouble! To maintain bone density, strong muscle tissue, healthy blood and general good health; the body needs moderate *regular* exercise for the whole of its lifespan.

Many confess how easy it is to get into a 'couch potato' lifestyle and sit for hours on end snacking whilst watching television. Apart from piling on the pounds, sitting for lengthy periods of time is seriously bad for our health whether we are a desk-bound computer operator or on a long-haul flight.

Walking, swimming, gardening and cycling are regarded as the easiest ways of keeping the majority of us physically fit. I have personally found Hatha Yoga to be one of the most effective and gentle body revitalising systems. Yogis versed in the 'Laws of Life' formulated this ancient Eastern and Oriental exercise technique over 4,000 years ago, which brings mind, body and spirit into perfect harmony as well as exercising every bone, muscle and organ in the body. This should help to keep us fit and in good health well into our twilight years. In yoga classes I have seen many an 80-year-old move with more agility than some half their age.

Whilst standing at a supermarket checkout, a *very* elderly lady dropped some small change. I bent down to retrieve it for her but, to my amazement, she beat me to it. I had no idea if she practised yoga, but that's the way it should be!

Breathing: To maintain good health we must breathe *clean* air. Our system was never meant to take in toxic by-products such as benzene, carbon monoxide exhaust fumes, dust and cigarette smoke. Added to that, our households are full of toxic chemicals in such things as cleaning agents, air fresheners, hair lacquers, deodorants, perfumes, paints and solvents, all of which we are breathing in every time they are used. No wonder we have an epidemic of asthma and other respiratory problems.

Strange as it may seem, few people in the Western world know how to breathe *correctly*. We are, apparently, lazy, shallow breathers and don't take enough air into the lungs to clean out the toxins and oxygenate and cleanse the blood. This allows contaminated blood to circulate throughout the body which, over a period of years, can have serious consequences.

There is an ancient yogic tradition that regards correct breathing as a prelude to a long and healthy life. We should, apparently, inhale through the nostrils and fully inflate the lungs by distending the chest and abdomen. The breath should then be held for a second to oxygenate the blood, and then fully exhaled, again through the nostrils, thus expelling stale air and other debris from the respiratory system. This, we are informed, should become the natural and habitual way of breathing – just as it is with babies and animals.

Deep breathing, or pranic breathing as the yogis call it, is also renowned for energising the body, calming the mind and giving greater clarity of thought. Two books that I found useful are *Breathe Better Feel Better* by Howard Kent and *Science of Breath* by Yogi Ramacharaka.

Drug Addiction: Drug taking and general substance abuse is widespread across the social divide. With 3.5 million of its population regularly taking drugs, causing over 1,500 premature deaths every year, the UK is now the 'drug capital of Europe' according to a EU survey and a Home Office report. The taking of hard drugs is usually started on a 'try it for kicks' basis, boredom, or because it's the 'in thing to do'. Some even blame a lack of love and affection and parental disinterest in their lives for their incursion into narcotic substances. Many victims succumb to premature ageing and an early death, particularly when the addiction is combined with alcohol. Unfortunately, when we have 'celebrities' and prominent members of society admitting that they have taken hard drugs, then that is the role model image they present to today's youth.

For several years I sat on various committees that had police and Social Services representation as well as being a Governor on two educational establishments. It brought home to me the devastation caused by drug addiction both to the community and to families, with 14 to 20-year-olds causing most local crimes to fund their drug and alcohol related habits. Naïve parents are horrified when they find their children are taking drugs, with many dealings done at school gates and in parks as pushers look for potential 'victims'. Thankfully, drug education is a priority in most schools. The most heart- breaking cases are the children that have to be taken into care by local authorities when their parents are addicted to hard drugs, alcohol or both.

The detrimental long term health effects of taking hard drugs such as crack cocaine and cannabis are well known, but little is mentioned of the million and a half Britons who are addicted to prescription drugs, such as painkillers, antidepressants, sleeping pills and tranquillisers, as a result of long term medication! That aside, death caused by the side-effects of prescription drugs is thought to be the third biggest killer in the UK. In 2002, according to the National Audit office, nearly 20,000 people died from doctors' prescriptions and another 415,000 suffered severe disabilities that ruined their lives. If that doesn't shock, then *CURED TO DEATH – The Effects of Prescription Drugs* by Dr Arabella Melville & Colin Johnson (Secker & Warburg 1982) certainly will!

Money cannot buy health, but I'd settle for a diamond studded wheelchair.
Dorothy Parker 1893 – 1967 (American writer and humorist)

Summary:

The few topics covered here are merely the tip of a very big health iceberg and to the health conscious minority will not be new. But since our health statistics are appalling, I hope it will make you more aware of how we can prematurely age our bodies, alter and deform our genetic structure, make ourselves terminally ill and depart this life earlier than necessary. Very often with great suffering, not just to ourselves, but to our loved ones who have to cope as best they can when *their* lives are dramatically changed as a consequence, often with feelings of helplessness.

In a society where we consume painkillers and other prescription medicines by the truckload, I'm sorry to say, that despite volumes of recommended health do's and don'ts, our Mr and Mrs Average are not very health conscious. Many of us have yet to learn that health *is* wealth, and that prevention really *is* better than cure. In the Western world very few of us die of old age – most of us commit slow 'suicide' by adopting irresponsible lifestyles!

We have a physical body that has to last us a 'lifetime', however long or brief that may be. Something worth looking after, wouldn't you think? Apparently not! We take drugs, over-eat, binge drink on alcohol, smoke, neglect exercise, put 'rubbish' into our mouths, worry and complain of stress. All negative lifestyle traits and habits that age us quickly, gain us weight and make us ill – and then we spend a small fortune on anti-aging creams, diet regimes, medicines, gym subscriptions and health insurances!

Scientists have long known that certain populations in the East and the Orient are blessed with good health and long lives. And, thanks to their environment and natural diets, don't suffer from the degenerative diseases that plague our Western 'civilisation'. That is, until they come here, live in our polluted towns and cities and adopt our destructive 'processed chemical diets' and lifestyles! What should that tell us?

One in three of us will be diagnosed with cancer and one in four will die from it. Horrendous statistics, but if you are serious about keeping and maintaining your health, you will find books by Phillip Day of great value, particularly *Health Wars* and *Cancer – Why We're Still Dying to Know the Truth*. Day doesn't mince his words in his writing or lectures, and tells the truth about the dangerous chemicals in our society that are making us *very* sick.

Aches and pains, fatigue and not feeling well are warning signs. That's why we have thousands of nerves all over our body to tell us that something is wrong! Unfortunately, good health is something that we take for granted and is only appreciated when we have lost it! Just as we trash our streets with rubbish and have to pay someone to clear it up, so we trash our bodies with rubbish and have to pay someone to 'clear up' our inevitable sickness. It would seem that we are our own worst enemies. If we have inherited good genes and an efficient immune system then we are blessed. Scientists are now finding that the detrimental gene damaging effects of some of our bad habits, traits and addictions can be genetically passed on to future generations. If that doesn't make us think, then nothing will!

It's quite noticeable, when people who have recovered from serious health problems – particularly if they had a close brush with death – adopt a different attitude to life, as if they have been given a second chance. They are much happier, tend to live each day as it comes, adopt a more laid back attitude, eat and drink more sensibly and don't get anxious or worry about trivia as they realise how short and precious life is.

Many people are confused by the apparent paradox of a loving God and sickness and disease. We seem to blame a God – or even deny the existence of one – because of the very health conditions that we, with our freewill, have created. And don't we criticise this God for failing to heal us or stop us from irresponsibly wrecking our body? No Divine Deity causes sickness, disease or personal accidents. Common sense should tell us that no big hand will come out of the sky and knock that cigarette out of our mouth or stop us consuming excessive alcohol. And no supernatural voice will boom out, '*Don't eat that junk food!*' Or, '*Stop taking drugs!*'

When we are feeling fit and well, we have a better outlook on life that

gives it more meaning and purpose. We are therefore happier and more able to cope with everyday living to pursue the things that are important to us.

Understanding that lack of personal responsibility in our lifestyles creates most of our health and social problems, represents another piece of the jigsaw. Health and happiness go hand in glove, so let us now investigate as to why happiness can seem so elusive.

If the diet is wrong then medicines are of no use.
If the diet is right then medicines are of no need.
Ayurvedic text (500BC)

We squander health in search of wealth; we scheme and toil and save.
Then squander wealth in search of health and only find a grave.

3 Happiness – *Why is it so elusive?*

There is only one happiness in life, to love and be loved
George Sand 1804–1876 (French novelist)

True happiness (if understood)
Consists alone in doing good.
William Somerville 1675–1742 (English gentleman)

Happiness is that Holy Grail, that elusive state of mind that is dangled in front of us like a carrot on a stick. To many it seems so near but always just out of reach. Many seek it, but so few find it. Why? Do we really know what happiness is, and if we found it would we recognise it? Let us investigate.

If 'One person's meat is another's poison', then one person's definition of happiness can literally be another's idea of misery. Over the years I have asked numerous people if they were *really* happy, and waited for the usual reply of, 'Oh yes – very.' The reason for asking was because their eyes and attitude portrayed a different story. It's quite intriguing when few people admit to being unhappy – even when they look miserable! Happiness shows in the eyes – they sparkle. On the other hand, honest ones admitted that they were not very happy and stated that they would be a lot happier:

- If they could get out of debt.
- If they could get a decent job.
- If they could retire early.
- If they could have children.
- When the children leave home.
- When they are married.
- When the divorce is settled.
- If they could put on a bit of weight.
- If they could lose some weight.
- If things were 'different'.
- If the 'neighbours from hell' would move.
- If they weren't so miserable and depressed.
- If they could have better health.
- If they could change their looks.
- If they could stop worrying.
- If they could have more time to themselves.
- If they weren't so lonely.
- If they learnt to like themselves more.

Such answers imply that their happiness is going to be 'tomorrow' and dependant on 'if' and 'when' and other external factors. There are those who rely on other people to bring them happiness, but in the long run it inevitably leads to disappointment or heartbreak when the relationships go sour or death intervenes. However happy people *think* they are, many imagine they could be happier – wondering, if the grass really is greener on the other side of the fence.

Even advances in mechanical and electronic technology don't seem to have brought about a corresponding increase in happiness. Perhaps it has made life too complicated, which is why so many people caught up in today's hectic and stressful rat-race long for the more laid-back simple life – manana, as the Spanish say!

Surveys show that we are less happy now than we were 30 years ago despite being twice as affluent. And statistics reveal that happiness declines from childhood and reaches an all time low at the age of about 38 before gradually rising again. Apparently, those over the age of 60 are the happiest. Perhaps being retired on a pension is the answer! Seriously, something is dreadfully wrong here if we have to be more than halfway through our life before we start to regain any resemblance of happiness. And if we are not happy, then life can seem monotonous or pointless.

Indigenous tribes in remote parts of the world often seem far happier than most of the children and adults in the Western world. I feel it's the simplicity of their lives and their closeness to Nature that makes this so. The emphasis also seems to be on family life and laughter. Which is probably why the 220,000 Melanesian islanders of Vanuatu in the South Pacific, were recently voted the happiest people in the world, despite their poverty – whilst Britain, one of the richest nations in the world, was not in the top 100!

Observation reveals that the happiest people are those who laugh a lot. Laughter is one of the major keys to happiness because it releases endorphins in the brain that create a feeling of wellbeing, which is also crucial to health – another factor in the happiness league. Research has shown that children laugh about 40 times a day, whereas adults only manage an average 14 laughs.

Of all days, the one most surely wasted is the one on which one has not laughed.
Nicolas-Sebastine Chamfort 1741–1794 (French writer)

A child's world is one of innocence with pretend and make-believe and laugher at the simplest of things. This is because children live for the moment, and have not been contaminated by the politics of an adult world. It is quite amusing to watch a young child get more pleasure out of a cardboard box than the expensive high-tech toy that was inside it! Adults, on the other-hand, can take life much too seriously with their fears, anxieties and paranoia. Laugh at the world I tell them. 'What is there to laugh about?' came one reply, 'It's not the sort of place you'd want to come to for a holiday, let alone a lifetime!'

It's quite noticeable that unhappy people don't seem to laugh much, and when they do it is usually pseudo-laughter, often with the aid of alcohol. They fail to see the funny side of life and have lost any sense of humour they may have once had. I did mention in the *Introduction* that a sense of humour in this crazy world is essential as far as happiness is concerned.

All the genuinely happy people that I know have a delightful sense of humour. And many of them have suffered tremendous grief and personal tragedy, but they have learnt to overcome it, get on with their lives and laugh at the world. Hopefully, by the time you have finished this book you will understand why it doesn't pay to take this world too seriously. People can be very funny without realising it – even in their seriousness.

I say that, because very few people truly understand themselves and quite often put on a façade to the world by pretending to be something they are not. Thus we get the snobs, the drama queens, the serial adulterers, the confidence tricksters, the celebrity scandals, the lying politicians, the drunks in the pubs trying to forget, and all the other 'actors' on the stage of life ad-libbing as the 'play' unfolds before them. This is how observant cartoonists and comedy writers make us laugh by picking up on, and exaggerating, the 'characters' in the 'soap-dramas' of everyday life.

Some years ago, I was in a coach party travelling back from a London theatre, whereupon a middle-aged gentleman entertained us by telling the most hilarious jokes. He had us all in stitches for virtually the whole journey. When we got off the coach I said to his wife, 'Your husband's quite a character.' To which she replied, 'You should see him at home, he's as miserable as sin!'

There is much truth in the saying, 'Laugh, and the world laughs with you – cry, and you cry alone'. Genuine laughter, like happiness, is infectious; and they are the only infections we should be glad to catch and pass on!

If you are feeling a bit sorry for yourself at the moment, could I ask you to try a little experiment? When convenient, with no one else in the room, stand in front of a mirror and pull a miserable face – a great big frown. How does it look? Not a pretty sight is it? Now try a big smile. Do you see the difference? Now I would like you to try a little giggle – now a big one – and now a good hearty laugh. Much better isn't it?

No one can be truly happy unless they understand and love themselves for who and what they are, otherwise they will become confused and unable to comprehend what roll they are meant to play in a world full of false values. The false values of hype, for example, where fantasy advertisements for 'dream cars', 'dream houses' and 'dream holidays' seduce us into borrowing large sums of money to appease our egos and materialistic urges. 'Dreams' that are supposed to make us feel happy and one of the 'in crowd'.

We are now up to our eyeballs in debt, aided and abetted by plastic credit cards that encourage us to purchase the latest gadgets, gizmos and designer gear with money we haven't got because of the 'must have it now' mentality. A mentality that can quickly turn a 'dream' into a materialistic nightmare and burst our pseudo happiness bubble! Everything has its price – as many realise when they catch the consumer 'spending virus' and dive into the trough of materialism. Those who can't afford to play this game often become disappointed and unhappy. For many, it can become an insatiable never-ending quest, always wanting the latest status symbol or trying to keep up with the Joneses. Material happiness never lasts and the wise ones soon realise that physical objects can never bring real and lasting happiness.

Never keep up with the Joneses. Drag them down to your level. It's cheaper.
Quentin Crisp 1908–1999 (English writer)

Some turn to alcohol or drugs to blot out or run away from their unhappiness, thinking that a few hours in a drunken or dazed stupor will give them the 'bliss' they so desperately seek. On sobering up, realisation sets in that the price to be paid is sinking even lower into the depths of depression and despair. And so the vicious circle continues until they become alcoholics or drug addicts. Genuinely happy people have no need to take drugs or consume vast amounts of alcohol to 'escape' into their own little world.

Neither, it seems, is happiness a question of wealth. Money can buy us anything we want, but happiness we will have to find for ourselves. Countless wealthy people are dreadfully unhappy and even suicidal, with many venturing onto the slippery slope of drugs and alcohol, often having to book themselves into clinics to be 'dried out'.

For some, the accumulation of vast wealth destroys their ability to be truly happy. They find the lack of genuine friends and the ability to buy anything they like quite depressing. Perhaps Michael Gardner-Jones was right when he remarked: *'Happiness is a state of mind, not a state of bank balance.'*

I am reminded of the time when Patricia and I were holidaying in Spain and happened to meet an Irish property millionaire in a local coffee bar, whereupon he openly confessed that he was depressed and very lonely. He had many pseudo-friends but no genuine ones he could confide in or trust, and was convinced that if he lost all his money his 'friends' would disappear overnight. We were due to have dinner with English friends that evening, so we asked if he would like to join us. He gratefully accepted the invitation and later joined the seven of us in a little Spanish restaurant in a cobbled courtyard.

Some of our friends lived in the area and knew the owner and chef very well, so the hospitality was second to none. We laughed and joked most of the evening as well as telling some hilarious stories. Finally, when the time came to depart, our guest – with tears in his eyes – gave his thanks for one of the best evenings he had experienced for many-a-while. But what struck home, was when he confessed that it was an absolute pleasure to meet and converse with such '*genuine salt-of-the-earth people' who had let him be himself and shown him a kindness and happiness that had long been missing from his life.* We never kept in touch, but I have often wondered if he ever found what his wealth had denied him – the priceless things in life that money can never buy.

There are numerous reasons why some people are genuinely happy, whilst others seem to have 'lost the plot' and wallow in the misery of their unhappiness. First, let's have a look at the following characteristics and see if they are conducive to happiness or unhappiness in people who:

- Frown a lot, rarely smile or laugh, and are full of fear, worry and anxiety.
- Have little or no genuine sense of humour.
- Have no set goals in life.
- Are lethargic and apathetic (can't be bothered attitude).
- Enjoy scandal and often gossip and tittle-tattle about others behind their backs.
- Are pessimistic and whinge and moan about people and things (attitude problem).
- Carry chips on their shoulders about past grievances.
- Are obsessed with money and material things.
- Are possessive with people and things.
- Are extremely selfish and continually take from life.
- Find it difficult to show love, affection or compassion.
- Find it difficult to live with themselves (don't like themselves or the way they look).
- Are short tempered and vent their anger and frustration on others (bullying).
- Are full of ego, desires and self-importance ('I want, I need, I have').
- Laugh and gloat at other's misfortunes.
- Continually criticise others.
- Are racist.
- Are argumentative, sarcastic and cynical.
- Lead complicated lives.
- Drink to excess or take hard drugs to escape the realities of life.
- Binge eat to find comfort in food.
- Are hypochondriacs or succumb to frequent illnesses.

- Show jealousy and resentment at other's success or achievements.
- Have very few genuine friends.
- Suffer from low self-esteem and take remarks or comments personally.
- Talk abruptly and are often rude.
- Take life too seriously.
- Think that happiness is outside of themselves.

It would be virtually *impossible* to find lasting happiness if we harbour many of these negative characteristics. That is because they emanate from our lower materialistic nature, and therefore violate the Cosmic Law of love, peace and harmony, which *must* be present within us if we wish to be happy. Such behavioral patterns are an inevitable giveaway, and we might as well have *'I am unhappy'* tattooed on our foreheads.

Anyone can be happy for five minutes or even five hours under favourable conditions. Others manage two weeks or more during a good holiday but find themselves living their old frustrated and unhappy lifestyles when they return home. Many seek for peace and tranquility within Nature but are unable to find or retain such peace. I have found through experience that it is best to clear our minds of all negative emotions and selfish wants and desires. Then we may approach Nature with the love, compassion and reverence that she demands of us. Only then will she divulge her secrets of lasting peace and happiness.

> The man who casts off all desires and walks without desire,
> with no thought of a mine or of an I, comes unto peace.
> *The Bhagavad –Gita*

So what *is* the happiness secret? Let's have a look at some of these characteristics in people who:

- Smile and laugh a lot.
- Have a lovely personality, genuine humility and sense of humour.
- Always talk kindly of others.
- Never carry chips on their shoulders or harbour past grievances.
- Live in the *now*, because they realise that happiness *is* now.
- Realise that happiness comes from *within*.
- Accept that people are more important than things or money.
- Give to life by helping and thinking of others (unselfish).
- Show love and affection to people and animals.
- Accept and love themselves and other people just the way they are.
- Take life as it comes and rarely complain.
- Never take things personally.

- Let the fears and anxieties of everyday life go over their head.
- Have plenty of patience and understanding and rarely argue.
- Are optimistic about life and offer words of comfort and encouragement.
- Never dwell on their ailments or problems.
- Lead uncomplicated lives (a 'keep-it-simple and moderation-in-all-things' policy).
- Look after their health.
- Have open minds about life in general (no comfort zones).
- Never force their way of life on other people.
- Set themselves achievable goals in life.
- Have varied interests and hobbies.
- Have an awareness of Nature and the oneness of all life.
- Have soft, sparkling and compassionate eyes.
- Have lots of genuine friends.
- Have that 'What you see is what you get' personality (heart on their sleeve).
- Realise that life is much too short to be miserable.

If we have many of these positive characteristics, traits and lifestyles we are well on the road to genuine happiness. Simply because they emanate from our higher spiritual nature and we are consciously, or otherwise, living in accordance with the Cosmic Law of love, peace and harmony. You may wonder if such people are an endangered species, but in fact, they are in great abundance all over the world, and it has been my pleasure to have met countless numbers of them over the years.

A sure-fire recipe for happiness is to recognise any negative characteristics that we may have and gradually 'dissolve' them by making an effort to adopt the positive characteristics. Those who have a mixture of both tend to be on alternate highs and lows – the 'yo-yo happiness syndrome!' The highs *will* win in the end, and maybe, for the first time, the secret of genuine happiness will be revealed.

What we give to life we will get back. If we emanate love, peace, laughter and happiness that is what we will receive in return. That is why *optimists* are always right when they say *'I told you so'*. If on the other hand we whinge and moan, and continually find fault with life and people, then life will give us plenty of things to find fault with and frustrate us, thus causing us to be unhappy and miserable and see life as meaningless and pointless. That is why *pessimists* are always right when they say *'I told you so'*.

The happiness of your life depends on the quality of your thoughts.
Marcus Aurelius 121–180 (Roman Emperor and philosopher)

It's very easy to be down, sulk, or adopt a 'throwing our toys out of the pram' attitude when life is not as we want it to be, but it is often the result of our own negative thinking. So, would it not make sense to change our thoughts if we wish to bring happier circumstances into our life? Because we *have* the choice we can therefore be as happy or unhappy as we like and if others can be happy after suffering dreadful calamities, then so can we.

If we wish to make excuses for being unhappy then there are hundreds to choose from. For many there will always be someone or some trauma to blame. This may sound strange, but I am convinced that some people just love being miserable. They are never 'happier' than when they are whinging or moaning. Thankfully, there is an art in being 'deaf' if you are ever forced to endure such company!

It's very sad, but so many carry grievances from the past to haunt them in the present. I have met people who have ruined, and therefore wasted, much of their lives by carrying the mental burdens of guilt, anger, regret or blame for something that happened 40 or more years ago – with a painful past being given an 'action replay' at periodic intervals.

Some blame an unhappy childhood for their present attitude to life. A few being abandoned at birth and brought up in foster homes, whilst others had no love or affection from cruel or alcoholic parents. And numerous numbers said bullies made their school days a nightmare that still haunted them, particularly when sexual abuse from those in authority took place. Difficult though it was, some decided that the best policy was to forgive, even if they couldn't forget, saying that the past was the past and no way was it going to ruin future happiness.

Past hurts and grievances of *any* kind are expensive and heavy baggages to carry. And sound advice for anyone so afflicted is to lighten your load by mentally dumping them *now*, and get on with the life you were meant to live. To those still affected by childhood traumas, books by David Pelzer will be invaluable – see *Bibliography* (Child Abuse).

Some have confided of their difficulties in finding happiness again because of traumatic events that have happened in their lives. 'How can we be happy when we have just lost our child with cancer?' 'My mother's suicide has devastated me, it has destroyed my life.' 'I am dreadfully unhappy in my marriage.' 'I am so distraught; my husband has left me for another woman.' 'How can I be happy when I have been out of work for so long and there are no jobs?' 'I have been so lonely and unhappy since my wife's death.' 'I am so depressed and unhappy I can't see the point of anything any more.' 'I don't know what we are going to do. We have lost everything – our home, our business and all our savings.'

There are millions of stories like that from all around the globe. I don't know many families where tragedy hasn't struck at some time or other. It's part and parcel of life's harsh lessons. Life goes on – even after wars and earthquakes. Today will be the unhappiest day of many peoples' lives – it will also be the happiest for countless more. From time to time traumas and tragedies happen that can make large dents in our happiness quota when life hits us below the belt and takes us from laughter to tears within a short space of time. No one is immune, as history confirms.

Let us look at it this way. How would we appreciate real happiness if we didn't sample the opposite from time to time? The art is to learn and accept what life is trying to teach us. Once we have done that, with wisdom and humility, and not harbouring bitterness, guilt or other feeling-sorry-for-ourselves emotions, then future happiness will follow, just as day follows night – and I am speaking from experience here.

100 per cent happiness all the time is impossible for the vast majority of us, but if we can achieve 80 per cent on average then we will be doing well. It's not the circumstances or problems in our lives that cause us to remain miserable or unhappy; it's our *attitude* to them. Those who adopt positive attitudes and have many of the happiness attributes mentioned soon bounce back, with acquaintances not realising the tragedies they had suffered unless it cropped up in casual conversation.

Some of the happiest people I have met – and with a good sense of humour – are wheelchair bound, many since childhood and others as a result of illness or accidents. In many ways I feel that Nature has compensated them, since they seem far happier than many of their able-bodied counterparts.

The root causes of unhappiness are, unfortunately, inherent in much of the human race. It is selfishness and greed. This encourages us to dwell on self, with our self wants, self needs and pet hates. Happiness is *Love*, and thinking positively about life and what we can *give* to it by helping others, not negatively about what we can *take* from it or what it owes us. As the poet John Ruskin wrote: *'When a man is wrapped up in himself he makes a very small package.'*

Like many things in life, unhappiness comes with a price tag, and can be *very* expensive. Expensive in terms of potential mental and physical health due to self-destructive periods of negativity. The paradox of true happiness is that it is *priceless,* and yet *free* and for the taking. Despite what life throws at us from time to time we really *do* have that choice, and those who have made it certainly have no regrets.

Where there is peace there is harmony;
Where there is harmony there is Love;
Where there is Love there is happiness.
Buddha Maitreya (Koji Takeuchi)

Summary

To understand the jigsaw of life one of the essential necessities is to cultivate happiness. When we are genuinely happy we are truly *'alive'*. We are enthusiastic and optimistic and therefore have a better outlook on life and *want* to know what makes it tick. Miserable people are rarely interested in becoming Seekers of Truth!

When we grasp an understanding of the meaning and purpose of life, we will realise that all the fears, hurts, grievances, anger, resentment and boredom that daily rob our Mr and Mrs Average of happiness are but trivia in the great Cosmic Plan.

The only thing we need do to be happy *today*, right *now,* is to decide that we are *going* to be! My recipe for happiness is in making a conscious effort to give and receive love, and to laugh at life by finding humour – every day. When we cease to love and laugh we cease to live and will be unhappy. And when we are unhappy we become old.

Happiness is the birthright of all human beings and is the *natural* state of being. Our true (higher) nature is love, peace, harmony and joy, and when we are not at peace within ourselves due to anxiety, worry, stress or a dozen other earthly factors then we will not be happy. But life will, sometime, somewhere, somehow, 'guide' us away from the selfish life to the selfless life. Its eternal message being: *'Unconditional Love is Happiness – and it is now!'*

Understanding the 'secrets' of happiness and the conditions that cause unhappiness, represents another piece of the puzzle. We can now proceed on the quest where we will put religion up for scrutiny and analyse faith and knowledge.

Happy is he who has overcome his ego;
Happy is he who has attained peace;
Happy is he who has found the Truth.
Gautama the Buddha (C.563 – C.483 BC)

All those who suffer in the world do so because of their
desire for their own happiness. All those happy in the world
are so because of their desire for the happiness of others.
Shantideva C.685 – 763 (Indian poet and scholar)

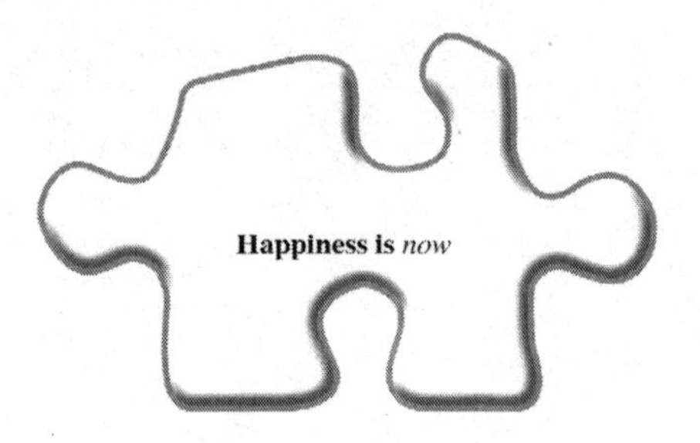
Happiness is *now*

4 Religion – *Faith or Knowledge?*

Do not believe in the strength of traditions even if they have been held in honour for many generations and in many places; do not believe that which you yourself have imagined, thinking a God has inspired you. Believe nothing which depends only on the authority of your masters or of priests. After investigation believe that which you yourself have tested and found reasonable and which is for your good and that of others.
Gautama the Buddha (C.563 – C.483 BC)

Those who seek a meaning and purpose to life eventually include religion on their investigation agenda, since it has been a fundamental part of human life for thousands of years. Many, from birth, have no freedom of choice and are obliged to follow a family or state religion. In that respect, I can thank my parents for not indoctrinating me into either religion *or* politics, leaving me an open mind to draw my own conclusions in later life.

Apart from church primary school as a child, my first introduction to religion was at the age of 17 when applying to join the local church youth club. The conditions for joining were confirmation into the Church of England faith and attending regular church services. I didn't have a problem with that at the time – I just wanted to play snooker and table tennis.

It was duly arranged for me to have chats with the vicar for confirmation lessons. He was a very amicable gentleman and we met for an hour each week. He talked about Jesus and God and read relevant chapters from the Bible and cordially invited me to ask questions. I remember asking such questions as: 'If there is a God, why are babies born handicapped?' 'Why do children have to die?' 'Is there an afterlife and, if so, what is it like?' and 'Why does God takes sides in war?' And why this and why that.

Over the weeks, the expressions on his face were priceless as he struggled to answer my questions. He talked and talked and talked, but what I received was politicians' answers. I never got a direct answer to a direct question, and believe me I really wanted to know. After six weeks I was more confused than ever, and was more or less told that I must have faith and believe in the Bible, because what happens in this world is only for God to know and not for us to question. I was disillusioned. Here was a man who had been preaching from the pulpit for many years but couldn't answer the basic questions of life from a 17-year-old. Yes, I *did* get confirmed – I really *did* want to play snooker and table tennis!

Because of that experience I remained agnostic and never gave orthodox religion much thought for the next 18 years. I felt that it had stayed in the dark ages for too long, and was all faith and belief without offering any proof or giving acceptable answers to sensible questions. I could never understand why, if there *was* a God, 'He' would wish humanity to remain in ignorance of the laws governing life and death.

Blind Faith and Belief

Many who read this book will have been touched by tragedy, and often left 'cut and bleeding' or maybe just 'badly bruised' when life suddenly pulled the rug from under their feet. Very few of us will escape a battering on this Earth in one form or another. When traumatic things happen and, happen they do, I feel that knowledge is more comforting than blind faith or ignorance. I have talked to many whose blind faith has been rocked to the core or destroyed by life's sudden tragedies. 'Why is this happening to me?' we cry out, naively thinking that death and destruction, murder, rape, divorce, accidents and terminal illnesses only happen to other people.

During a television programme about the devil and evil, a devout Jewish gentleman who survived the Nazi concentration camps during World War Two particularly moved me. One of his very pertinent questions was: 'Where was God when six million Jews were being gassed?' It was evident by the tears in his eyes and the tone of his voice that the question had rocked his faith and haunted him for over 50 years.

One could equally ask: 'Where was God when World War 1 started?' Or 'Where was God during the Catholic Inquisition, when hundreds of thousands of men, women and children were tortured and murdered in '*His*' name?' 'Where is God when thousands are dying every day of starvation and disease?'

Should we just have blind faith and accept that such horrors are the will of God and that we mustn't question? Is that an easy cop-out to pacify our ignorance, or have the knowledge and answers been there for thousands of years staring us in the face?

Many religions are based on belief systems that accept alleged events as being true and factual without definitive evidence or proof. Thus belief systems, by their very nature, invite doubt, and tend to be matters of opinion or subject to argument or disagreement. Perhaps that is why numerous individuals throughout history have interpreted their scriptures in different ways, thereby creating numerous offshoots and variations on a theme. Each one believing that they are right and all the others wrong, thus requiring their followers to believe and have blind faith without questioning.

Why so many interpretations if there is only one Truth? Two plus two equals four in any language in all parts of the globe. It cannot be altered or varied in any way, or subjected to different opinions or interpretations. Neither does the answer require faith or belief because it is the truth and provable.

Truth stands on its own evidence, it does not require
any other testimony to prove it true, it is self-effulgent.
Swami Vivekananda 1863 – 1902 (Hindu missionary)

Faith is required when we are ignorant of facts and experience. Knowledge, on the other hand, is to understand by investigation and experience that someone has integrity or something is working in accordance with a law or formula. Knowledge thus replaces ignorance. Design engineers wouldn't dare say to a client: 'Have *faith* that the machine will work' or 'I *believe* it will work.' He would want to *know* that his machine was going to work properly and ask to see design schemes and calculations as evidence.

The eminent philosopher and psychologist Carl Jung was once asked if he believed in God, to which he replied: 'I do not *believe,* I *know.*' Jung distinctly knew the difference between believing and knowing. There is nothing wrong in having a faith or belief, it's just that having knowledge and experience is infinitely better. We are now living in an age of unprecedented scientific knowledge waiting to be investigated, but we will put a ball and chain around our mind if we keep it closed or blinkered. I never unduly concern myself with what others *believe*, only with what they *know* through direct experience, and only then can I be sure that it resembles the truth.

Many have confessed that their faith sustained them in times of trouble and that is good. Equally, knowledge and experience kept me afloat when life dealt blows below the belt. Similarly, others have stated that it was purely a belief in themselves and a sheer determination to succeed that helped them through a crisis. A few find none of these 'lifeboats' and, unfortunately, drown in their own sorrows as we will see in later chapters.

It is not faith in an all-powerful deity that enables us
to move mountains, but faith in our own abilities.
David Brandon-Jones 1936 – 1986 (Practical Palmistry)

Well-intentioned people have expressed how wonderful their local vicar or priest is and what a pillar of the community they are. I appreciate that and, over the years, have had many a discussion with clerics on social occasions. Some admitted that they had a great interest in metaphysical matters – such as discussed in this book – but daren't preach them from the pulpit for 'fear of repercussions from their superiors'. Others chose to change the subject when 'awkward' questions breached their comfort zones.

I recently attended a Catholic funeral service and found the ritual and dogma rather impersonal regarding the deceased. During the reception afterwards, the priest came and sat next to me. We got chatting about this and that and, eventually, I asked him if he really believed what he had read out in church. He looked around over the top of his glasses, leaned towards me and whispered: 'It's a job.' The answer spoke volumes.

The American writer and journalist, Ambrose Bierce (1842–1914) wrote with a rather dry wit in *The Devil's Dictionary* that faith was a 'belief without evidence in what is told by one who speaks without knowledge of things without parallel'.

'Where is my Daughter?'

As an example of blind faith and belief, let me recount a personal and touching story of a gentleman who, in 1974, crossed my pathway and influenced my life. At the time I was studying Raja Yoga meditation and spiritual healing at a sanctuary in Buckinghamshire. These are subjects that we will be looking at in later chapters.

One evening, after meditation, I became engaged in conversation with a gentleman by the name of Fred (I have refrained from mentioning his full name for reasons that will become obvious as the story unfolds). Fred, who was small in stature, of slim build, balding with grey hair and in his mid-sixties, was staying at the sanctuary for a few days of rest and study. I enquired as to why he was studying philosophical teachings, whereupon he suggested we go to his room where it would be quieter to tell me his story.

Leading the way up the stairs of the old low-beamed cottage, Fred entered his room and sat down on a comfortable chair. I followed, closed the door, and upon turning, saw an amazed expression on his face. This quietly spoken gentleman was literally lost for words. I asked him if anything was the matter, and he said that as I entered the room he had seen, quite clearly, a Zulu warrior from one of the spiritual worlds follow me in. This is another piece of the puzzle that we will be investigating.

This warrior, Fred explained, was at least 213cm (seven feet) tall, and his head had passed through the oak lintel and brickwork above the doorway and was almost at ceiling height. He described him as being about 40-years-of-age with a rounded face and prominent cheekbones, wearing a band of ostrich feathers around his head and carrying a spear and large shield. I asked Fred if he was clairvoyant, and he explained that he wasn't really, but occasionally when he was relaxed he saw and sensed things beyond the norm. This brief episode had sidetracked him for the moment, but he soon felt obliged to enlighten me as to his predicament.

It turned out that Fred was a retired Anglican clergyman with a long ecclesiastical background. Apparently, many months before he retired from the ministry, he had taken a funeral service for a fellow cleric whose 19-year-old daughter had died tragically. After the service the two men were in the vestry, and whilst Fred was hanging up his cassock, his friend, in a rather perplexed voice, asked him a very pertinent question. Because the question and the answer that followed had such a profound impact on the two friends, I have repeated it word for word. I have never forgotten it and it has spurred me on to find such answers for myself.

Friend: Fred, where is my daughter?
Fred: In heaven of course.
Friend (Louder and more accentuated): Fred, *where – is – my – daughter?*
Fred: I told you – in heaven.
Friend (Much louder and exasperated): Fred, WHERE – IS – MY – DAUGHTER?
Fred: (Quietly and sadly after a long pause for thought): I don't know!

'Brian, can you imagine the impact that had on me?' confessed Fred, in an emotional voice. 'It was like a sledgehammer blow. Here was I, a clergyman of some 30 years standing, been through theological college, was a missionary in the Congo for 12 years, read the Bible from cover to cover more than 20 times – memorising most of it chapter and verse – but couldn't answer a simple and perfectly natural question.' He paused considerably before continuing, 'And what made it worse, was the fact that it came from a fellow cleric who didn't know the answer either!'

I could see that he was a very sensitive and sincere man who had been emotionally scarred by the experience. 'What have I been telling people all these years?' he asked. 'I just took it for granted and never questioned as to where people went when they died. I never thought deeply about what I was saying – I told people exactly what I was taught to say.' Visibly upset, he continued: 'I was a professional clergyman, so wasn't I supposed to be an authority on the subject?'

You may wonder how the five simple words 'Fred, where is my daughter?' could have had such a profound effect. But words can, and do, change people's lives and, once heard, cannot be taken back. Imagine how you would feel, for example, if you had been a professional chef or motor technician for 30 years and couldn't answer a logical question about food or car engines!

Over the years Fred had glibly used the word 'heaven' countless times without thinking about where or what it was. Those five words started an avalanche inside him as he realised everything about his crumbling faith had been learnt 'parrot fashion'. 'I have to find the *Truth* – I cannot live with myself until I do' he exclaimed. 'I am researching life after death and building up an evidential dossier on the subject.'

He went on to tell me how his change of thinking had cost him dearly in marital and financial terms. His wife had given him an ultimatum, having told him that if he pursued this change of direction which, incidentally, she couldn't understand, then their marriage would be over as she couldn't live with him any more. 'What could I do? It was like a gun to my head,' he said, 'she couldn't live with me if I continued, and I couldn't live with myself if I didn't.' He explained that after much deliberation he signed his house and most of their savings over to his wife. 'We had a final hug and thanked each other for 40 years of marriage' he said, with tears in his eyes. 'I walked away with what I could pack into one suitcase and enough money for a few months, after that I had to rely on my pension.'

I wondered what I could say to comfort or encourage him on his quest, but I was still a novice myself. He was a brave man and I admired him, but I suppose we have to learn to live with ourselves, and if we cannot do that then how can we successfully live with anyone else? Because of his quest for Truth he had sacrificed a lot, gained emotional humility and had now become a nomad.

It was no coincidence that our paths crossed. I too had recently set out on a pathway to try and find a meaning and purpose to life and death and here was a fellow traveller I could relate to. Over the next eight years, until his death, we were to become very close friends, giving each other moral support and encouragement as we compared experiences and evidence to crosscheck for accuracy. I will be mentioning Fred from time to time, and have included this episode of his life as an example of going from blind faith and belief to knowledge – albeit the hard way!

Investigating Religion

Investigating world religions and their multiple offshoots of different sects and denominations is a mammoth task. Most religions, over the centuries, have been tampered with, some more so than others, and very little of what 'truth' they originally had is evident today. Volumes have been written on religious history by unbiased scholars who paint a broader and harsher picture than I have space for here.

The acknowledged atheist and rationalist, Professor Richard Dawkins from The University of Oxford, has likened organised religion to a 'virus' that spreads to others by indoctrination and conversion. In his highly acclaimed book *The God Delusion,* he scientifically demolishes faith and belief religions. The historian and philosopher Arthur Findlay in *The Curse of Ignorance* in

1947 and Thomas Paine in *The Age of Reason* in 1793 did precisely the same. The latter incurred the wrath of priests and their allies and barely managed to escape with his life!

It is not my intention to offend those who find comfort in their religious beliefs, only to point out historical facts that scholars have known for decades. The evidence is there for anyone to research. But it is surprising how many are ignorant of the *true* history and origins of their religion, and will become easily offended, defensive or even violent if they feel their faith is under threat or in danger of being disproved. Years of observation has taught me that people will believe what they want to believe, whether it is truth or lies, and this is particularly evident when religious indoctrination has occurred during early childhood.

> Even when presented with measured and reliable factual information, many persons' religious beliefs have forced them to reject the logical and obvious truth in favour of the teaching of their religion, some not even daring to read material which questions the beliefs of their religion.
> *James McQuitty (Religion: Man's Insult to God)*

When self-confessed agnostics and atheists frequently pose the question: 'What has religion done for the benefit of the world in the last 2,000 years?' Personal observations supply them with the answer. Namely, that *politics* within religion has been the cause of most of the world's problems, leaving the planet in a bigger mess than it has ever been. To a limited extent, and I repeat, *limited,* I can sympathise with atheists. Many openly state that it is the extremists, fundamentalism and religious gobble-de-gook that have made them so – truly a sad testimonial for institutions that have had centuries to get their acts together.

Some religions and sects are money and power driven and have *divided* the human race not *united* it. Reason and logic dictates that if people are herded into different camps with religious labels round their necks they become segregated through dogmas and doctrines. And to prove the point, there is plenty of historical evidence that religions have promoted hatred, manipulated and controlled people's lives, started wars and caused untold suffering. They were known as religions of the sword and it was a question of 'convert or die'. Seemingly, one country could invade another and slaughter in the name of religion without a conscience. The early Church got much of its wealth and power through plundering land and gold from other nations. The crusades and the rape of South America are two prime examples. They have yet to comprehend that *hatred divides and destroys*, whereas *love unites and heals* – a philosophy that we will be discussing in later chapters.

Bloody religious wars were fought for centuries as the different religions attempted to gain total domination of the known world.
John A Keel (Our Haunted Planet)

Where was the love and compassion? I mistakenly thought that religion was supposed to lead by example. Perhaps it has, and that is why we are never free of wars and violence perpetrated in the name of God. In the past, those who opposed this theological madness were classed as heretics or blasphemers and burnt at the stake or tortured to death. Not having the answer to its critics, the Church found it easier to exterminate them. Today, such practices are the politics of autocratic regimes.

It would seem that we are free to question, criticise or oppose political parties should we disagree with their policies (doctrines), but if we dare to question or criticise the doctrines of some organised religions we are branded as heretics and accused of blasphemy. I was baffled as to why institutions that claimed to be spokespersons for God and offer salvation would need a law of blasphemous libel to protect itself, with talk of 'defending the faith'. Truth doesn't need defending and it certainly doesn't care what we say about it or whether we accept it. Writer and playwright, George Bernard Shaw, once stated: *'All great truths begin as blasphemies.'*

Down the centuries, many organised religions exploited the fears and superstitions of the vulnerable and uneducated masses, and took advantage of their fear of death, fear of God or a devil and created mysteries that didn't exist. But their greatest crime is *intolerance*, particularly with other faiths and unbelievers. The long history of religious violence and persecution is disturbing and, unfortunately, it will plague us well into the future until Truth prevails. We have witnessed Catholics and Protestants, Hindus and Muslims, Christians and Muslims, Arabs and Jews (Islam and Judaism) and Muslim Sunnis, Shiites and Kurds trying to verbally demoralise or physically destroy each other whilst continuing to patronise their one and the same God. What a wonderful example religious hypocrisy portrays to the world!

Violence in any form is bad enough, but when extremists perpetrate it in the name of religion, it only serves to highlight their spiritual and moral bankruptcy, with little understanding of forgiveness, love and compassion or the true nature of God. Perhaps if they understood Spiritual Truth instead of relying on blind faith and belief we would be free from religious conflict. Spiritual Truth aside, common sense tells us that it is better to work together as one race with wisdom, love and compassion, and create a better world for our children and grandchildren rather than destroy it!

As long as people believe in absurdities they will continue to commit atrocities.
Voltaire 1694 – 1778 (French writer and philosopher)

It is only since the last century, when the masses became more affluent, learnt to read and write, think for themselves and ask serious questions, that orthodox religion, mainly in the Western world, has been so exposed to scrutiny, doubt and the inevitable decline.

In the UK, dwindling congregations are causing at least 50 churches or chapels to close every year through lack of support. If a well-established corporate company was losing that much business after umpteen years of trading, it would surely take a long hard look at its products, sales staff, and management structure.

Because of its plight the Church is desperately seeking a new image in the hope of attracting newcomers. Had it told the truth about life after death, the *real* God and the purpose of life instead of suppressing them to protect vested interests, the window dressing of out-dated dogmas and doctrines would not be necessary. Neither would the introduction of religious indoctrination groups.

Dogma is the curse of all systems of thought; once a system or religion gets bogged down in a printed book, once the pundits and priests lay down that you *must* believe such and such a statement or be guilty of heresy, then that system or religion has begun the process of ossification which will end in death.
Air Chief Marshall Lord Hugh Dowding 1882 – 1970 (The Dark Star)

The Church, with its massive financial assets of land and property is, unfortunately, hastening its own self-destruction with frequent arguing, bickering and backbiting as bishops and other senior clergy become involved in power struggles and theological differences within its ranks. This goes on whilst followers leave in droves – attracted to the evolving 'religions' of *Materialism* and *Atheism*.

People now worship money, power, property, cars, and technology. Encouraged by the media, pop stars, film stars and sports stars are the new celebrity icons – idolised and worshipped instead of Saints and gods. And many state that music, culture and sport have done far more to unite the world than religion has ever done.

Several years ago, the Rev G. L. Carnes, Vicar of Hampton Wick, aptly summed up the situation when he wrote: *Today, with its power over individuals gone and with science toppling its shibboleths, the Church promotes only a blurred vision of the truth. It makes no impact on the deadly disease of our time; over-secularisation of society with its heady emphasis on money, power, prestige, sex and video.*

Science v Religion

Science is based on reason, enquiry, research, facts, evidence and proof – or it *should* be! Religion on the other hand is based on opinions, myths, faith and belief. Hence science and religion have been seen to be in conflict for hundreds of years. Particularly so, when astronomer and mathematician Galileo and philosopher Giordano Bruno, dared to defy the Church's theory of the Earth being the centre of the Universe. Both suffered the wrath and torments of religious fanatics during the Catholic Inquisition, the latter being burnt to death in 1600.

In 1858, professional Naturalist Alfred Russel Wallace, pre-empted Charles Darwin by propounding the theory of 'evolution by natural selection' and subsequently sent Darwin a brief essay on the subject. Having worked on the same theory himself for decades, this spurred Darwin to complete his own studies, and on the 24th November 1859 his book *On the Origin of Species by Means of Natural Selection* was published. This demolished the Biblical theory of creation and sent shock waves of seismic proportions through religious establishments. This begs the question; did Darwin and Wallace inadvertently take God out of the equation? We will see!

Even today, the argument continues. Religious 'Creationists' believe that God *created* the world in six days and all life instantly by 'intelligent design'. Whereas scientists (heretics), with the knowledge of genes, DNA and carbon dating, continue to endorse Darwin's theory. They offer evidence that all life on Earth is related and *evolved* from single cells hundreds of millions of years ago due to natural selection and survival of the fittest. Scientific studies of primates on the human branch of evolution inform us that we are only one gene away from an ape, and that we started walking upright 3.2 million years ago!

Despite its materialistic image and venture into weapons of mass destruction, science, with the advent of the electron microscope, radio telescopes, satellites, space travel, quantum mechanics and complex computer systems, has taught us more about the origins of the Universe than religion.

Disillusioned Youth

Youngsters are observing the present state of the world and the impotence of science, politics and religion to solve self-created problems or *truthfully* answer their questions. So should we be surprised when they turn to alcohol and drugs to drown their confusion, pessimism, apathy and depression; or take their own lives because they see no meaning and purpose to life?

Some years ago, a humorous, but deadly serious American gentleman spoke on the radio about religion. He bet that if he were to cut three holes in a sack, paint 'I am Moses' on the back and front and wear it walking along a

Californian beach, he would have at least 30 followers within the hour! He maintained that because there are more lost souls than ever before looking for answers to life's suffering, or something or someone to believe in, they would follow like sheep without questioning his motives or integrity. These are the ones, he felt, who need to 'belong' and risk becoming gullible prey to the vultures of divisive religious sects and cults that manipulate minds and split families.

Many, of course, do find comfort and a form of security in the faith of their religion, particularly during distressing times, and are quite content to use it as a crutch and not question it too deeply. The need to sing and pray in the social companionship of others I respect, and would certainly not wish to rock boats or disturb long-held beliefs.

For the benefit of novice seekers – and even agnostics and atheists who have ventured thus far – let me give a synopsis of four major religions and what knowledge I gleaned from their study. I may well surprise you with a fifth and, although it is not a world religion, thousands throughout the world now revere its philosophical wisdom.

Hinduism

Religion runs through the very heart of India, and for thousands of years it has been the home of numerous spiritual masters, swamis and gurus. And, as my mentor Dr Paul Brunton found, sorting the genuine from the fake and deluded is a veritable minefield. It was from India that much of the world's accumulated spiritual knowledge and wisdom spread to form part of the culture and religions of other continents.

For many years I developed an interest in the ancient Indian teachings found in the Vedas – perhaps the oldest of all spiritual teachings, the Upanishads which contain the philosophical aspect of the Vedas, and the Bhagavad-Gita which embraces Universal Truth in the moral dialogues between the human incarnation Lord Krishna (who was credited with virgin birth) and his disciple Arjuna. This philosophy – known as Hinduism – acknowledges no founder or formalised doctrines, dogmas or a human personalised God. It embraces unconditional love, the Universal Law of Karma and the evolution of the human soul (consciousness) based on meditation and diverse yoga disciplines. This is spread over many lifetimes (reincarnation) until total enlightenment (merging back with the Godhead) is achieved – philosophies that we will be investigating in later chapters.

On a visit to the Punjab in Northwest India in 1990, I was honoured to converse with Hindu holy men (Sadhus) and Sikh teachers who spoke about the necessity of humility and devotion regarding the study of such spiritual matters. It was also interesting to be informed that ancient Indian scriptures mention the atomic structure of the Universe, its vastness, and the Earth's relationship within it.

Throughout its long history, India has seen countless religious wars involving Hindus, Muslims, Sikhs and Christians. And since independence in 1947, Kashmir has suffered continuous religious conflicts causing the deaths of over 60,000 people.

> He who experiences the unity of life, sees his own self in all beings, and all beings in his own self, and looks on everything with an impartial eye.
> *Bhagavad-Gita (6:29)*

Islam

The religion of Islam, with its one and a half billion followers, worships Allah – the One God – and reveres the prophet Mohammed (570 – 632 AD). At the age of 40, after prolonged periods of spiritual experiences, soul-searching and a yearning to understand God and life's meaning and purpose – in desert and mountain solitude, he eventually received illumination from a spiritual presence which he later identified as the archangel Gabriel. The words conveyed during many such encounters became the teachings as written in the text of Islam's holy book the Koran or Qur'an – this being a code of laws and ethics and the Word of Allah (God). At the time, this was much needed for unification of the lawless tribal factions that dominated the territory, causing the inevitable conflicts until the religion became established in the region.

Islam also reveres Jesus as a prophet, and its doctrines, similar to Christianity, teach of a hell of fire and eternal torments for sinners and a paradise (heaven) that rewards the just and faithful. The birth place of the prophet Mohammed – The Holy City of Islam – is Mecca in Saudi Arabia, and all devout Muslims are expected to make the Hajj pilgrimage to the Grand Mosque at least once in their lifetime,

Islam embraces strict disciplines – prayer, five times daily; fasting (Ramadan); cleanliness and other aspects of daily living. I am informed by Muslim friends that Islam is a religion based on love, worshiping Allah and caring for the poor and needy. But they are saddened by the hatred and violence perpetrated by extremists in the name of their religion – also the divisions and conflict between Sunnis and Shiites. This was also evident whilst talking to Muslims in the Punjab.

I am a particular admirer of the Sufis who represent the mystical and pacifist aspect of Islam. Their writings have shown great wisdom and spirituality down the ages. The Sufi philosophy is one of pure love, and their one aim is to purify themselves from negative earthly contamination in thought, word and action and achieve the wisdom and bliss of complete union with God (total enlightenment) – a common theme in many religions.

> Say: 'O men, I am the Messenger of Allah to you all, from him who rules over earth and sky. There is no God but he. He ordains life and death. Believe in Allah and in his Messenger, the gentile prophet who believes in Allah and in his words. Follow him, and no doubt you will be well guided.'
> *Koran (vii, 155-8)*

Buddhism

Like many religions, Buddhism's, early years were not without internal conflict, power struggles and persecutions from tribal factions. Although, to the best of my knowledge, it is one of the few religions that has never raised a fist against another religion or forced its doctrines on any other country. It teaches tolerance of other religions and that alone makes it worthy of investigation.

Although derived from Hinduism, Buddhism is a scientific philosophy rather than a religion, particularly as it doesn't embrace a personalised God, only Cosmic Law. This appealed to my enquiring mind and encouraged me to investigate Buddhist philosophy in its various formats for pieces of life's puzzle. And what better role model could one have than to witness His Holiness the 14th Dalai Lama (Tenzin Gyatso) embrace unconditional love, compassion, wisdom and happiness.

> My religion is very simple. My religion is kindness.
> *The Dalai Lama (Tenzin Gyatso)*

Prince Siddhartha Gautama (C.563 – C.483 BC) was born in India, and at the age of 29 is reputed to have left a life of great wealth to seek spiritual enlightenment – the ultimate Truth. He questioned as to why there was so much suffering in the world when he had been born into a life of riches and splendour. During his quest, Siddattha conversed with Hindu holy men who advised him to follow the strict and austere yogic discipline of contemplation and meditation to tame the ego's earthly desires. After six years of devotion, whilst meditating under a Bodhi tree by a river in Bodh Gaya, Bihar, he achieved his objective of enlightenment – absolute bliss – Nirvana.

Henceforth he became known as Gautama the Buddha (the Enlightened One) and taught others how to attain the same goal following his experiences. Hence meditation and contemplation play a large part in Buddhism – similar to the Hindu and Sufi philosophies of enlightenment. Probably two of the best known treatises on the Buddha's teachings are the Pali Canon and The Dhammapada.

Buddha preached non-violence to all living things and left us the legacy of the *Four Noble Truths* and the *Eight-fold Path to Enlighten*ment. These teach that we can eventually become free of the Law of Karma (sowing and reaping) and Rebirth (reincarnation) by renouncing materialistic desires, adopting the middle way, keeping good thoughts, telling the truth and showing love and compassion. They also explain the reasons for our suffering and how we can avoid it. Buddha maintained that by following these principles we will eventually *know* and have an understanding based on *experience*.

> The religion of the future will be a cosmic religion. It should transcend a personal God and avoid dogma and theology. Covering both the natural and the spiritual, it should be based on a religious sense arising from the experience of all things natural and spiritual as a meaningful unity. Buddhism answers this description ... If there is any religion that could cope with modern scientific needs it would be Buddhism.
>
> *Albert Einstein1879-1955 (Physicist)*

Christianity

Today, all schools embrace multi-faith religious education, but in my day, Christianity was the *only* religion taught at school. As the adopted religion of my country, I decided to subject it to closer scrutiny, wondering if it would also yield pieces of life's jigsaw. Its book, The Holy Bible, consists mainly of the Old Testament – a Hebrew history book, and a much slimmer New Testament – the story of Jesus Christ.

According to most Biblical scholars, Paul (Saul of Tarsus) invented the Christianity that we know today. It was he who turned the simple words of Jesus the man into a saviour-god sacrificial religion, giving Jesus – whom he never met – the appellation of Christ. This has caused scholars to comment on the two conflicting gospel characters. One, being the gentle Jesus who healed the sick and talked of forgiveness, love and compassion, and the other, the stern theological Christ, the Saviour, the Son of God.

When we die, Christianity preaches that those who had faith and believed in Jesus Christ will go to heaven (paradise) and be with God, and an eternal torment in a hell of fire and brimstone awaits sinners and unbelievers – despite the Bible also informing us that God is all loving, forgiving and merciful!

Jesus is an enigma. The three gospels (according to) Matthew, Mark and Luke were written 30 to 70 years after his death, and the gospel (according to) John, written at least 100 years after Jesus' death, tell us precious little of his life from birth to 12-years-of-age, or from 13 to about 30-years-of-age. And what they do are a series of contradictions.

Unbiased scholars have long regarded Jesus as a non-historical character by the fact that no eminent writer at the time, Greek, Roman or Jewish, wrote about him or his activities – which is extremely curious if Jesus was such a prominent character. The Jewish historian Josephus (38–107AD) was credited with mentioning Jesus in his writings, but critical examination concludes that it is an interpolation. Which, according to the historian Gibbon, was added in the fourth century and definitely not in Josephus's style.

The historian Arthur Findlay wrote of the 17 saviour-gods in recorded history, and according to their followers all 'died to save the sins of the world'. Most were credited with virgin birth, were persecuted and died fateful deaths. Some of their stories are virtually identical. To further confuse the issue, scholars have also noted that the life of Jesus seems to share an uncanny resemblance to the life of Apollonius of Tyana, one of the wandering Pagan philosophers of the first century. He had disciples, healed the sick, raised the dead and condemned evil. Apollonius, who also rode into Jerusalem on an ass, was revered by some emperors as a god.

Although religions may claim their teachings are unique, Christianity has certainly been guilty of plagiarism, having copied from Zoroastrianism, Mithraism, Judaism, Hinduism, Buddhism and ancient Egyptian texts. Centuries ago the Church 'absorbed' the natural philosophical religion of Paganism (Pagan means 'country folk or dwellers') and Christian conquerors built churches on Pagan sites and adopted Pagan symbols. The Pagan Sun-God festival at the winter solstice on the 25th December became Christmas, and the Pagan fertility festival at the spring solstice became Easter. Paganism embraces a natural relationship with the Earth and its energies, and has grown tremendously over the last 20 years as followers become disillusioned with outdated and inflexible dogmas and doctrines of organised religion.

Various teachings from the Essene community (an ancient Jewish sect) were also copied word for word in the New Testament, as scholars found when they translated some of the hundreds of ancient Jewish scrolls that were found in caves at Qumran, near the Dead Sea in 1947. Many question why, after all these years, only 25 per cent of the translations have been officially released? Could it be because they were written at least a century earlier than the New Testament proclaims?

In 325 AD, at the Council of Nicaea, the Roman Emperor Constantine formulated what is known as the Nicene Creed. He, and the majority of the Council, decided which writings should form the gospels so as to form a unified religion of the Roman Empire, and any clergy who opposed this doctrine were imprisoned, tortured or murdered. And to further prove a point, the ruthless Constantine instigated the murder of his wife Fausta, son Crispus and numerous other unfortunates who dared to disagree with him. From that moment, Christianity became a power structure and a 'convert or die' religion.

It seems incredible how, from that meeting, 1,700 years ago, the simple teachings of a humble, wandering Jewish preacher and healer, have escalated into a multi-billion dollar business, with lavish cathedrals, bedecked with priceless gold and silk ornaments and icons. This has created a veritable army of cardinals, archdeacons, deacons, archbishops, bishops, deans, canons, priests, vicars and rectors, and spawned numerous cults, sects and sub-divisions within the Christian movement. How ironic, when the Biblical stories of Jesus depict him as a heretic who came into conflict with the priests and orthodox religion of his day for frequently exposing theological hypocrisy and bureaucracy!

If we take the basic teachings accredited to the man Jesus, they simply state that we should treat others as we would wish to be treated ourselves, that what we sow we will reap (Karma), and that God, being in each and every one of us, is our spiritual parent and permeates *unconditional* love. Therefore, we in turn should show love, compassion and forgiveness to one another. This makes perfect sense, but at the time, it contradicted the Old Testament writings depicting 'an eye for an eye and a tooth for a tooth', a fearful God of wrath, vengeance and jealousy who slaughtered without mercy. This angered the religious 'establishment' that wanted Jesus silenced!

The Jesus story is an excellent example of how enlightened seers, sages, masters, prophets, mystics and philosophers have, down the centuries, suffered persecution and premature deaths for attempting to bring Spiritual Truth to an ignorant planet. The man Jesus did not found a religion – he taught a way of life.

> The great sages do not identify themselves with any particular religion or creed. They are above all such distinctions. They belong to all humanity.
> *Swami Rama 1925 – 1996 (Living With the Himalayan Masters)*

For those who wish to further their enquiries there are numerous books that discuss the pros and cons of the authenticity of Christianity, whether Jesus ever existed and whether he was God or man. The Bible states that Jesus was crucified and his body placed in a tomb, and then confuses the issue by telling us that he was buried (1 Corinthians 15:4). Revelation 11:1 even tells us that Jesus was crucified in Egypt! And what are we to make of Acts 5:30 that states: 'The God of our fathers raised up Jesus, whom ye slew and hanged in a tree'? The hanging of Jesus is again confirmed in Acts 10:39 and 13:29.

Some scholars state that Jesus survived the crucifixion, married, had children and died of old age in Kashmir, India – with pictures of his tomb and family lineage to prove it. (Citing historical sources, convincing evidence is given in *Jesus Died in Kashmir* by A. Faber-Kaiser and *A Search for the Historical Jesus* by Professor Fida Hassnain). Kashmiri friends confirm the existence of Jesus' tomb at Rozabal in Srinagar, Kashmir.

Other researchers are convinced that Jesus died in 73 AD whilst helping the Zealots defend their last stronghold against the Romans at Masada. Others maintain that he survived the crucifixion, married Mary Magdalene, had children, fled across the Mediterranean and finally died in France – the bloodline surviving to this day.

Mary Magdalene is a fascinating character, and plainly not the 'whore' as portrayed in the Bible. Many historians believe that she was deliberately written out of the Jesus story, as talk of a 'Saviour' being married with children didn't sit comfortably with clerics 1,700 years ago! *The Mary Magdalene Cover-Up* by Esther de Boer makes intriguing reading.

In 1945, during an archaeological dig near Nag Hammadi in Upper Egypt, an earthenware jar was found that had been buried since the fourth century. In the jar were thirteen papyrus books, known as the Gnostic Gospels. These are alternative Christian texts that challenge those of the New Testament. In one of the books Mary Magdalene is described as Christ's companion whom he loved more than the other disciples, and places her at the forefront of early Christianity.

So, where do we go from here? Well, any organisation within the Christian movement that adopts the simple humble teachings of Jesus, without all the dogma, pomp and glory and masses of icons, has my admiration. The Salvation Army and The Society of Friends (Quakers) are good examples. The Quakers, founded by George Fox (1624 – 1691) have no sacraments or ministerial dogmas and doctrines and are total pacifists who believe solely in peace, love, respect, compassion and forgiveness. Wonderful!

This is my commandment, that ye love one another.
John (15: 12)

Native American Indians

The Native American Indians are a race for which I have great admiration and affection. Many now consider them to have been and, probably still are, despite past negative propaganda and lies, one of the most spiritual races ever to set foot on this Earth. They looked after and educated their young, revered and tended their elders and nursed the sick with love and natural healing, thereby making them truly civilised. In that respect I feel they put our Western society to shame.

Because they were at one with and, fully understood Nature (Pagans), their religion was simple; it was to honour the Great Spirit – Wakantanka (God) and respect Mother Earth. Their temples were simply the mountains and pine forests. They knew from *personal experience* that every living thing was connected and had a spirit (soul) and that there was an afterlife which they called the Happy Hunting Grounds (spirit worlds). The wisdom of some of their chiefs would do justice to the world's greatest philosophers.

Pause awhile over the profound words of the Native American Indians' 'Ten Commandments':

- Treat the earth and all that dwell therein with respect.
- Remain close to the Great Spirit.
- Show great respect for your fellow beings.
- Work together for the benefit of all mankind.
- Give assistance and kindness wherever needed.
- Do what you know to be right.
- Look after the wellbeing of mind and body.
- Dedicate a share of your efforts to the greater good.
- Be truthful and honest at all times.
- Take full responsibility for your actions.

If we discarded the entire world's religions and lived by these rules alone we would have a Utopia here on Earth, so why does the human race find it so difficult to live by such values? For 28,000 years the Native American Indians didn't, until the violent Europeans tried their ethnic cleansing tactics on them some 400 years ago, taking their land and forcing them to accept a belief-system religion. It virtually destroyed a race that could have taught us so much.

The Indians couldn't understand why, if the white races had but one religion, one God and one Holy book, they should differ so much about it, or behave so badly if this religion talked about a God of love. They witnessed the white races' broken promises, jealousy, selfishness and abuse, their violence and ability to wantonly destroy, their greed for money and land, sexual lust, disrespect for life and all living things, the need to constantly stupefy themselves with alcohol and a total lack of personal responsibility. And they called the Indians savages!

I am poor and naked, but I am the chief of the nation. We do not want riches but we do want to train our children right. Riches would do us no good, we could not take them with us to the other world. We do not want riches. We want peace and love.

Red Cloud 1822 – 1909 (Oglala Sioux chief)

Moral Guidance

It has been uttered, albeit by a tiny minority, that we need religion to give us moral guidance and values to live by. Those who have studied the history of religious intolerance, violence, cruelty and suppression might well dispute such statements. Blaise Pascal (1623 – 1662), the French mathematician and physicist, aptly stated: *'Men never do evil so completely and cheerfully as when they do it from religious conviction.'* And in 1999, when Professor Steven Weinberg, the 1979 Nobel Laureate in Physics, received the 'Emperor Has No Clothes' award from the Freedom From Religion Foundation, he said, *'Religion is an insult to human dignity. With or without it you would have good people doing good things and evil people doing evil things. But for good people to do evil things, that takes religion.'*

After decades of reporting religious (sectarian) violence, the media has now exposed numerous perversion scandals by making the masses aware of child abuse within main-stream religion. Thousands of priests and other clergy have, in recent years, been accused and charged with paedophile activities which, according to statistics, are rife in over 23 countries. Various commissions have been set up to investigate the problem, particularly in the UK and USA. This has inevitably led to secrecy and cover-ups by senior clergy that have deliberately turned a blind eye and moved *known* child-abusing priests from parish to parish where they have continually re-offended! Many abused victims, whose lives have been ruined, have come forward after as long as 50 years to expose the scandal. This has cost the Church huge sums of money in compensation. The media has called it 'a ticking time-bomb'. Globally, it's the tip of an iceberg that has shattered the faith of thousands of people who trusted these clergy with the religious education of their children.

A typical infamous organisation exposed for cruelty was the Magdalene Asylums – laundries run by nuns for 'fallen women' in Ireland. The nuns adopted an uncaring and brutal regime against thousands of unfortunate women who were forced to endure humiliation, torment and suffering for decades. These cruelties continued until the Asylums were closed in 1996.

In 2009, the media reported that Church leaders had covered up 'endemic' and 'ritualised' abuse of thousands of children in Roman Catholic schools and orphanages in the Irish Republic. It stated that for *six decades*, priests and nuns terrorised boys and girls with sexual, physical and mental abuse. The 2,600 page report by Ireland's Commission to Inquire into Child Abuse – which took nine years to complete – was damning in its condemnation of paedophile priests and the cover-up of their atrocities. Voltaire, the 18th century writer and historian, summed up such activities when he wrote: *'As long as people believe in absurdities they will continue to commit atrocities.'*

As well as thousands of documented cases of child abuse by clergy; some going back 60 years, there are numerous cases of vicars and priests being convicted of downloading child pornography from the internet. Many were involved in such depravities for years, even though they still continued to conduct church services.

Many have difficulty in accepting that such immoral acts of degradation are committed by clerics who preach faith and belief whilst threatening the masses with 'hell and damnation' if they dare break the Ten Commandments! Such hypocritical actions simply confirm that they don't believe a word of what they preach. They also offend the genuine and sincere Christians who try to live their lives according to the teachings accredited to Jesus. There are also numerous documented reports of such atrocities being committed by individuals within other faith systems, sects and cults.

Sadly, after considerable investigation, I reluctantly admit that I cannot find one iota of evidence that would substantiate any religion, sect or group – including politics – that attracts or perpetrates violence or abuse – in *any* shape or form – giving humanity a moral lead.

Organised religion has only been around for about 3,000 years, whereas archaeological evidence, published in Time and Mind, showed that even the earliest humans in Europe between 500,000 and 40,000 years ago showed a concern for the welfare of others. We now know that Neanderthals displayed compassion similar to us, as do many animal species; particularly when it comes to caring for their young and other family members. Love and compassion is the basis of all life throughout the Universe – that is Spiritual Law.

So who *will* give society a moral lead and set an example? Perhaps it could be you and I, and all the millions like us, just by being happy, showing love, compassion, kindness, forgiveness and patience to all who come into our lives!

Example is a living law whose sway,
Men more than all the written laws obey.
George Sedley 1639 – 1701 (English dramatist and poet)

Light-hearted

I have had many light-hearted discussions on my doorstep with well-meaning people who wish to introduce me to the Bible and save me from my sins. They thumb through literature and try to answer profound philosophical questions. Sadly, they never do, since their faith and belief is based on yet another individual's differing interpretation of the Bible – which is merely an opinion. I am informed that things are 'true' because they are in the Bible which is the word of God. When I question the evidence for such a statement, they usually reply: 'Because it is' – which always ends the conversation! They invariably leave promising that someone with more knowledge and experience will call on me. I am still patiently waiting!

Some years ago I encountered a student who was a member of a Church youth group. The conversation somehow got around to metaphysical subjects, of which she was extremely interested and wanted to know about life after death, reincarnation, God, healing and everything under the sun. Eventually, she asked if I would give a talk to her group. And so, with the vicar's permission, it was duly arranged.

I arrived at the church hall with a selection of books on the aforementioned subjects. Whilst placing them on a table, I noticed the vicar sitting in the front row with his arms folded and legs crossed – an interesting posture for connoisseurs of body language! After introductions, I launched into my presentation and talked about many personal experiences regarding the meaning to life and death, as well as any relevant scientific evidence.

Questions were invited at the end of the session, with a suggestion that they might like to browse through some of the scientifically inspired books on the subjects. I won't mention the response, but try to imagine an astronaut talking to the Flat Earth Society or a vegetarian lecturing to the Meat Marketing Board!

A very nice lady brought a cup of tea, thanked me for the talk, and said: 'I understood every word you spoke my dear, but the trouble with this lot is they are so blinkered.' The vicar also thanked me and rushed off to the local pub 'to get a couple of drinks in before closing time' as he put it!

I have frequently been asked my opinion of certain Evangelists who wear expensive clothes and jewellery, drive luxury cars and have expensive houses in acres of land. 'Alleluia brothers, the Lord needs your money' seems to bring out the wallets and chequebooks like moths to a flame. If I had that sort of mind and wanted to get rich quick, I would join them. The Lord doesn't need your money – *they* do!

I think religion would be very good for training athletes, particularly atheists, since whenever the subject is mentioned most of them want to run a mile!

Summary

Some religions have more to offer the individual than others, and if one offers peace and security and helps us to understand the spiritual values in life then it is right for us at the time. Despite what they may say, no institution or organisation has the monopoly on Truth, and we should have the freedom of choice to accept or reject any religion. Especially when we feel that we have outgrown belief systems, doctrines, creeds, dogma and ritual or have a need to know more.

Perhaps clerics of all faiths should seriously consider what they are asking people to have faith in and believe and, what *evidence* they can offer to substantiate it? Saying that such things are true and must not be questioned because they are written in old scriptures promotes numerous questioning minds in the twenty-first century.

> Any philosophy or belief system that cannot stand up to questioning or honest criticism is not worthy of further investigation and deserves to fall by the wayside to make way for those that can by reason of demonstrable facts.

When surveying our troubled world and noting the fear, hatred, cruelty, materialism, greed, corruption, crime, violence, unrest, poverty, racism, sexism, and drugs and alcohol abuse within those countries professing allegiance to certain religions, I cannot but observe how little their religions have helped their cause and how much they have hindered it. On studying organised religion's lengthy track-record, I don't think it would look too good on their CVs. One would expect religions to compliment each other like various orchestral instruments playing the same symphony from the same musical score. But it appears they all want to play different tunes in different tempos! Perhaps that is why we live in such a discordant world!

Neither am I impressed that some religions still demean women by treating them as third class citizens and denying them the privileges that men think are their own God-given right! It's not very spiritual when we read: '*But I suffer not a woman to teach, nor to usurp authority over the man, but to be in silence*' (1Timothy 2:12). And I don't suppose the Women's Liberation Movement was around when Paul penned: '*Let your women keep silence in the churches: for it is not permitted unto them to speak; but they are commanded to be under obedience, as also saith the law*' (1 Corinthians 14: 34). Had Paul written those words today, he would probably have found himself in court on a sexism charge!

It has been said that we should look for the common theme in all religions and not the differences. Krishna, Buddha, Jesus and the Prophet Mohamed, as *well* as the 6th century BC Chinese philosophers Confucius and Lao-Tzu, all taught a way of life in that we should practise love, humility, respect, kindness, compassion and forgiveness, as well as heal the sick, comfort the bereaved, help the poor and generally treat others as we ourselves would like to be treated. In that way, we would be living in accordance with God's Universal Laws. An amazingly simple common theme! But after centuries of religious turmoil, the 'theme' becomes increasingly difficult to find when it appears to have fallen on so many 'deaf' ears that practise 'lip-service' religion.

Blind faith and belief are not on my agenda – knowledge, facts and evidence are and, in that respect, I prefer to remain freelance in my outlook without religious labels round my neck. It is my policy to investigate, observe, accept what truths I feel may be offered and move on. In that way our minds are open to further knowledge and experience.

I also investigated Theosophy and Spiritualism, neither of which relies on blind faith since they are both scientifically and personally provable philosophies. I will expand on these as the quest unfolds as I found them to be excellent stepping stones in the search for the pieces of life's jigsaw.

Understanding that knowledge is a natural progression from blind faith and belief, represents another piece of the puzzle. We can now investigate whether there is any evidence for life after death.

> The mind of man, once released from the suffocating complacency of man-made religion, is ever-enquiring, always looking for answers and if released it will find them.
> *David Wood (Genisis: The First Book of Revelation)*

> Whenever you want to know the truth about any religion, all you have to do is to watch those who practise it with sincerity.
> Gordon Smith (Spirit Messenger)

5 *Life After Death* – *The Evidence?*

Part One

A Personal Search

The Search Begins

I was, and am convinced that there is an existence beyond so-called death, and that there are means of communication between the so-called dead and ourselves.
Sir Edward Marshall Hall 1858 – 1927 (English lawyer)

Living on this planet should carry a health warning since it will be the death of us all! Death is an irrevocable fact of life, and yet in the Western world in particular, we try to brush it under the carpet, treat it as a taboo subject and regard anyone who investigates it as weird. Despite the fact that over 500,000 of us die every year in the UK, we pretend it only happens to others and ignore it for as long as possible in the hope that it will go away and not affect us. Of course it never does, and when the inevitable happens to someone we love we are devastated and wracked with grief, particularly if the circumstances were tragic.

In our moments of despair we look for answers and comfort, but to whom and where do we look? To religion? If being told that our loved one is in heaven with Jesus or God gives us comfort, then that is fine – unless, of course, we have an enquiring mind. But as my dear friend Fred found out – the hard way – the Church is as publicly ignorant about life after death as it is about God. And let's be honest, if there is no life after death, just oblivion, then what is the point of religion – or life?

If I explain my own personal search for evidence *and* proof that we survive the death of our physical body, it will help you to understand how 'doors' open, and how pieces of the jigsaw fall into place for those who *seriously* and *sincerely* want to know. One of the early lessons my quest taught me was that answers are not given on a plate. Life will make us search for them, as any engineer or genuine scientist will tell you. So, if we do not *search* then we will not *find*, and if we do not *question* then we will get no *answers*.

Look and you will find it – what is unsought will go undetected.
Sophocles C.496 – 406BC (Greek dramatist)

My parents had recently retired from their 'open all hours' corner shop and moved to Hitchin in Hertfordshire. In the late 1960s my mother had received healing for osteoarthritis of the hip by the laying on of hands. It was because of this that they wished to remain in contact with healers for regular 'top-ups' as they put it. They wrote to the National Federation of Spiritual Healers who informed them that their nearest venue was Hitchin Spiritualist Church, a short walk from where they were living.

On Easter Sunday in the spring of 1973, the family and I visited my parents who asked if we would like to attend the evening meeting. They explained that the evening would consist of singing, healing prayers, a reading, a philosophical talk and a demonstration of clairvoyance (evidence of survival) by a guest medium. Never having seen a clairvoyant demonstration before, I jokingly suggested that a medium was midway between a small and a large. The joke was to be on me. As we walked to the meeting, little did I realise that it would *totally* change the direction of my life.

Hitchin Spiritualist Church was a modern purpose-built brick building, and as we entered the foyer we were given a warm welcome by committee members who made a great fuss of our sons Ian and Kevin. On entering the main hall I was surprised by the amount of conversation and laughter, it was certainly not the sombre atmosphere I had imagined at such gatherings. With over 70 people present that evening most of the seats were taken, so we had to split up with us at the front and my parents at the back.

The visiting medium was introduced as Mr Alan Chantrey from Peterborough. In his early forties, slim, dark haired, 183 cm (six feet) tall and very well dressed in a dark blue blazer. Not my stereotyped image of a medium; which goes to show how wrong preconceived ideas can be!

After harmonious singing and healing prayers, Chantrey gave a philosophical talk about life, and spoke for an impressive 20 minutes in a positive and passive voice without notes or falter. Every word rang true. This man spoke my language! I was even more intrigued when he was later asked to give 'evidence of survival' with a demonstration of clairvoyance. Approaching the front of the platform Chantrey went to various people in the audience giving them what I assumed to be descriptions of departed loved ones. Most of these were accepted by the recipients. Finally, pointing to me:

A.C: I'm coming to you young man – I have your grandmother here with me.
B.S: Which one?
A.C: (Without hesitation) Your mother's mother. She's about 90-years-of-age, five-foot nothing, with greying short curly hair. She has a pronounced curvature of the spine and has got very rosy cheeks – it looks like rouge. She wants to say to you: 'Wake up my lad, you're only half alive, and that's not you my lad'.

The medium continued to give more personal details from Gran, punctuated every so often by the words 'my lad'.

Facts: Gran was 92-years-of-age when she died. She was five feet tall (152 cm), and her short curly hair was *going* grey, not totally grey or even white haired, which was almost unique for a woman of her age. She *was* rounded of spine (osteoporosis) and did have *very* rosy cheeks. Whenever Gran was going somewhere special she always overdid the rouge making her look a little bit like a clown. But the icing on the cake was the frequent use of the words 'my lad'. Gran always referred to me as 'my lad', very rarely Brian. It was always, 'leave the cat alone my lad' or 'would you like a drop of port my lad?' in later years. And yes, on reflection at that time, I *was* only 'half alive'. My thinking and awareness of life has changed beyond recognition since then.

Impressive though this evidence was, Alan Chantrey continued by describing two 'deceased' uncles – one dressed in merchant navy uniform and the other a tall white-haired stocky gentleman. I couldn't recall either of them, as the uncles I knew were still alive at the time. Nevertheless, I accepted what they had to say as being relevant to my personal life. Chantrey thanked my three relatives for being there, ending with a 'God bless you'. The chairman then closed the meeting with thanks to all concerned.

That was my first experience of clairvoyance, and I remember sitting there thinking that it could be telepathy – this guy had just read my mind and that's all there was to it. On the way out my mother remarked: 'That was Gran to a tee wasn't it?' I agreed wholeheartedly. 'And the other two were *my* Uncles,' she said emphatically. 'The white haired one was Uncle Bob and the other was Uncle Harry who *was* in the merchant navy.' That demolished my telepathy theory as I had not been thinking about Gran and I never knew of my great Uncles.

For the rest of the week, that evening dominated my thoughts, because, if it *was* telepathy, why wasn't Alan Chantrey earning good money appearing on television or other venues? Enquiries revealed that he worked in an engineering company, didn't own a car and only charged train fare expenses for having given up a Sunday evening.

I decided to pursue the subject further – I was intrigued. It appealed to my inquisitive engineering mind that wanted to know the 'nuts and bolts' of it all. Armed with mild scepticism, I was determined to either expose the whole thing as a load of rubbish and leave well alone, or devote the rest of my earthly days to investigating life after death and all that it implied. After all, if my Gran *was* still alive somewhere in another dimension, with all her faculties and the same personality, then that means we *all* survive the 'death' of the physical body – and that must give a whole new meaning to *this* life.

We attended the Hitchin meetings every time we visited my parents, as I wanted to study the various mediums and converse with them on a scientific level. Male, female, young and old, they all had their individual styles. Some were full time, others part time with daytime jobs such as accountants, engineers, policemen, airline pilots, nurses and every other job and profession you could think of. Many were extremely positive and accurate with their survival evidence. The few nondescript 'messages' that didn't make sense seemed par for the course, and I was determined that such hiccups wouldn't put me off or deflect me from my objective.

In the autumn of 1973, out of curiosity, I visited the Spiritualist Church in Chesham not far from where we were living. This was an older building, rather like a very large garden shed but tastefully done. We sat at the back of the hall and waited for the meeting to commence. After what seemed like ages, the chairman looked at his watch and announced: 'It doesn't look as if the medium is going to turn up, so would you like to take the meeting Eileen?' He gestured to an elderly lady in the front row who made an effort to stand but had to be helped to the platform. She was wearing a leg iron, walked precariously with crutches and made bronchial wheezing noises. I was aghast, and felt that she should be in hospital not taking a meeting.

It took quite an effort for her to get up the steps and into a sitting position. The chairman introduced Eileen and invited her to open the meeting. She arose, walked *unaided* to the front of the platform, said a beautiful little prayer without any sign of a wheeze and returned easily to her seat. This was repeated without any problems whilst giving a short philosophical address and, again, when asked to give evidence of survival. She stood once more with ease, pointed to various people in turn and gave them what I considered to be excellent evidence, with full descriptions and personalities of departed loved ones. I cannot recall *any* that were not recognised by the recipients.

Eileen, pointing to me, said: 'I'm coming down to the gentleman at the back of the hall.' I remember thinking that she shouldn't risk it and that it could take an age for her to reach me in her condition. But I was amazed when she alighted from the platform unaided, refused offered help and, with a slight limp, walked up the aisle without crutches to where I was sitting. I was dumbstruck!

Standing by my side and with a lovely smile, she said: 'I have your Grandmother here on your mother's side of the family.' She went on to give another perfect description of Gran, complete with rosy cheeks and rounded back, just as Alan Chantrey had done at Hitchin several months before. The description was given without as much as a wheeze. 'She is showing me blueprints (engineering drawings) and is saying that you do these, don't you my lad?' said Eileen. Giving a little chuckle she continued: 'Your Grandmother is very proud of you and loves you very much (admittedly this could have applied to anyone, but it's a perfectly natural thing for a Gran to say). 'She finds it easy to come back because she was interested in life after death when she walked this Earth, and she is pleased that you are also. I will leave you with her love – God bless you.'

With a parting smile, Eileen walked back to the platform unaided and climbed the steps to her seat. The chairman announced that due to the late start they had run out of time and asked Eileen to say the closing prayer to end the meeting.

Facts: My profession *was* in engineering design, thus I was involved in creating drawings (blueprints to my Gran). The description of Gran was 100 per cent correct, complete with 'my lad' again. Also, Eileen's little chuckle was *identical* to Gran's – Eileen didn't have a natural chuckle. My Gran *was* interested in life after death, as I later found out, and had visited a London medium several times after the death of my Grandfather in 1955.

I made my way to the front of the hall after Eileen had been helped down from the platform. It was difficult to believe that it was the same women who had stood by my side only minutes before. She looked considerably older, was wheezing and had a job to walk, even with crutches. I introduced myself, thanked her for my 'message' from Gran and informed her how accurate she had been.

Eileen was only too pleased to talk with me and, as I caught a vague smile, I wanted to give her a big hug; she was in such a sorry state. She confirmed that she had no idea she was going to be asked to do the clairvoyance (which gave the messages more credibility), and had only come to enjoy the peace and receive healing. I asked how she could walk and breathe so easily whilst giving clairvoyance, to which she explained that when working with the 'power of the spirit' her physical problems didn't exist. In later years I was to confirm this phenomenon when observing disabled mediums who needed wheel chairs and crutches in normal life, but walked without them during clairvoyance.

Eileen was to be of great help to me over the next few years – although I felt it was mutual. I shall say no more, other than to add that she was a great lady and I shall be forever indebted to her. She once confessed that she had more love given to her from the spiritual worlds than she had ever known from this sad world.

For the rest of 1973 I continued to attend both Hitchin and Chesham Spiritualist venues whenever time allowed. I was determined to get to the truth of 'survival' come what may, and felt that the Spiritualist movement was the best bet at the time and worthy of further investigation. As I saw it, there was no other organisation that *attempted* to prove or *could* prove that death was not the end and that life had a purpose.

I became an avid reader on the subject, scouring bookshops – new and second hand – and libraries for any books that would help me. I found some absolute gems in the most unlikely places and digested the information like a starving man would food!

Over the following months I accumulated a wealth of survival evidence from various mediums. This included my 'deceased' grandmothers and grandfathers as well as other relatives, friends, acquaintances and old work colleagues. Some I had to enquire about – which subsequently proved correct – again demolishing my telepathy theory!

One evening, after a Hitchin meeting, the family and I were walking towards the exit when someone touched my arm and called my name. On turning, I found myself next to a lovely elderly lady who introduced herself as Mrs Tullet, the wife of the chairman (I was subsequently informed that she was a very accurate medium – keeping her clairvoyance strictly for friends and family, and not wishing to work in public unless asked to do so should the guest medium be unavailable).

'I'm being asked to tell you that you will do a lot for the Spiritualist movement in the 1980s,' she said. 'A likely story' I thought, since I had no intention of becoming involved in anything – after all, this was 1973. 'It's coming from a Tibetan guide,' she continued, 'and he says that he is going to show himself to you very soon.' Well, that certainly made the hairs on the back of my neck stand up. Receiving 'messages' from deceased loved ones was one thing, but guides *showing* themselves to me sounded scary. I look back now and smile, but for the next few weeks I slept with one eye open!

Weeks later, at another Hitchin evening, the medium was Mr Michael Gardner-Jones. He was of average height and build, in his early fifties, and sported a magnificent head of grey hair. I sat at the back of the hall quite content to just listen and observe when, half an hour or so into the clairvoyance, Gardner-Jones pointed to me:

M.G-J: I would like to come to the gentleman in the 'Jazzy' shirt at the back.

B.S: Who me? (A daft reply, as I was the only one at the back wearing a 'Jazzy shirt).

M.G-J: Yes 'Mr Jazzy' (much laughter) I have your grandfather here. He's mid- seventies, about six foot tall, slim built, quite bronzed, has a distinguished Roman nose and a large moustache. He's also wearing a 'cheese cutter' cap. I'm now getting terrible chest pains – he says he went with a humdinger of a heart attack!

Facts: This was a perfect description of my mother's father, so I didn't need to ask which one. My grandfather was 75-years-of-age when he departed this

Earth. He was six foot (183cm) tall, slim, and had tanned skin due to working outside nearly all his life. Although the nose description and large moustache were correct, his trademark was his 'cheese cutter' cap. Grandfather never went *anywhere* without it. We used to joke that he even slept with it on, and he did pass with a massive heart attack.

I was then given personal details, allegedly from my grandfather, which was factually correct, followed by:

M.G-J: You have a great healing ability; I see a lot of blue in your aura.
B.S: I've been told this many times but don't know what to do about it.
M.G-J: See me afterwards.

I took an immediate liking to this medium, he was different. With a cracking sense of humour he made people laugh without detracting from the underlying seriousness of it all as well as giving good evidence that 'death' was not the end of living. When the meeting closed, I joined a group of people waiting to speak with him.

Introducing myself, I reminded Michael of his request. 'I run healing and meditation groups at my sanctuary, would you like to come along?' he asked, and then added, 'Unfortunately, it's some distance from here. I live at Chesham in Buckinghamshire.'

'So do I,' I replied, amazed at the coincidence. When informed that the sanctuary was only a couple of miles from where I lived, I agreed to join his group the following evening. Once again, a life-changing experience beckoned.

The Sanctuary

The sanctuary was a lovely old cottage situated down a winding country lane on the outskirts of Chesham, and it was here that I found myself knocking on the rustic front door that Monday evening. Vera, Michael's wife, gave me a lovely warm welcome followed by a warning to duck my head as I entered the low hung doorway. Vera, in her early fifties, was of stocky build with greying auburn hair tied at the back. I immediately felt at home as she and Michael introduced me to the group.

Mike (as he preferred) had been clairvoyant from early childhood, had studied major world religions and philosophies and was also a renowned healer. He was a very spiritual man with an abundance of love and compassion for suffering humanity and, coupled with his esoteric knowledge and sense of humour, he seemed an ideal teacher. I would be learning both Raja Yoga meditation and healing by the laying on of hands. I will be expanding on these intriguing subjects in later chapters as they are important pieces in the jigsaw.

On numerous occasions I went to the Sanctuary armed with dozens of questions on metaphysical and esoteric subjects that I had thought of during the week. My mind was like a sponge soaking up the knowledge, which inwardly made sense as to why we appear to be living in such a world of turmoil and chaos. Week after week, month after month, Mike never failed to give me plausible answers to my searching questions – even when I jokingly tried to catch him out!

Psychic Visions

The meditation exercises gave me priceless moments of indescribable inner peace and awakened within me an awareness and intuition that had long remained dormant – but something else began to intrigue me. Quite often, when coming out of meditation, I would 'see' very clear and defined faces – male and female, young and old – with style of hair, colour of eyes and every line and wrinkle. Sometimes words came into my head; not thought words or through the ears, but a clear inner voice, often with an accent or dialect.

At the end of each meditation Mike would ask how we got on and what we experienced. Whilst describing the faces and repeating the words, many in the group recognised them as 'deceased' parents, grandparents, aunts, uncles and friends, and accepted the words as being meaningful to them.

When I asked why I was 'seeing' these faces and sometimes complete people, Mike explained that one of the 'by-products' of Raja Yoga meditation can be the development of the psychic faculty, which, apparently, most of us have. This would appear to be a common phenomenon and was mentioned extensively in Indian yogic philosophy. The yogis were advised to ignore it as it was purely psychic and considered a distraction on the spiritual pathway to God Consciousness. His advice was to do the same, as he only taught meditation and not psychic development – unless I wished to become a medium, which I definitely didn't. But once again, my engineering logic switched to a scientific wavelength when contemplating the possibility of 'seeing' and 'hearing' people who once lived on Earth.

A Bedroom Vision

In the autumn of 1973, I awoke in the early hours to see the most amazing figure of a Tibetan, or Mongolian, warrior standing at the side of the bed. Although the bedroom was almost pitch dark, he was luminous in brilliance and as solid as any human I have ever seen. His face was handsome and his smile radiant as he stood there with his arms folded across his chest. I estimated that he was at least 183cm (six feet) tall, about 40-years-of -age and wearing what looked like a leather body-warmer over his tunic. On his head was the most amazing gold-coloured domed helmet, slightly pointed on top and cut-away round the ears and over the eyes, culminating at a point on the bridge of the nose.

Surprisingly, I wasn't the least bit frightened, since he emanated an incredible radiation of peace and love. I did the usual routine of pinching myself and looking away, and was even aware of the clock ticking and a tiny chink of light through the curtains from a nearby streetlight. Being definitely awake and in full control of my faculties, I looked back to my left expecting him to be gone, but he was still there smiling at me.

We continued to look at each other for what seemed like minutes as, spellbound with awe, I analysed every line on his face. Eventually, he faded from my vision until I could see him no more. I was extremely disappointed and mentally pleaded, 'Please come back, where are you?' But he was gone. Was he the Tibetan guide that Mrs Tullet had spoken of many months before? Some might say that I was hallucinating, but I know what I saw and what I experienced. I would have accepted this as an isolated and non-provable incident, but a few months later a surprise awaited me.

We had invited friend Fred (who I mentioned in the previous chapter) to stay for the weekend, and although we corresponded regularly we did enjoy our philosophical chats. After lunch we settled in the lounge to update each other on our researches. Fred was telling me how he was investigating reincarnation, when in the middle of his dialogue he suddenly paused with an open mouth and stared at me intently. 'I'm sorry to break off our conversation,' he said excitedly, 'but I must tell you what I'm seeing.' Adjusting his gaze and seating position he continued, 'Standing at the side of you is a magnificent Tibetan warrior with the most incredible golden helmet, and ….' On hearing that, I couldn't wait for him to finish, and jumped up and got a pencil and paper. 'Draw him,' I said, eagerly awaiting his sketch.

Fred drew *exactly* what I had seen at my bedside months before, complete with the identical shaped helmet. When I told him the story of my 'vision' he was elated at having given me further evidence, and I was pleased that someone else had seen him. 'He certainly has a lot of love and spiritual power,' said Fred, 'and he will look after you and help you with the philosophy.' At that time, I had never told Fred that I was already drawn to the philosophy of Tibetan Buddhism. Fred's clairvoyant faculty was beginning to open up and he told me of the many spirit people he had seen over the last few months.

The weekend went all too quickly and, whilst driving him to the station, Fred told me that after all his years in the Ministry he had only just realised that we are surrounded by invisible worlds full of people. 'I have been blind to the truth all my life,' he said, 'what a terrible waste – I'm just beginning to wake up.' He paused as he got out of the car, 'And the sad thing is Brian, the masses are still asleep.' With that, he bid me farewell, shut the door and walked into the station.

Life Goes On

I was by now technical director of an engineering company with the responsibility of obtaining design projects and finding the right personnel to carry them out. Foolishly, and against my better judgement, I mentally brought the work home in my mind, causing me many sleepless nights. Often I would burn the midnight oil trying to work out difficult designs to save lost hours the following day.

This became mentally tiring and preoccupying, and meditation helped to keep me in check at a difficult time. To make matters worse, the managing director was 'borrowing' funds from the company accounts to prop up another business. Warning signs were flashing so, after twelve months, I left for better prospects, vowing never to let myself get into that situation again – but that was easier said than done.

My next employment was similar in nature but as a freelance Design Consultant. I continued to go to the Sanctuary for meditation and healing classes, read relevant books and attend Spiritualist venues at Chesham and Hitchin. This, coupled with increasing psychic experiences, gave me invaluable knowledge of life's laws and the meaning to life and death.

Material Changes

May 1975 saw us moving into a large house on the other side of Chesham as the bungalow was now too small for our growing family. Later that same year I was offered a contract with a local engineering company. It was in the countryside, which gave me ample opportunity to meditate or read by the side of the nearby canal during lunch breaks – weather permitting.

Humorous Moments

Being a student of life is not without its humorous moments. Having attended Chesham meetings frequently, I was invited to go on the committee. This entailed a rota system for chairing the platform for guest mediums and making them feel welcome on arrival. This gave me a chance to have in-depth talks with many of them as well as giving me confidence to speak from the platform during introductions.

On one such occasion I was chairing for the medium Bob Haynes from

Camberley in Surrey. During his clairvoyant demonstration I was relaxing with my eyes closed, when I became aware of two figures from the spirit world walking towards me. As they got closer I could see they were Chinese. One, a tall thin gentleman and the other short and rotund. Upon reaching me they smiled and bowed, just as the medium turned to me and said: 'Excuse me Mr Chairman, but two Chinese gentleman have just come to greet you. I don't know who they are but they look like the Laurel and Hardy of the spirit world.' This caused laughter in the hall, but it was interesting that the medium saw them as well.

Another humorous incident occurred at my first AGM which was held in the healing room. Just as the meeting was about to start, we heard footsteps coming down the aisle and stopping outside the healing room door. I got up to let whoever it was into the room, and imagine my surprise when, upon opening the door, found no one there. I closed the door only to be greeted by raucous laughter from committee members. Apparently a much loved and long 'deceased' committee member always turned up at AGMs and that year the joke was on me.

A month or so later, another strange but amusing incident happened. The large Ascot water heater in the bathroom had started to leak, so I decided to take it to pieces and investigate. Upon removing the cover and disconnecting the water pipes, I discovered the problem was a leaking heat exchanger that was beyond my repair capability, so decided to reassemble it and call a qualified heating engineer.

Try as I may, I could not get the pipes back together. A pipe had sprung and I was beginning to lose my patience. Suddenly, out of the corner of my eye, whilst lying in a prone position on the floor, I 'saw' the spirit form of a Native American Indian chief, complete with a magnificent feathered headdress. He was standing in front of the bath with his arms folded and laughing. Despite my sense of humour I was not amused, and even said out loud: 'OK clever-dick, how would *you* get it back together?'

'Why not put a large spanner under the fixed pipe and lever the other into position' was the Indian Chief's quick reply. Following his instruction, I had the whole thing back together in minutes. The 'apparition', still laughing, faded before my eyes. I had to smile; I had been in the world of engineering for over 20 years and had just been put in my place by a Native American Indian. The moral being, that if I had kept my cool I would have seen the answer to the problem myself! This 'vision' caused me to become interested in Native American Indian culture.

Clairvoyant Training and Discipline

One of the mediums who frequented both Chesham and Hitchin venues was Derek Markwell, a smart gentleman of slim build in his late thirties. His mediumship demonstrations were positive and accurate, giving excellent evidence of an afterlife, with full descriptions, personalities, ages and names. I admired this approach and made an effort to observe him whenever possible.

After one of Derek's Chesham visits, a mutual friend invited us, and Derek, back to their house for a drink and a chat. Half an hour later we were laughing and joking, when out of the blue, Derek remarked: 'You are very psychic Brian – would you like to sit in my development circle?' I was taken aback but gratefully accepted. Yet another life-changing experience was about to unfold!

The following week I joined Derek's development circle at his house in Ruislip, ready to be trained as a medium. The only drawback being, that I didn't want to be a medium – just a healer with clairvoyant ability. Being psychic or clairvoyant is one thing, but standing on a platform in front of lots of people offering them evidence of an afterlife was not really my scene. I was merely after personal proof that what I was seeing was real living people from another dimension who had once lived on this Earth. But life, as you probably know, doesn't always go according to *our* plans!

Eight of us were in Derek's group, and after initial introductions, strict procedures regarding the training and development of the psychic faculties were spelt out for my benefit. It was drummed into me that love, humility, integrity and discipline are essential for safe and accurate contact with higher astral dimensions. Arrogance and ego combined with psychic development, I was informed, was like playing with matches and dynamite. 'Do it properly or leave it alone', was Derek's philosophy.

After an opening prayer to the Great Spirit (Derek's favourite term) we were instructed to enter the meditative state for about 15 minutes to lose the sense of 'self', after which, Derek would expect us to demonstrate clairvoyance. That shouldn't be too difficult, I thought, after what I had been 'seeing' over the last few months; but I was in for a shock when it came to my turn! I was asked to stand up, go to at least two people in the group and give them evidence of survival. Derek told me to tune in, describe *exactly* what I saw and speak clearly as if I were on the platform in a local hall. I felt nervous and self-conscious standing in the middle of the group realising, for the first time, that this was a whole new ball game.

'I would like to come to you Vince,' I said, in a soft voice. 'Speak up!' interrupted Derek quite firmly, 'they can't hear you at the back of the hall.' 'I would like to come to you Vince,' I repeated in a louder voice, 'There's an elderly gentleman with you – I think he has a moustache, and…' 'You *think?*

Either he *has* or he *hasn't*,' interrupted Derek once more in a firm but friendly tone. Tuning in a bit more the spirit gentleman became clearer. 'Yes, he has a little grey moustache,' I said, hesitating. 'Has he any other distinguishing features, how old is he and what's his height and build?' asked Derek, interrupting yet again. 'He's about 75-years-of-age and I think he has a bald head with …' 'You *think*?' asked Derek, interrupting for the fourth time. 'You think too much – sit down, that's not good enough,' he said, smiling, 'but I trust that's proved to you that it's not as easy as you thought when under pressure.'

I reflected on how often I had seen spirit people so clearly when not under pressure and now I couldn't do it when eager to impress my teacher. Derek completed my poor attempt by describing to Vince who I was supposed to be 'seeing' and gave him a very relevant message from the gentleman. He then asked Harry to stand up, tune in, and give some *good* evidence of survival, which didn't do wonders for my self-esteem as he accentuated '*good*'.

'I have your Mother here,' said Harry, almost shouting as he pointed to John, 'she's 80- years-of-age, about five foot six inches in height, slim figure with a very pretty elfin face and curly white hair down to her shoulders.' Now that did impress me. 'She tells me that you have been sleeping badly due to financial problems on your mind,' continued Harry, 'but you mustn't worry as it will soon resolve itself.' John accepted the message as being accurate. 'Sit down big-head,' joked Derek, as he interrupted Harry. 'That's how it *should* be done Brian, but don't worry, we'll make a good medium of you yet!' said Derek with a broad grin on his face.

The training was extremely disciplined, as Derek wouldn't accept shoddy mediumship. There were far too many untrained mediums giving non-descriptive messages, he maintained, and stated that being able to play 'Chopsticks' on a piano was as far removed from being a concert pianist as being psychic is from being a good and accurate medium.

The weeks and months went by and we were taught how to tune in correctly by changing our consciousness to a different frequency. Very much like daydreaming or that state of mind when we are just waking up from, or going into, a deep sleep. It's that in-between state of consciousness when we are neither asleep nor fully awake. Many people have stated that is when they have seen spirit loved ones. That is the clairvoyant state that can be achieved from a normal conscious mode by proper training if a natural psychic ability is present.

One group evening, Derek wanted to prove the point that several people can see the same spirit person at the same time. He asked me to tune in and identify a spirit guide standing next to me, but not to mention who it was. This I did and could 'see' an Arab with a flowing white headdress held with a black band around the forehead. He then asked Eileen to tune in and tell the group who she could see. 'It's a lady with long blonde hair and a headband,' said Eileen. *'Wrooong!!'* retorted Derek, shaking his head and chuckling, 'try again.' After a long period of silence Eileen suddenly exclaimed: 'It's an Arab!' *'Correct!'* said Derek, 'Because you didn't tune in clearly the first time, you mistook the white headdress for long blonde hair.'

One foggy winter evening, I arrived at Derek and Eileen's only to be told that the meeting had been cancelled because of the bad weather. I had left home before Derek had telephoned. It was a nightmare journey but that was how dedicated I was in those early days. Having turned up, the three of us decided that we would just have an informal chat. After about an hour and feeling very relaxed, I 'saw' the solid form of an elderly 'spirit' gentleman sitting on the sofa next to Eileen. I described his personality and distinguishing features (including some black teeth) and mentioned that he was offering her a large bunch of chrysanthemums. She came over very emotional and said that I had just given an excellent description of her father.

Eileen explained that her father used to grow prize chrysanthemums as a hobby when he was on Earth, and by offering them to her was his way of saying he loved her and was still 'alive'. That experience made my journey worthwhile!

A Lady in Distress

It was about this time that Mary, one of the secretaries at my workplace, asked if I would have a chat with her elderly mum Bertha and hopefully give her some healing to perk her up. She had recently lost her husband and was feeling a bit down and sorry for herself. I met Bertha at her house in Thame in Oxfordshire and found her to be a lovely lady but very lonely. After a brief chat I suggested that she might like to receive some healing, so I sat her on an upright chair, placed her hands on her lap and asked her to relax as best she could.

I had just placed my hands above her head, when I 'saw' the spirit form of an elderly gentleman walk through the doorway, put his arms around Bertha and say: 'Hello me ducks, how are you today?' After the healing I told her what I had seen and heard, giving her a full description of the gentleman complete with cheese-cutter cap, rolled up sleeves and waistcoat. She was overjoyed and told me that it was a perfect description of her late husband and that he had always affectionately called her 'me ducks'. Bertha was still grieving and had never got over his death.

I visited Bertha many times over the months and she loved the chats and healing. On one occasion she became extremely upset whilst telling me the story of her brother- in-law Cyril who had been staying with her. Apparently, she was awoken in the early hours by a loud thud and a groan, and being very tired, thought she would investigate in the morning and promptly fell asleep again.

The next morning, when venturing downstairs, she found Cyril lying dead on the floor. Whilst she was telling this story, I 'saw' the solid form of a very overweight spirit gentleman, wearing a suit that looked too small for him, sitting in a chair by the fireplace rocking backwards and forwards with laughter. A very strange thing to do under the circumstances I thought.

Bertha went on to tell me that she had suffered terrible guilt ever since, and wondered if she had investigated when she first heard the groan he might still be alive. At that moment the gentleman stopped laughing and rocking and shook his head from side to side several times, whilst a voice in my head clearly said: 'She could have done nothing, it was very quick. Tell her not to worry – I'm fine.' With that, he faded from my vision. Upon explaining to Bertha what I had seen and heard, her tears ceased and was replaced with a lovely smile.

She confirmed that it was a perfect description of her brother-in-law Cyril, and went on to tell me that he had a terrific sense of humour and would rock backwards and forwards with laughter many-a-time. The chair that I had seen him in was his favourite, which he always sat in it when visiting her – and he had a suit that, due to his size, *was* too small for him! That was the way I envisaged using clairvoyance and healing, and it made me feel very humble and grateful. That evening, going to Bertha's house straight from work, I had managed to help her immensely. It gave her more evidence of the afterlife and took away years of guilt.

'That's My Pet'

Some weeks later I was helping at the weekly healing clinic at Chesham Spiritualist Church, and one of my 'patients' was a lady in her mid thirties. After introductions, she sat down in front of me and I channelled the healing energies around her head and shoulders. As I did so, I 'saw' the spirit form of a very handsome and distinguished looking gentleman, in his late fifties. He was wearing a blazer and tie, had a good head of grey Bryl-creamed hair with a quiff and sported a little grey moustache. He then said to me in a *very* posh voice: 'That's my Pet, you know, and I love her very much.'

After the healing I described who I had seen and what he had said. The look on her face was priceless and, with tears of joy, she told me that it was her deceased father exactly, and that he had always called her his 'Pet'. She was very emotional, and after she had left, it caused the other healers Madge and Les to enquire why. I was politely told not to give clairvoyance to people when they had only come for healing. I had been put in my place for doing what had given Bertha so much comfort – but I learnt a lesson!

A Door Closes

I was under Derek Markwell's strict guidance for two years, during which time, most of us had mastered the art of giving accurate clairvoyance with fine attention to detail. After one group meeting in the autumn of 1977, Derek informed some of us that he could teach us no more and needed to make way for newcomers to the group. 'I would be proud to book you for any Spiritualist platform,' he said. 'Get out there and do it, that's the only way you are going to get more experience.' Good advice, but I had no wish to be a platform medium. Neither did Harry, whose clairvoyance was some of the most accurate I had ever witnessed. I didn't remember much of the drive home – I was too much aware that another chapter in my life had just ended.

I still went to the sanctuary for meditation and healing instruction and, although I loved Mike and Vera dearly, I felt that grass was beginning to grow under my feet and that it was time to move on – but how and where?

Looking back to that particular time, I realise how many 'rough edges' had to be knocked off before travelling further on the quest. My spiritual education over the next five years was to be traumatic and painful, but what it taught me was priceless and absolutely necessary for a 'diploma' from the University of Life.

Disaster Looms

My job was rapidly becoming mentally tiring and, once more, I fell into the trap of taking work home and sketching designs on endless pieces of paper. The warning signs were repeating themselves – of which I should have been more aware. Waking in the night with design problems on my mind and finding it difficult to get back to sleep again was a recipe for disaster!

Well, disaster did strike in October1980 when my marriage hit the rocks. Sheila admitted that there was someone else and that it was serious. How could I have been so blind? Very easily it seems. Sheila decided to stay for Christmas for the sake of our two boys but would leave in the New Year when I returned to work. None of my pleading made any difference, and 21 years of marriage finally came to an end – I was devastated.

On the Sunday prior to her leaving, I loaded Sheila's car with suitcases and odds and ends that she wanted to take with her as tears rolled down my cheeks. When I went back to the house Sheila was also crying. The next morning we were very civilised and gave each other a big hug and a kiss and said thank you for those 21 years. We parted good friends, but I left for work knowing that another chapter in my life had ended and things would never be the same again.

Contemplating Life

That evening found me sitting alone in a large empty house contemplating life with a very uncertain future. I was hurting badly inside, wondering what I had done wrong, feeling rejected and a thousand other emotions, realising that everything I had worked for had collapsed around my ears. What worldly goods I had meant nothing to me now. Bricks and mortar, cars, money and career status didn't seem important any more. Although I didn't realise it at the time, it was another important and *priceless* lesson that I had to learn.

Our two boys, Kevin and Ian, aged 17 and 19, both stayed with me, and although they were out more than they were in, they gave me love, affection and sympathy as well as a good reason to get out of bed in the mornings and cook for them.

The weeks that followed left me feeling extremely sorry for myself, and it was compounded when my dear friend Fred telephoned to say that he had been diagnosed with terminal stomach cancer and was not expected to live much longer – another emotional blow when I was already on my knees. I have said many times that very few ever question life when it's 'hunky-dory', and seekers of Truth are not spared its traumas. Knowledge and experience merely softens the blows and heals the wounds a little faster.

'Laughing Boy'

I hadn't long joined a new meditation group in Harrow, and one evening I concluded that I wouldn't be in a fit state of mind to attend. I didn't want to spoil the evening for the others and rang my friend Pauline to tell her so. 'You get yourself over here,' she said in a firm voice, 'and don't you dare hang up on me.' She wouldn't take no for an answer, so I relented and went.

The group was very consoling, but I really didn't feel like participating. My negative attitude over the past week had caused me to feel distant from any spiritual help being offered. But I was mistaken, and what was to follow took me completely by surprise.

Within minutes of meditating, with my eyes closed, I 'saw' clairvoyantly an elderly Chinese gentleman standing in front of me. He was of lean build, at least 70-years-of age, had a long grey beard and wore a black hat and long gown with a cord at the waist. He literally emanated love as he stood there with hands tucked into his sleeves in typical Chinese tradition. He bowed, smiled and said: 'Greetings; you will not be lonely – and now I will make you laugh.' I felt that he was wasting his time as I was not in a laughing mood. He continued: 'Then I will make everyone laugh – our love and blessings to you all.' With that he bowed once more and faded from my vision.

As he did so, my lips broke into a smile with a distinct upward curvature exposing my teeth. I deliberately tried to stop it but couldn't. Then came a little chuckle, followed by a laugh, and before long I was laughing hysterically. I thought how ridiculous it was, when Ron, on my right started to chuckle which also progressed into hysterical laughter. Pauline next to him started until she too was in hysterics, and then Jean, followed by the rest of the group. One by one in anti-clockwise rotation we were laughing uncontrollably. The tears of laughter and joy were rolling down my cheeks until after many minutes duration I eventually stopped, followed by all the others in strict rotation. After a brief silence, Ron asked: 'What the heck was that?'

I explained what I had seen, what had been said, and how I had tried to stop laughing but couldn't, whereupon the others confessed the same. None of us could help ourselves or stop laughing until the 'power supply', or whatever it was, ceased. We were all taken aback at what had happened and marvelled at the amount of love that had been given. Ron suggested we call the Chinese gentleman 'Laughing Boy', and from that moment my sadness left me. I came away from the meeting on a spiritual high, instinctively knowing that everything was going to be all right.

From then on, 'Laughing Boy' was with me frequently and, right to the present day, I have regarded him as a very dear, wise and knowledgeable friend who, with love, compassion and wisdom – together with other spiritual helpers – has stood by me in times of concern. Knowing my strengths and weaknesses, he has encouraged me to move forward on the narrow path of Spiritual Truth. I have 'seen' him and experienced the laughter and love countless times since that memorable day, and will be mentioning him from time to time.

Matchmaking

On 31 January 1981, after their class had finished, I was invited to the Sanctuary for a chat and a cuppa. Mike and Vera welcomed me with the usual bear hugs and introduced me to the group. The next two hours passed quickly and just after midnight people started to disperse. I was about to leave when Vera reintroduced me to a young lady. 'Patricia is having trouble with her car,' she said, 'and I was wondering if you would follow her home to make sure that she gets up the hills.'

Smoke? I had never seen anything like it coming from the exhaust of Patricia's battered old Hillman Imp. I tried to follow closely but couldn't see the car or the road for smoke. After a couple of miles, knowing that she was safely up the hills, I abandoned the chase, and when the smoke had cleared, turned round and went home.

The following evening I received a telephone call from Vera saying that Patricia had offered to cook me a meal. She gave me her number and suggested I call her. This I did, and asked Patricia if she got home OK and thanked her for offering to cook me a meal. 'I didn't *offer* to cook you a meal,' she replied, 'Vera *asked* me if I would cook you a meal because you were not eating properly and had lost weight.' We both laughed when we realised that Vera was exercising her matchmaking skills!

The meal invitation became a reality and, despite my nervousness, the evening was a success. Patricia was 39, slim, pretty, and had an abundance of love and kindness. She had been divorced for three years and was living on her own with her two children Mark and Neil aged eight and nine. After a few weeks of regular dating, we grew very fond of each other, and our meeting was to change both our lives for the better – but testing times were to come.

How Did I Get Sweet-Talked Into This?

In February 1981, I received a letter from Alan Chantrey, the first medium that I had seen at Hitchin in 1973. He had taken the liberty of recommending me as a guest medium to Boston Spiritualist Church in Lincolnshire for a date in April. Apart from exchanging Christmas cards and the occasional chats when he visited Hitchin, Alan knew very little about me. I decided to call him, ask why me, and mention my reluctance to be a platform medium – and the fact that Boston was 130 miles away!

'Of course you can do it,' said Alan when I rang him. 'You can stay overnight at my place in Peterborough and I will go with you the next day for moral support.' In a moment of weakness, and not wishing to offend, I relented and agreed to do it. On putting the phone down, I made up my mind that it was *definitely* going to be a one-off booking.

Have you ever had a cold sweat, when your body and hands felt chilled but the perspiration was running from your brow? That was how I felt whilst sitting on the platform of Boston Spiritualist Church in front of 60 people who were expecting me to give them evidence of 'survival'. 'How did I get sweet-talked into doing this?' ran through my mind. I remembered the years of training I had been through in Derek Markwell's group and asked my guides and mentors in the spirit worlds for their assistance.

My face immediately started to grin from ear to ear, and culminated in a feeling of peace and love beyond description. It was 'Laughing Boy', the Chinese gentleman who had given me such reassurance, and there he was, standing in front of me as I heard the president introduce me. My next impression was that of an American Indian who 'appeared' by my side – the same one who had given me plumbing advice many years before, and what a tower of love and strength he was now. From that moment, all fear vanished!

I didn't remember much of the next hour or so, but I was relieved when it was all over. Alan Chantrey made his way towards me and said: 'Well done, you've proved you can do it. Did you know you had an Indian chief and a Chinaman with you tonight?

'They really liked you,' said the president as she handed me a cup of tea and some biscuits. 'Thank goodness for that,' I thought, 'now I can go home.' 'Can we book you again for later this year?' she asked. I was taken aback by the question and proffered the excuse of time and distance. 'How about just one booking for next year then?' she asked in such a sweet voice – a voice that I just couldn't refuse. I had, there and then, committed myself for next year, but what I didn't envisage was Boston giving my name and telephone number to other spiritualist venues!

For the next week or so I was inundated with calls for bookings and, once again, I didn't have the heart to say no except to those who were too far away. To compound the situation, Mike had also given my details to dozens of spiritualist venues when he realised I had accepted bookings. I was now booked to the end of 1981 with hardly a spare weekend, but thankfully Patricia backed me all the way. She was to become my most ardent fan and my most constructive critic. I had unwittingly and, against my own initial wishes, launched myself as a platform medium!

Little did I realise at the time what plans 'Laughing Boy' and other spirit helpers had in mind. They were to make it perfectly clear that I needed to do my 'apprenticeship' as a platform medium to enable me to meet thousands of people, to comfort the bereaved, give evidence to seekers of Truth and understand for myself the philosophy behind suffering, death and dying.

A Favour Returned

It was about this time that Bertha made contact again. She was saddened by my marriage break-up and wanted to meet Patricia. We spent a Saturday afternoon with her at Thame where she was so pleased to see us. It was quite noticeable that she was a much stronger and happier lady than when I first met her. As Patricia and I were leaving, Bertha took me to one side and whispered in my ear: 'You'll be all right with this one my dear.' How ironic that I had comforted Bertha for nearly five years and now in my predicament she had given *me* loving words of comfort and reassurance.

Not long after that meeting Bertha moved to Devon where she lived for over 20 years until she joined her husband in one the spirit worlds in 2005 at the age of 92. I bet his first words to her were: 'Hello me ducks, how are *you* today?'

Health and Work Problems

For some months before we met, Patricia had been having occasional bouts of nausea and internal pain. In May 1981 she collapsed and was rushed into hospital. A gallstone problem was diagnosed – which they eased – but she was sent home and put on a waiting list for an operation. I will tell you the outcome of this story in the chapter on Healing, as something remarkable happened whilst Patricia was in hospital.

Things were changing rapidly in my material life and, in the June of 1981, negative problems at work reared their ugly head. I had, unknowingly, got sucked into a 'political' situation within the company. Being in a senior position I was asked to resign. I refused, and said they would have to sack me. They obligingly did!

A Vision Makes Me Cry

The recession was beginning to bite hard and engineering design work was difficult to find. It was a time of industrial doom and gloom. Although it was still early days for Patricia and I, I now had no wife and no job. Two large doors had firmly closed behind me. By now, I was beginning to understand how the laws of the Universe operate and trusted them implicitly by adopting a positive attitude and acceptance of the situation. It meant taking one day at a time, living for the moment and enjoying our time together.

I had been in regular contact with my agent to see if any freelance engineering contracts were available. He wasn't very optimistic, so we decided to take a few days break. Patricia's mother offered to look after Mark and Neil so we headed for the south coast and found a suitable bed and breakfast at Selsey in Sussex. The following day we visited Chichester cathedral and noticed posters advertising a Janet Baker concert scheduled for the following evening.

The cathedral was packed to capacity and we were right at the back. The music was magnificent and Janet Baker sang many arias in different languages. Half an hour or so into the concert whilst staring at the floor by my feet, my mind drifted into thinking about my strange and uncertain predicament and how my world had totally changed in the last few months. At that moment, I became aware of healing hands being placed on my back and shoulders. The heat was amazing and the whole of my spine was glowing. Don't ask me why, but I instinctively knew that three monks from the spirit realms were standing behind me and administering healing.

I continued to stare at the floor and was amazed to see, very clearly, a pair of sandalled feet protruding from under a white robe. Then a hand was placed under my chin and very gently lifted my head. As my head came up I could see the folds in the robe and a cord around the waist. Eventually, I looked into one of the most spiritual faces I had ever seen. It was that of a bearded young man, probably in his mid-thirties with the hood of the white robe about his head. The brilliant radiance around him was incredible, the smile on his face was of pure wisdom and his eyes were the most loving and compassionate. The amount of love pouring into me was indescribable. As his hand stayed under my chin, I felt absolute humility in his presence. Then, very clear and distinct words came into my head: *'I will not let you down.'*

The vision slowly faded and, as I came out of the trance-like state, could hear once more the orchestra and Janet Baker's beautiful voice. Tears of emotion had run down my cheeks and soaked the front of my shirt. Any doubts as to my future had disappeared, knowing all was well and under control. I had literally been supercharged with energy and was on a spiritual high, the like of which was beyond words. Patricia was staring at me in a look of amazement. 'Are you OK?' she whispered, 'You are glassy-eyed and have been crying.' 'I will tell you about it later,' I whispered in reply.

The concert over, we joined the queue for the exits, and felt as if I was 'floating' instead of walking. I was so happy inside with not a care in the world and couldn't stop smiling. What a contrast to how I had felt on first entering the cathedral.

On the way back to our B & B we stopped at a restaurant for a bite to eat and talk about the experience. My first question was obviously 'Who was it?' Had I been of a religious faith, presumptuous or on an ego trip, I could very easily have said it was Jesus. It was certainly the stereotype image of him. But on the other hand, I was aware that very high spiritual beings wear white robes – often referred to in esoteric literature as 'The White Brotherhood' – which appears to be the dress code of their status. White-robed 'spiritual guardians' greet many people when they have a near-death experience (NDE) – a phenomenon that we will be looking at in the next chapter.

I had a completely open mind as to who it could have been, but I was curious as to why he had said '*I* will not let you down' instead of '*We* will not let you down.' Guides and other teachers of spiritual truth invariably say '*we*' and not '*I*'. They talk in the plural not the singular, so who could it have been that would have said '*I*'? Of all the visions that I have been privileged to see, this one was to have the most profound effect on me, even as I write those words all these years later. Here is a brief account of how issues fell into place after that memorable event in Chichester Cathedral:

'I will not let you down'

• The following day I telephoned my agent who informed me that he had arranged an interview with a client who was interested in my design experience. Having been out of work for five weeks this was a welcome sign. On the Monday morning I went for the interview. The Project Manager was impressed enough to start me immediately.

- Soon after, Patricia's friend Bill called on us. By a remarkable 'coincidence' he had been in a similar position to myself and dismissed in a similar way. Having taken his company to an Industrial Tribunal and won the day with agreeable compensation, he advised me to do the same since I had nothing to lose. I did, and the tribunal found in my favour. The company admitted full liability and an 18-months-old Ford Capri was offered as compensation.

- One evening, I received a telephone call from a very distressed Sheila, saying that she would like an amicable settlement to the divorce, as things were getting out of hand with the solicitors who seemed to relish the 'battle' that neither of us wanted. We met at the house, decided who wanted what in the way of furniture and knick-knacks, and had the whole thing sorted within the hour. We finished with a meal and a chat down the local pub and agreed to put the house on the market. The divorce was finalised within a few weeks and, we are still, to this day, very good friends and meet at social occasions.

The house took ages to sell. It was now the autumn of 1982, the recession was in full swing and 12 months had rolled by since we had set wheels in motion. The chain had broken *four* times, putting us back to square one each time. This was very frustrating, as after weeks of house hunting we had finally put a deposit on a new one being built in Bedfordshire. We were determined to trust the promise of the 'vision' and not get disheartened. I had asked Patricia to marry me and we were looking forward to starting a new life together in our new house.

The house build had reached first floor window level and the builder would soon be asking for his money. At this stage there was a risk of losing the house, but fortunately Nature intervened. Thanks to heavy rains, the first few months of 1983 were some of the wettest on record – which put the builder well behind schedule.

- Our wedding day was looming, it was still raining and there were floods everywhere. Our concern was for good reason. We were getting married at the Sanctuary, Mike Gardner-Jones was taking the service and the reception was to be held in the Sanctuary garden. On June 3rd the rain was torrential. On June 4th, our wedding day, it was the sunniest for weeks and we had an amazing day to remember.

- Our honeymoon was to prove quite eventful – in a spiritual manner of speaking – and a phenomenon occurred that was to have a profound life-changing effect on me. I will share this with you in the chapter *Is There a God of Love?*

We returned from honeymoon to find a letter from the builder demanding full settlement for the new house and wanting to sign contracts within three weeks or it would go back on the market. With no buyer in sight for the Chesham house, *'I will not let you down'* looked very precarious. I finally decided to borrow the money.

- The next morning I visited my local bank to ask for a bridging loan for £50,000 – a considerable sum to borrow in 1983. 'I'm afraid we don't do bridging loans for people who haven't sold their house,' said the manager. The disappointment on my face must have prompted him to pause and say: 'Just a moment sir, I'll review your case again.' He was gone ages and, finally, on his return, said: 'You have been a good customer with our bank over many years, so in your case we have decided to make an exception.'

'*WHAT!* Are you mad?' said my solicitor when I telephoned him the next day. 'If you can't sell that house for months you will be financially crippled,' he stressed. 'Why on earth did you do it without consulting me?' I never told him of my trust in a vision, since he would never have believed me and would probably have had me certified!

- Mowing lawns and cutting hedges was a regular chore at the empty Chesham house. I was doing just that on the day following my solicitor's ranting, when a middle-aged gentleman and his wife opened the side gate and walked across the lawn towards me. 'Is this house still for sale?' he asked. I informed him that it was and invited them to look around. After a brief viewing he approached me. 'We like it,' he said, 'are you open to offers?' 'Try me,' I replied. He offered less than the asking price, but I accepted it – I just wanted to get rid of the house and close that chapter in my life.
  'We've already sold our house, so it will be a cash purchase.' After some hesitation he continued: 'There's only one snag – we want to move in within three weeks.' Amazing! That was the time the builders wanted to sign contracts for our new house. 'Do you think the solicitors will be able

to complete in time?' I asked. 'Well, we want to, so that's good enough isn't it?' he replied with a grin.
'Impossible!' said my solicitor when I confronted him the following morning. Well, I'm normally a very placid person but I found his attitude tiresome. 'Look, *I* want to move in three weeks, and *he* wants to move in three weeks,' I said, *'SO JUST DO IT!'* And guess what? He did!
We moved into our new house in August 1983. I formally adopted Patricia's two sons, Mark and Neil, and thereby became a 'new' Dad. The love and affection I have received over the years have been priceless!

I often think of that highly evolved soul that I 'saw' in Chichester cathedral all those years ago, when we trusted his words *'I will not let you down'*. In past history when people experienced such 'visions' and 'heard' voices, they started a religion. As for me, I just signed a bridging loan!

Time to Move On

By now, I was fully booked for mediumship two years ahead with hardly a spare weekend to ourselves. Who said they had no wish to be a platform medium? Even midweek was booked for clairvoyant demonstrations, Question and Answer evenings and lectures. Despite demanding jobs, we often rushed home from work, grabbed a bite to eat and drove for miles to meetings, frequently staying on afterwards answering questions from people who had been severely battered and bruised by life. We looked upon it as a labour of love – for which they were always grateful.

I continued with the clairvoyance in halls and spiritualist venues until 1996 when, after 15 years on the circuits, I declined further bookings, having felt that the time had come to move on and concentrate on the higher philosophies. Communicating with loved ones and friends in the astral worlds is as natural as talking to them when they were with us on Earth but, as we will see, there are many more pieces to the jigsaw of life.

Over the years, Patricia and I met numerous people who had had psychic and spiritual experiences or who were interested in the philosophy, so we started regular discussion evenings for those with open minds who wanted to talk about such subjects, share their experiences with others and ask questions. We did this for over 20 years until work and committee commitments hogged our diaries!

Let us now hear from others who would like to share their experiences with you, and look at some of the scientific evidence for life after death.

Spiritualism is not a religion; it is a discovery – the discovery of an actual fact in nature. Like other facts in nature it always existed and operated, even before it was discovered.
John Butler (Exploring the Psychic World)

Spiritualism is the scientific explanation of the Christian belief and faith in survival of life after death.
Canon Harold Anson (Master of the Temple)

Patricia and I signing the marriage register in the Sanctuary – witnessed by Michael Gardner-Jones

Sketches of four guides as seen and drawn by the author.
Note the Chinaman, affectionately known as 'Laughing Boy'.

Life After Death ***– The Evidence?***

Part Two

Evidential Experiences and Scientific Research

Communication Between Worlds

I am absolutely convinced of the fact that those who once lived on Earth can, and do, communicate with us. It is hardly possible to convey to the inexperienced an adequate idea of the strength and ultimate force of the evidence.

Sir William Barrett, FRS 1844 – 1925 (Professor of physics)

Millions of people the world over have, for centuries, experienced spontaneous psychic encounters. Here are typical examples:

Less Sceptical Now

Eric Davis, 65, a retired company director recounts:

I had never really given any thought to ghosts or spirits or anything spiritual, and in that respect I suppose you could call me a sceptic – that was until my first encounter. This was the sudden and very clear vision of a young girl of approximately nine years-of-age. She had long scraggy hair and was wearing a grey tattered dress with a ragged cut bottom. I would guess the period to be sometime during the Middle-Ages. She often stands by the head of my bed looking or waiting for something. There is no communication, just a happy little girl. Over a period of four years she has visited me seven times.

Some years ago I was having a nightmare which really scared me. Suddenly, I heard a voice say: "Don't worry I will take it away." I woke up with a fright, and saw a man in the old style sailor's uniform sitting on the bottom of the bed. He was about late fifties in age with a big bushy beard. He was wearing a blue and white striped T-shirt, a red cravat and a black berry hat. The type of person you would expect to see on a pirate ship. He looked at me as he waved his hand in the air. Immediately all the fear and panic left me and I felt peaceful and calm. I have seen him several times over the last four years.

I have no opinion either way about these visions – but I know what I saw. I'm a little more open-minded and less sceptical on such matters now!

'How did you get into the house?'

There are numerous accounts of young children seeing spirit people, and this story comes from 50-year-old David Walsh:

When I was 10-years-old, I woke up one morning in the early hours and saw an elderly gentleman with long white hair and bushy white beard standing at the foot of the bed. We just stared at each other, and I thought: "How did you get into the house?" I woke my 12-year-old sister Karen, and said: "What do you think of this?" She looked and saw him and said: "Oh yeah!" When I realised she could see him as well, I hid under the covers!

'That's him!'

When six-years of-age, our son's nephew, Matthew, came rushing in from the garden one day, all out of breath, shouting: 'Mummy, mummy, I've just seen great, great, great grandad.' 'What on earth are you talking about?' asked his surprised mother. 'I've been talking to him,' said an excited Matthew. To which his mother asked: 'How did you know who he was?' 'Because he told me,' said the lad. 'What sort of things did he say?' asked his mother. 'He asked me how I was and what I was doing and if I was happy,' replied Matthew.

His mother placated him at the time, not wishing to hurt his feelings or accuse him of imagining such things, but later searched through some family photograph albums. She found some old sepia photographs showing elderly men and women, and asked Matthew if he recognised any of them. He immediately pointed to a particular gentleman, saying excitedly, 'That's him! That's him!' Matthew had pointed to his great, great grandfather. And had, in the excitement of his garden 'vision', added too many 'greats', but he had correctly recognised a photograph that he had never seen before!

'Who are you talking to?'

In the summer of 1972 we were invited to a party in a large Victorian house in Luton. The hostess called everyone into the dining room where the buffet had been prepared, and it was then that we noticed our eight-year-old son Kevin was missing. I went to look for him and eventually found him in the lounge. This was an extremely large room with a high ceiling and ornate fireplace. Kevin was completely alone, and yet he was talking to someone. I caught him by surprise when I said, 'So there you are. Who are you talking to?' 'These people,' he replied. 'What people?' I asked, humouring him.

Kevin started to describe men with 'funny' whiskers wearing dress suits, bow ties, and butterfly collars. Some were smoking cigars and others strange pipes. The women were wearing ball gowns with bustles. Some of the people were drinking wine, he informed me. 'What did they say to you?' I asked. 'They just asked me my name and if I was enjoying myself,' he replied, 'and they had *very* posh voices,' he added.

At the time, and much to my regret, I was ignorant of such experiences and just told him to come and have some food. What Kevin had 'seen' and 'heard' was a typical Victorian party in a typical Victorian house! He couldn't have invented such a story because he knew nothing of that period or the style of clothing.

'Very, very sorry'

Whilst collecting her young daughter from nursery school, Mary Slater was a witness to the following:

A four-year-old girl told her teacher that she needed the toilet. After several minutes of absence the teacher went to investigate. On approaching the toilet door, the teacher heard the child holding a conversation with someone inside the toilet. She immediately knocked on the door, opened it, and found the child on her own. She asked the child if she was all right and enquired as to who she was talking to. "My daddy," replied the child. "Your Daddy?" asked the sceptical teacher. "Yes, he said he was my daddy and he was very sorry for dying," said the child. "What do you mean?" the stunned teacher asked. "My daddy said he died in a car with a hose and was very, very sorry," replied the child.

When the girl's mother arrived to collect her, the teacher decided to tell her what had transpired. On hearing the story the mother went ashen and had to sit down. She explained that her husband (the child's father) had committed suicide when she was pregnant by sitting in the back of their car with a hose connected to the exhaust pipe. The mother had never mentioned the cause of the father's death to the child for fear of upsetting her.

'Man!'

Carol Swann tells of her granddaughter's experience:

Back in the 1980s, my daughter Dawn lost a dear friend and colleague. His name was George and he was only 26 when he died. One day, when my granddaughter Anya was only a few weeks old, barely able to focus and wrapped in a blanket on the settee beside me; I became aware that George was in the room and walking towards Anya. I mentioned this to Dawn, who was sitting beside me, and she said, "I know! I saw Anya smile and follow something across the room to right beside her."

Dawn continues the story:

Anya was about 18-months-old and lying on our bed waiting to be put into her own, when I sensed that George was around again, and asked Anya if she could see anyone. Anya starting smiling and waving, and pointing her finger said: "Man!" She would not have done that voluntarily, and I guessed that

George was smiling and waving at her.

When Anya was about three and a half-years-of-age, I took her on a visit to my friend Faith in Watford. Although not mentioning it that day, Faith had recently lost her little dog and was still upset about it. Anya suddenly said that she could see a little dog and described him in great detail. Faith remarked that it was an extremely accurate description of the dog, and that where Anya was pointing was exactly the spot the dog always went to.

> Long before they shed their mortal figment, souls that have done naught but good, acquire the faculty of conversing with those souls that have preceded them in the spiritual life.
> *Lord Krishna (Bhagavad-Gita)*

With the Gita's 2,000-year-old message in mind, let us now look at other forms of psychic phenomena.

Orbs

In recent years the subject of orbs has come to the fore. These are the mysterious balls of light, like miniature moons, that thousands of people are discovering on their family photographs. In the vast majority of cases the orbs were not obvious to the naked eye when the photographs were taken, although a few people have confided that they have seen them visibly since childhood and take them for granted. Several recent photographs of myself also contain orbs of various sizes

It doesn't seem to matter whether the photographs are from 35mm roll films, digital cameras or even single use throw-away cameras, the orbs continue to appear. So much so, that scientists are taking the subject seriously – some having experienced the phenomenon personally – and are scrutinising the images in their laboratories, having ruled out faulty cameras, moisture, dust and other obvious influencing factors.

In 2007 an Orb Conference took place in Sedona, Arizona, where scientists openly declared that they believed orbs to be of paranormal interest worthy of serious investigation. Many orb pictures have been considerably enlarged and found to contain images of humans and animals – some recognisable as 'deceased' relatives and pets. Many believe them to be spiritual in origin and are an intricate part of life after death.

Peggy Weber, who visibly sees orbs, took a photograph of one in her bedroom, and when enlarged on her computer, recognised the image as that of her beloved husband Tony who 'died' some years before. Having seen the orb picture of Tony, I can verify that it was a perfect likeness of him when he was alive on Earth. Peggy, who is writing a book on the subject, has thousands of orb photographs, many of which are currently being studied by scientists.

Direct Voice

This phenomenon is where 'deceased' relatives and friends from the spiritual worlds are able to speak to a gathering of people via a mechanically contrived voice box – usually trumpet shaped – with the help of an accomplished medium. One world famous direct voice medium was the late Leslie Flint who, for 60 years, gave evidence to thousands from all over the world that the communicators were who they said they were. Most giving full names, nicknames and highly personal details that only the recipients and communicators knew, often speaking in their native dialect or accent.

Many of Flint's meetings, mostly held in small private gatherings, but sometimes held in large halls over periods of up to two hours, were frequently attended by clergy of all ranks, including priests, vicars and bishops, as well as politicians and other notable members of society. Over the years, Flint voluntarily subjected himself to rigorous, often scientific, examination prior to meetings to safeguard against accusations of trickery or fraud.

Transfiguration

Transfiguration is another form of mediumship where people from the spiritual worlds superimpose themselves over the face of a sensitive person so that they can be recognised by a third party. My first experience of this was in 1975 when I was asked to join a regular group who were sitting with a developing transfiguration medium by the name of George Bone.

Bone sat in a chair with a low-wattage lamp placed on his lap so that it shone up into his face. The main light in the room was switched off, and I waited in anticipation of what would happen. Moments later Bone's face was completely overshadowed. Firstly, there was the face of a very elderly lady with white hair who was recognised immediately by one of the group as a much-loved grandmother. This lasted for several seconds before fading. The face of a much younger bald-headed gentleman immediately followed and was recognised as a father. For the next hour faces continued to come and go, with all shapes and sizes, young and old, male and female, with many recognised.

Sitting in a meditative state with his eyes closed, not once did Bone's facial expression change as we counted over a hundred different faces in the hour. For me, the most fascinating ones were the different nationalities that superimposed, including Arabs, Chinese, Black Africans, Native American Indians, Egyptians and Indians with and without turbans.

One evening, whilst sitting at home reading, my face started to tingle and felt as if it was covered in cobwebs. Before I could say anything, Patricia exclaimed: 'Good heavens, my father has just transfigured over your face.'

In the late 1980s, I attended a transfiguration demonstration given by the Welsh medium Ray Williams at a public hall in Markyate. During the demonstration the hall was in darkness except for the weak light placed under the medium's chin. Dozens of different faces transfigured, with Williams calling to the area in the hall where the recipients were sitting. Most faces were recognised, but a few not.

One of the faces that transfigured looked familiar. It was the face of an old Chinese gentleman with a black hat and a long stringy beard. Williams' voice boomed out: 'I want the tall bearded gentleman at the back of the hall.' No one answered, although I did fit the description. After an uncomfortable silence, I shouted out: 'Me?' Back came the reply: 'Yes, *you*. There is a Chinese gentleman here who says that he makes you laugh – is this so?' 'Yes,' I replied, recognising Laughing Boy's face. '*Good*,' said Williams, 'because he has some spiritual advice for you.'

An accented voice then spoke from the mouth of Ray Williams. It was Laughing Boy's humorous but deadly serious tone, and what he had to say was uncannily accurate. I had never met Ray Williams before or since, and he couldn't possibly have seen me at the back of the hall in almost pitch darkness with a light shining in his face.

Carolyn Mutter tells of her transfiguration experience:

On Friday 16 February 2007, Andrew, my best friend and confidant, died in a car accident on the way home one evening, on a road he had driven many times over many years. Some weeks later, a friend mentioned that in the past she had seen a lady called Heidi, a spiritual medium, and suggested that we try to see her in the hope that she would be able to make contact with Andrew. An appointment was made, and little did we know it would be a time that changed my belief and thoughts about life after death.

My fiancé (also called Andrew), Rachel and Holly (our deceased friend's daughters) and myself approached the front door, and although I felt scared and uneasy, we were warmly greeted by Heidi. Within minutes we were in the kitchen chatting and drinking tea.

A short while later we sat on a sofa in the front room of the house. Red candles were burning on the mantelpiece and the shelf behind us, casting a peaceful and gentle light into the room. Heidi sat on a dining chair about three feet in front of us and was clearly visible to all. I was asked to move so that I would be sitting on her left side. Upon asking why, I was told that it was the side my folks would appear.

Being ready to commence, Heidi tied her long hair back to expose her face, whereupon and amazing event began. Her face became empty and a black swirl replaced her beautiful features. On the left side of her face an image of a woman appeared. Instantly I said: "It's my mother." Heidi nodded in agreement. I felt peace but also sadness because I miss her so much. The image was as clear as looking at a live person or photograph. Her features were just as I remember them; a beautiful smile and gentleness.

Moments later she seemed to change from the forehead down, to be replaced by a deep forehead and eyes, which we all recognised as our friend Andrew who had died in the car accident. We naturally asked him what happened and told him we missed him. He smiled as his image moved over to the right side of Heidi's face, to be replaced by a young male who I recognised from photographs as my fiancé's brother James who died when he was 21. He leaned towards me and said: "I like you," then turned to face my fiancé Andrew. Andrew asked him how he was getting around (due to a brittle bone disease, James had spent all his life disabled, in pain and wheelchair bound). He replied: "It's ok; I can do what I want now." He then made reference to Andrew not eating his (James') food now. Since James had been unable to feed himself properly, Andrew would oblige and occasionally helped him finish his meal.

Friend Andrew appeared again, and Heidi said he had been having fun with me. Another change came when my granny appeared and I spoke about shared memories. Friend Andrew then reappeared – which he constantly did after every person – smiled, as only he could, and was immediately replaced by a female face. Heidi then scratched the backs of her hands alternately and said that I would recognise the gesture. I immediately knew it was my step-grandmother, an ex-school mistress, who I called Aunty Mary.

Aunty Mary was then replaced by friend Andrew who was very persistent, as though he was trying to tell us something. Next, came a lady with high cheek bones, white hair and very dark skin under her eyes. I recognised her, again from a picture, as Andrew's grandmother who passed when she was 101-years-old. She moved off to the right side of Heidi's face as friend Andrew appeared again. We told him he ought to give others a chance, but he seemed reluctant to leave, even when Heidi cast her head downwards. Then, an Egyptian looking gentleman rushed from left to right and escorted Andrew from the scene. I asked who it was, and Heidi replied: "He's my spirit guide – he's a good man."

A male face then appeared that we thought could be my fiancé Andrew's father. I said: "It can't be Frank; he doesn't have a beard or glasses." Heidi nodded and said: "You want a beard and glasses?" Right before our eyes the image morphed a beard and glasses – it was Frank as I knew him. He turned to Andrew and said: "You are a good boy." Emotions were very high! Then my mother came back and told us that she had someone with her – it was my father. I was tearful when I told him I loved him, and said that I was sorry I didn't stay with him at the hospice where he passed. I didn't know if he was cross with me. I had just travelled from the Hospice in Camberley in Surrey, to my home in Norwich, when the phone call came to tell me that he had just passed away – alone. This had always been my regret and made me very sad.

Heidi then ended the evening and said that our friend Andrew mentioned something about tyres – a new car maybe? We also thought it could be something to do with his Austin Champ. As we left the house, I had the feeling that all was not sorted.

The following day, Rachel rang and said that Heidi had called her to say that she had been woken early that morning by our friend Andrew, and that he was cross with her because she had got it wrong, and should not have told us that we were going to get tyres or a new car. The reason for his accident involved tyres. Andrew had purchased new tyres from the internet a week or two before he died. The inquest verdict was accidental death, but the only thing they could find was two split tyres.

Materialisation

Materialisation is the name given to physical mediumship as distinct from the mental mediumship of clairvoyance (seeing), clairaudience (hearing) or clairsentience (sensing). With this phenomenon, people who inhabit the spiritual worlds can materialise in solid form so as to be fully recognised by friends and loved ones here on Earth, often in broad daylight. Imagine the thrill of being able to hug and talk to a dear friend, a mother or father and other loved ones who have 'died'. There are numerous documented cases where this has happened. In fact, spirit people materialising after they have 'died' has been a phenomenon for thousands of years in most cultures. In many instances the presence of a physical medium is not always required. Here are a few typical examples:

A Surprise

In September 1983, my mother started to lose her memory, and on two occasions was found wandering in the town not knowing where she lived. She was medically diagnosed with severe dementia. Within one month she was 'dead', and the autopsy revealed a massive brain tumour. A few days later, I was walking home from work across my local park thinking about a problem that had occurred with one of my design prototypes, and barely noticed a tall elderly woman walking towards me. We were within a few strides of each other when I recognised her as my mother, wearing slacks and coat. 'That was a surprise wasn't it Brian?' she said. 'Yes, for you or me Mum?' I replied, as we embraced each other with a hug, absolutely stunned at how solid and real she was and how radiant she looked. We both cried tears of joy, saying how much we loved each other, and I could even smell her perfume. The shock of seeing her snapped me out of my work worries, and as I gazed at her wonderful smile, she gradually 'dissolved' in a faint mist. That was *three days before her funeral!* At my request Michael Gardner-Jones took the service.

A Teeth Occasion

In May 1984 I was asked to be best man at a friend's wedding, and during the rehearsal a rather humorous incident occurred. The future bride and groom were standing at the altar with the Pastor, rehearsing their commitments, and I was a few metres away directly behind them. Suddenly, I received a sharp nudge in the ribs from someone's elbow. Looking to my left, I saw a very tiny grey haired elderly lady, in her late seventies, standing by my side. 'I'm going to put my teeth in for this occasion,' she told me, in a delightfully extrovert manner. 'Are you really?' I whispered back in amusement. She gave a lovely smile, nodded and faded in a ball of mist! Solid though she was, I realised then that she must have come from one of the spirit realms.

After the rehearsal I told Bob of the experience and described the lady in detail hoping he would know her. He was 'shell-shocked' and informed me that it was a perfect description of his long deceased grandmother. He explained that she had a habit of elbowing people in the ribs when she wished to attract their attention. He also added that her false teeth spent more time in a glass than in her mouth, and that her gums were so hard she could chew toast. He also confirmed that she only put her teeth in for special occasions. Bob asked me to repeat the story to his brother at the reception the next day. I did, and he confirmed every detail. We joked about people in the spirit worlds suffering from bruised ribs since she went over there!

'What Yer Doing Boy?'

In the spring of 1985, I was servicing our Ford Capri, and had the cam-cover removed trying to set the tappets. I was vaguely aware of someone walking across the lawn and poking their head under the bonnet. Looking up, I expected to see my neighbour, but to my surprise it was Patricia's father who had 'died' in March 1984.

'What yer doing boy?' he said to me in a curious voice. Once again I was caught off guard seeing Harry, quite solid, leaning on the wing smiling at me. 'Trying to fix this,' I replied, as I watched him disappear in a white mist. I put the spanners down, rushed indoors and told Patricia what had happened. She explained that her father was very interested in working on cars and motorbikes and used to do all his own maintenance. He also had a habit of calling men he knew as 'boy'. I knew none of this as I had only met Harry a couple of times prior to his passing.

A Prison Vision

Not long ago, 'Jim' – a friend of an acquaintance – was 'set-up' on a drug charge and was consequently given a three year prison sentence. One morning he told a prison officer: 'I had an elderly man talking to me all night, and among other things he said he hung himself in my cell, is that true?' (The apparition was physically solid).

The officer was visibly shaken but confirmed 'Jim's' description of the man, who he was, and what he had told 'Jim' about his conviction, before adding: 'We don't talk about it – he was a nice old boy and we liked him. We don't like prisoners to know which cells occupants have committed suicide in.'

Flight 401

This is a fascinating true materialisation story which became a best-selling book and Hollywood film. It concerns an American Eastern Airlines jumbo jet, Flight 401 which, in December 1972, crashed in the Florida Everglades killing 99 passengers and crew. There were 77 survivors.

In his intricately researched book, *The Ghost of Flight 401*, John G. Fuller explains how salvaged non-structural parts were used as spares for the maintenance of similar Eastern Airlines planes. Not long after this tragedy, Captain Bob Loft and Second Officer Don Repo, both having 'died' on the ill-fated flight, materialised in solid form in full uniform on various Eastern Airlines' planes that had utilised the salvaged parts. They appeared so normal that they were accepted as part of the flight crew – that was, until they dematerialised, causing panic and upset amongst passengers and crew!

On an incoming flight to Phoenix, a woman passenger became hysterical when she saw the empty seat next to her suddenly become occupied by a crewmember – he immediately 'disappeared' when she started screaming. She was removed from the plane in a straitjacket!

On another occasion, Don Repo materialised on the flight deck of an L1011 aircraft, warned the crew of an impending malfunction and then 'vanished'. The flight was aborted and a subsequent maintenance check confirmed the malfunction. On another flight, a malfunctioning galley cooker was repaired by a fully materialised Repo after the stewardess had asked for a maintenance engineer. She thanked the Captain, who then stated that an engineer had yet to attend. When the stewardess described the repairer, the Captain immediately recognised him as the 'deceased' Don Repo.

Fuller further explains how they contacted Don Repo through several experienced mediums, with proof that he was who he said he was. Repo also gave intricate flight take-off and landing procedures for his aircraft, why it crashed, as well as imparting highly personal details of his life and family. All this was unknown to the mediums and author but subsequently proved correct upon investigation.

The following examples of materialisations require the presence of physical mediums. That is to say, mediums who produce a substance known as ectoplasm – which comes from the Greek *Ectos* (outside) and *Plasmo* (to shape) – and can exude from the nostrils, mouth, ears or stomach. Ectoplasm forms into bodies of the deceased which makes them solid and touchable to loved ones, friends and other onlookers.

Minnie Harrison

Materialisation medium, Minnie Harrison, ran a weekly Family Home Circle from April 1946 to the mid 1950s in which 'deceased' family members and friends would materialise in solid form in the Harrison's living room. Two regular visitors were Mrs Agnes Abbott (Aunt Agg), one of Minnie's elder sisters who passed over in 1942, and Granny Lumsden, Minnie's daughter-in-law's grandmother who passed over in 1930. They, and others who materialised, would chat, laugh and joke with their family members just as if they had never 'died'. All concerned looked forward to their regular visits.

One of the sitters in the Home Circle was Mrs Florence Hildred whose husband Sam had 'died' suddenly in December 1945. Imagine her wonderment when Sam became a regular communicator at the Circle and spoke with his wife as only he knew how, with the love, affection and humour that he had shown when on Earth.

Another regular sitter was Mr William Brittain Jones, F.R.C.S., a man of the highest integrity with years of investigative experience in such matters. He was also a highly respected surgeon and Superintendent of Middlesbrough General Hospital. On one occasion, Mr Jones' held hands with his materialised mother who, before she left, referred to him as 'Brittain my boy'. Mr Jones later confirmed that this was what his mother always affectionately called him – personal information that no one else in the room knew.

Minnie Harrison passed over to the spiritual realms in 1958 and her son Tom – another attendee at the Home Circle – kept regular notes of events for many years and, in his booklet *Visits By Our Friends From the 'Other Side',* Tom recalls a son who fully materialised and comforted his mother and father who had been grieving for nine years since their son Bruce's death. That emotional encounter changed their lives for the better. Tom maintained that it would be wonderful if all grieving parents, relatives and close friends could experience such comfort and reassurance.

Helen Duncan

Scottish Helen Duncan is, arguably, one of the most publicised of all the world's materialisation mediums. Not just in the many books written about her, but in various press articles over numerous years. Alan Crossley, one of Helen's biographers and close friend for many years, was a recognised leading expert on materialisation phenomena with well over 40 years experience of the subject. Alan witnessed up to thirty fully materialised figures at many of her public meetings with identification evidence, often spoken in Russian, Spanish and other languages and dialects, given to loved ones and friends present.

One of Mrs Duncan's controversial meetings took place during World War ll, when a young sailor fully materialised and stated that his battleship, H.M.S. Barham, had been sunk by enemy torpedoes (Mediterranean – November 25, 1941). The sailor's mother, who was present at the meeting, refused to accept that her son was dead and wrote to the Admiralty for confirmation. Because of the news blackout, they replied, asking her where she had obtained the information as they had not been officially notified that HMS Barham had been sunk. When the Admiralty *were* finally notified, it was established that the sailor had materialised at the exact moment the ship went down.

From then on, Mrs Duncan was closely monitored by the authorities. At a séance in Portsmouth in January 1944 Mrs Duncan was arrested, and in March 1944 at the Old Bailey, was charged under the 1735 Witchcraft Act but, in reality, she was sentenced for security reasons amidst claims that she had been in possession of classified information. The authorities fearing that she might divulge D-Day plans! Mrs Duncan offered to demonstrate her materialisation phenomena to the court but the request was refused.

Russell Byrne

This is one of life's classic love stories between two worlds. With Gwen Byrne's permission, here is a brief account of the story of nine-year-old Russell Byrne who 'died' of cancer in August 1963. In August 1982 Russell communicated via automatic writing at a meeting (séance) in Leicester, gave his parent's contact details and asked if someone could get in touch so that he could be reunited with them. Despite the 200 mile journey to Leicester, the outcome was that Alf and Gwen Byrne were reunited with their son who 'died' twenty years before. Over many months, Russell materialised hundreds of times for his parents as they hugged and kissed him, often sitting on their laps reminiscing about personal details of his childhood on Earth.

Alf and Gwen's other son, Kevin, a scientist, also witnessed the materialisation of his brother on many occasions and confirmed without doubt that he was Russell. One may question as to how and why a little boy, who died 20 years earlier, would materialise as a nine-year-old and not a 29-year-old. The answer being, that although he would be 29-years-of–age in the spiritual worlds, his parents and brother may not have recognised him at that age. According to researchers, this is typical of most child materialisations. Gwen wrote of their wondrous experience in her book *Russell.*

Two other parents present at the Leicester meetings were Mr and Mrs Jefferys who embraced and spoke with their materialised 16-year-old son Michael who 'died' in a motorcycle accident. Again, their experience was repeated numerous times, not just at Leicester, but in their own home where meetings were also held.

Alan Crossley also spoke and embraced his 'deceased' wife at the Leicester meetings, and stated: 'I know what I know and no one knew my wife better than myself.' Alan also added: 'I have been privileged to witness four such mediums who have adequately proved to my satisfaction that psychic phenomena is a reality and demonstrates the ability of those who have died to return and hold a normal conversation as well as appear in full human form. It is not a question of belief as far as I am concerned – I KNOW!'

The Leicester materialisation meetings, like many others today, eventually restricted the phenomena just to family and close friends to avoid hostile harassment from the narrow comfort zones of those who criticise without bothering to investigate.

Alec Harris

Alec Harris who, apart from being an established healer, was a highly respected Welsh materialisation and direct voice medium, and for nearly 30 years, both in his own home and in public venues, demonstrated beyond any doubt, that under favourable conditions, those who have 'died' have the ability to materialise in solid form enabling them to be recognised and converse with loved ones and friends here on Earth.

At one meeting thirty recognised figures, many of different nationalities, materialised and spoke with family and friends in their native language, often in rare dialects. Many professional people attended Alec's meetings, both in the UK and in South Africa, where he and his wife Louie went to live in 1957, and vouched that the evidence they received from materialised friends and relatives was genuine.

Louie Harris recalled attending a very emotional Helen Duncan meeting where her father materialised and embraced and conversed with her mother (his wife) and Louie. Alec 'died' in 1974 aged 77.

Isa A. Northage

Isa Northage was a highly gifted healer, direct voice and materialisation medium who, from the age of three, heard spirit voices and played with spirit children and animals. In 1949, Isa founded the *Pinewoods Healing Church* where spiritual healing was given to seriously ill patients – the recovery rate was impressive. The healing was administered by one of Mrs Northage's spirit guides by the name of Dr Reynolds, who practised on Earth in the early 1800s. He would fully materialise to do the 'surgery'.

From 1938 – 1958, Isa Northage was instrumental in proving that persons from the spiritual worlds can materialise solid and be recognised, conversed with and hugged by loved ones on Earth. To do justice to such evidence and honour the memory of Isa Northage and *Pinewoods,* Here are brief extracts from Allan Macdonald's self-published book *A Path Prepared.*

Then there was the young man, badly injured in a mining accident near Doncaster, who had been treated in hospital for a fractured skull, injured pelvis, and severed nerve tissue, and was unable to move arms or legs. He had been sent home as nothing further could be done for him, and was not given long to live. As a last resource he was brought to my surgery in an ambulance by his father and uncle to see if anything could be done for him. After two spirit operations he was able to get on his feet again. For these operations Dr Reynolds again fully materialised and was assisted by Dr Hollander whom I have mentioned previously. One operation was performed on the skull and another on the pelvis. Within a year this young man was again able to walk and play games.

MAI FENG SHANG. – The beautiful form of this Chinese girl emerged from the mists which seemed to rise from the floor, and spoke as follows: "Survival is no new revelation as you people of the West seem to think. We Chinese have known and practised communion with spirits for thousands of years. I passed over to the world of spirit six hundred years ago and it was practised thousands of years before my time.... Trance utterances and materialisation of spirit forms are all known to the Chinese.... With these words Mai Feng Shang dematerialised, leaving behind a lovely perfume of incense.

I am Mrs E.... H.... of Rubery, Birmingham, and since 1948 have witnessed wonderful and, to me, evidential phenomena. At my first sitting my mother materialised and spoke of intimate family matters, and my niece Hilda, who had been unable to walk some time before her death, also materialised and danced before us,.......

It's a wonderful little book, and full of witnessed materialisations of a personal nature that were extremely evidential to the people concerned. Like all personal materialisations, it would be extremely naive and crass of critics to suggest that sitters are fooled by imposters posing as long-deceased loved ones and friends.

They whose minds scorn the limitations of the body,
are honoured with the frequent appearance of the spirits.
Their voices have been often heard, and they have appeared
in forms so visible that he who doubts it must be partly bereft of reason.
Cicero 106 – 43BC (Roman lawyer, politician and philosopher)

Scientific Research

I have come to admire all the serious researchers on the subject of survival and feel that we should owe them a debt of gratitude for proving that life is not futile, and that we do indeed live on in another dimension. For readers who may be interested, I have compiled a list covering the last 150 years of persons, many of great scientific and intellectual standing that have investigated and researched physical mediumship (materialisation) and many other aspects of metaphysical phenomena. Their names are in alphabetical order:

Professor Alexander Aksakov (Russian scientist and psychic researcher)
Dr Hernani Andrade (Psychic researcher – Brazil)
John Logie Baird (Pioneer of television and psychic researcher)
Dr Douglas M. Baker, B.A., M.R.C.S., L.R.C.P., F.Z. (Scientist, writer, lecturer and psychic researcher).
Lord Arthur Balfour, KG, OM (Prime Minister 1902 to 1905 – Chair of the Society for Psychical Research [SPR])
Sir William Barrett, FRS (Professor of physics – Royal College of Science, Dublin and Member of the SPR)
Professor Henri Bergson (Scientist and Member of the SPR)
Professor Ernesto Bozzano (Italian scientist and psychic researcher)
Professor Angello Brofferio (Scientist, philosopher and psychic researcher)
John Butler (Psychic researcher and writer)
Dr Hereward Carrington (Psychic researcher and writer)

Professor Ercole Chiaia (Scientist and psychic researcher – Naples)
Dr W. J. Crawford (Engineer and psychic researcher – Queens University, Belfast)
Dr Robert Crookall (Doctorate in science and philosophy – psychic researcher and writer)
Sir William Crookes, FRS (Physicist and psychic researcher)
Alan E. Crossley (Psychic researcher and writer)
Dr Cyriax (Scientist and psychic researcher – Berlin)
Air Chief Marshall Lord Dowding G.C.B., G.C.V.O., C.M.G. (Psychic researcher and writer)
Sir Arthur Conan Doyle, M.D., LL.D. (Psychic researcher and writer)
Professor Hans Driesch D.Phil., LL.D., M.D. (Philosopher and psychic researcher – Leipzig University)
John N. East (Psychic researcher and writer)
Sir Arthur Eddington (Scientist and psychic researcher)
Harry Edwards (Spiritual Healer, psychic researcher and writer)
Professor Arthur Ellison DSc(Eng), F.I.MechE (Scientist, electronics engineer and psychic researcher)
Dr Ermacora (Physicist and psychic researcher)
Professor Gustav Fechner (Physicist, philosopher and psychic researcher – Leipzig University)
Everard Fielding (Psychic researcher)
Arthur Findlay (Historian, businessman, psychic researcher and writer)
Dr G. Fingi (Physicist and psychic researcher)
F.W. Fitzsimmons F.Z.S., F.R.M.S. (Curator: South African Zoo, and psychic researcher)
Nicolas Camille Flammarion (French Astronomer, writer and psychic researcher)
Professor Theodor Flournoy (Psychologist and psychic researcher – Geneva University)
Dr Pia Foa (Professor of Pathological Anatomy, Turin, and psychic researcher)
Sir Archibald Geikie (Geologist and psychic researcher)
Dr Gustave Geley (Scientist and psychic researcher – University of Lyons)
Professor Gerosa (Scientist, physicist and psychic researcher)
Dr Paul Gibier (Scientist and psychic researcher – New York)
Sir Richard Gregory (Editor and psychic researcher)
Dr Edmund Gurney (Member of the SPR)
Sir Edward Marshall Hall K.C. (Lawyer and Member of the SPR)
Dr Glen Hamilton, F.A.C.S. (Scientist and psychic researcher – Member of Canadian Parliament)

Professor Robert Hare (Chemist and psychic researcher – University of Pennsylvania)
Rev. Professor Henslow (Psychic researcher)
Dr Richard Hodgson (Chemist – Cambridge University – Member of SPR)
Professor James H. Hyslop (Scientist and psychic researcher – Columbia University)
Professor William James MD (Psychologist and psychic researcher – Harvard University)
Sir James Jeans (Physicist, Astronomer and psychic researcher)
Raynor C. Johnson M.A., Ph.D., D.Sc. (Physicist, psychic researcher and writer)
Allan Kardec [Leon-Denizarth-Hippolyte Rivail] (French metaphysical philosopher, psychic researcher and writer)
Montague Keen (Farmer, writer and Member of the SPR)
Elizabeth Kubler-Ross, M D. (American psychic researcher and writer)
Lord Lindsay (Psychic researcher and writer)
Sir Oliver Lodge D.Sc., LL.D., F.R.S. (Physicist and psychic researcher)
Professor Cesare Lombroso (Italian Criminologist, Anthropologist and psychic researcher)
Joseph Maxwell LL.D., M D. (France)
Professor William McDougall (Psychologist and psychic researcher – Duke University)
George Meek (American engineer and psychic researcher)
Professor Milesi (Psychologist and psychic researcher – University of Rome)
Carlos Mirabelli (Psychic researcher – Brazil)
Vice-Admiral W. Usborne Moore (Naval Officer and psychic researcher)
Professor A. De Morgan (Psychic researcher – President of the London Mathematical Society)
Professor Morselli (Scientist and psychic researcher – University of Geneva)
Professor Mosso (Physiologist and psychic researcher – Italy)
Professor Gilbert Murray (Scientist and psychic researcher)
Professor Frederic W.H. Myers (Cambridge University lecturer and psychic researcher)
Dr Julien Ochorowicz (Scientist and psychic researcher – University of Warsaw)
Dr Karlis Osis (American Society for Psychical Research)
Dr Eugene Osty (Scientist and psychic researcher)
Robert Dale Owen (Scientist, Diplomat, writer and psychic researcher)
Professor F. W. Pawlowski (Scientist and psychic researcher – University of Michigan)
Dr Ronald D. Pearson, BSc. (Engineer, lecturer, writer and psychic

researcher)
Professor Raoul Pierre Pictet (Physicist and psychic researcher - Geneva University)
Carl du Prel (Scientist and psychic researcher – Munich)
Edward C. Randall (Lawyer, psychic researcher and writer – Buffalo, U.S.A.)
Dr Konstantin Raudive (Psychologist and psychic researcher – Germany)
Lord Rayleigh (Physicist and psychic researcher)
Professor Charles Richet, Ph.D., MD. (Physiologist, Nobel prize-winner, psychic researcher and writer – Paris medical facility)
Michael Roll (Lecturer, writer and psychic researcher)
Professor Archie E. Roy ((Professor Emeritus of Astronomy, writer and psychic researcher – Glasgow University)
Professor Giovanni Schiaparelli (Scientist, Director of Milan Astronomical Observatory)
Baron Albert von Schrenck-Notzing, M D. (Physician and psychic researcher – Munich)
Dr Gary Schwartz, Ph.D. (Scientist and psychic researcher – Arizona University)
Michael Scott (Astrophysicist and psychic researcher – Edinburgh University)
Professor Henry Sidgwick (Scientist and psychic researcher – Cambridge)
Emanuel Swedenborg (Scientist, writer and psychic researcher)
Rev. Charles Drayton Thomas (Psychic researcher and writer)
Sir J. J. Thompson (Scientist and psychic researcher)
Professor Marc Thury (Physicist and psychic researcher – Geneva University)
William Tiller, Ph.D. (Psychic researcher – America)
Dr R. J. Tillyard, F.R.S. (Entomologist and psychic researcher – Australia)
G.N.M. Tyrrell (Physicist, mathematician and psychic researcher)
Professor Ulrich (Scientist and psychic researcher – Leipzig University)
Peter Wakeham (Psychic researcher and writer)
Dr Alfred Russel Wallace LL.D., F.R.S. (Scientist, Naturalist and psychic researcher)
Professor William Edward Weber (Scientist and psychic researcher – Leipzig University)
Dr Carl Wickland (Physician and psychic researcher)
Gary Williams (American writer and psychic researcher)
Professor Christian Winther (Psychic researcher – Copenhagen University)
George Woods (Psychic researcher)
Dr Victor Zammit (Australian Lawyer, writer and psychic researcher)

Professor Zollner (Astronomer, scientist and psychic researcher)
Professor Zolluce (Physicist and psychic researcher – Leipzig University)

These eminent scientists, physicists, doctors of medicine and seasoned psychic researchers considered life after death *proven.* They personally directed or witnessed very exacting experiments with genuine direct voice and materialisation mediums that were, in most cases, conducted under the stringent laboratory conditions with every conceivable precaution taken to guard against fraud and deception. So sceptics and debunkers, should they so wish, can take issue with the likes of them.

Some would no doubt argue that these scientists and researchers were self-deluded and tricked by frauds, or give other non-viable and laughable reasons as to why they think they were duped. Describing them as nutcases, cranks, and dabblers in the supernatural would also be on a character assassination agenda. But, I would point out that many of these researchers were and, are, some of the greatest minds this planet has ever seen. And many, by their own admissions, were highly sceptical, and even disbelieving, prior to their investigations. Neither do I think that any of them would have suffered fools gladly.

Frauds exist in all walks of life, and mediumship is no exception. Money, ego trips, or both usually motivate the frauds, but the genuine *always* comes before the fraud, since the fraudulent must always have someone or something to *copy*. And they do say that imitation is the sincerest form of flattery!

Prominent members of society also witnessed many of these experiments, with the results often published in newspapers and magazines. What they found to be true in the way of survival evidence has been duplicated, proven and documented thousands of times the world over. Why is it, do you think, that so many of the world's top scientists have, over the years, investigated mediums and the whole of the 'life after death' phenomenon? It is because they recognised it as a legitimate branch of *science* when they realised that they were dealing with sub-atomic phenomena, or quantum physics – the study of atoms – the building blocks of life.

> Survival after death is not a matter of belief, it is
> a scientific fact supported by sub-atomic physics.
> *Peter Wakeham (Psychic researcher and writer)*

What could be more exciting to a scientist than investigating the possibility of multiple worlds on different frequencies that are populated by people who claim to have once lived on Earth? Think how that evidence could change the world for the better, give a whole new meaning to life and save millions from grief and depression.

So were all of these investigating scientists mad? Numerous psychic researchers have said that they think it is the pseudo-scientists and debunkers who refuse or are afraid to investigate such an important subject that are mad. A classic example of this was when Sir William Crookes invited Sir George Stokes, who was then the Secretary of the Royal Society, to visit his laboratory and see the evidence of survival for himself – but he refused. This has been likened to the priests who refused to look through Galileo's telescope for fear it would upset their belief systems, dogmas, vested interests and preconceived ideas and prejudices about the Universe. By ignoring or denying such phenomena doesn't mean it ceases to exist! As the famous author and 'survival' researcher Sir Arthur Conan Doyle once wrote:

It is possible to write down the names of fifty professors in great seats of learning who have examined and endorsed these facts [survival evidence], *and the list would include many of the greatest intellects which the world has produced in our time – Flammarion and Lombroso, Charles Richet and Russel Wallace, Willie Reichel, Myers, Zollner, James, Lodge and Crookes. Therefore the facts* ***have*** *been endorsed by the only science that has the right to express an opinion. I have never, in my thirty years of experience, known one single scientific man who went thoroughly into this matter and did not end by accepting the Spiritual solution. Such may exist, but I repeat that I have never heard of him.*

There is a principle which is a bar against all information, which is proof against all arguments, and which cannot fail to keep a man in everlasting ignorance – that principle is contempt prior to investigation.
Herbert Spencer 1820-1903 (Engineer, journalist and philosopher)

Summary

I have tried to convey my personal quest for the proof of a life after death, and evidence from various sources, that all the suffering and joys of humanity, many over such brief lifetimes, are for a good purpose and do not end meaninglessly at a grave.

Quite often I hear people who have never given the question of survival much thought, or even bothered to research it; make comments like: 'Nobody has ever come back to prove there is a life after death.' To which I would light-heartedly respond: 'How do you know they haven't?' And the usual stereotyped reply, being: 'Because if they had we would all know about it wouldn't we?' What can one say to such ignorance when the evidence is under their very noses!

Nature will eventually force most of us, at some time, to question death. Like all those brave and honoured scientists and researchers who studied the subject thoroughly, often risking their careers or suffering ridicule from the ignorant, I am only interested in provable facts. I have proved life after death for *myself* thanks to numerous personal experiences. I *know* what I have experienced is the Truth, and the mass of scientific evidence has merely confirmed it for me.

Knowing that life after death is a *scientifically proven fact* provides us with another vital piece of the jigsaw. We can now move on in our quest and analyse why so many fear death and dying?

I tell you we *do* persist; communication ***is*** possible. I have *proved* that the people who communicate are who and what they say they are. The conclusion is that survival is *scientifically* proved by *scientific* investigation.
Sir Oliver Lodge D.Sc., LL.D., F.R.S. (Physicist)

The evidence of Spiritualism is too strong, too widespread and accepted by too many sober minded people for hasty rejection. Scientific men accustomed to dealing coolly and accurately with phenomena have pronounced in favour of the truth of Spiritualism.
Rt. Rev. Bertram Pollock 1863 – 1943 KCVO, DD, Bishop of Norwich

The evidence for survival is exceedingly good and only a second rate scientist would be absurd enough to dismiss the paranormal.
Professor Arthur Ellison DSc(Eng),C Eng., F.I.MechE (Scientist and engineer)

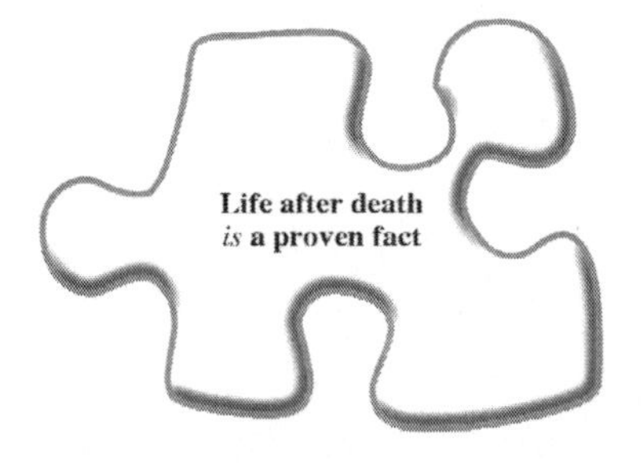

6 Death and Dying *– Why the fear?*

Never the spirit was born; the spirit shall ceases to be never.
Never was time it was not; end and beginning are dreams.
Birthless and deathless and changeless remaineth the spirit forever.
Death has not touched it at all, dead though the house of it seems.
Bhagavad-Gita

Nothing in life is to be feared. It is only to be understood.
Marie Curie 1867 – 1934 (Physicist)

Despite scientific evidence that life continues beyond the grave, an irrational fear of death, known as necrophobia, is not uncommon. If the knowledge of death and dying was fully understood, perhaps even taught in educational establishments – as it once was in ancient Greece, India, Egypt and Tibet, for example – then the ignorance, fear and paranoia connected with it would virtually cease to exist.

My father-in-law Harry came into the fear category and, even on his deathbed in March 1984, he was afraid. I only had the pleasure of meeting him twice, so the subject of my research into such matters never arose. It was a great pity, because Harry was a lovely, kind and sensitive man in his mid seventies, and I never learnt of his fear until he entered hospital for the last time. It was there that Patricia held his hand while he was dying and talked to him about what would happen at the moment of death.

Harry was in an intensive care unit at Orpington in Kent, and had saline and glucose drips in his arm and up his nose. He would drift in and out of consciousness at frequent intervals with each interval getting increasingly longer and deeper. It was during his lucid moments that he would become frightened and grip Patricia's hand hard. Even during his lapses into coma we spoke words of comfort, and explained that death was nothing to be feared but something to be looked forward to as a great adventure, and that loved ones from other frequencies would come to meet him at the moment of his transition.

He was, in reality, having a crash course on the 'facts of death' as opposed to the 'facts of life'. We had no idea if he understood what we were saying, but after many hours in coma a truly wonderful sight gladdened our eyes. Unaided, Harry, suddenly sat up and, still attached to the drip, opened his eyes wide and looked straight at the blank wall next to his bed. With the most beautiful smile of surprise and recognition, he reached forward with his free arm in a loving gesture as if greeting an 'invisible' person who had come to escort him to his 'new' home.

'Someone's come for him, I can sense them,' said Patricia – just as I 'saw' a very pretty, elegant elderly lady with outstretched welcoming arms, wearing a black silk dress with matching hat. 'It's Nan – dad's mum,' said Patricia, very excited. Harry slowly closed his eyes, and still smiling, lay gently back onto his pillow. He never regained consciousness – to this world.

In 1968, my Grandmother on my mother's side (yes, the one with the rosy cheeks), was staying with my Auntie and Uncle in Berkshire. Gran was sitting in a comfortable chair and appeared to be drifting off to sleep. Suddenly, she opened her eyes and, with a look of surprise, reached forward with both arms in a welcoming gesture. A huge smile beamed across her face as she whispered, 'Why Ted, you've come for me, and you've brought Edith and Macky.' With that, she sank back into the chair and breathed no more. Uncle Tom had just caught her last words. It was a lovely way to go!

Ted was her husband (my Grandfather) who passed to the spirit world via a heart attack in 1957. Edith was her daughter who had 'died' at the age of twenty from diphtheria, and Macky was her dog that had passed over many years before.

I have talked to many people who were nearing the end of their life. Most were suffering from terminal illnesses and asked if I would give them healing to alleviate discomfort or pain and reduce their fear of dying. I often knew when their 'departure' was near, as they became quite clairvoyant and 'saw' people and animals that they had known and had since 'died'. Many talked of conversations with a deceased mother or father or other close relatives. Their passing usually occurred within a few days of this happening and is perfectly natural. It is merely Nature's way of telling them that there is no such thing as 'death' and that they will not be alone when their time is up.

Some years ago I spent an evening with friends who told me this rather amusing story. Bob's frail and elderly mother was living with them at the time, and one evening he saw her nearly jump out of her chair. 'What's the matter mum?' he asked. 'I've just seen an American Indian walk through that wall and stand in front of me staring,' she exclaimed in a startled voice. 'Did he say anything to you?' asked Bob, trying to humour her. 'No, he just smiled and beckoned me to follow him,' she replied. 'And then would you believe it,' she said, pointing, 'he walked straight through that wall over there.' Within two days she 'died'.

Now this prompts the question, why would an elderly lady who knew nothing about the afterlife or American Indian guides, see one walk through a wall two days before she died? Sceptics might argue that she was hallucinating or that it was the brain's way of gently easing her into oblivion. But what is hallucinating? Seeing something that isn't really there? Who says it isn't? And what is reality? I have 'seen' thousands of 'invisible' people and animals over the years and most of them have been recognised from their descriptions – and they were certainly real to me.

When a change of consciousness occurs, such as sleep, meditation or daydreaming, we can pick up frequencies that are not sensed by our five physical senses. When 'death' is near it can bring about a more serene nature and therefore a change of consciousness, so many people will experience some form of clairvoyant activity when they are near the end of their life. But don't panic if it happens to you when you are feeling fine, it doesn't mean to say that your 'sell by' date is near – there are a dozen good reasons why this can occur.

One has to ask why a brain would want to protect its owner from oblivion and show them pictures of deceased relatives, friends, pets or American Indians? Particularly in cases where the dying person was not aware that some of them had died! I think nature would just flick the switch without the necessity to deceive.

Sceptics are a wonderful bunch and their explanations can be quite humorous at times, particularly when it becomes obvious that they themselves are frightened of dying. The subject is treated as taboo because if they deny it, ridicule it, put forward an unprovable daft theory or totally ignore it then it will go away or cease to exist!

Just Dying to See You!

This touching story of a deathbed experience happened to the father of Maureen Palmer (affectionately known as Mo), a long-time friend, healer and medium:

My father, Harold Turner was 88-years-of-age when he passed to the other side of life. He had been profoundly deaf most of his life and consequently had learnt the skill of lip reading. But in later years his sight began to fail so we had to communicate by writing in very large letters on pieces of paper. It was very difficult to get through to him, and because of this he never understood my work with spirit helpers and guides. Unfortunately, he was one of the "When you're dead you're dead" brigade and knew nothing of the existence of the spirit worlds or their way of life.

My mother went over 17 months prior to his passing and I tried to explain the truths of life after death to him and that he would be with her again one day. He wanted to believe but had trouble accepting it. But three months after her passing he told me that one night, when he was wide-awake, he had seen her come into the bedroom and smile at him. She was wearing her pink dressing gown and carrying her hot water bottle under her arm. After this he used to ask questions, and I feel that my answers gave him some degree of comfort.

My father was in hospital for the last month he was with us, and a few days before he passed he told me that the room had been full of people, some he knew and others he didn't. He even mentioned that some babies were there. I knew that he was seeing friends and family from the spirit worlds and not hallucinating, because I was very much aware of them myself.

A few days later I visited him again, but he had his eyes closed and was unaware of my presence. It seemed that he was talking and having a joke with someone. Suddenly, he held up his arms and seemed distressed, saying "I can't, I can't." I knew he was terrified of going because he thought that if we sat on the settee in the place where mum had been at her moment of passing, we might get "zapped" as well. He also thought that if mum had been anywhere else she wouldn't have gone!

Two days prior to my father's passing he was sitting in a chair, and being pleased to see me he gave me a lovely smile and a kiss. After chatting for a while and being quite lucid, he looked at me and said: "Your mum is here such a lot; I see her and hear her so clearly." Here was a man who had heard nothing with his physical ears for most of his life now ***hearing*** *very clearly and with his deteriorated physical sight* ***seeing*** *clearly.*

He then fell asleep, and moments later he was again talking to those from the spirit worlds that had come close. It appeared to me that someone had offered him a cup of tea, as he made the action of holding a cup and drinking from it, saying that it was a "lovely cuppa". It was then that my mother came close to me, as I could see her and feel her hand on my head as she said: "I'm here, he'll be alright, don't worry."

Two days later he passed over. I know he struggled to stay because of his fear of dying. I have been privileged to have seen and spoken to both of my parents since. I was so happy to know that after 61 years of marriage in this world, they are happily together in the next.

I have often wished that those who are afraid of dying could have seen what I saw with my father. They would have no doubt that we are never alone at our moment of passing, and that life is continuous. We have nothing to fear – in fact, quite the opposite!

This story of a dying experience happened to 65-year-old Eve O'Sullivan, a family friend, healer and psychic (Eve never did want to be known as a medium!):

I was sitting at the hospital bedside of Ron, a 39-year-old acquaintance who was suffering from an incurable brain tumour. Ron had been in a coma for many hours and was not expected to live much longer. It was then that I saw an elderly gentleman from one of the spirit worlds standing at the foot of the bed. I instinctively knew that it was Ron's father. Almost immediately, Ron came out of the coma, opened his eyes, smiled and pointed to the bottom of the bed. "You've just seen your father haven't you?" I asked him. He managed a little nod. "He's come for you – there's nothing to be frightened of," I told him. Then, with a lovely smile on his face, Ron closed his eyes for the last time.

Sue Norton, a retired Care Home Manager, shares this story with us:

My son Paul was 33-years-old when he died of cancer and it was a very traumatic time for us all. He was very frightened of dying and would often cry as he didn't want to leave us. From diagnosis to his passing was only three months.

Paul was in a hospice for a week before he died and was still a frightened young man until he went into a coma. We thought this was going to be the end, but he came out of the coma for a few hours while I was at his bedside. He then said to me, "Mum, I'm not frightened of dying now because I have seen Grandad and my dog 'Trampas'." He then looked at the doctor and said: "I have seen your brother with his small dog and he says that you must ring your other brother." Paul then looked towards the doorway, smiled, and went back into a coma – he died the next day.

The doctor confirmed that he did have a brother in spirit, and acknowledged Paul's description of the dog. He said that he wasn't surprised because that sort of thing happens a lot in hospices before people die. This gave me a lot of comfort, even though I believe in an afterlife.

Two years later, when staying in York, I decided to see a medium. She gave a good description of Paul, confirmed what he had died of and said that he was very happy. She also told me that my mother would go over soon (this proved correct), and that a baby would be born soon that would help me. I just couldn't think how that could be – until my 15-year-old daughter got herself pregnant! My little grandson has been a treasure.

I would like to tell you of a strange incident that happened recently. My husband Paul, two friends and myself visited our local Spiritualist Church. Paul was told by the medium that the power of love, and how to love, conquers all things. We both agreed that the message could be for anyone. That night, in the early hours, we were awoken with the music-centre playing "The Power of Love" at full volume. This spooked us out because we ***always*** *take the plugs out at night. Paul went down to investigate and found the music centre still playing although it was switched off. The plug was in the socket but the socket* *was also switched off.*

Paul pulled the plug out and came back to bed. At that very moment we could hear more music, this time coming from the loft. Paul again investigated and found that it was dozens of our daughter's music boxes that she used to collect all playing at once. I shouted, "If that is you Paul (the son who died) please stop – I do understand your message at the Spiritualist Church last night." The music boxes suddenly stopped.

My husband Paul is a qualified electrician, and the next day he stripped the music centre down to see if there was a fault. He also checked the plug and socket, but in each case found nothing wrong.

Even death is not to be feared by those who have lived wisely.
Gautama the Buddha

Behind Myself

One warm evening in the spring of 1973, I was in a deep meditation at the Healing Sanctuary in Chesham. I remember having the sensation of travelling backwards at tremendous speed with a whistling noise in my ears. Suddenly, I found myself standing across the other side of the room, about 4m (13 feet) from where I had been sitting. I wasn't dreaming or imagining this, and had all the faculties of memory, thinking and reasoning. Everything was much clearer than normal and the peace and tranquility was amazing. I was aware of being in a body and could see my hands and arms. I could also see the other meditators and hear their breathing, wondering why I was wide-awake and standing, whilst they were sitting. Then it dawned on me – *I was out of my body, standing behind myself and looking at the back of my own head!*

Panic set in and, with a sudden jolt, I was back in my physical body sitting on my chair. Afterwards, I explained to Mike what had happened, and was informed that I had experienced an astral projection, or what is known as an out-of-body experience (OBE). 'It's a perfectly natural phenomenon,' he said, 'and nothing to be frightened of. Now you've had proof that your consciousness can exist outside of your physical body.'

At the age of 35, I had just found out that we all have an *astral body*, and wondered why this important information was not discussed at school despite volumes of literature on the subject – as I later found out! It would have made a lot more sense and helped me to have understood the immortality of life better than knowing that Moses was found in the bulrushes and that Daniel was thrown into the lion's den umpteen thousand years ago! The astral body is a major factor in the dying experience, and understanding why we have one and its function, will make the life after death enigma much clearer.

The Astral Body

Down the ages the astral body has been known as the soul body, the spirit body, the etheric body, the phantom body, the emotional body, the celestial body, the fluidic body, the bioplasmic body and the quantum body. Whatever name scientists and philosophers use, this 'invisible' body is the exact replica of the physical body. It was also mentioned in esoteric teachings in ancient China, Greece, India, Tibet and Egypt (where it was known as the 'ka'). So if it was taught thousands of years ago, why are we in the Western world so ignorant of it today? It is even mentioned in the Bible where Paul informs us that we have both a terrestrial body and a celestial body.

As scientists are aware, everything in life is made of positively charged particles of matter known as atoms. The astral body is no exception, and it too is made up of a mass of vibrating atoms that are on a different but harmonic frequency to the physical body, hence both bodies can co-exist within the same space.

Our astral body is our *real* body, in the sense that it survives the 'death' of our physical one and has two main functions. First, it enables us to live on this dense planet of matter we call Earth by animating our physical body (our spacesuit). And, as we are all too aware, our 'spacesuit' body of flesh and blood is biological and prone to wearing out – a process we call aging. Second, our astral body is the receptacle for that spark of pure consciousness that we call the soul, or the energising life force, that is in each and every one of us. This entire neat little package is the real us which we call our personality.

Our astral body is connected to our physical body via an invisible 'electrical' cable known as the astral, or silver cord (also mentioned in Ecclesiastes 12:6), that is attached at the back of the head. This enables the astral body to energise and control the brain (computer) of the physical body. The cord is extremely pliable and stretches like a piece of elastic to an almost infinite length, thereby allowing the astral body to travel vast distances from its physical counterpart. Figure 1 shows the initial process of the astral body disengaging from the physical – usually when we go to sleep.

The astral cord acts in a similar way to the umbilical cord lifeline that connects the foetus to its mother's womb. The umbilical cord is cut to allow the baby to leave the underwater world that it has been living in for nine months and be born into this world. Similarly, when the astral cord dissolves, 'death' to this world takes place, enabling the astral body to be 'born' into the next frequency.

As far as 'death' is concerned there are dozens of ways we can go. It doesn't matter to Nature how we 'die'. Whether it is a disease, malnutrition, heart attack, a bullet, a mugger's knife, burning, drowning, an accident or old

Figure 1. The Astral body leaving the physical

age – the end result is always the same. Namely, our astral body can no longer operate our now defunct biological body, so it 'abandons ship', dissolves the cord and automatically heads for its allotted astral frequency. Hence what we call 'death' takes place, leaving our grieving relatives to dispose of our defunct physical body to Nature's recycling plant. 'Death' is merely a *permanent* astral projection! It is the *astral* bodies of 'deceased' loved ones, friends and acquaintances that are seen and communicated with by people who are sensitive enough to 'see' them psychically.

Fear of death is fear of the unknown and, once that fear is removed, then peace of mind will be assured. You may think that there are no dress rehearsals for dying – but there are. Every time we go to sleep we have a mini 'death', because our astral body has left our physical body. Hence we are as good as 'dead' to this world until it returns and we regain consciousness (wake up). In reality, we have astral projected, and in an average lifetime we will do this at least 30,000 times!

Whilst we are asleep and our physical body is resting and repairing itself, our astral body visits some of the many astral worlds that surround and interpenetrate our Earth. Thus we are living in many worlds at the same time – this world during the day and the astral worlds at night. Many remember their night-time sojourns and frequently tell of conversations with departed loved ones now living in these astral worlds – some being given verified information they otherwise had no access to.

Because our *consciousness* is in our astral body, it is inevitable that we will become *unconscious* when it moves out of alignment with our physical. Apart from sleep; a blow on the head, an electric shock, anaesthetic or fainting can cause this. When our physical body recovers, our astral body will automatically return to reanimate it, thus allowing it to regain consciousness – assuming that we are in a reasonably healthy condition!

I have concentrated mainly on the astral body, since that is the vehicle the vast majority of us will use in the immediate afterlife. Housed within our physical body, are six interpenetrating 'higher frequency' bodies that play a part in our cosmic evolution through the various planes (worlds) of existence. They are: The Etheric body, the Astral body (as discussed), the Mental body, the Causal body, the Celestial body and the Soul body.

All leave the physical as one unit after discarding our worn-out, damaged or diseased physical body. The Etheric body – often referred to as the 'astral shell' or 'husk' – usually disintegrates after about three days, once its function of being a protective sheath between the astral body and physical body is no longer necessary. The Mental, Causal, Celestial, and Soul bodies are only used in the higher frequencies should progression from one plane to another be favourable. To reside in astral or spiritual world we have to 'die' and 'lose' a body – as we will see in the next chapter,

Coma

Many ask what happens to the astral body of someone who is in a comatose state. All the while the physical body is breathing, either normally or on a life support machine and taking sustenance, then it is technically still 'alive'. The astral cord will still be intact but the person concerned will be living more in the astral worlds than on Earth. They will be fine, but it is we who should understand this phenomenon, as they will probably be observing and listening to our every word during our hospital visit.

Many survivors have confirmed this, which is why it is vital to talk to them as if they were fully conscious. Providing the physical body is not badly damaged, playing their favourite music or asking them if they would like to regain consciousness here, or live permanently in the astral planes has often achieved results – one way or the other!

Experiments

Many scientific experiments have been conducted on the astral body. And some of the early pioneers were two Dutch Physicists, Dr Zaalberg Van Zelst and Dr Malta of The Hague. They were amongst the first to analyse the atomic structure of the astral body by first theorising and then proving that it must have some mass and therefore its weight could be calculated. After lengthy and laborious experiments they concluded that the average astral body weighed about 69.5 grams (2.25 ounces). This apparently agreed with the experiments conducted by Dr Duncan McDougal of Haverhill, Massachusetts. He found that by putting the beds of dying patients on a finely balanced scale, at the moment of death the scale reacted dramatically – recording weight losses of between 62 – 77 grams (2 – 2.5 ounces). This suggested to him that some substance having mass (weight) had left the body at 'death'.

Out-of-Body Experiences (OBEs)

During presentations on metaphysical subjects I am always impressed by those who have had out-of-body experiences. Many of whom have never spoken about it for fear of ridicule or wondering if they were having a nervous breakdown. They never realised that it was a perfectly natural phenomenon. One moment they were in bed trying to sleep, and the next, they were fully conscious floating at ceiling level looking down upon their 'lifeless' body. This can be quite scary the first time it happens, but some are fascinated by the experience and want to study the subject in greater depth. One such person was Richard Chetland, a 52-year-old Graphic Artist:

Between 1989 and 1992, I devoted many hours of spare time to techniques that would allow me to separate my astral body from my physical body at will whilst fully conscious. I had read Robert Monroe's book "Journeys out of the Body" which involved deep meditation and mind focusing.

The first stage of the projection would start with a high pitched whistling sound followed by a wave of vibrations that swept through my body. These vibrations brought about a state of paralysis, which initially caused me to panic. I found the high pitched whistling to be directly linked to the paralysis, and experienced this stage at least 50 times.

In December 1991, I attempted the second stage whilst lying on my side on the double bed. I had already spent a frustrating two and a half hours trying to induce the first stage, when suddenly there was a high pitch whistling noise and paralysis. I immediately pushed, and simply floated sideways out of my body across the bed. I could clearly see the bedroom around me, and soon realised that I possessed two bodies at the same time. I reckoned that about two per cent of me was monitoring the physical body, while 98 per cent was focused in the second body – my astral counterpart. At that point, I regarded my physical body as you would dirty clothing.

This first experience lasted a matter of seconds, during which time I had noticed my wife's digital alarm clock that read 16:38. I had made a mental note of this because I couldn't see this from my side of the bed due to the obstruction caused by the pillows. The moment I separated, I was aware of an irresistible force pulling me back to my physical body. I used every essence of will-power to stay projected, then – blackness. I was suddenly thrust back into my physical body that had its eyes shut. I opened my eyes and sat up immediately to check the alarm clock that was reading 16:38.

This experience proved to me that an element of me had non-physically acquired this information. But more than that, it was a demonstration of a non-physical existence and that the mind, personality and character had a vehicle for transportation in this non-physical realm. What was unexpected about this experience was that the body I was floating in felt solid, in fact, identical to my physical body. The only difference being that it felt weightless.

From that moment at 16:38 on the 19 December 1991, my search into the afterlife ended. I knew without question that when my physical body – for whatever reason – cannot support my subtle astral body, my astral will permanently separate and reside in another dimension. Since then I have had hundreds of partial and full out-of-body experiences. I am aware of the first stage of a projection virtually every night, and the now familiar floating in and out of my physical body just before sleep.

During the autumn of 1992, I experienced a spontaneous astral body projection. I had been asleep for a couple of hours when I awoke to get a drink of water. I sat up in bed but was acutely aware of something lying behind me. Suddenly, I realised that I had sat up in my astral body, and the 'thing' lying behind me was my physical body. The shock of this sudden realisation sent me reeling into the air. I gently floated upside down and came to rest about 2.5cm (1 inch) above the floor. My legs were bent akimbo and I was rotating slowly, one moment looking under the bed and the next along the hallway.

I was, by now, very excited and extremely wide-awake in my astral body with immediate thoughts of exploring this new dimension. I tried to pull myself upright by using my astral arms and legs, but they just passed through the bed and floor. No matter what I tried I just carried on spinning. I was so frustrated that I asked for assistance from higher forces, and, mentally called out, "If there are any kind and loving individuals that are watching over me and can help, please put me upright."

Immediately, I became upright and was facing the bed looking at my physical body – It was like meeting a twin for the first time. I then felt the magnetic pull of my physical body drawing me closer. My natural reaction was to push against this force to stay out longer and explore. Out of desperation I thought of projecting to the author's house to try and make contact with him.

Suddenly, I found myself downstairs in Brian's lounge. I was upright, about 30cm (12 inches) above the floor and facing the inglenook fireplace. Although it was the early hours and dark, I could see the room clearly. There was no sense of travelling the 10 miles from my house to his; it was instant, exactly like an edit on a film. I then had the sensation of being on autopilot, because I gently floated upwards and felt that I was about to pass through the ceiling and make contact with Brian.

Suddenly, and unexpectedly, I felt a force gently push me back down. I was determined to make contact with Brian, so, once again, I drifted upwards, and at about the same point this force, again, gently pushed me back! It was like the repelling action between two magnets – the harder I pushed the harder the force pushed me back (I have since felt this force on many occasions, particularly when I have tried to astral project to someone in the privacy of their own home).

I made one last attempt to contact Brian but was again pushed gently down. Suddenly, I found myself back in my own bedroom looking at my sleeping physical body. I was then aware that my astral hand was pressed against the left side of my face and my knees were bent. It appeared that I was mirroring my physical body below me. Suddenly, I was relocated back in my physical body, remembering every vivid detail. About two weeks after that experience,

I read in a book on astral projection that it is quite normal for the astral body to mirror the physical when in close proximity for alignment purposes.

Not all of my out-of-body attempts have been 100 per cent successful, and sometimes I am only able to move an arm or a leg. Such was the case in 1995 when I had dedicated a complete weekend to practicing coming out of my body. I had spent the Friday evening and Saturday morning working through my techniques without success. By mid-afternoon I had reached the first stage (paralysed physical body), but, for some reason, I couldn't fully separate and only had my astral arms free to move. A few weeks before, I had read that reaching out and asking for help often brings results, so I did just that. I sent out the thought, "If there are any kind and friendly people around, could you please help me gently out of my body?"

I repeated the request a few times; not knowing whom a hand would belong to. Suddenly, I felt a hand place itself in my astral hand, and immediately knew this was my dad who had passed over in 1979. In that loving touch I had felt his whole personality and character come through to me. It all happened so quickly that, in shock, I returned to my body. An instant involuntary return happens automatically, like some built-in safety device, whenever a sudden or unexpected event takes place. Unfortunately, this excitement ended any further OBE that day, but at least I had made contact with my dad.

Since 1992, I have experienced many varied projections. I have passed through our physical plane, unseen and not sensed, whilst moving through material objects. During some projections I am in the astral copy of our world where things appear solid to me. Several times I have found myself in a much higher plane; I think it is known as "Summerland" in spiritualist philosophy.

During one projection, I was standing in a field and utterly awe-struck by the vibrancy of the grass. It gave off a colour that affected me emotionally. There appeared to be an apricot golden glow and warmth that permeated everywhere, and a feeling of absolute bliss and complete contentment. No worries or fears, just a simple feeling of being at home – I didn't want to leave. I remember bending down to touch the grass and becoming distracted by the sight of my astral hand – it was perfect. With no blemishes or scars my skin was as pure as an infant's. Everywhere I looked it was immaculate. The pavement had no cracks and the plants, bushes and trees were in their prime condition. My senses had become heightened and somehow fused together. The whole environment felt as if it was an energy that I had an empathy with because I was made of it too.

Because of my out-of-body experiences, I know that we all survive the death of the physical body and live on in other dimensions. There is nothing to fear about dying. This Earth is not our home and what lies beyond is marvellous.

Much of Richard's metaphysical knowledge has been gained by personal experience and, like myself, he is only interested in provable facts. I would add that his integrity is outstanding and that he has an abundance of love and compassion for all life.

45-year-old Bill Gill tells of his out-of-body experiences. Bill was born in the Punjab, India, but came to England when he was three-years-old:

Since the age of 12, I have had three out-of-body experiences that I can vividly recount. The first was very brief, but I can remember floating upwards and looking down at myself asleep and noting the sheet covers and the style and colour of my pyjamas. The second was when I floated out of my body and passed through the walls of my bedroom and travelled down the street examining neighbours houses and cars.

The third time it happened I was 26-years-old. I floated out of my body, left my house, and instantaneously found myself outside my Grandparent's house in India. It was early morning there, with dawn about to break, and what I witnessed still gives me goose pimples. A burglary involving two men was taking place. They had broken into the house and were dragging my Grandfather outside where they beat him up and left him immobilised. They ran back into the house and left carrying a bag and other items. I watched all this happen and felt powerless to do anything.

Upon awakening the next morning, I received a telephone call from my mother who was very distressed at the news that my grandfather had been badly beaten and robbed of a large amount of money and other possessions. I feel that it was this last OBE that germinated my spiritual awakening and caused me to look at deeper meanings to life.

Janet Bowers, a 45-year-old mother of two, recalls childhood experiences:

I was aged about nine or ten when I started having out-of-body experiences. Many times I would leave my body sleeping and sit on top of the wardrobe looking at myself in bed or float around the bedroom. Sometimes, when out of my body, I would see spirit people in my bedroom. On one occasion I saw a middle-aged man with dark hair and a beard and dressed very smartly in a suit and tie, sitting on the edge of my bed cross-legged looking at me. I had the feeling that he once lived in the house. Even though I was a child, I wasn't at all frightened and just accepted it as natural, even when I saw the gentleman psychically on one occasion when I was fully awake and dressed.

My mother got concerned when I told her these things so she took me to the doctor. He just recommended sleeping tablets!

This spontaneous out-of-body experience happened to Margaret Withers when she was 62-years-of age:

My out-of-body experience happened in the summer of 1988 when I was having my usual morning meditate at home. I was just starting to get the peace and harmony feeling when I suddenly found myself out of my body floating up to the ceiling and observing my physical body sitting in the chair below me. Then, and I don't know why, but these words of Robert Burns came into my head, "Oh, that some power the gift would gi'e us, to see ourselves as others see us." The next thing I knew, I was back in my physical body.

Peggy Weber, a near neighbour, shares her out-of-body experience:

I was in my early thirties at the time and my husband Tony had just come home from work. In his usual playful mood he chased me round the dining room table to give me one of his 'scary' fun greetings. He inadvertently caught my throat, causing me to black out and fall to the floor. The next thing I knew, I was hovering at ceiling height looking down on Tony as he went into panic mode trying to revive my lifeless body. I observed him moving my limbs and calling my name.

From where I was hovering I could also see my brother – who had a plaster caste on one leg – round the corner of the L-shaped room. He had heard the commotion but couldn't see what was happening from where he was sitting. I saw him trying to lift his leg off of the coffee table and bend forward to see if he could help. Suddenly, I found myself back in my body as Tony tried to stand me up. My brother later verified my description of his frantic efforts to get his broken leg off of the coffee table!

All the while I was out of my body I had a wonderful feeling of indescribable peace and love. It was truly a meaningful and vivid experience that I will never forget.

Near-Death Experiences (NDEs)

This is another phenomenon involving the astral body. Although similar to OBEs, it happens to people who are near death, hence the term 'near-death' experience. Most happen in a hospital environment whilst undergoing surgery or in intensive care when all the normal functions of life suddenly cease. That means no visible signs of life such as breathing, heart beat or brain patterns on the oscilloscope. Under these circumstances patients are classified as 'clinically dead'.

Many have spoken of floating out of their body and hovering at ceiling height whilst observing doctors and nurses trying to resuscitate their 'dead' body lying on the operating table or bed. They also claim to have observed certain emergency medical procedures that they couldn't possibly have seen from their physical body had they been conscious. Apart from having the ability to see and hear from a remote corner of the operating theatre or ward, many patients experienced incredible peace and love and, ironically, because of this, didn't want to be resuscitated!

Another fascinating feature of this phenomenon is when patients claim to have floated through the ceiling into the room above the ward, or through the walls into an adjoining corridor and witnessed confirmed conversations and events they couldn't possibly have seen or overheard. Some describe floating through the roof of the hospital and into the street below where they observed happenings that were subsequently proven correct. Some of the best evidence comes when patients claim to have projected to the home of a friend or relative and observed events and conversations taking place that were later verified – events that occurred whilst they were officially declared clinically dead!

Many NDE patients speak of leaving their bodies and travelling down a long dark tunnel towards a brilliant white light. A light into which many enter and are overwhelmed at the magnificent sight that greets them. Often they are met by 'enlightened spiritual beings in white robes', whilst others speak of being greeted by loved ones who 'died' years before.

A typical example was Rosina (Rosie) Nutting, a life-long friend of my parents whom I called 'auntie'. At the age of 66, Rosie suddenly became delirious, not knowing where she was and seeing and hearing 'invisible' people. She was rushed to hospital and went into a coma almost immediately. Rosie was put in intensive care and given various tests that eventually diagnosed the onset of Diabetes. Despite repeated attempts to revive her, Rosie was eventually classified as 'clinically dead'. This is her story:

I suddenly found myself floating above my body, and could see myself lying there surrounded by doctors and nurses who were trying to resuscitate me. The next moment, I was travelling very fast down this long dark tunnel from which I emerged into a world of such beauty and magnificence. The light was absolutely radiant and the atmosphere was of indescribable love and peace. The colours and smells of the flowers were truly amazing, the like of which I had never experienced before.

I was greeted by, what I can only describe as, two "transparent beings" dressed in long white robes. They bathed me in the most incredible love and had the most compassionate smiling eyes I have ever seen. When they spoke to me it was in such a comforting, kind and gentle way. They told me that I had nearly died on Earth and that my visit here would be brief because I still had work to do there and lessons to learn.

They showed me some of the beauties of their world and gestured to two figures that seemed to be gliding towards me. When they got closer I could see that it was my mother and father who had died some years before. We hugged and kissed and tears of joy flowed down our cheeks; it was wonderful. For a while we just talked and talked, and then they took me to meet some old friends and other relatives who had passed over. It was so vibrant and real, I could have stayed there forever.

Then, the two "transparent beings" told me that I must go back, and I immediately felt a strong pulling sensation as the scene around me faded. The next thing I remembered was waking up in a hospital bed surrounded by doctors and nurses. But the amazing thing was that I could still see the "transparent beings" standing next to one of the doctors. I don't think I was fully conscious but I can remember trying to tell the nurses what I had experienced. The vivid memory of it will live with me always and I now have no fear of dying.

A few years later I was to nurse my brother Ted who developed terminal cancer and was frightened of dying. I told him what it was like in heaven and what it was like to die. Just before he passed, in July 1977, he lost all fear of dying and said to me, "You have been such a comfort to me Rosie; I don't know how I would have coped without you." I knew then why I had to come back and the work that I had to do.

Rosie also nursed her husband Bill when his time came to depart this Earth. Prior to her NDE, Rosie was not particularly religious and knew nothing, or very little, about an afterlife or spirit worlds. I was intrigued when she told me of her experience, and smiled when she called the white-robed enlightened gentlemen 'transparent beings', but I knew exactly what she meant!

Martin Nathanael tells of his near-death experience, and although it is reminiscent of a Cosmic Consciousness experience, as explained in the chapter *Is There a God of Love?* I have included it here for reasons that will become self-explanatory:

It lasted for a few moments. But in that brief span of time I was enfolded in a most profound experience. Without a shadow of doubt, I came to know that:

- *I am not this body; I inhabit a body which exists for my use.*
- *My sense of personal identity is not dependent on the body.*
- *I have subtle senses which bypass the brain and the physical sense organs and whose modes of perception are more penetrating and versatile.*

- *There is one consciousness, one life, which becomes differentiated through the various forms of life, which makes all creatures one in essence (on that level).*
- *My essential nature is indestructible, invulnerable, and immortal.*
- *Everything I do and how I respond to events is inwardly recorded.*
- *The inner content of these actions, the relevant purity of intent, is under 'judgement' born of love and wisdom.*
- *There is a mighty pure and loving Presence, for whom no words can do justice, who is available to me, especially in moments of crises and danger.*

I came to know all this, and much more, as a result of a near-death experience. But I could at first communicate none of this to anyone, for I was only seven-years-old when I nearly drowned after falling out of a boat. It was over 10 years later when I first related this experience to another. It took another 10 years before I would attempt to convey the experience in writing. This account was published about two years before Dr Raymond Moody's popular study of near-death experiences.

Over the years Martin has made a serious study of near-death experiences as well as other metaphysical subjects on which he lectures and writes. He is also a spiritual counsellor.

45-year-old Janet Bowers suffered a major heart problem and describes her NDE:

Two years ago I had two cardiac arrests within the hour. During the first one I felt myself floating out of my body and found myself in a cloud of white mist. I knew I was dying, but at the same time I was strongly determined that I wasn't going to let it happen. I felt responsibilities to my family and there were things that I still wanted to achieve in my life. I could feel a cord (my astral cord) and held on to it for dear life. Then the light became clear and bright and I was desperately trying to pull myself back to my body. I couldn't see the cord but I was aware that it was there – like an invisible rail.

Eventually I made it, and vaguely became aware of being back in my body when my second cardiac arrest struck. Again, I felt myself being sucked out of my body through my back and travelling very fast in what felt like a downwards direction. Once more, I knew that I was dying and I didn't want to. Apparently, I was 'clinically dead' as doctors gave electric shock treatment to my chest to start my heart beating again. The next thing I knew I was thrown back into my body and, on regaining consciousness, could see the medical staff bending over me with concerned expressions on their faces.

The eminent Swiss psychologist, Carl Jung (1875 – 1961), had a near-death experience after a heart attack and afterwards wrote: *'What happens at death is so unspeakably glorious that our imaginations and our feelings do not suffice to form even an approximate conception of it.'*

Margaret Withers writes:

In June 1960, I was rushed into hospital to have my spleen removed. I was pregnant at the time, which made it more complicated. During the operation I floated out of my body and found myself travelling down a long dark tunnel. Although I was in this dark void, I felt very peaceful and happy with an amazing feeling of love all around me. I knew I was still in a body because I could see it and feel it, but I didn't want to go back to my physical body because I felt I was where I should be.

I then felt myself being pulled back along the tunnel to my physical body, whereupon I regained consciousness and was aware of being in a hospital bed. A nurse told me that they staged an all night vigil because they thought they had 'lost' me. I remember thinking at the time that if dying was that easy and so full of love and peace, then what's all the fear and fuss about?

The doctors told me that because I nearly died during the operation there was a good chance that I would lose the baby, but in the December of that year our healthy baby boy Julian was born. In December 1944, our baby daughter Sandra was born prematurely, but she only lived for 20 minutes. Because I have been psychic from birth, I have clairvoyantly seen her many times, and so has my other daughter Marion who is also very psychic. I am so privileged in that respect because I know that my darling daughter is still alive and well and growing up in her other world. Our astral bodies live on in another universe after we die here.

I'm not afraid of dying – I just don't want to be there when it happens.
Woody Allen (Film producer and actor)

Interesting Facts

- Surveys reveal that nearly 8 million Americans have had near-death experiences.
- In the People's Republic of China, a questionnaire given to university students revealed that 58 per cent had had an out-of-body experience and 40 per cent had had communication with the dead.
- The Greek philosopher Plato (429 – 348 BC) mentions NDEs and OBEs in his writings.

- Near-death experiences can happen at any age, but out-of-body experiences are usually prevalent from early childhood to about 40-years-of-age.
- Conscious astral projection techniques can be learnt and practised at will.
- NDEs and OBEs are natural scientific phenomena experienced by all cultures and by both religious and non-religious people.
- Blind people can see other people and things when they have an OBE or NDE.

Scientific Studies

It is encouraging that, worldwide, many doctors are seriously studying NDEs to obtain scientific evidence that patients could have experienced an afterlife whilst pronounced clinically dead prior to resuscitation. Researchers at Southampton University have shown that lack of oxygen to the brain is *not* responsible for these experiences as some sceptics claim, since most of the NDE patients had more than adequate supplies. Doctors have also discovered that it should not be possible for the brain to have such lucid experiences, or the lasting memory of them, when brainstem activity has been lost at clinical death.

In September 2008, at the United Nations in New York, an international consortium of doctors and scientists held a symposium titled 'Beyond the Mind Body Problem: New Paradigms in the Science of Consciousness'. Amongst those present were Dr Sam Parnia from the Southampton NDE research team, Dr Pim Van Lommel from Holland who, after 20 years of research, wrote *The Science of the Near-Death Experience*, and world renowned authority on NDEs, Dr Bruce Greyson.

The conclusion of these, and other eminent professionals present, was that human consciousness (mind) appeared to exist separately from the physical body and brain when the latter are classified as 'clinically dead', thereby complimenting what was known in the east and the orient thousands of years ago!

Another scientifically researched book on the subject is *Science and the Near-Death Experience: How Consciousness Survives Death* by Chris Carter. Sceptics' arguments crumble as Carter presents empirical data to prove that the mind is separate from the brain, and that it is this mind that experiences, remembers and survives the 'death' of the physical brain and body.

Near-death experiences have been reported in many countries over the last 100 years, particularly in America, which prompted Dr Raymond Moody to write *LIFE AFTER LIFE*, published in 1975, in which he outlines graphic accounts of patients describing their near-death experiences. This was followed by *The Light Beyond* in 1986. Dr Moody's studies have shown that the vast majority of near-death survivors state that *love* and *knowledge* are extremely important, because they are the *only* things that we take with us when we 'die'.

Although different in approach, another informative book is Phyllis Atwater's *Coming Back to Life*. Atwater survived three near-death experiences and, as a consequence, researched the subject in great depth by interviewing over 200 near-death survivors and their families. Once again she found that survivors *know* that there is a life after death, are not afraid to die, and confirm that material things are not important – *love* is all that matters!

> What is interesting is that so many men of medicine and science have come away from their research believing in life after death, even if they entered the study of near-death phenomena with no disposition to such a view.
> *D. Scott Rogo (Writer and psychic researcher)*

A Good Send-off

In the April of 1992, I was contacted by a Mrs Betty Bolton who asked if I would take the funeral service of her husband Alan. She explained that Alan had been interested in metaphysical subjects for many years and had an extensive knowledge of life after death. Consequently he was not in the least bit worried about dying, even when he was terminally ill and transferred to a hospice. In fact, he was in good humour, even telling the intrigued nurses about the astral body, the spirit worlds and what it was like to die!

Alan had never been impressed by religion and had made it quite clear to Betty that he didn't want an orthodox funeral service as he had found most of them 'impersonal, archaic and depressing'. On the 16th May 1992, I took Alan's service at the local crematorium, mentioning his love and understanding of metaphysics and his knowledge of death and dying.

I explained to a large congregation that what was in the coffin was not Alan, but only a worn out vehicle that he had used to get around on this Earth, and that he was still alive and well living in his 'real' body in another dimension. Pressing the button to close the curtains around the coffin, I raised a symbolic glass of wine and, together with the congregation; we gave a toast and blessing to Alan, wishing him well in his new life.

Afterwards, the Funeral Director and some of the congregation approached me, saying that it was the most interesting funeral service they had ever attended. Apparently they were fascinated by my talk on the metaphysics of life and death, stating that it made a lot of sense.

In the spring of 1993, a dear friend, Trish Parker, was rushed into hospital. She was diagnosed with terminal cancer of the liver and given just two weeks to live. Resigned to an imminent departure from this planet, 56-year-old Trish began to plan her own funeral service and, via her daughter, I was asked to take it. Trish was fully aware of the laws governing life and 'death' and everything discussed in this book, hence she was not afraid to 'die' and peacefully looked forward to 'going home'. So much so, that whilst propped up in her hospital bed, she was telling her sons and daughter all about the process of 'dying' and of life in the various spirit worlds. The doctors and nurses were amazed at her cheerful composure right up to the day of her passing.

At home, that very evening, Patricia was ironing and I was engaged in paperwork when, simultaneously, we felt a loving surge of energy pass through us, and just for a brief moment the room seemed to be full of radiant light. 'Trish has passed over,' said Patricia. 'Yes,' I replied, glancing at the clock, 'that was amazing.' It was later confirmed to have been the *exact* time of Trish's transition from this world to the next.

The crematorium was packed to capacity with many having to stand - such was the popularity of a truly spiritual person who gave nothing but love and affection to all who came into her life. Trish maintained that death was not to be treated with doom and gloom and asked for a cheerful service, so I spoke about the 'nuts and bolts' of death and dying in an easy-going scientific format. Once again many of the congregation expressed how interesting it was for a funeral service and what a good send off we gave Trish.

In April 2000, Patricia's 86-year-old mother, Eileen, suffered a major heart attack in the care home where she resided, having had a major stroke the year before. We knew her time was up, and as her quality of life was non-existent, 'death' would be a blessed release. Patricia talked to her during her last hours in coma and explained the 'dying' process and how she should accept it and go with it. Eileen 'died' in Patricia's arms with a look of peace on her face that she had rarely shown in life.

Patricia asked me to take the funeral service as we were determined to give Eileen a light-hearted send-off in celebration of her life. At the crematorium Irish medleys were played before and after the service as that was the country of her birth. Once again I talked about the transition of her astral body from this world to the next dimension, and that the real Eileen was not the worn out earthly body in the coffin. There was also a lot of laughter when I spoke of amusing incidents in her life.

Afterwards, during the reception, guests and family remarked that they thoroughly enjoyed the service, and stated that they should all be of that format. Now it may seem strange that people actually enjoyed a funeral service, but why not?

One of the guests at the service was a disabled friend, Mike Collins. Mike suffers from Cerebral Palsy and has been wheelchair bound virtually all his life. He has also been psychic from childhood, and later told Patricia that he had seen her mother standing in front of the coffin smiling during the service. He described her perfectly, and mentioned a blue and white outfit she was wearing. Mike had never met Eileen, and certainly didn't know that Patricia had asked the undertaker to dress her mother's body in a *blue and white outfit*. Apparently, her body was deformed and very stiff so they couldn't put the suit *on* her without the risk of breaking some bones, so they had to *lay* it on her. And there she was, alive and well at her own funeral - *wearing it!*

Poked With a Stick

For many years, whenever Patricia's mother Eileen wanted to stress a point, she would playfully poke me in the chest or stomach with her walking stick. Also, whenever Patricia and I bought something long-term for the house, I had a habit of jokingly saying: 'That will see us out.' Patricia was never amused with the remark and would say: 'Stop saying that.' No one outside of our immediate family knew of either of these habits.

Some weeks after Eileen's funeral, we were enjoying an afternoon chat with Mike Collins at his Bungalow, when he suddenly closed his eyes and said: 'Your mother is here Patricia. She is poking Brian in the chest with her stick and saying: 'You *must* stop saying, "That will see us out!"' Hand on heart; I have not said it since!

'Laughing Boy' Attends

George Hunter, a 73-year-old father of three, was dying of terminal bowel cancer, and it was his wish to vacate the hospital and spend what time he had left at home with his family, who took it in turns to sit by his bedside.

I asked George's daughter Liane and her husband Andrew if they would like me to ask my Chinese spiritual helper 'Laughing Boy' to stay with George and guide him over to the 'other side' when his time came. They gratefully agreed. A few days later, with Andrew by his bedside, George opened his eyes from a semi-comatose state, chuckled, and whispered: 'I can see a Chinaman.' It was the familiar involuntary 'Laughing Boy' chuckle that means, 'I am here'. With that, he closed his eyes once more and, several days later, passed peacefully away.

George's family asked if I would take the funeral service. And so, at the local crematorium on the 12th January 2009, George was given a fitting tribute to a life well lived. Although I had never met George, he was described as being the most loving and devoted husband and father who saw the good in all and never had a bad word to say about anyone. Doreen, his loving wife for nearly 50 years, informed me that they were not particularly religious and that George believed there was nothing after death. Death was not something they liked to talk about, as the thought of one of them being left on their own was too distressing to contemplate.

Having said farewell to George and Doreen's family and friends after the reception, the 90 mile journey home had all the makings of a 'white knuckle' drive. It was dark with torrential rain and high winds when we joined the waterlogged busy M1 Motorway. The spray was horrendous and visibility near zero, especially when overtaking drivers sent bow-waves of water across our car. After a few miles, Patricia asked: 'How are you coping with these conditions? 'Fine', I replied, 'I feel remarkably calm and peaceful, just as if we are driving down a country lane on a sunny afternoon.'

'That's just how I feel,' said Patricia, who would normally have been uncomfortable under such conditions. 'Have you noticed, there's an overpowering atmosphere of love and peace in the car?' she continued. 'Yes', I replied, 'It's as if there's a powerful spiritual presence sitting on the back seats.' 'Exactly', was Patricia's response. Two hours later we arrived home still cool, calm and collected, and decided to have an early night after a busy day. Patricia went upstairs to prepare for bed whilst I unloaded the car. Here is her description of what happened next:

I was sitting on the bed in my nightdress, thinking about how well the day had gone when, from behind, I became aware of hands gently touching me on both shoulders. At that moment, I was infused in a wonderful atmosphere of indescribable love, and then a kind and gentle voice whispered in my ear, "Thank you, thank you – thank you so much." I got into bed just as Brian came into the bedroom and said nothing of what I had experienced, wondering if it was my imagination. Brian continues the story:

As I came out of the en-suite, a powerful shudder ran down my spine causing me to burst into uncontrollable laughter. As the characteristic and indescribable wave of love enveloped me I knew it was 'Laughing Boy'. Still laughing I got into bed and, as soon as I switched off the light, the bedroom became bathed in a radiant golden glow. At that instant, I was both laughing and crying with ecstatic bliss. Just as Patricia asked what was happening, a loving, gentle voice said: 'Thank you. Thank you so much for what you did.'

Amidst the ecstasy and the tears, I said: 'It's George, he's fine and in a wonderful world of love and light. He's with 'Laughing Boy' and has come to say thank you for taking the service and for comforting Doreen and the family.' Then Patricia told me her experience of hearing virtually the same words. The following day we telephoned Andrew and Liane to tell them of our experience. They were delighted to hear it, and although they fully understood, they suggested that it was early days to tell Doreen as it might be out of her comfort zone to comprehend such phenomena. Time will be the deciding factor!

> Do not stand at my grave and weep; I am not there. I do not sleep.
> …. Do not stand at my grave and cry; I am not there. I did not die.
> *Anonymous British soldier (First World War)*

Summary

A truism of life's enigmas is that one good experience is worth a thousand words, as those who have had OBEs and NDEs will tell you. These experiences impart knowledge. Knowledge that individual consciousness can exist separate from the physical body. Above all, knowledge that 'death' is an illusion and something to look forward to and not feared. The fear is born out of the unknown, but once the unknown is known, then the fear will dissolve. Once again, you will appreciate that the prime factor in all these experiences is love, peace and harmony.

Finally, for readers who would like to study the enigma of the astral body in greater detail, *Journeys Out of the Body* by Robert Monroe, *The Study and Practice of Astral Projection* by Dr Robert Crookall, *The Projection of the Astral Body* and *The Phenomena of Astral Projection* by Sylvan Muldoon and Dr Hereward Carrington are timeless classics on the subject.

If you now feel more reassured about 'death' and dying, then I offer you another piece of life's jigsaw. We can now proceed on our quest and investigate the whereabouts of invisible worlds and their inhabitants.

> Death is merely a more advanced form of living.
> *Richard Wilkins (Philosopher and writer)*

> Are we humans simply a collection of chemical processes or do we have a separate component that gives us life? What is the relationship between the mind and the brain and what happens to our mind and consciousness at the end of life?
> *Dr Sam Parnia (Horizon Research Foundation Mission Statement)*

> While you do not know about life, how can you know about death?
> *Confucius 550 – 478BC (Chinese Philosopher)*

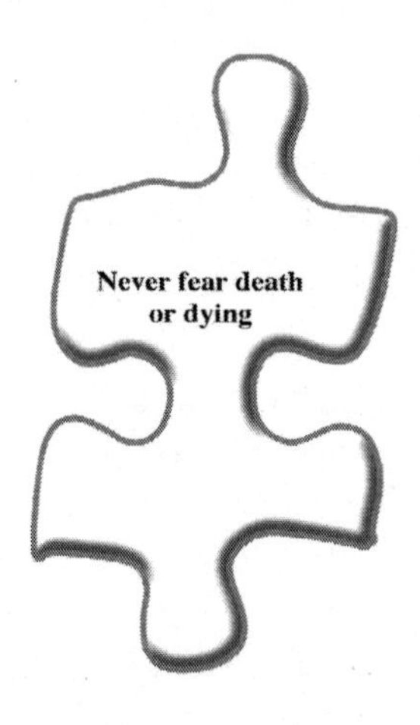
Never fear death
or dying

7 Invisible Worlds – *Where are they?*

Those who hold erroneous views regarding the body
consider the body real and are relentless in their pursuit
of sensory pleasures. Little do they know of other
dimensions beyond that of the physical body.
Venerable Master Hsing Yun

There is no death, only a change of worlds.
Chief Seattle 1786-1866 (Suquamish tribe)

Our world, the Earth, is surrounded and interpenetrated by other invisible worlds. This fact is not very well known in the West, but in the East and the orient they have known, for thousands of years, that we live in a multidimensional universe. The ancient Egyptians, Chinese, Tibetans, Greeks and Indians were fully conversant with these other dimensions of existence, as were the North and South American Indians, the Maoris, Aborigines and many of the African native tribes.

Down the ages, in virtually all races and cultures, there have been those who, either by accident or design, found that they could change their state of consciousness by trance, secret herbal potions, whirling or otherwise and tune in to these 'invisible' worlds. They were known as the oracles, witch doctors, medicine men and shamans. These other dimensions have been called Heaven, Paradise, Nirvana, the Happy Hunting Grounds, the Abode of the Gods, the Spirit Worlds, the Astral Worlds, Planes or Realms, Etheric Worlds, Celestial Realms, Svarga (Hindu), Devachan (Theosophical), Sukhavati (Buddhist), Valhalla (Viking) and the Unseen Universe. I sometimes refer to them as 'Head Office'!

Worlds within Worlds

As a designer, if I could maximise the amount of life in the Universe, I would create a world that vibrated at a very low frequency (the rate of vibration of atoms). Then, if I chose to create another world in the same space, all I would have to do is raise its frequency above the previous one. I could keep doing this ad infinitum until I had hundreds or even thousands of different worlds all co-existing within the same space but on different frequencies. Therefore, they wouldn't interfere with each other because they would each have their own personal frequency.

Now, if I were to populate these worlds, I would have to make sure that the inhabitants vibrated at a similar rate to the world they were living in so that they could see each other and their environment as solid. In our world we see and feel people and objects as solid, hear sounds and smell odours. What we are doing with our senses is tuning in to the frequency rates of the vibrating atoms in the objects, sounds and smells. Everything in the Universe is made up of atoms, and it is only the rate of vibration (frequency or wavelength) of those atoms that determines whether things appear solid, soft, opaque, liquid or 'invisible'.

Just because we cannot see or hear something doesn't mean that it doesn't exist. The human eyes, ears and nose have a very limited frequency range, whilst most animals and other creatures can see, hear and smell far beyond our range. Why can't there be a tree, a house or people that you cannot see, in front of you right now – even in the middle of your lounge or bedroom? They would just be vibrating at a different frequency that's all.

In our 'modern' world we have come to accept radio and television as part of our everyday lives, but how many of us have given any thought as to how it all works? At this very moment there are thousands of pictures and sounds being transmitted around the globe, many by satellite, yet they are all on different frequencies. They are passing through our bodies and the walls of our houses, but unless our television and radio receivers are switched on and *tuned in* to the required frequency, then we will be unaware of their existence. Once our sets are operational we can see and hear these signals as programmes of entertainment and, should we wish to change the programme, then we simply retune to a different frequency by flicking the channel-changer or turning a tuning dial.

The invisible worlds interpenetrating our Earth are very much like that. Many people today, including children, can, by intuition, extra sensory perception (ESP), second sight or whatever, from time to time, sense, 'see' or 'hear' things beyond the normal senses. What they are doing, knowingly or otherwise, is tuning into these invisible worlds and 'seeing' or 'hearing' their inhabitants. They have become receivers, just like televisions and radios and picked up some of the astral and spiritual world frequencies seeing them as images or visions. These are the people we now call psychics, mediums and clairvoyants; although I feel 'sensitives' would be more apt and appropriate because we have to be sensitive to these other dimensional frequencies to pick them up.

Ancient man knew that smashing the atom yields pure energy.
He knew that human eyes could only see a tiny portion of the
electromagnetic spectrum (visible light), and he believed that other
worlds or realities existed beyond the limitations of his sight.
John A Keel (Our Haunted Planet)

Many Dimensions

There are probably billions of 'invisible' planet worlds and other dimensions of consciousness within the Cosmos. Scientists are already talking about 'multiverses' and speculating on the 'string theory' of other dimensions, often quoting the third, fourth, fifth and even the tenth and eleventh dimension and beyond. They also suspect that these 'worlds' may conform to unknown laws of physics. Today, physicists have confirmed what the mystics and philosophers of old have been saying, namely that there is a link between the microcosm and the macrocosm. That is, a relationship between the smallest atomic particles and the vastness of the Cosmos.

Some physicists studying sub-atomic particles (a branch of quantum mechanics) are now looking at our Universe as a vast intelligent grid system that is organised like a giant computer complete with memory banks. They see the grid as being programmed to continuously recycle matter in various forms, thereby speculating that the existence of invisible worlds can be calculated mathematically. This was what Pythagoras (581-497 BC) the Greek philosopher and mathematician implied when he said that the secret of life was numbers. He was, like many of his contemporaries, fully aware of invisible worlds and their occupants. Likewise, at the beginning of the last century, Sir Oliver Lodge D.Sc., LL.D., FRS, one of our greatest physicists, was a pioneer of modern sub-atomic phenomena. He was also convinced of the reality of an afterlife and that the secrets of the atom would eventually mathematically prove the existence of etheric worlds as he called them.

For readers interested in the above subject matter at a scientific level, *Intelligence Behind the Universe* by Ronald Pearson, BSc. will provide more food for thought.

In simplistic terms, according to the Ancient Wisdom occult teachings (occult simply means secret knowledge) and Theosophist philosophy, there are seven basic astral planes surrounding this Earth with each one subdivided into seven planes, and each of those subdivided into seven more and so on until the seventh subdivision. Each plane vibrates on a different frequency; hence they don't interfere with each other and can therefore occupy the same space (see Fig. 2). They are shown as separate bands for the sake of simplicity but in reality they are interpenetrating spheres.

The vibrating frequencies of these planes are graded according to the manifested amount of love within them. The lower frequencies have the least amount of love and the higher frequency planes of consciousness the most. The Earth, or material plane as it is known, is one of the lowest and densest frequencies, which is why we need a dense physical body to exist here. The astral planes are designated as the lower, intermediate and higher, whilst the

Cosmic Planes
These are ultra-high frequency 'worlds' known to exist but beyond our comprehension at our present stage of spiritual evolution on Earth.
Souls at these levels are thought to be pure Mind and have no physical form.

Celestial Planes
These high frequencies are often referred to as Heaven, Paradise and Nirvana, and are where spiritual masters and Avatars reside. The Light and energies of Love at this level defy description

Mental and Causal Planes
These are worlds of almost unimaginable beauty and indescribable energies of love and tranquillity. This is where spirit guides and inspired teachers of truth reside, as well as highly evolved beings that have no negative karma and no longer need to reincarnate on Earth. Progress from here is dropping of the causal body to enter the Celestial Planes. These are the last levels for reincarnating on Earth.

Higher Astral Planes
These are inhabited by those who showed an abundance of unconditional love and compassion when on Earth - very often living selfless lives to help others, despite any personal suffering. The landscapes here are an incredible variation of breathtaking beauty, with energies of love and tranquillity truly earned by those living here. Advice from enlightened spiritual mentors is given regarding possible rebirth on Earth or progression to the Mental and Causal planes.

Intermediate Astral Planes
These levels are where the majority of Earth's inhabitants will reside after they shed the physical body. Contact with Earth is within frequency range of sensitive people (psychics) and experimental electronic equipment.
The landscape varies enormously between these astral frequencies, but it is generally in accordance with the beauty and splendour on Earth and therefore comfortable to the inhabitants. This is where patients that have near-death experiences temporarily meet with loved ones.

Lower Astral Planes
These are where the astral bodies of the Earth's troublemakers and undesirables are segregated after the 'death' of their physical body. The frequency levels are low and the terrain is grim and depressing. This caters for the mind-set of the inhabitants that have shown no love or compassion in their often violent and confrontational earthly lives. They have merely reaped what they sowed – cause and effect

Earth Plane
Here we live in our physical body (spacesuit) that enables us to interact with our own kind at all levels of spiritual growth, from the truly enlightened to the ignorant, confrontational, violent and cruel. Earth is a spiritual training school for us to learn the lessons of cooperation, love, peace and harmony.
What we learn here befits us for life in one of the other frequencies (planes) after the 'death' of our physical body.

Figure 2. Multidimensional Planes of Existence.
(Not separate as shown, but interpenetrating each other)

frequencies above these are known as the spiritual worlds and called the mental and causal planes with the highest being known as the celestial and cosmic planes.

The frequencies above this are beyond the scope of most of us mortals to fully comprehend at our level of spiritual development and are the subject of advanced esoteric teachings as taught by highly evolved Spiritual Masters. The astral and spiritual planes are mainly inhabited by the astral bodies of people and animals that once lived on Earth, but we will be considering other life forms and entities that also inhabit these regions.

A Great Man Investigates

During the Second World War, life expectancy amongst aircrew was not good, particularly for rear gunners in the bomber squadrons. Many were shot to pieces when their turrets received a direct hit. As a consequence, there were numerous reports of bomber crews seeing and talking to materialised dead crewmembers during their flight home. Many crews never realised this at the time and were stunned when they landed back at base. Aircrew also told of 'seeing' the astral bodies of 'dead' airmen following stretcher parties carrying their shattered bodies after they had been extracted from damaged aircraft.

It was stories like these – often talked about in the Officer's Mess – that intrigued Air Chief Marshall Lord Hugh Dowding G.C.B., G.C.V.O., C.M.G. Dowding was in charge of the British air force during the war and masterminded the Battle of Britain. In fact, he was so interested in the subject of the astral body and life after death that he did what any genuine scientist would do – he investigated and proved it for himself. I have the highest admiration for people of his calibre who, at great risk to their careers, investigate such important and worthy subjects.

To comfort the bereaved and demystify the fear of death and dying Lord Dowding wrote of his knowledge and experience in his books. In the *Dark Star* he speaks of communicating many times with his deceased wife via direct voice mediumship and the highly personal evidence received, as well as descriptions of the spiritual world in which she was living. In his book *Many Mansions*, he describes the astral planes and how they are interlinked with the astral planes of planets in other solar systems – knowledge that was written in ancient Indian scriptures and known by the Greek philosophers.

All things are infinite and eternal, even matter, for through it and by it are engendered innumerable worlds, which exist simultaneously and consecutively in space and time. Not only is the whole of Nature infinite, but all that is comprehended in it is infinite in number and dimensions.
Anaxagoras 503-428BC (Greek philosopher)

Who Goes Where?

You might well be wondering what determines which plane (frequency or world) we go to when we 'die'? Quite simply, we are graded according to the amount of love we have shown whilst living on Earth. The atoms in our astral body vibrate in accordance with our thoughts, hence, the more loving and compassionate (spiritual) we are, the *faster* our astral body vibrates. Conversely, the more hateful, bitter and materialistic we are the *slower* our astral body vibrates. Love speeds it up and hatred slows it down! Now, if you are one step ahead of me here, you will realise that at the moment of our 'death', whenever that is, we will automatically go to the astral world that is vibrating at our own personal frequency. In other words, the one with which we are most compatible.

As an example, let us assume that when our hypothetical Mr Arthur Ritus dies of a heart attack, his astral body is vibrating at a frequency of say, 40 megahertz (MHz). This will qualify him for an afterlife in a plane of consciousness that is vibrating at a similar frequency. Consequently, all the people, animals, trees and houses in that world will appear solid to him because they are all vibrating on a compatible frequency.

The bonus for our Mr Ritus being that the people in his new astral world will be kind, loving and compassionate – just like him. Whereas the rotten elements of society that create most of the Earth's problems will have astral bodies that vibrate at very low frequencies. And since 'like attracts like', they will probably inhabit one of the lower frequency astral planes.

We grade and segregate ourselves in the 'afterlife' simply *by the way in which we have lived our lives here* – not by what political party or religion we belong to, or how much money we have accumulated or how many houses or cars we own. There is no 'hell' for unbelievers or 'heaven' for believers. No 'Pearly Gates' (although I am sure they could be arranged if we really want to see some) and no St Peter with a clipboard checking our names on a list. As we will see during our quest for life's meaning and purpose, there is a highly intelligent process governed by the *Spiritual Law of Love*. This, when you think about it, would appear to be the perfect solution!

Terrain in the Astral Worlds

The astral worlds are as varied as this Earth when it comes to terrain. For example, Eskimos would expect to see snow and ice in their 'heaven' when they 'die', and Arabs would probably expect to see deserts and palm trees in theirs, because that is what they have been used to. They would probably feel out of place in each other's landscape. Because there are thousands of astral planes interpenetrating this Earth, there is a place for each and every one of us.

The landscape in each plane is formed by the *thoughts* of the people living there.

The mystics of old and teachers of ancient wisdom gave these multi-dimensional frequencies Sanskrit names, whilst some modern day researchers have given them numbers such as plane 1, 2, 3, 4 and so on. This is rather like differentiating radio and television frequencies by calling them Channel 1, 2, 3, etc. For conformity I will call them by their most popular terminology.

> Wherefrom do all these worlds come? They come from space.
> All beings arise from space, and into space they return; space
> is indeed their beginning, and space is their final end.
> *Chandogya Upanishad 1.9.1*

Earth (material) Plane

We all know that we are walking around on a spinning ball of rock called a planet which is covered with soil, grass, sand, snow, ice and water and permeated with vegetation of every description. To do that – as we have seen from the previous chapter – our astral body has to wear a biodegradable 'spacesuit' that we call our material or physical body. We are experiencing life here with thousands of other species that also wear 'spacesuits'. Unfortunately, many think that our 'spacesuit' is the real us, and when it gradually wears out through old age, gets diseased or damaged and is no longer wearable, we die – and that's the end of it. They are known as the 'When you're dead, you're dead!' brigade that have chosen not to investigate, or are frightened to, yet seem to know all the answers!

We need a material body made of dense matter to live in a world made of dense matter. This is one of the few worlds where the good, the bad and even worse, can mix and live side by side to experience and learn. When we 'die' to this world and go into the next by dumping our 'spacesuit' we are *automatically segregated*. We need our astral body to live in the astral planes, but as we have seen, we are segregated by the amount of *love* – or lack of it – that we have shown on Earth. So let's have a brief look to see what sort of life we are likely to live after 'death' when we are segregated into worlds of like minds.

Lower Astral Planes

These low frequency planes are very close to the Earth's vibrational frequency and many investigators have likened them to a hell or purgatory because of the atrocious conditions there. Imagine a world totally devoid of love, with no colour, no trees, flowers, birds or anything of beauty, just a dark, dismal, murky terrain with putrid smells. Add to that a depressing negative atmosphere of gloom, despondency and hatred and you will get some idea of the prevailing conditions.

So, who are the unfortunates that live there? Most are the Earth's troublemakers and undesirables. They are those who are corrupt, have committed murder, been responsible for wars, terrorism, child abuse, sexual depravities, drug dealing, torture and every conceivable atrocity that vile and depraved minds can commit. These are the ones who showed no mercy, love or compassion to any human or animal – just love of self-gratification. They have only themselves to blame, since their very thoughts and actions on Earth will produce a low frequency astral body and hence a low frequency world awaits them after death.

For those who have minds like cesspits, then what better place for them to live than in a cesspit? And if that wasn't bad enough, they will be mentally tormented by guilt for every human that they wronged. They will also experience the wrath and hatred of their own kind who are trapped with them in their vile world. It is simply their minds, and nothing else, that become their 'jailers'!

Many of these wretched inhabitants were extremely wealthy and abused positions of trust and power when they lived on Earth. These are the corrupt, violent and callous ones that ruined peoples' lives. They and their ilk have paid the price of ignorance. Had they made the effort to study the laws of life they would have realised that breaking human laws may have been easy, with lenient punishment, but in the afterlife we get away with *nothing!*

This would seem an opportune moment to offer a timely word of warning. Unless you are an experienced psychic investigator, if you have ever been tempted to use the Ouija board, then *don't!* It is the lower astral inhabitants that *dabblers* are most likely to invite into their lives and very much regret it. Yes, they *are* 'evil' spirits, simply because they were 'evil' when they lived on Earth – nothing changes after 'death'. It has been likened to dialling a telephone number at random and inviting the person into your home – a risky business!

Because the lower astral planes are closest to Earth frequencies, many of the inhabitants can, and do, attach themselves to weak and like-minded individuals here. They prey on alcoholics, drug pushers and addicts, child abusers, muggers, and all the other corrupt and rotten despots of society to encourage them in their depraved way of life. Over the centuries, many such individuals have heard 'voices' telling them to commit atrocities. Such is the influence of these lower astral entities on our Earth, that I will be highlighting it again in the chapter *Good and Evil.*

For several years, I belonged to what is known as a Rescue Circle. That is, a group of mediums who sit together at periodic intervals to help those who, although 'trapped' in the lower astral frequencies, are willing to be persuaded that better worlds exist for them. This is achieved with the combined help of the more spiritually enlightened from the higher realms who have compassionately chosen to help their fellow beings 'escape' from their self-created torment.

This work is a serious and dangerous business requiring the highest of morals and great strength of character from all who undertake it, as Lord Dowding explains from his own rescue circle experiences in his book *The Dark Star.* Contact can be made with *any* of the immoral, depraved, foul-mouthed or violent inhabitants wandering around in the lower frequencies. Many refuse help at the time of contact, since they don't realise they are 'dead'. Why should they? They never believed in a life after death when they walked this Earth, and no amount of reasoning will convince them otherwise.

Thankfully, many *are* willing to listen, subdue their anger and bitterness and have their questions answered. They are asked if they can see a bright light. If they can, then we know they are ready to go with the loving helpers from the higher spiritual worlds that have come to take them to a more comfortable frequency. It is extremely rewarding work and is a combined effort in the name of love between those of us living in the physical world and those in the spiritual frequencies. There is hope and help offered to all – none are abandoned. It is only our attitude of mind that enslaves us!

Intermediate Astral Planes

These regions are where the majority of the Earth's inhabitants reside after the 'death' of their physical bodies. They will find themselves in one of the thousands of sub-divisional frequencies within the intermediate astral plane system, and it is from these levels that most clairvoyant communication takes place, simply because most Earth psychics are compatible with these frequencies.

The lower of the intermediate astral regions often accommodates those who are neither good nor bad but who have generally lived irresponsible or selfish earthly lives. These are the unhappy ones who wasted their lives moaning about people and life in general, often hurting others by spreading tittle-tattle, rumours and lies. They probably had children but gave them precious little attention, love or affection – simply because they were never given any when they were young. As parents, they would have probably been classed as failures by their offspring. Nevertheless, they have been known to show signs of love on the odd occasion – particularly where animals are concerned – proving that most of us have a soft-spot somewhere! The terrain at this level is much the same as on Earth, with similar vegetation and habitation as the limited mind of such persons can envisage. Once again they would have earned an environment that would be in keeping with their thoughts and the way they lived their earthly lives.

Also within these regions are what is known as rehabilitation centres or 'Summerland'. These cater for people who had prolonged and serious illnesses or a severe mental or physical trauma prior to passing over. They are rather like our hospices and are staffed by compassionate volunteer doctors and nurses. Many inhabitants on these levels are not aware of, or cannot accept that they have 'died' from the Earth plane and therefore need counselling before they can join loved ones in other frequencies.

The landscape here is generally of great beauty with flowers, trees and shrubs of all varieties forming the right environment for recuperation and is equivalent to the best that the Earth plane has to offer. As well as diverse recreational facilities there are schools, colleges and libraries for the continued education of the inhabitants, and houses of all descriptions that have literally been built by the thoughts of those who inhabit them.

Travel in the astral and spiritual worlds is instantaneous and achieved purely by thought. People merely think of a place and they are there, including any return trips to the Earth plane from time to time to visit loved ones. Those who are returning for the first time will be guided or shown how to 'bypass' the dreadful lower astral regions, since they are extremely unpleasant places in which to get lost! It is easier for people to go 'down' to a lower frequency world rather than 'up' to those vibrating faster than their own astral body.

Living in the highest levels within the intermediate planes are those who would have been aware of their earthly faults and tried to correct them. Genuine love and affection would have been given to most who crossed their pathway on Earth. They would also have an enquiring mind and be aware of the spiritual side of life – generally, very loving and compassionate people.

These regions are pulsing with high frequency love energies, and the landscape is one of magnificent beauty, with lakes, mountains and meadows full of exotic flowers and shrubs. The air here is permeated by wonderful floral smells, and birds of all descriptions and colours are in abundance with choruses of song fit for such realms. It is here that many loved ones arrange to meet should they be on different levels after 'death'. It is also the region where those still living on the Earth plane can visit friends and relatives in their astral body whilst their physical body is 'asleep' in bed, or meet them during a near-death experience (NDE). I would suggest that the 'dark tunnel' through which most NDE patients travel is to guide them safely through the dismal lower astral planes.

Higher Astral Planes

These frequencies are often referred to as the start of the spiritual worlds, as they are populated by those who showed an abundance of impartial and unconditional love and affection when they were on Earth. They would have generally led selfless lives and, more often than not, put other people's happiness and welfare before their own, despite any personal hardship and suffering. Humility and lack of ego will be their hallmark as they live in a world permeated with the most incredible frequencies of spiritual love. These are wonderful people and, when they left our planet of suffering, many would have considered them too good for this Earth. They would have truly earned their new world of Love!

Many children are termed as 'old souls in young bodies' because of the amount of love, compassion and wisdom that they show from a tender age. Subsequently, when they leave the Earth plane prematurely they often come to this level to live. As we build the puzzle of life, you will see that it is the age of the *soul* that matters not the age of the physical body.

The landscape at these levels is one of incredible beauty, with a tranquillity of which we can only dream. There are the most amazing buildings of shimmering gold and cities the like of which we can only imagine. They have been designed with great wisdom by the loving thoughts of those who inhabit these levels, and are nothing like the polluted cities of architectural and planning chaos that we have here. Rivers meander through the most magnificent meadows lined with trees, exotic flowers and shrubs of all descriptions, many of which have never been seen on Earth. Gorgeous smells and intoxicating music permeate the air, and shimmering lakes amidst breathtaking mountains complete the backdrop to worlds of unimaginable peace.

Universities, or halls of learning as they are often known, are in abundance as the inhabitants realise that knowledge is part of spiritual growth. Every subject fit for those with an elevated and enquiring mind is available. Music, mathematics, physics and spiritual philosophy are just some of the many subjects offered at this level of consciousness. Here the scientist can still have his laboratory and the musician can still listen to or play in orchestral concerts.

Recreational activities are also to be enjoyed, and laughter and happiness are taken for granted in these higher spiritual planes where thoughts of the Earth, with its negative atmosphere, are few and far between. And the amusing thing is, that we cry and mourn for loved ones who leave the Earth for worlds like this! Do we really cry for them – or for ourselves?

If we have loved ones living at these levels, visits to Earth will be rare – simply because it will hold them back from their studies and spiritual progression. During my clairvoyant days, those whom I did encounter and describe from these elevated spiritual frequencies were always encased in white and golden auras and literally emanated love and compassion. It was always a humbling experience and a great pleasure to meet such lovely people.

All this would seem a far cry from the cartoonist's 'death' jokes of us becoming angels playing harps whilst floating on clouds in a mythical heaven. Or even some religionists' views that, after death, we enter into a deep sleep whilst waiting for trumpets to sound for the chosen few to awaken from their graves to take possession of the Earth. Apart from giving children nightmares, the latter would make a good script for a horror movie!

Mental and Causal Planes

These almost unimaginable worlds are even higher frequencies of spiritual love, peace and harmony and are truly awesome in their magnificence. The landscape, by what accounts we have, is even more breathtaking than the higher astral planes. Those who live here are the inspired philosophers, healers and teachers of Truth, as well as artists and creators of all that is of interest for the spiritual growth of humanity. How often have we been uplifted by music, art, poetry and spiritual writings that have moved our very soul? It is from these levels that such inspired thoughts percolate down through the various frequencies to uplift and encourage those who are of like mind to write, compose and create at elevated levels of consciousness.

Many of the wonderful souls that live here are the spirit guides and teachers of diverse Earth nationalities. It is their unconditional love and spiritual inspiration for the human race that has earned them the right to live here. Many volunteer to descend into the lower astral regions on rescue missions.

Spiritual entities known as angels and archangels are also inhabitants of this and other frequency levels. They have never lived on Earth in physical form as they are of a different evolution to the human race. Nevertheless, they are highly spiritual by nature and act as messengers and helpers between the various planes of existence. Many books have been written about angels and how to make contact with them.

Celestial Planes

These planes of existence have often been referred to as Heaven, Paradise, Nirvana and 'the abodes of the gods'. It is from here that many of the great spiritual masters, seers, sages and other teachers of Truth reside, as they have much closer links with the Supreme Spiritual Power of the Cosmos – another piece of the puzzle that we will be investigating.

For the vast majority of us, such frequencies defy description, but esoteric teachings talk of total and absolute bliss. These higher teachings, which represent another piece of the puzzle for advanced seekers of Truth, state that these levels are not the *end* of our spiritual quest, but only the *beginning!*

Cosmic or God Consciousness Planes

These frequencies, although we know they exist, are quite beyond our present comprehension and, apart from highly evolved spiritual masters, we could no more understand them than an earthworm or beetle could understand us. The love energies at these levels are so powerful that the vast majority of us from human evolution would be unable to absorb them. It has been likened to plugging a five-volt bulb into a trillion-volt supply!

Where Will I Go?

If you are now wondering which astral plane you might go to when your time comes to vacate your physical body, then don't worry, everything will be fine. As I will repeat as often as necessary, those who are of a hard and unscrupulous nature with a greedy and materialistic frame of mind are not interested in books of this nature. You *are*, or you would not have read this far. That tells me that you have within you – in whatever degree – love, humility, kindness and compassion. If so, you will probably be in the top frequencies of the intermediate astral planes, if not higher. You will find yourself in a beautiful environment with your own kind of people, the ones that you love and who think like you do. Look forward to it – you'll love it!

The above are merely brief descriptions of other frequencies and the lifestyles of the people living there. If this has interested you in learning more about the astral and spiritual planes, then *Life in the World Unseen* by Anthony Borgia, *A Soul's Journey* by Peter Richelieu and *Saved by the Light* by Dannion Brinkley and Paul Perry are good books to start with.

> Today we realise our Earth is not the centre of Creation but a grain of dust in a space-time universe, including universes of various dimensions co-existing within our own, all paralleled by a possible universe of anti-matter.
> *W. Raymond Drake 1913 – 1989 (Gods and Spacemen in the Ancient East)*

Electronic Communication

What would you think of the idea of turning on your television set, tuning it in to one of the astral world frequencies, and be able to see and speak to your 'deceased' loved ones? Wishful thinking? Not according to American George

W. Meek. It was his dream to do just that, and over the last 50 years of electronic communication research and development that dream is beginning to turn into reality.

Meek was a very successful international designer and consulting engineer with many worldwide industrial patents to his name. He retired from engineering in 1970 at the age of 60 to devote his time to the research of life after death and other metaphysical phenomena, a subject that had held his interest for many years. In 1971 he set up an organisation called *Metascience Foundation* in which he invested over half a million dollars of his own money to fund the research. Meek eventually formed a team of like-minded technical and scientific personnel from many countries. His travels took him all over the world as he and his scientific colleagues meticulously investigated countless numbers of mediums and healers of all abilities.

In Pennsylvania in 1974, Meek and some of his team met a brilliant, temperamental clairvoyant medium by the name of Bill O'Neil, who was also a ham radio buff and electronics expert. O'Neil claimed that he had made psychic contact with a fellow radio ham and doctor known as 'Doc Nick' who stated that he had 'died' five years previously. This 'Doc Nick' had given O'Neil instructions on how to adapt a tape recorder and radio equipment so that they could hold conversations from the astral worlds other than through conventional mediumship.

The apparatus was built, and the two men, both in different dimensions, held many hours of taped conversations. Months later another deceased voice came on the scene and identified himself as Dr George Mueller. Mueller gave O'Neil instructions for up-grading the electronic equipment to achieve better communication as well as personal details about himself for identification. Mueller stated that when he lived on Earth he was a physicist, and gave O'Neil details of where he could locate his death certificate issued in 1967. He also gave intimate details of his personal family life, his activities at Cornell and Wisconsin Universities, his social security number and three unlisted telephone numbers of the top security establishments where he had worked prior to his death. All these personal details checked out when thoroughly investigated, causing the top security establishments to question how Meek had obtained the 'secret' telephone numbers!

By September 1980 Dr Mueller and O'Neil were holding clear and intelligent conversations regarding complicated electronics as well as what life in Mueller's astral world was like. The electronic device used for this communication was dubbed 'Spiricom' because of its ability to communicate with the spirit worlds, and the scientific research was known as the 'Spiricom Project'. Twenty hours of documented recordings were eventually made on the device with excellent evidence and identification given by the communicators.

Having listened to some of these recordings I felt that they were the early pioneering days of radio communication with the astral planes.

Dozens of 'deceased' people from the astral planes made contact. They gave their names and details of their lives when on Earth, with some proclaiming that they had been in the astral planes for hundreds of years. Meek's team also received collaboration from several scientists residing in the astral planes. They stated that they were working in their laboratories to perfect easier and clearer devices for communication with the Earth.

In July 1990, I met George Meek when, at the age of 80, he came to England to lecture about the astral body and the Spiricom Project. I spent a very memorable two days in his company when he enlightened me as to the scientific progress he and his team had made in their investigations into life after death. Meek's sincerity and integrity were impressive, as was his kindness, compassion and humility. Should you be interested in comprehensive details of the Spiricom Project, *The Ghost of 29 Megacycles* by John G Fuller is very informative (see *Bibliography*).

29 Megacycles (megahertz) was the initial frequency that Mueller and other astral inhabitants were picked up on after painstaking experimental research. Meek informed me that the project had been set back several months when frequency interference from the lower astral planes occurred, allowing some of the depraved and foul-mouthed inhabitants there to wreck the broadcasts. This problem caused Dr Mueller and other scientists in the intermediate astral planes to search for a better communication frequency.

In 1984 Hans Otto Koenig of Moenchengladbach in Germany, took his sophisticated electronic equipment to the studio of Radio Luxembourg where, helped by studio technicians, he successfully communicated with 'deceased' persons residing in the astral planes. The broadcast was heard by an estimated two million people. Koenig returned to the studio several times with great success, each time managing to hold verifiable conversations with astral residents. This gave encouragement to Meek's Spiricom team and spurred them on to further research.

In Luxembourg, from 1985 –1988, Metascience Foundation members Jules and Maggy Harsch-Fischbach, with the aid of spirit technicians, developed advanced systems of electronic communication with the astral worlds that were superior to anything else at the time. This enabled verifiable, clearer and longer two-way conversations to take place. It was no coincidence that the favourable transmitting frequency they used was also 29 megahertz! As a consequence, they were regarded as one of the worlds leading electronic astral plane communicators.

Early days

The early pioneering of radio contact with the astral and spirit worlds was known as Electronic Voice Phenomenon (EVP), and has a history of experimentation going back to the days of Marconi, Edison and Tesla at the beginning of the 20th century. EVP was limited to voice contact and numerous audible spirit voices were picked up on early gramophone recordings and tape recorders.

Most great discoveries in life are found by accident, and such was the case with Friedrich Juergenson, a Swedish film producer and artist. In 1959 he went into the woods to record bird songs, and later, when playing back the recordings, heard human voices that were not in the woods at the time, and which he subsequently described as paranormal. Juergenson was so intrigued with this phenomenon that he devoted years of experimentation to the subject before concluding that the voices were from the spiritual worlds.

In 1965, Dr. Konstantin Raudive, a Latvian psychologist, visited Juergenson. After extensive enquiry Raudive declared that the spirit voices were genuine and returned to Germany to start his own experiments. Over the following years he recorded more than 70,000 paranormal voices, and his book, *Breakthrough: Electronic Communication with the Dead may be Possible*, is now regarded as a classic on the subject.

Juergenson and Raudive alerted the public's attention to the phenomenon of recording spirit voices on tape recorders. Subsequently, thousands of people all over the world found they could achieve similar results and, as a consequence, started EVP organisations. Even the Vatican has experimented with the subject with positive results!

I have personally spoken with some who achieved repeatable conversations with 'departed' loved ones, but they stated that it takes a lot of patience, perseverance and determination to get acceptable voices. They found that when a new blank tape was inserted into a tape recorder and left running in a closed room overnight (preferably without a ticking clock or noisy budgie), recognisable 'deceased' voices were often heard on playback the next morning. The voices would frequently ask questions, or give answers to questions put by loved ones. Very often, it would only be necessary to ask a question in the room *before* the recorder was switched on to get a reply on the tape. In many cases the replies would be in six words or less and barely discernible. The old 'reel-to-reel' tape recorders were deemed the best as they could be left running for hours instead of the conventional 60 minutes. I am not aware of DVDs fulfilling the same function!

An informative book on the subject is *Voices from Paradise* by Judith Chisholm. Judith investigated EVP phenomena after suffering the devastating loss of her 29-year-old son Paul in 1992. She obtained evidence of his survival after receiving many taped messages.

Telephone Calls

How would you feel if you received a telephone call from a loved one on the 'other side'? Shocked? Not surprising – but many people have, and I am not referring to sick hoax calls here. Genuine telephone calls from the likes of Auntie Flo and Uncle Joe on the 'other side' have been received. And, once again, highly personal questions were asked that only they would have known. This is, apparently, a world-wide occurrence, and in 1980 two highly respected psychic researchers, D. Scott Rogo and Raymond Bayless, wrote a book called *Phone Calls from the Dead.*

More recently, scientists have achieved excellent conversations with 'departed' loved ones, friends and colleagues using modified fax machines and printers. Highly personal questions were asked and detailed evidential replies were received that only the genuine 'departed' could have known. Meek's wife Jeannette 'died' in 1990 following a series of strokes, but via specially designed electronic systems he managed to hold more than 100 conversations with her from her new astral world abode. In 1992, George obtained astral plane pictures of Jeannette together with their 'deceased' daughter Nancy Carol, via a receiving station in Luxembourg. Meek's last book *Enjoy Your Own Funeral* was published shortly after his 'death'. It contains diagrams and details of his electronic communication experiments and research into every known aspect of life after death.

To my friend Brian Sadler – with the hope that in the
years ahead he will provide still more answers to the age-
old questions regarding the continuity of human life.
With love and best wishes – George W. Meek

George wrote those words on the back of his Metascience business card and presented it to me as we parted company after our meeting in 1990. I am doing my best to live up to those words but George is a hard act to follow. George and I kept in communication until he vacated his physical body in 1999. His legacy lives on.

Instrumental Transcommunication

With scientists and technicians in the astral planes and several countries on the Earth working together, great advances are being made with visual as well as audio contact with the astral planes. Since 1985, this more advanced technology has been known as Instrumental Transcommunication (ITC).

Continuing Meek's research into ITC is his partner and colleague Mark Macy. Since 1992, Macy has published various journals and books on the subject of electronic communications with other dimensions. *Conversations Beyond the Light,* that he co-wrote with Dr Pat Kubis, shows photographs of the various astral planes together with friends and colleagues now living there. Not only does ITC record visual contact, but also audio contact where voice patterns scientifically match recordings made when the 'deceased' lived on Earth. A detailed study of the terrain in these other dimensions has also confirmed what mediumistic contact with the spirit worlds has been saying for decades – once again, making life after death in a multidimensional Universe a scientific fact.

Macy's *Miracles in the Storm* details some of the problems encountered during ITC research and the conditions required for setting up the necessary equipment. In 1995, fellow researchers and scientists from various countries founded the International Network for Instrumental Transcommunication (INIT). This is known as World ITC and has a website www.worlditc.org for up-to-date information.

Based on 15 years of research, Macy's later book, *SPIRIT FACES – Truth about the Afterlife*, contains 70 colour photographs of people living in the astral planes.

> I'm involved in a controversial field of communication research called ITC, or Instrumental Transcommunication. It's not your normal everyday type of communication; it involves the use of technical instruments to get information from the worlds of spirit in the form of voices, images and text. Effectively, my fellow researchers and I are in contact with departed colleagues and loved ones by various means – primarily telephone, radio, television, computer and camera.
>
> *Mark Macey (Miracles in the Storm)*

At least 20 countries host research groups set up to seriously investigate the phenomena of electronic communication with those we call 'dead'. Many of these groups consist of respected academics who state that the evidence is 'very compelling'.

'Deceased' Earth scientists now living in the intermediate astral planes inform us that their electronic and frequency knowledge is far greater than ours, hence the link-up problems. They say it is like trying to pick up our modern UHF and HD signals with an old 'cat's whisker' radio (wireless). Electronic communication with the astral worlds is still in its infancy, but thanks to the concerted efforts of hundreds of scientists, in this world and the next, the breakthrough is gradually being achieved.

Although it grieves me to say this, there are various vested interests that, over the centuries, have done their best to debunk, ridicule and suppress the facts about life after death. It may sound incredulous that there are those who do their utmost to keep such information out of the public domain, but as any serious seeker of Truth will tell you – *it is a fact*. It is, apparently, in their interests to keep the masses ignorant of such information 'otherwise the rulebooks and textbooks will have to be re-written!'

> The first and most important secret that has been carefully guarded and withheld from the public at large is that two or more worlds exist, composed of different forms of matter but occupying the same space.
> *John A. Keel (Our Haunted Planet)*

Summary

Until recently, we have had to rely on sensitive human beings picking up voices and visions from the astral worlds and translating what they heard and saw. Although perfectly natural, this method has always been open to error and fraud – but science marches on. The last hundred years has given us electricity, cruise liners, fast cars, trains and aeroplanes, space rockets, mobile telephones, radios, television, DVDs and compact disc recorders, electronic robots, computers and more. We can now speak to our families in Australia as clear as if they were in the next room, and command centres can see and speak to astronauts in space.

Eventually, with enough time and money devoted to scientific research, ITC technology *will* be perfected and, like other everyday electronic wizardry, be taken for granted. Hopefully, our Mr and Mrs Average will then lose their fear of death. No longer will they grieve for their 'deceased' loved ones because they will still be able to see and talk with them. They will know *exactly* what the intermediate and higher astral worlds look like and where they themselves *could* be going when they eventually 'die'. The lower astral frequencies that caused havoc in some of George Meek's early EVP experiments, for obvious reasons, will in all probability, not be part of any foreseeable electronic linkup!

Hopefully, because of this knowledge, our world will gradually become a more peaceful place in which to live, with wars and violence a thing of the past, and politics and religion having to drastically rethink agendas.

Once again, Love is the 'theme tune' running through a chapter and, coupled with the philosophy that we live in a multidimensional Universe, represents another piece of the jigsaw. We can now proceed on our quest and investigate as to whether a benevolent force of good – whatever we conceive it to be – governs this multidimensional Universe.

The future lies with instruments capable of recording
vibrations or radiation emanating from the spirit world
which are not normally receptive to man's five senses.
Maurice Barbanell (Writer and editor)

The development of radio science will enable you in the future, I hope, to get in touch with your fallen comrades. Radio link with the dead *is* coming.
Sir Ernest Fisk (President of the Institute of Radio Engineers)

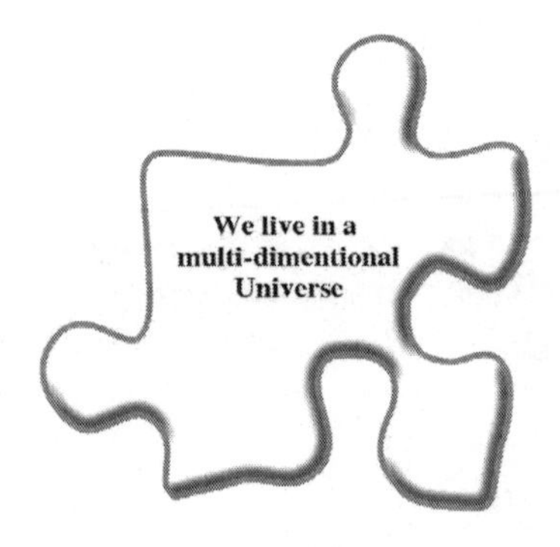

8 Is There a God of Love?

If God did not exist, it would be necessary to invent him.
Voltaire 1694 – 1778 (French Philosopher and writer)

After many years of personal evidence and proof that life is continuous, that we survive the death of our physical body and live on in an 'invisible' multidimensional Universe, I still had a deep yearning to prove the existence of a loving God. Why? I suppose, to be reassured that some superior intelligence of infinite love and wisdom was really in charge of the Universe, rather than humanity being a freak accident of Nature on a doomed planet and victims of our self-created conflicts, greed, ignorance and stupidity!

I had a good job, a very loving family, a large circle of marvellous friends, a nice house with all the material comforts to go with it and really wanted for nothing, but something inside me wouldn't let me rest until I had some answers. It was part of an inner desire to know if life had a meaning and human suffering a purpose. I reckoned that if life after death was fact, not fiction, then it must be for a very good reason, and that there must be more to life than meets the eye.

At the time, I had no idea of how or where I was going to get my evidence of God, and why should I succeed when millions have failed? I decided that the best thing to do was just go along with life and let things happen. If I were meant to know these things then life would show me. Experience dictated that my guiding lights should always be *love and compassion*, as the pathway to a loving God would *not* be where there was conflict.

Killing for God

- 'Thus saith the Lord of hosts [to King Saul]….now go and smite Amalek, and utterly destroy all that they have, and spare them not; but slay both man and women, infant and suckling, ox and sheep, camel and ass.' (*1 Samuel 15: 2-3*)

- 'Happy shall be he that taketh and dasheth thy little ones against the stones.' (Psalm 137:9)

- 'Break their teeth, O God, in their mouth ….let them be as cut in pieces.' (Psalm 58:6)

- ‘Let his days be few ….Let his children be fatherless and his wife a widow. Let his children be continually vagabonds and beg; let them seek their bread also out of their desolate places.’ (Psalm 109:8)

- ‘Thus saith the Lord God of Israel …. slay every man his brother, and every man his companion, and every man his neighbour.’ (Exodus 32:27)

- ‘And Joshua at that time turned back, and took Hazor ….And they smote all the souls that were therein with the edge of the sword, utterly destroying them: there was not any left to breathe: and he burnt Hazor with fire. And all the cities of those kings, and all the kings of them, did Joshua take, and smote them with the edge of the sword, and he utterly destroyed them, as Moses the servant of the Lord commanded.’ (Joshua 11:10 –12)

- ‘Their children also shall be dashed to pieces before their eyes; their houses shall be spoiled, and their wives ravished.’ (Isaiah 13:16)

- ‘When thou goest out to battle against thine enemies ..... the Lord your God is he that goeth with you, to fight for you against your enemies.’ (Deuteronomy 20:1 – 4)

- ‘Their bows also shall dash the young men to pieces; and they shall have no pity on the fruit of the womb; their eye shall not spare the children.’ (Isaiah 13:18)

- ‘…. thou shalt save alive nothing that breatheth: But thou shalt utterly destroy them; namely the Hittites, and the Amorites, the Canaanites, and the Perizzites, the Hivites, and the Jebusites; as the Lord thy God hath commanded thee.’ (Deuteronomy 20:16 – 17)

Here we have examples of horrendous atrocities committed in the name of a cruel and avenging god, with rape, the wholesale mass slaughter of men, women (many pregnant), children, babies and animals, and the total destruction of their towns and villages. Today, this could be classified as terrorism with the perpetrators of such genocidal acts wanted for war crimes.

From 1482 until 1834, with God as the excuse, the Catholic Inquisition used every torture and torment imaginable against unbelievers, psychics and freethinkers. And down the centuries virtually every army claimed God was on their side, with both sides convinced they were doing ‘His’ will by slaughtering the infidels and blasphemers. Hence countries could be invaded and conquered with the inhabitants tortured and slaughtered in the name of

God without a conscience. Even during civil wars it was amazing how many commanders brought God into the equation.

> All wise people throughout history have gone through great pains in order to know truth directly. They were not satisfied by the mere opinions of others. They were not frightened off from this quest by the defenders of orthodoxy and dogma, who persecuted and sometimes even executed them because their conclusions were different.
> *Swami Rama 1925 – 1996 (Living with the Himalayan Masters)*

Right up to the early 20th century, hell-fire and damnation was preached from the pulpit until the very mention of God put fear into every man, woman and child. If God didn't punish them a devil would – a 'catch 22' situation. Even today we have 'just wars' fought in God's name, with prayers offered for a safe return and the granting of victory. I would think God must be very battle weary by now!

Let me, just for a moment, put things in perspective. Our Earth is an insignificant little planet in a galaxy we call the Milky Way. And our little galaxy is like a speck of dust in the desert in comparison to the Universe, and the Universe is like a speck of dust in the Cosmos. At the moment of writing, astronomers at their observatory in Hawaii have found a galaxy 12.3 billion light years from Earth. A light year is the distance travelled by light in one year, and is used as a unit for measuring distances in space. Since light travels at a known speed of 186,300 miles per second, that means in one year it can travel over 5,880,000,000,000 miles. If we multiply this figure by 12.3 billion you will have some idea of the distance involved between this 'new' galaxy and Earth.

British astronomers are now saying that at least a *billion* Earth-like planets exist in our own Milky Way galaxy, and have mentioned constellations a mere 51 light years away as an example. This is virtually on our doorstep in galactic terms.

Now, if we are so minute compared to the vastness of the Cosmos, do we really believe that the wisdom and 'Intelligence' that brought all this into being would want to get personally involved in our private lives, pathetic wars and squabbling religions here on Earth? An important piece of the jigsaw is at stake here, so let me offer you further food for thought.

Astute observation should tell us that Nature is no respecter of persons. She cannot be pleaded with or bargained with and she certainly doesn't discriminate. The virus will kill or maim just as impartially as electricity or gas. Fire will warm us or burn us to death. Rainwater will refresh us or drown us in a flood. Soil will sustain our crops or bury us in an avalanche or mudslide. Wind will cool us and sail our yachts, or destroy us and our environment with hurricanes or tornadoes. The Sun, which is vital for life on Earth, will burn our skin, start forest fires, and if we get lost in the desert or bush without water it will show no mercy and quickly become our 'enemy'. Why? Because the Law of Nature is *impersonal!*

For generations we have been brought up to believe in a *personal* God to whom we should say our prayers to every night. To many children, and even some unquestioning adults, 'He' was a medieval archetypal old man with a long white beard somewhere up in the sky listening to every spoken word. 'He' was a God to be feared – one who got jealous and angry, intervened in our private lives, fought our enemies, healed our sickness, sorted out all our problems, rewarded or punished us, had racial and religious discriminations and protected us from evil and danger. Well, let's have a look at just a few 20th century statistics and see how much evidence there is for such a notion.

- Martinique May 8, 1902: A volcanic eruption killed an estimated 40,000 people.

- Namibia (Africa) 1907: In an act of genocide by the German occupation, 66,000 men, women and children of the Herero tribe were taken into the Kalahari dessert and left to die.

- Italy (Avezzano) January 13, 1915: An earthquake killed more than 35,000 people.

- World War 1 (The Great War) 1914 – 1918: An estimated 14.6 million people died, with 30 million wounded.

- Russian Civil War 1917 – 1922: An estimated 10 million people died as a result of civil war, terror, famine and disease.

- Influenza outbreak 1918: This pandemic killed an estimated 40 million people in five months and preceded an outbreak of encephalitis which affected a further five million.

- Japan (Tokyo and Yokohama) September 1923: An earthquake killed an estimated 142,800 people.

- Japan (Kwanto) 1923: A fire killed more than 60,000 people.

- China (Nan-Shan) May 22, 1927: More than 200,000 people died in an earthquake.

- Spanish Civil War 1936 – 1939: An estimated 370,000 people died.

- World War ll 1939 – 1945: Over 50 million people died, including the gassing of six million Jews and the atrocities of Japanese and Nazi concentration camps.

- Chechnya (Russia) 1944: Stalin approved the deportation of the entire nation. More than 500,000 people died.

- Korean War 1950 – 1953: Over 4.8 million people died.

- Vietnam War 1965 – 1973: An estimated 3.5 million people died as a result of the war and political violence.

- Aberfan, Wales, October 1966: 116 children and 28 adults were suffocated or crushed to death when a 30 foot high coal waste tip moved like a land slide and engulfed a school and cottages.

- Nigeria, Biafra 1967 – 1970: Civil war killed over one million people.

- Northern Ireland and UK 1969 – 1998: Over 3,000 people died due to sectarian violence.

- Peru, May 1, 1970: More than 50,000 people died in an earthquake and landslides.

- Uganda 1972 – 1979: An estimated 100,000 people died due to the atrocities of Idi Amin.

- Cambodia 1974 – 1997: Pol Pot's Khmer Rouge Communist organisation killed more than 1.5 million people in an act of genocide.

- Guatemala, February 4, 1976: 23,000 people died in an earthquake.

- China (Tangshan) July 28, 1976: An earthquake killed more than 250,000 people.

- Iran, September 16, 1978: 20,000 people died in a one minute earthquake.

- Iraq and Iran War 1980 – 1988: Over one million people died.

- Afghanistan 1979 – 1989: The Soviet invasion led to the deaths of over 1.5 million people.

- Bhopal, India, December 3, 1984: 40 tons of toxic gas leaked from a chemical factory. It killed almost 25,000 people and caused over 500,000 to suffer severe and dreadful after-effects that they are still dying from.

- Mexico City 1985: An estimated 10,000 people died in an earthquake.
- Almero (Columbia) November 13, 1985: A volcano eruption killed over 20,000 people.
- Armenia 1988: An estimated 100,000 people died in an earthquake.
- Hillsborough (UK) April 15, 1989: 96 fans were crushed to death at a FA cup semi-final. One of our sons was there on that fateful day. He survived with just a twisted ankle, but thought that the, trapped, elderly gentleman who helped him over the wire didn't.
- Iran, June 1990: Over 40,000 people died in an earthquake.
- Iraq / Kuwait (Gulf War) 1990 – 1991: More than 200,000 people died.
- Bangladesh 1991: A cyclone and floods killed 140,000 people.
- Bosnia / Kosovo (Yugoslavia) 1992 – 1999: More than 200,000 people died in a political / religious / ethnic conflict.
- India 1993: 7,600 people died in an earthquake.
- Rwanda 1994: 800,000 men, women and children were shot or hacked to death in an act of genocide.
- Japan 1995: Over 6,400 people died in an earthquake.
- El Nino (destructive forces of nature) 1998: Over 10,000 people died in 12 months of drought, floods and pestilence. In Papua New Guinea, over 7,000 people were killed when a tsunami suddenly engulfed them.
- Afghanistan 1998: A total of 9,000 people died in two earthquakes.
- Afghanistan, August 1998: More than 5,000 unarmed Hazara men in the Mazar-i Sharif region were massacred by the Taliban.
- Turkey, August 17, 1999: An estimated 17,000 people died in an earthquake.
- Iraq, August 1999: A UNICEF report stated that over 500,000 children died after the 1990/91 Gulf War as a result of sanctions.
- Indonesia (East Timor) September 1999: Armed militia went on the rampage after a referendum vote for independence. Aid agencies reported that at least 20,000 people were massacred in an act of genocide.

- Venezuela, December 1999: Torrential rain caused floods and mudslides that killed an estimated 50,000 people.

- All over the world, *every day*, hundreds of thousands of men, women, children and babies suffer injury and death because of wars, terrorist activities, murders, accidents, earthquakes, floods, mudslides, famines, hurricanes, avalanches and volcanic activities. And we could also include sickness, disease, poverty, neglect and abuse.

These are just a sample of the facts and figures highlighting the stupidity of the human race and the ferocity of Nature during the last century. Many more could have been added, but evidence of the intervention and protection of a loving personal God (Theism) is not obvious. If it was, then all these everyday atrocities and disasters would not befall us. Hopefully, it has given you the promised food for thought.

On December 24, 2004, an Asian earthquake triggered a tsunami that killed an estimated 240,000 people and injured thousands more. The media reported that, as a consequence of the catastrophe, untold numbers around the world, including clerics, deeply questioned or abandoned their faith. Due to the lack of intervention by their personal God, many concluded that we live in a pitiless Universe where innocent people become victims of Nature's awesome power. And in Haiti on January 12, 2010, an earthquake killed more than 200,000 people, causing thousands more to wonder where their protective God was when needed.

Some might argue that such atrocities are the work of a devil, which would imply more knowledge of a devil than that of a God of love. Surely, we ask, wouldn't a loving God intervene and save his creation from a devil's torments, or stop him doing it in the first place? As a responsible and loving parent, would you knowingly let your offspring be tormented and abused and do nothing about it? Of course you wouldn't – so let us investigate further.

Wars, murder, accidents, disease and catastrophes of Nature have plagued this planet since time immemorial. In fact, it's just one big hellhole of a 'war-game' here. When Nature erupts and people are killed and injured we strangely call it an 'act of God'. But do we really think a God kills and injures people and animals by hurling rocks, trees, and horrendous volumes of air and water at them, or inflicting plagues, famine and pestilence on them for amusement?

Over the years I have sought to find acceptable answers that are not an insult to the intelligence. So with tongue in cheek, let us ask a few more questions.

Why would a loving God let tens of thousands of men, women, children and babies die horrible deaths every day, but heal Mrs Green, up the road, of her arthritis? Or, why would a God help Mr Brown, down the road, find a good job, yet let thousands of nice people be mugged, raped and brutally murdered every day? Millions of people around the world believe that a personal God intervenes in their personal lives and does the most trivial things for them. 'I believe God wanted me to do this work,' some say. Or, 'I believe God saved my life and was with me at the time.' And even, 'I know I am going to win because God is with me.'

Does that mean that God has favourites? Well if that's the case, the 19,240 soldiers that died horrible deaths on the Somme battlefield on July 1st 1916 must have been well out of favour. Or perhaps the 35,000 or so children who die through poverty, starvation, neglect, abuse and disease *every day* on this planet are unlucky because God is too busy sorting out Mr and Mrs Average's petty problems. Unfortunately, it is usually the first personal catastrophe to hit them hard that causes many people to think otherwise and abandon the personal God mentality.

If you are with me so far, you will realise that any sensible judge or jury would throw the childish notion of a personal and intervening God out of court through lack of credible evidence. Unfortunately it is the cold hard statistics of everyday living and dying, coupled with the personal God scenario, that has turned so many of today's generation into atheists or agnostics. Genuine teachers of philosophical Truth have known for centuries that a God does *not* interfere in the affairs of the human race, so why have their teachings been falsified or fallen on deaf ears?

> You will see God in every thing and every body – *after* you have seen God in yourself! Thus, after following other gods, after believing in a multitude of deities, Man finally understands that there is but one spirit behind all creation, and after believing in a personal spirit, a personal God, he ultimately realises the Truth that the highest Deity is Impersonal and Universal
> *Paul Brunton 1898 – 1981 (Discover Yourself)*

Over the years I have met many people who have had shattered lives from disasters that came out of the blue. Perhaps you have experienced this yourself when life suddenly collapses around your ears and things go horribly 'pear-shaped'. Many have been mentally or physically scarred for life, and cannot relate to a God of love because of what has happened to them or their families. Some even believe they are being punished by God for something they have done wrong in their life – the very antithesis of those who think that God *helps* them every day in their personal life.

I well remember, many years ago, giving healing to a young woman who was the sole survivor of a car crash that had killed her husband and child. She herself had suffered a fractured skull, and thereafter blinding headaches and depression for which her doctor had prescribed a heavy dose of tranquillisers. She was angry with God, and had tried to take her own life because, as she put it, her purpose for living had been taken away. She also wanted to know why she was left to live without them. A very good question that demands a very good answer.

As another example of how life can change from idyllic to a nightmare scenario in a brief moment of time; a lady, who had also come to me for healing some 20 years ago, explained what happened to a family that she knew.

Her friend, a young mother of two children, was washing her 10-month-old baby in the bath when she realised that she had left the clean towel at the bottom of the stairs. She called to her four-year-old son, who was playing in his bedroom, to fetch the towel. This he promptly did, but seconds later the mother heard thumping noises and a muffled cry. She immediately rushed to the scene only to find her son lying unconscious at the foot of the stairs. She was unable to revive him, and after several minutes, realised that she had left the baby in the bath.

Rushing upstairs the mother found her baby lying face down in the water unconscious, and once again tried revival techniques without success. By this time, as you can imagine, she was hysterical but managed to telephone for an ambulance. Whilst waiting, she rang her husband at work and asked him to come home immediately, but in his panic he drove too fast, ran out of road on a bend, hit a large tree and was killed instantly.

The outcome of this tragedy was that the baby died as a result of drowning and the young son died of a brain haemorrhage after hitting his head during the fall. The mother had a mental breakdown as a result and six months after the event was still under medical sedation. My lady patient asked how God could let such a tragedy happen to such a nice family – a question that must echo the sentiments of thousands throughout the world every day.

There are no quick five-minute 'off-the-cuff' answers for such personal tragedies, any more than there are for death and destruction catastrophes that decimate families. What we are looking at here, and all other aspects of life, are not the actions of chance, good or bad luck, a devil, or a personal God, but the actions of an *impersonal law* – the law of *cause* and *effect*. Just as the law of Nature is impersonal, so are all the other known laws of life such as the laws of physics, for example.

Should you wish to foolishly experiment, throw a brick into the air and then plead with the law of gravity for it not to hurt you when it falls to earth. You will quickly realise that you are wasting your time pleading when you note that the brick is still on collision course with your head. Split seconds before you are rendered unconscious – with an impending visit to a casualty department – you will have realised three very important facts:

1. A crash helmet would have been a wise investment.
2. Learning to run would have been even wiser.
3. Not tempting impersonal laws in the first place would have been the wisest.

NB: The author accepts no responsibility for this experiment should you be out of favour with the law of gravity.

I trust that you are not sitting in an ambulance with your head bandaged reading this paragraph or I would have to deduct points for stupidity. Hopefully, you are now more aware of the law of gravity and the law of cause and effect. The effect was a potential headache and the cause was throwing a brick!

Is There a God of Love?

The Infinite, The Absolute, Brahman, Allah, Yahweh, Jehovah, Ptah, Shiva, Vishnu, Universal Mind, The Great Spirit, Wakantanka, Ahura Mazda, The Divine, The Force, Mother-Father, Ra, Tao, Zeus, are all names that, down the centuries, have been attributed to an all-powerful, omniscient, omnipotent deity that is believed to be in charge of the Universe. This 'Power', whatever we conceive it to be, has been credited with having created the Earth, all life on it, and supposedly spawned the various religions.

Does a God of love exist? The ultimate and age-old question, and the best way to give you an answer in simplistic terms is an explanation of a '*Cosmic Consciousness*' experience. Since the dawn of recorded history – and probably before – countless men and women the world over have experienced Cosmic Consciousness. Even today, reports of it are manifest and virtually all tell a similar story. Let me tell you how it happened to me and how it presented the personal evidence and proof that I had been searching for.

It was June 1983, Patricia and I had just got married and, because we had spent our last penny on the wedding and new house that was being built, we couldn't afford a honeymoon. Mother-in-law Eileen suggested that we spend a week in Norfolk at her bungalow whilst she looked after Patricia's two boys, Mark and Neil.

Driving around the Norfolk countryside one sunny afternoon, we approached the lovely village of Deopham. We paused awhile to look round the old village church and, later, being hungry and thirsty, came across 'The Victoria Inn'. Once inside we were immediately aware of a peaceful and inviting atmosphere, with the olde-worlde charm of oak beams, low ceilings and a fireplace with a log-burning stove. Apart from the lady behind the bar we were the only customers.

On ordering food and drinks we sat at a table offering a beautiful view of the winding country lane with its lush hedgerows, magnificent trees and the most perfect cloudless blue sky. Add to this the singing of multitudes of birds and the picture postcard scenario was complete. What peace and beauty it all was, and goodness knows we had earned it, as we were both exhausted from the hectic rushing hither and thither on the run-up to the wedding. At that instant, at the other end of the bar, I became aware of a translucent, egg-shaped, shimmering white cloud (a phenomenon that I was to later know as an orb). It was approximately 1.8m (6 feet) tall by about 90 cm (3 feet) wide, and made its way towards me *between* the tables, not *through* them. I stared in amazement as it hovered about 60cm (2 feet) in front of me for a few seconds. Suddenly, it engulfed me. What happened next is difficult to put into words.

At that instant, I became totally 'at one' with the Cosmos and knew *everything* there was to know. I knew the *meaning and purpose of life* (hence the title of this book). I knew the blueprint of life itself and that I (consciousness) was immortal and, in numerous forms, had always existed, and that 'death' was the great illusion of our physical world. I knew that a loving God existed and what God was. I was part of God and God was part of me – my very soul. I was loved beyond measure and I loved God equally so.

I knew that everything from the smallest microbe to the largest galaxy is part of an incredible Cosmic Plan and that everything is linked. All is perfect and in accordance with a beautiful simplistic *Law* – the Law of *Love*. That which we call 'evil' did not, and *could* not, exist at this level – neither does time as we know it. The radiation of peace and love was incredible, so much so that it was almost unbearable, if that was possible. It was like a trillion volts of love – absolute bliss, total ecstasy. Earthly love is but a pale reflection by comparison.

This was where I belonged; this was coming 'home'. This was my source; this was where I came from and this is to where I will return after a great cosmic journey. It was so incredibly real, and I was far more 'alive' and aware than I have ever been in my earthly body.

Gradually the scene faded, and once more I was aware of my surroundings and sitting next to Patricia. 'Are you all right?' she whispered, staring at me. 'You were miles away and the tears have been streaming down your cheeks.' I looked at the front of my shirt and it was soaking wet – similar to my experience in Chichester Cathedral.

Had I been able to put my hands on a terminally ill person during that experience I knew, without a doubt, that they would have been instantly healed. And I say that with all humility and the greatest respect for the higher powers.

I had no idea of the time interval – it was irrelevant. I tried to explain what had happened, but words failed to express the indescribable and *totally silent* experience. It will live with me forever, and taught me more in that brief moment about the meaning and purpose of life than a million books or lectures could have done. Now I can truly say, like Carl Jung, that I don't *believe* in God – I *know* there is a God – of unimaginable Love and knowledge!

God's one and only voice is silence.
Herman Melville 1819 – 1891 (American poet and novelist)

The author pictured in the Victoria Inn immediately
after the Cosmic Consciousness experience.
Note the look of ecstatic bliss – which lasted for hours afterwards.

Cosmic Consciousness experiences seem to happen at a certain stage in people's lives, and are personal proof to the individual that a God of love exists and what 'It' is. At lectures I have asked audiences if any of them have had a Cosmic Consciousness experience, in one form or another and, on average, about 10 per cent respond. Most are overjoyed to speak afterwards and the feeling is always mutual. They too had the all-knowing, the radiation of love, being at one with everything in the Cosmos, and knowing that a loving God exists. I could tell by their eyes and they could tell by mine that we had all had a little taster of the TRUTH.

Perhaps you have had such an experience yourself, or many, in which case you will understand. If you would like to contact me via the publisher please feel free to do so, particularly if you have not been able to talk about it. Many are glad to make contact with like minds to reaffirm that they didn't hallucinate or suffer a mental problem.

It was, incidentally, many years after the experience that I read my first account of one in *Fourteen Lessons in Yogi Philosophy* by Yogi Ramacharaka. I could have written the very words and it gave me great comfort to know that what I had experienced was perfectly normal and well known in both ancient and present day esoteric teachings.

I have since been honoured to make the acquaintance of a Japanese Buddhist monk – Buddha Maitreya (Koji Takeuchi) who, over a period of 25 years, has built the most beautiful Japanese garden at his sanctuary in Nottinghamshire (see *Bibliography*). Whilst discussing the cosmic consciousness experience, he told me that it was a partial enlightenment that should encourage me to seek for the ultimate Truth of *total enlightenment*. That is what he had personally attained through 'sacrifice and dedication' over many years using the discipline of meditation. This is what he teaches, maintaining that the Truth is here now and can be experienced in everyday life. I felt most humble in his presence knowing how much I still had to achieve.

For me, like others, cosmic consciousness is a life-changing experience, and for many years afterwards I found it difficult to settle down to everyday life and accept it for what it is. Let me give you a symbolic example.

Suppose we took a poor, lonely, filthy, starving wretch – poor in health and clothed only in rags – from the gutters of Calcutta in India, and instantaneously whisked him to some luxurious paradise island. There he was bathed, healed, and dressed in the most expensive clothes, given the best of food and drink, shown unconditional love by everyone there, told that this was his real home, that nothing would be too much trouble - just to ask if he needed anything. Imagine him being in that new environment for a few weeks and absolutely ecstatic with happiness and security.

One day the scene fades, and he wakes up clothed once more in his rags back in the gutters of Calcutta with all the filth and stench. How do you think he would feel? And how do you think he would explain it to others? Life for him would *never* be the same again. Before, he would have known no better, but now he does – *much* better.

More Cosmic Consciousness Experiences

Virtually all who have had a cosmic consciousness experience tell the same story, and how they found it difficult to settle down and relate once more to this world – a world where very few of its inhabitants have experienced or know the true meaning of life, love, health or happiness. I can do no better than let others explain in their own words. Mark Lathwell, a Bespoke Cabinet Maker shares this experience:

In 1995, at 23-years-of-age, a sudden revelation overshadowed my mind as I found myself alive in a new atmosphere, where I was enlightened beyond all imaginings and aware of a place I never knew existed. All thinking ceased, as did the ideas that normally reigned in my mind – they just melted away into insignificance. Therein a heightened control of the 'animal' nature came over me and I felt set free from all earthly attachments. My whole being was filled with the most wonderful feelings of joy and happiness.

In this glimpse I saw the world as a giant living organism evolving through various stages of growth. I was aware in that moment of a super-intelligent MIND pervading all that is, and that all things emanate from it, and that it is my origin. I also had an insight into the significance of all things (an all knowing).

I was also aware that the Truth about Life is right here and now, and that it is our true business here on Earth to discover our true identity by following the tender feeling in the heart to its source – the Real 'I' – the DIVINE SELF, and to live accordingly. Therefore we have to take more notice of the experiences in everyday living, for it is they that provide the means for us to uncover and unfold this divinity within us.

After this experience it took me a long time to come to terms with living on this Earth, but it has given my life a new meaning and perspective that has wiped away much illusion that I was living under.

Jeff Watts, an Engineering Manager shares his Cosmic Consciousness experience:

From the beginning of this birth I had been searching for something I knew but had temporarily forgotten. When I was 14-years-of-age there was an experience that can only be said to equal Cosmic Consciousness. For many weeks prior to this experience I had been listening to Beatles' Albums, and I realise now that this played an essential part in lifting my consciousness to a higher level of thinking.

The Cosmic Experience manifested itself within a split second. Suddenly my consciousness expanded into nothing – and then everything. The experience was beyond all known parameters and cannot be fully expressed with words as they have finite limitations. I was aware of being pure consciousness (soul), and instantaneously having absolute knowledge of everything – an all knowing. Knowing of the existence of the Absolute and the connection of all life. I was ageless and totally beyond being male or female, and I was aware of my immortality (deathless), and that my consciousness would always be. I was infused with love – absolute ecstasy and bliss.

I seemed to be stationary in the present moment, and time didn't exist. Gradually, a sense of our dimension returned, but the experience will remain with me always. It is difficult to readjust to this world or see life as 'normal' again after such an expansion of consciousness. It was totally unlimited and more real than the physical world.

This experience taught me so much, but these are my observations:

- *The universe is sustained by love – it is eternal.*
- *The intelligence governing all things is the Absolute.*
- *Physical reality equals a temporary costume. The costume can die – but I cannot.*
- *Soul growth is the essence of life.*

This cosmic consciousness experience happened to 52-year-old Michael Collins, who was introduced in the chapter on *Death and Dying*:

I was in my bedroom on the afternoon of 15th May 2000 wondering where my life was going and what it was all about. At the time, I was looking at a picture of Sai Baba, and just happened to glance through the doorway into the hall of my bungalow when I saw coming towards me a pulsing white light in the shape of an egg. It seemed to hit my forehead and encompass me. The light and I were one.

I then had the most tremendous feeling of peace and love and I seemed to know everything. If I had been asked any question I would have been able to answer it. The meaning to life was so clear. I had a sense of my own immortality and knew that I would always be. I also knew the nature of God. Time and space stood still and the peace and love was beyond description. This was reality!

As the light faded and I became aware of myself once more, tears of joy and sadness ran down my face. Joy at what I had experienced and sadness at having to return to a world of strife. This experience will stay with me forever. I am now trying to accept this world for what it is – an illusion!'

It is interesting to note that again we have an egg-shaped pulsing white light as a precursor to the Cosmic Consciousness experience. Although Mike's 'egg' differed greatly in size from my own experience, the effect on us both was identical. Mike has been an ardent seeker of Truth for many years, and he has an abundance of love, kindness and compassion. You will be hearing from Mike again in later chapters since he would like to share other experiences with you.

Hallucinating Drugs

Over the centuries, many indigenous races have taken hallucinating herbal potions to induce changes in consciousness to either make contact with the spiritual worlds or achieve God Consciousness. These have included everything from 'magic' mushrooms to smoking 'whacky-baccy'. Today, drugs such as LSD and psilocybin have been experimented with to try and produce the same experiences, although many mystics have stated that drug-induced cosmic consciousness experiences are but a pale reflection of the natural spontaneous experience.

Who or What is God?

For the vast majority of us, we are trying to grasp the indescribable, but I will attempt to put into simple words my understanding of the nature of God based on my own experiences. God is the Infinite Spirit of Love that pervades the Universe. God *is* the Universe in all its vibrating and manifested frequencies and forms. God is neither male nor female but embodies the qualities of both. If you like, it is the 'mother-father' principle, and is continually manifesting life (consciousness) throughout the Universe.

There is one Divine Mind which keeps the Universe
in order and one providence which governs it.
Plutarch C.46 – C.120AD (Greek philosopher and historian)

Life (consciousness), although perfect at every stage of its being – like a seed for example – starts in simple form and *evolves* through experience over aeons of time (billions of years) in countless forms, and upon reaching 'perfection' (total enlightenment) merges back into God from whence it came. Thus God, although perfect, is experiencing life through us and all other life forms. And just as much as we need God, so *God needs, and loves, each and every one of us*.

All life forms throughout the Universe have consciousness, and that consciousness comes from and, is part of, the Universal Consciousness – God. Thus *all* living things have the essence of God in them, which is spiritual and known as the soul or spirit.

Enlightened spiritual masters, philosophers and mystics maintain that God cannot be taught – only experienced. It is a vast Cosmic Intelligence, vibrating on the frequency of *Love* – it is our Spiritual Parent – The Great Spirit, The Infinite, The Absolute! This is the *real* God that enlightened humans throughout history have experienced and speak of, and is a far cry from an invented, personal, jealous, violent and vengeful 'god' that portrays the worst traits of the human race. Down the ages, religious extremists have abused, defiled and destroyed the very meaning of the word God, so much so, that it now means nothing to our Mr and Mrs Average. So if we must give the unnameable a name, then I prefer the term *The Absolute*. This is what my mentors use and I can understand why.

The Absolute manifests equal and unconditional love to *all* living things throughout the Cosmos – *including* our Earth's undesirables. You may find that difficult to accept or comprehend at this moment in time, and probably think that they don't deserve it, but The Absolute neither judges, condemns, threatens nor punishes – it is *totally impartial and impersonal* (Deism). The Law of Love is programmed into the Universe and any violation of that Law requires the 'violator' to put things right – a philosophy that we will be looking at in later chapters.

> Many people do not believe in God because they think that
> if he existed he would intervene. But the reality is that he has
> placed natural laws into operation to bring order out of chaos.
> *James McQuitty (Religion: Man's Insult to God)*

So that you will better understand the meaning of impersonal unconditional love, let me recount a spontaneous spiritual experience that happened some years ago.

One sunny morning, Patricia and I were strolling down our local high street which, being market day was very crowded, with dozens of stalls selling all sorts of everyday wares. Suddenly, I was overcome with an incredible feeling of love and peace. It was so magnificent and ecstatic that, still smiling, tears of joy ran down my face. And although I was walking it felt more like floating or gliding.

The strange thing was, that whilst looking at people – stall holders and customers alike, I knew them intimately – *every minute detail of their lives* – both good and bad, together with all their problems, grief and heartaches. Whichever person I looked at, it was the same – an instant and intimate life review. At the same instant, I was aware of a total and unconditional love for them all. I loved them beyond words – young and old alike – just as if they were my own offspring, despite knowing that some of their characters left a lot to be desired!

All of them were learning about Love through the experience of life. It was not necessary for me to interfere with their lives at a personal level because the Spiritual Law of Love and Harmony governed every one of them.

Throughout the experience I was fully aware of what was happening, and even gave Patricia a running commentary. Every so often she would ask if it was still with me. The experience lasted for at least an hour before it gradually dissipated and everyone once again became a total stranger.

In 1998, Jean Raza, a 50-year-old mother of two children, had a similar experience:

I was travelling on the tube in London, a journey that I had undertaken many times. I was absorbed in my own thoughts until the train stopped at a station when I looked up to see where I was. A man entered my compartment, and as he sat down I immediately recognised him. But it puzzled me how I knew him so well. I looked around the carriage and saw another face I recognised. This time it was a young black woman.

I was just thinking it was an incredible coincidence, when I happened to glance around the rest of the carriage and recognised all of them intimately, and somehow felt a deep and loving connection with each and every one. I felt very uneasy about all of this, and panic started to set in. When the train arrived at my stop, I jumped up and made a quick exit out of the doors, not wanting to look at anyone in the process.

I came out of the station and walked quickly down the road, and as I did so I recognised and knew each face that passed me. I found this difficult to handle and tried to keep my eyes on the ground until I reached my destination.

It took me a few days to come to terms with my experience as it had come unannounced and unbidden, but I feel so privileged to have had it. I have had this happen to me several times since, and have gradually come to feel comfortable with it as well as a sense of love to all mankind.

Once again we have this instant and intimate knowledge of people and the unconditional love felt for them all. Here is another experience that happened to Jean in 1985:

After practising yoga for an hour in a public sports hall, my class always spent the last 15 minutes in a meditation, lying on our backs with eyes closed and wrapped in a blanket. On this particular occasion I was lying down and relaxing, as I had done many times before, when suddenly I was overcome with a feeling of great peace and joy. I felt totally and unconditionally loved and completely safe and secure. I knew that all was well and as it should be.

This was not a day-to-day love, or even the feeling of being loved by a partner, parent or child – but a deep spiritual love. As the tears streamed down my face I felt so blissful, and knew that whatever path my life took it was meant to be, and was part of a greater plan.

I never spoke to anyone about this experience until I attended one of Brian's discussion groups. There I met a lady who spoke of having a very similar experience, and for the first time in many years I found I could talk about the wonderment of that experience with people who understood.

I think of it as my "near God" experience, and although over the last 15 years I have brushed against this feeling of total love, I have never felt so absorbed by such bliss and joy as that first unbidden experience.

Jean has had many such experiences, but this one made her realise the truth of the Absolute's unconditional spiritual love for us all.

God is the expression of the intelligent universe.
Kahlil Gibran 1883 – 1931 (Syrian writer and poet)

Summary

I know without doubt that a loving spiritual power of good governs the Universe. It is the only power that I respect and trust. This has nothing to do with faith, books or what I have been told – it is based on personal knowledge and experience. This has indicated to me that, for however brief, it is possible for each and every one of us to have direct contact (mind to Mind) with The Absolute whilst we are still in our physical body – mystics have often referred to this as 'God's Grace'. Realisation of the Absolute is possible through contemplation, meditation and cosmic consciousness experiences; thus the Absolute becomes a *reality* rather than a theoretical 'He' in a faith and belief system. The disciplines required to do this on a more permanent basis are extremely strict and require the help of a spiritual master, teacher or guru.

At our present state of spiritual consciousness it is virtually impossible, for most of us *finite* mortals to comprehend the full power and nature of the *Infinite* God – The Absolute, just as an earthworm or beetle cannot understand us. Only the Absolute can fully understand the Absolute! But, down the ages, countless thousands have experienced glimpses of such bliss and splendour and, as a result, have had their lives changed for the better.

We will see in the next chapter that the communicating language between *all* forms of life is *LOVE*. And the elevated human mind that manifests unconditional love and immeasurable compassion is much nearer to understanding the Mind of the Absolute than the lower nature minds of the selfish, greedy, corrupt and violent. *Like minds attract and understand like minds* – think about that for a while!

The man Jesus was purported to have talked of a spiritual God of Love and Gautama the Buddha was credited with teaching compassion and respect for all living things and the Eight-fold Path to Enlightenment (merging with the Godhead). The Native American Indians embrace the universal Love of The Great Spirit, and Hindu and Sufi mystics speak of the bliss of complete union with God. This concept of proving to the individual that God exists, and the nature of God, goes back thousands of years to the 'Mystery Schools' of ancient Greece, Egypt, India and Tibet. It is pure unadulterated *spirituality* – totally devoid of all dogma, doctrines, ritual, superstition, threats and other divisive and invented gobbledegook that was added and preached down the centuries.

God has no religion.
Mahatma Gandhi 1869 – 1948
(Indian nationalist leader)

I now understand and love the Absolute more than words can express. It has touched my very being for which I am eternally grateful. It is the most wonderful and loving presence one can ever encounter and its Spiritual 'Power' and 'Intelligence' is awesome. The great Indian Masters and Gurus have said that the Absolute radiates with more light than that of a trillion suns!

If we are of a loving and compassionate nature, then spontaneous spiritual experiences can happen to *any* of us, at *any* time and *anywhere*, particularly if we have a sincere desire to understand these things. In his much acclaimed *Cosmic Consciousness,* Richard Maurice Bucke describes his own cosmic consciousness experience and of those throughout history who are known to have had one (or more), including many well know poets, writers and other prominent members of society.

Phyllis Atwater, in her book *Coming Back to Life,* interviewed over 200 near-death survivors and, apart from most floating out of their bodies, entering a long dark tunnel and emerging into a spiritual world of love and light to hug and converse with deceased loved ones, many also spoke of having a God Consciousness experience. After discovering that death isn't and God is, they talk of an 'all-knowing' and 'falling in love with God'.

We are all on an exciting, evolving journey towards enlightenment and due to our ignorance of Spiritual Laws that process can be long and painful at times.

But let me reassure you that despite any problems, traumas and grief that you have experienced, you are loved and guided more than you will ever know. Your consciousness (soul or Overself) is immortal and can *never* die because it is part of the Absolute's consciousness. If knowing that doesn't give you comfort, then experiencing it most certainly will!

We are *all* sons and daughters of the Absolute, which means that we all have a Divine inheritance. The pathways to a loving God are many – the pathway to Truth is but one. Much of the world desperately hungers for Spiritual Truths, and when that hunger within us cries out in anguish for answers and sustenance, then Cosmic Law – as decreed by the Absolute – will oblige us. From my innermost being I wanted to know if the Absolute existed and what it is – now I *know*!

We have now come to the end of a very profound and essential chapter, and if this is your first step onto the spiritual and philosophical pathway, perhaps it has encouraged you to think a little deeper about life. Understanding that a loving, intelligent, spiritual principle of good governs the Universe represents a vital piece of the jigsaw. We can now proceed to the chapter on Love and investigate Spiritual Laws.

Wars are not made by the Great Spirit. Disease is not given by the Great Spirit. These are the things that the children of matter have brought upon themselves by the misuse of their freewill. There are lessons to be learned, but they can be learned without the brutalities and the hideous cruelties that the children of the Great Spirit perpetrate against each other. Do not mistake the doings of man for the acts of the Great Spirit.
Silver Birch (Spirit guide and teacher)

Ask of those who have attained God; all speak the same word. All the enlightened have left one message. It is only those in the midst of their journey who hold diverse opinions.
Dadu 1544 – 1603 (Sufi mystic)

There *is* A God
of love

9 Love – *The Law of Life*

Though days and seasons soon are gone,
a love that's true lives on and on.
Robert William Lawrence

We have just fitted a vital piece of the jigsaw explaining how and why an impersonal Universal Intelligence vibrates energies of Love throughout the whole of space – that which we call The Absolute, or God, governs the Universe. So let us now investigate how and why that principle applies to our everyday lives.

Once we understand and put into practice the principle of unconditional love, then we are well on our way to discovering one of the greatest 'secrets' of life that, unfortunately, for reasons that will become evident, seem elusive to our Mr and Mrs Average.

Apart from the word God, love is probably one of the most abused and misunderstood words ever uttered by the human race. It is often used to convey a gambit of fickle emotions involving relationships with people, animals, music, art, food, Nature and every conceivable materialistic object imaginable. We fall in and out of love in the blink of an eye, discover that 'love' can easily turn to 'hate' and get confused between love and lust!

A Universal Language

Love (harmony) heals and unites, whilst hatred (disharmony) destroys and divides – we can observe this in everyday life on a global scale. Anything that is not in harmony with itself will self-destruct. Countries, companies, institutions, families, marriages, health and happiness will all deteriorate and fall apart if disharmony is constantly present. Lack of harmony is lack of love! This is not just a fact of life it is an easily observed example of Cosmic Law.

Without love, life becomes meaningless and pointless. Love, like music, is a universal language that can be 'spoken' and understood by all living creatures – plants, insects, animals and humans – all have the ability to respond to love. Love is a language that we can express anywhere in the world, and even if we don't understand the spoken dialect, a warm smile, a sincere handshake and a genuine hug or embrace are never misinterpreted by like-minded people. Like a diamond, love has many facets.

In the spring of 1990, Patricia and I visited the Punjab in northern India and stayed as guests of Indian friends. We were invited to the homes of many of our host's friends and relations and, without exception; these complete strangers welcomed us with as much love and affection as if we had been their own family.

On another occasion we visited an Ashram at Beas to listen to an Indian Master speak on Spiritual Discipline. We expected this to be the highlight of our holiday, but not so, as we found when invited to meet Bibi, an elderly lady who had lived in the Ashram for most of her life. Entering a small, basic humble brick dwelling in the Ashram grounds we sensed the most incredible atmosphere of love, and noticed a group of people sitting in front of an elderly lady who we instinctively knew was Bibi. Leaving our shoes in the doorway, not knowing what to expect, we made our way to a space on the floor and sat cross-legged.

Sweetmeats and drinks were offered and we ate and drank in silence. When we had finished, Bibi beckoned us forward and as we knelt before her and looked into her eyes; rarely have I felt such depth of soul, love, compassion and humility in a human being. Words could not describe that humbling moment as I realised that we were in the presence of a highly evolved soul. Laying my head on her lap, she placed her hand on my head whereupon incredible waves of love permeated my entire body. The tears ran down my cheeks until I was sobbing uncontrollably. I then realised that Patricia was having the same experience and, with her head on Bibi's lap, was also sobbing her heart out. She too had experienced those healing eyes and hands and the indescribable radiation of love.

We both had the feeling that Bibi had 'read' our very souls, and in that instant knew more about us than we knew about ourselves. She had in those few precious moments imparted to us both, a peace and understanding that was priceless. She loved us and we loved her. We were strangers in her country who couldn't speak her language or she ours. But that didn't matter, we had communicated via the universal language of *Love* – a language spoken with the eyes and hands.

Bibi was 92-years-of-age and as fit and agile as many half her age, with her love keeping her physical body in youthfulness and spontaneity. So it was no surprise when we later saw her jump side-saddle onto the pannier of a bicycle to be transported across the Ashram. Bibi left her body and passed to the higher life in 1997 aged 99 years. Always smiling and the epitome of Love – that is how we will remember her. We had truly been blessed with a powerful infusion of Love on that memorable day.

Love is the energising elixir of the universe... The cause and effect of all harmonies.
Jalalu'd Din Rumi 1207 – 1273 (Sufi mystic and poet)

Love and Children

Not all of us are destined to have children in this lifetime, for one reason or another – some through choice and others because of medical difficulties. But that shouldn't stop us from giving love and affection to a niece, nephew or a friend's or neighbour's child.

Having a baby is a serious commitment and not something to be used as a fast-track to subsidised housing as some youngsters seem to think! The raising of children is one of the hardest jobs and the greatest responsibility that we will ever undertake. It matters not whether children are our own flesh and blood, adopted or fostered; as parents or guardians we can make or mar their lives. Becoming a parent or guardian, despite any preconceived ideas, *will* change the lives of all concerned.

Children need to be brought up in a safe and secure environment. Lack of parental love is one of the most traumatic experiences children can ever suffer, and the attendant insecurity can affect them for the rest of their lives. It is the security of a family, hugs and cuddles and being told that they are loved that they will remember. What better gifts can parents give their children than their time and love? Love – or the lack of it – is what most adults remember of their childhood.

Genuine love and affection can never be bought, as many busy affluent parents seem to think when they lavish expensive presents on their offspring to compensate for lack of parental attention. Television, computers, mobile phones and play stations become the 'baby sitters' of stressed out parents when they relinquish their duties of one-to-one contact with their children. This becomes evident when surveys reveal that many people have lost the parenting skills that we once took for granted. If this is so, then what sort of role models will such parents be to their children *and* their grandchildren?

Raising children *is* hard work and there is no easy age range. The first lesson is trying to juggle the work-life balance and keep a happy and sane marriage. Babies are 'crying machines' and 'poo factories'. The constant attention, feeding and nappy changing can drive parents to distraction, with sleep deprivation being par for the course in most cases. You expect to have a baby *and* regular sleep?!! Didn't anyone tell you?

And then we progress to the 'terrible two's' stage when children start to walk and get a mind of their own, often with the art of making any room resemble a recycling centre within minutes of playing with their toys. Success comes when they have been educated to put their toys back when playtime is over! At this stage, eyes in the back of the head are a definite asset for parents when inquisitive little hands reach for any desirable object, or when they move out of sight within split seconds of parental distraction.

This is where grandparents can come to the rescue. Having been there and done it, they can have a vital role to play in the lives of children, often stepping in when parents are stressed out and reaching for the cyanide pills! Having grandchildren is a wonderful and special stage that keeps you young as you can often devote more time and patience with them than tired or busy parents. The bonus being that you hand them back at the end of the day – unless they are on a 'sleep-over' of course.

Because children seem to grow up more quickly nowadays, childhood is a precious time that can easily be lost by 'busy' parents. When it's gone it's gone! Quality time doing things as a family, having fun, being happy together, eating together, laughing and showing interest in their schooling is an essential part of bonding that will last a lifetime. One moment we are proudly watching them in the junior school nativity play and, in the seeming blink of an eye, we are proudly watching them walk down the aisle at their wedding.

Giving love and affection to children is common sense, but there is also the extreme to be wary of known as 'smother love' where we are in danger of producing 'cotton wool kids' who cannot fend for themselves without us fearing for their safety at every move. Children can thrive on a certain element of fear and danger, and it will make them more able to cope with the challenges of a pressurised, competitive and materialistic world in later years.

The teenage years need to be handled with the patience of a Saint, especially during any tantrums, slanging matches and door slamming episodes! This can drive parents to distraction and cause them to question why they ever had children, especially when they unwittingly drive a wedge between them by playing one parent off against the other. With raging hormones, many adolescents tend to grunt when spoken to by parents – who obviously live on another planet and don't understand them or the modern world with its music and technology!

Whatever their age, time, patience, a sense of humour, support and buckets of love and affection are priceless riches if we wish to avoid our offspring falling into the anti-social behavior category in later life by taking drugs and roaming the streets collecting ASBO's like educational qualifications.

Raising children can be a love-hate relationship for many, especially when their bedroom resembles a war zone, despite endless requests to keep it tidy. Mentally repeating the mantra 'this is my child and I love him/her unconditionally' over and over again may help to keep the blood pressure down!

In both time and money, children are a *very* expensive investment that we hope will pay dividends later in life, and we should never forget that they represent the future and that we are their teachers and role models. Which reminds me of a remark attributed to Jacqueline Kennedy-Onassis when she stated: *If we make a hash of bringing up our children, then what else we achieve in life doesn't much matter.*

Unfortunately, we are in the age of 'broken homes' when marriages and cohabiting relationships fall apart, and one parent – In many cases the mother – Is left to raise children on their own, often with the aid of state benefits and the occasional visit from the father. This is a common occurrence and can cause multiple social problems if the love, support and affection factor are missing. Youth Justice Board statistics found that 70 per cent of juvenile offenders were from broken homes, were more likely to drop out of school, suffer poor health, have little or no job skills and become involved with drugs and crime. Numerous single parent families cope extremely well – as evidenced during war times with fathers in the armed forces and mothers coping on their own. Many for considerably longer when fathers become war fatalities.

Some Nursery teachers claim they can spot future 'criminals' as young as three-years-of-age. They report that they will usually be the last children to be picked up and will scratch and kick anyone who tries to correct them. They are invariably like this because their home life is dire. Many come from deprived areas, know little of their fathers and the mothers are unable to cope. They will probably get 'lost in the system', grow up to be no-hopers and roam the streets at night showing disrespect to people and property because they are 'bored'.

As parents, we will all make mistakes and, as we can observe, every age brings its problems when raising children – particularly during times of sickness, when they can fall prey to every childhood illness known to medical science. Very often, it isn't until they grow up and have children of their own that offspring really begin to respect and appreciate the sacrifices that their parents or guardians made for them.

So, with tongue firmly in cheek, let me leave you with time-honoured advice from 'experienced' parents and guardians who jest: 'Don't worry – It's only the first 25 years that are the trickiest!' And, 'Be kind to your kids, because one day they may be choosing your Care Home!'

Your immortality is in a well trained child and small kindnesses.
Native American Indian philosophy

Caring For Others

To look after, or care for another in need, with a genuine love and compassion, whether we are a professional carer, nurse, friend or relative, is one of the highest services that we can give to life. It may well be a special needs child or an adult with learning difficulties or a debilitating or terminal illness. This is not an easy task, particularly for untrained relatives who cope as best they can in a home environment, often with limited or no funding, sleep deprivation and the knowledge that they are sacrificing their own life for the benefit of another.

I come into contact with so many inspiring unsung heroes who, often for decades, have unselfishly devoted their lives to caring for the under-privileged in our communities, and a whole book devoted to their cause would not do their numbers justice.

One such example is that of Idetha and Ron Harvey who, for many years, at their own expense, cared for the unfortunates who slept rough on the streets of London. For two days, once a month, they would prepare and take food, sleeping bags, blankets and clothing into the city and distribute it amongst the needy. They would spend the night with them, listen to their stories and often dress their wounds. The eldest being a 90-year-old war veteran with severe leg ulcers and the youngest would often be in their early teens having run away because of domestic violence and alcohol and drug abuse at 'home'. Some refused to go into hostels for fear of being taken back where they were abused.

Many of the homeless had once been respectable citizens with good educations and responsible careers. Their lives went pear-shaped when they were made redundant or their business collapsed. Many had lost their homes, became bankrupt and their partners (husband or wife) left them, and some were ex-service men who found it difficult to fit in with civilian life after leaving the services. The end result being that they turned to alcohol to blot out their nightmare and finished up sleeping rough on the streets – often in shop doorways for warmth.

Despite her own health problems, Idetha loved them all like a mother, and many told her that it was the first time in their lives that someone had shown them love and kindness and cared whether they lived or died. 'Bless them all, there for the grace of God go any of us,' Idetha would often say with tears in her eyes whilst telling their stories.

Idetha was also a volunteer with the Samaritans and would spend untold hours on the telephone talking to desperate callers on the other end of the line who, because of circumstances in their lives, often felt lonely, unloved, depressed and suicidal. Many thought life was cruel, Godless and pointless. 'I never put the phone down until I am sure they are in a better frame of mind,' she once stated. 'I would often wake up in the night wondering how they were,' she added, 'and pray that they were OK.'

In May 2009 at the age of 72, Idetha booked a one-way ticket to the spiritual worlds. I, for one, will miss her bear hugs, but for sure, the spiritual hierarchy on the other side will put her selfless, unconditional love and devotion to others to good use.

I have used Idetha as a typical example of the spirituality (goodness, love and compassion) in people in ordinary everyday life. Thankfully, there are untold millions of them throughout the world, and they make up for the greedy, cruel, corrupt, selfish, and violent minority who seek to disrupt, steal, manipulate, dominate or destroy rather than to care, comfort, heal or protect.

I am reminded of the touching story of the elderly gentleman who, every day, visited his wife in a local care home. She was suffering from Alzheimer's disease and had not recognised him for at least five years. When a neighbour asked him why he still went every day when she didn't know who he was, he replied: 'She doesn't know me, but I still know who she is.'

As we assemble more of life's jigsaw and begin to understand its Laws, we will see that nothing happens by chance or accident and that we are never in the wrong place at the wrong time. If life dictates that we care for another in need, and we do it with the right intentions, then we will be working with the Laws of the Universe, and the greatest of those Laws is Unconditional Love.

Only a life lived for others is worth living.
Albert Einstein 187 9 – 1955 (Physicist)

Love for Animals

Animals play a vital role in teaching us how to give and receive love, particularly domesticated pets. Unlike us humans, the animal kingdom doesn't seem to have many problems with natural parenthood when rearing its young. Observing animals and birds caring for their young can be both entertaining and enlightening. To see a child cuddling a puppy or kitten can be very moving, particularly when the animal responds with unconditional love in return and brings out the child's natural maternal or paternal instinct.

To the millions who live alone, particularly the elderly or those who have lost a loving husband or wife, the love of a pet can give a vital reason to get out of bed in the morning, knowing that a living creature depends upon them. Many such relationships are usually mutual. As well as being a companion, talking to a pet has kept many a lonely person sane. It is also comforting to know that a pet cat or dog will give a warm welcome when returning home to an otherwise empty house.

Domestic pets in particular can be quite human in their feelings and responses to love and affection, and it grieves many to see them treated cruelly, neglected or abandoned by a thoughtless minority. Despite being labeled as a nation of pet lovers, The Royal Society for the Protection of Cruelty to Animals (RSPCA) statistics don't make comfortable reading, and those who abuse animals are violating the Law of Love.

Until he extends the circle of his compassion to all living things,
man will not himself find peace.
Dr Albert Schweitzer 1875 – 1965 (Theologian and philosopher)

Love of Plants

'You are nearer to God in a garden than anywhere else on earth' so the saying goes. Although God, The Absolute, or whatever we care to call the Universal Intelligence, is everywhere, there is an element of truth in that statement. The sheer diversity of plants, shrubs, bushes and trees, and the intelligence behind Nature is a continuous wonderment to keen gardeners and horticulturists. They are never happier than when they have their hands in the soil (a miracle in itself) or are attending to their 'offspring' in the greenhouse, potting shed or garden. Those who love and nurture their plants or vegetables, are often credited with 'green fingers' and, in many cases, achieve abundant results.

Numerous worldwide experiments have shown that when plants and vegetables are given love and affection they thrive considerably more than those that have not. In 1974, American engineer and 'Life after death' researcher, George Meek, conducted a controlled experiment on newly-planted vegetable seeds. He found that those that were continually told they were loved grew in abundance and were above average size. The section of seeds that were shouted at and told they were ugly and useless, gave a very poor showing with small and often deformed vegetables.

Meek also repeated the experiment with 36 carefully selected gladioli bulbs. Half of the bulbs were encouraged to *'form buds and then bloom profusely'* – which they did. The other 18 bulbs, although only one metre (39 inches) away, were instructed to *'not form even one bud'*. They all obeyed!

Serious gardeners might be interested in reading *The Secret Life of Plants* by Peter Tomkins and Christopher Bird, and *The Psychic Power of Plants* by John Whitman. Evidence is produced that plants respond to positive human thought and harmonious music – the opposite having an adverse effect. It may also surprise many to learn that plants have retentive memories and, as many sensitive people are aware, trees give off an abundance of energy that can revitalise a depleted human body if the back, or hands, are placed against them. You will note the similarity with plant experiments regarding human thought and water sample experiments discussed later in the chapter. As our jigsaw pieces are assembled, this becomes another subtle reminder that ***all things are linked***.

There are more things in heaven and earth,
Horatio, than are dreamed of in your philosophy.
William Shakespeare 1564-1616 (Hamlet)

Love from the Spiritual Worlds

In previous chapters I have given examples of the wonderful and powerful love energies that emanate from radiant beings from the spiritual realms who return from time to time to encourage and guide us in our quest for Truth, knowledge and understanding. Those who are fortunate to have experienced such pulsating energies emitted by those who frequent the higher spiritual realms often state that mere words fail to express such blissful moments.

This applies not only to highly evolved beings that many call spirit guides, teachers of truth or guardian angels, but also to those departed loved ones who led unselfish lives of unconditional love and dedication to helping those less fortunate than themselves when they trod this Earth. During 15 years of public clairvoyance, I was honoured to meet numerous departed loved ones who emanated such indescribable love. Most had beautiful auras of white or golden light as they stood by my side to be described to relatives in the audience. Many confirmed that their loved ones *were* 'too good for this Earth'.

One of our spiritual mentors who comes into the former category is the highly evolved soul known to us as 'Laughing Boy', the elderly Chinese gentleman who, if you recall, made himself known to me in 1981 when, at a low point in my life, he made me laugh hysterically, along with all the other members of the meditation group. For the past 30 years, whenever he 'visits', the familiar shudder down my spine is always followed by the involuntary laughter and the most incredible waves of love making me cry with ecstasy as he imparts relevant words of wisdom and encouragement. Finally, let me leave you with one of the numerous memorable moments that Patricia and I have experienced over the years.

Some years ago, when entering our bedroom, I was surprised to see Patricia sitting on the edge of the bed sobbing. Sitting beside her, I put my arm round her shoulder and asked if anything was the matter. It was then that I became aware of a Native American Indian chief standing in front of her with his arms out-stretched. A wave of spiritual Love hit me like an avalanche and was so powerful and uplifting that I too cried tears of joy. 'Can you see the Indian?' asked Patricia, 'The Love is just amazing.' We were both seeing and experiencing exactly the same thing. Slowly the 'vision' faded, but it left us feeling supercharged with energy and Love.

We are all born for love. It is the principle of existence, and its only end.
Benjamin Disraeli 1804 – 1881 (English statesman and novelist)

Love for God (The Absolute)

To ask someone to love an 'invisible' or 'intangible' entity – something that they cannot experience with any of their five physical senses – may seem beyond the realm of credibility and, to a humanist, understandably laughable. But to those who are sensitive enough to pick up the immense waves of love permeating the Universe, often inducing a Cosmic Consciousness experience – as discussed in the previous chapter – then loving the very *source* of that experience becomes a perfectly natural response in return.

There are no words to describe the love of the Absolute, and all those who have experienced such bliss fumble for descriptive words to explain the inexplicable. The bottom line seems to be, 'Wait until you experience it and then you will *know*'. As we appreciate, love has many facets, and love for the Absolute is the highest manifestation of that love. But that doesn't mean to say that our love for a fellow human being, be it our mother, father, wife, husband, son, daughter, brother, sister is any the less, it is the same in essence – just different by degree.

For thousands of years, in diverse cultures, numerous mystical and esoteric writings speak of 'the absolute bliss of Union with the Divine' and talk about 'the love affair with God'. All this is far removed from the religious extremists that rant about a 'God' of jealousy, anger and revenge!

This invisible and subtle essence is the Spirit of the whole Universe.
That is Reality. That is Truth. THOU ART THAT.
Chandogya Upanishad 6:14

A Law Governed Cosmos

In the previous chapter we looked at why it isn't necessary for God, The Absolute, to personally interfere in the lives of its creatures because 'It' has programmed the Cosmos with the frequency of *Love* – which is *harmony*. It is this 'ocean' of Love that energises and sustains life everywhere.

Taking a thought-provoking look at Nature, do we need to tell an acorn how to grow into an oak tree or an apple pip how to grow into an apple tree? Even if we knew, there is no need, simply because they are *programmed* to grow into oak and apple trees. A pregnant mother has no need to tell her fertilised egg how to grow into a baby or her body how to heal itself when ill because she doesn't have that knowledge, but Cosmic Law does.

As a design engineer I was used to working with the laws of mechanics that governed the stresses and strains of various metals, and provided those formulas were utilised in the calculations then everything worked. Deviation from those laws was courting disaster!

When it came to the deeper and more meaningful things in life, I realised the possibility that *Law governed everything* – visible and invisible, material and spiritual. It seemed illogical to have laws governing some aspects of life and not others. Law, therefore, must govern the whole of the known universe – even planets in their orbits. Everything in Nature has intelligence behind it, whether it is a snowflake, a tree, a leaf, an insect, animal or the human body. Similarly, in our material world, everything that is manufactured has had intelligent thought and construction behind it. Behind every intelligent act is a greater intelligence. The intelligence of the Cosmos is the Absolute.

Everything that lives (consciousness) has a part of the Absolute within it, and it is known as the soul or Overself. It is the Overself that has the ability to tune in to the Love frequency, and it is our ego or body nature with its negative emotions of fear, worry, anger and hatred, that creates interference and blocks this energy. Hence we become ill, age quickly and self-destruct because we are not in harmony with the Cosmos or ourselves.

If there is righteousness in the heart, there will be beauty in the character.
If there is beauty in the character, there will be harmony in the home.
If there is harmony in the home, there will be order in the nation.
If there is order in the nation, there will be peace in the world.
Ancient Chinese proverb

The Power of Thought

We have looked at the power of thought and its affect on plants and water, so let us look at how it affects us in everyday life. Everything in the known Universe is made up of sub-atomic particles. These are programmed to vibrate in accordance with the Law of Harmony, and if they didn't then nothing would exist as we know it – we are literally a hologram of dancing atoms. Scientists have discovered that many of these particles are influenced by human thought. So if thought can manipulate sub-atomic particles then it doesn't take a genius to work out that every second, of every hour, of every day, we are constantly changing our lives with our thinking!

The beauty of this arrangement is that there is no such thing as good or bad luck, since all is in accordance with Cosmic Law. As we give out, so we get back. What we sow we reap. What goes around comes around. This is known as the law of Cause and Effect! What we cause today – for good or ill – will have an effect on us today, tomorrow, next year, ten years time or, as we will investigate in the next chapter, possibly even in the next lifetime. 'But that's not fair', some may say, 'I can't accept that'. Well, Nature doesn't have comfort zones, so why shouldn't we reap the rewards or suffer *self-inflicted* trials and tribulations according to the way we behave? As a designer, I think it's a brilliant system!

In Eastern philosophies this law of Cause and Effect is known as the Law of

Karma or the law of compensation and retribution. The word karma is derived from Sanskrit, meaning 'deed' or 'doing'. In ancient China it was known as the Tao, or 'the way'. Since we are personally responsible for our thoughts, words and deeds, then any consequences arising from them rests solely with us alone. Although ignorance of the Law is no excuse, it is the *motive* behind our thoughts and actions that determine our positive or negative karma and *not* the action itself.

Thoughts are living things, and since thoughts precede deeds (actions), then it is our *thoughts* that we should learn to control – hence the practise of meditation – a subject that we will be looking at later on. Once we learn to live in accordance with the Law of Love, peace and harmony, then everything in our life will fall into place and we will find life working *for* us and not *against* us.

Every thought of yours is a real thing – a force. Every thought of yours is literally building for you something for the future of good or ill.
Prentice Mulford 1834 – 1891 (Thoughts are Things)

Experiments with Water

Before we leave the subject of thought, I would like to mention the remarkable experiments of the internationally renowned Japanese researcher Masaru Emoto. Mr Emoto and his colleagues collected water samples from various sources such as lakes, rivers, streams and even urban tap water. The samples were then subjected to positive and negative thoughts and emotions. When these water samples were frozen, the results proved to be some of the most spiritually profound experiments ever witnessed.

Tap water that had been treated with chlorine, fluoride and other chemicals either didn't form ice crystals at all or produced grotesque shapes. Many mineral water samples didn't fare much better either. But when the samples were subjected to positive statements of 'love', 'peace' and 'thank you', either spoken or written on labels pasted to the sample bottles, the water formed *perfect* crystals when frozen.

But, when the same samples were subjected to negative statements such as 'hatred', 'evil', 'war' or 'fool', the resulting crystals were horribly deformed. It didn't even matter in which language the words were written, the water seemed to understand the essence of the words. Even *thinking* such statements produced the same results!

These experiments prove that, like plants, water is influenced by human thoughts, emotions and actions and, complete with colour photographs, are documented in Masaru Emoto's books *The Hidden Messages in Water* and *The True Power of Water* (See *Bibliography*)

Now, if we consider that the human body is at least 70 per cent water and our brain 90 per cent of the stuff, then guess what happens to us when we are constantly subjected to negative words of hatred and abuse, or positive ones of love, peace and harmony? We become depressed and ill or elated and uplifted accordingly. And here's a further thought. Knowing this, would you want anyone with an attitude problem to prepare and cook your food? Thoughts of anger and frustration will affect the very food they are preparing, which will eventually find its way into your body – with negative consequences. The moral being, *never* upset the chef – whether it be at home or in a restaurant! Oh, and by the way, the same applies to eating food if *you* are in a bad mood!

I will also be touching on Masaru Emoto's important findings in the chapters *Prayer and Meditation* and *Healing*.

What we are today comes from our thoughts of yesterday, and our present thoughts build our life of tomorrow: our life is the creation of our mind.
The Dhammapada (Buddhist)

Unconditional Love

Many will naturally find it difficult to show unconditional love to all and sundry as there will often be strings attached, conditions, likes, dislikes and subtle threats, particularly where injustices have been caused.

It is easy to observe that violence and hatred breed violence and hatred. In some countries children are taught to hate because of religious or political differences, racial intolerance or family feuds affecting generation after generation – a viscous perpetual cycle with many families never knowing peace or harmony in their lives.

As we have seen in previous chapters, to love one another as the man Jesus taught and to show kindness and compassion as the Buddha taught, should be the easiest thing in the world. But your observations will probably have confirmed that the human race finds it extremely difficult to put such profound and simple truths into practice.

How many husbands and wives find it difficult to talk to each other or show genuine unconditional love? How many parents find it hard to show unconditional love and affection to their children? When destructive criticism comes in the front door, love flies out the window!

When hugging people, the response tends to be a giveaway as to whether they have been used to getting hugs and cuddles as a child. With some, it's like hugging a gatepost – cold and unresponsive. Sadly, some people are unable to respond to love and affection because they have never been shown how – it's like a foreign language to them. And, if not corrected, it will go on down the generations. One of the greatest gifts that we can give to another human being, child or adult, is to put our arms around them to let them know how much they are loved. A hug can say a thousand words, but the problems of this world can be summed up in just *four* words – *Lack of unconditional love!*

At a presentation, some years ago, I touched on the above theme, and during the question and answer session that followed; a young lady expressed an opinion that she thought the world would be a boring place if we were all kind and loving to each other. I suggested that someone from a war-torn country could probably give her an appropriate response!

When the power of love overcomes the love of power, the world will know peace.
Jimi Hendrix [James Marshall] 1942 – 1970 (American rock guitarist and singer)

Where there is unconditional love there can be no anger or hatred, no resentment or jealousy, no thoughts of harm or revenge and no arrogance or selfishness. Where there is unconditional love there is peace, harmony, kindness, compassion and forgiveness. I have always felt that one of the best words in the dictionary is *sorry*. When said with humility its power to heal emotional wounds, end arguments and dissolve mistakes and wrong doings is amazing. All it takes is someone with wisdom and courage to say that magic word and all can be right with the world again if it is accepted as forgiveness, followed by a friendly hug to someone we love.

What has been hurt, our soul? No, our ego. That inflated ego balloon that life will sooner or later burst for us. It doesn't matter who is right or who is wrong, what happened in the past is past. Why not put it down to experience, start a fresh chapter and move forward with love, without grudges or resentment. The ego, or lower (animal) nature is continually centred on self. It is the 'self' that seeks attention, self-praise or self-pity. It is full of likes and dislikes and wants to be 'top dog' and win at all costs. It is easily offended, seeks for revenge, sulks, criticises and moans about life.

If very deep hurts, betrayal or physical violence are involved, it may seem impossible for some to express unconditional love or respect and accept forgiveness. In which case, the love will have died and prove difficult to resurrect. There are many recorded instances where victims have forgiven those who devastated their lives in one way or another and, as such, are deemed truly spiritual people. The act may have been forgiven, but not forgotten!

In the majority of cases, most of our sufferings are caused by our egos, in that we have become so body-conscious in our self-created materialistic world that we have forgotten who we *really* are, our spiritual heritage and the reason for our being here. As we get older and observe the suffering in life and watch the grief and tears of those whose loved ones have 'died', we realise that it is the amount of love and affection that we have been able to give and receive that is important, not how much we earn or how many material things we have acquired.

My mother loved my father, but after more than 40 years of listening to his repertoire of well-aired jokes at social gatherings, she would often remark under her breath, 'Oh no, not that one again.' Or, 'I don't know how many times I've heard that one.' Less than a month after he died, mum confessed that she would give anything to hear dad tell one of his jokes again! The moral here, is that very often we take people and things for granted and don't appreciate what we had until we have lost it!

How many fathers work long hours and never see much of their family, often arriving home when the children are in bed? The wake-up call comes when things eventually fall apart or go pear-shaped when they realise that they and their children have become strangers.

A survey conducted in care and residential homes, asked the elderly inhabitants if they had any regrets and what would they do differently if they could live their lives all over again. Virtually all of them said that they wished they had given more time and love and affection to their family and friends and not worried so much about life. Not *one* wished they had had more money!

A loving atmosphere in your home is the foundation of your life.
The Dalai Lama (Tenzin Gyatso)

Summary

Love has been the catalyst, or theme, if you like, that runs through every chapter of our quest to make sense of the meaning and purpose of life and death. Every piece of our jigsaw has that word impregnated in it like a stick of rock. The paradox of genuine love is that we have to give it away to get it back.

We are all on the cosmic journey of life travelling through space on our tiny ball of rock. It is a journey of blood, sweat, tears and laughter with a very steep learning curve where mistakes and regrets come by the bucket-load. That is the 'fertiliser' from which love and compassion can grow.

Some would no doubt argue that those who commit atrocities, lie, cheat, rob, bully, hate or threaten, don't deserve our respect, love or forgiveness. Be that as it may, all I would add is, that sooner or later – whether we like it or not – life will nudge us all onto the spiritual pathway to adopt the love, respect, kindness, compassion and forgiveness approach to each and every one – coupled with a genuine humility.

The egotistical and materialistic attitudes such as envy, greed, hatred, jealousy, revenge and cruelty that have wreaked so much havoc and caused so much suffering over the centuries will eventually be seen as outdated and superfluous as our Divine nature takes over. This is already in evidence as multitudes of unsung heroes help and comfort the traumatised, grief stricken and destitute amongst us. We see disciplines such as yoga, palates, Tai Chi and meditation gaining immense popularity, together with a far greater awareness of life's real values with an abhorrence of war and an overwhelming desire for world peace.

Love and humility are the 'keys' that will open 'doors' if we are sincere in our quest for Truth. And as we continue to observe – where there is *arrogance and ignorance* there is *weakness and stupidity*, and where there is *love and humility* there is *inner strength and wisdom.*

We are all going to 'die' – it's not negotiable, it's mandatory! It's the basis of our 'Contract' for being here. Once we become aware that we are spirits inhabiting physical bodies and that our souls need 'feeding' as well, then life will have a clearer meaning and purpose. The best food for the soul is unconditional Love and knowledge of the Absolute. That is why, when our consciousness expands, we long for and, thrive on, love, peace and harmony. So when mind, body and spirit are in total harmony we have a greater sense of wellbeing. Why? Because we are then in tune with the natural rhythms and Laws of the Universe.

Knowing that unconditional Love is the Law of the Universe and that violation of that Law, *in any shape or form*, is the root cause of all our sufferings, gives us another piece of the jigsaw. We can now proceed on our quest and investigate the possibility that we may have had more than one life on Earth – and why.

Life without love's load, and time stands still;
What we refuse to him, to death we give;
And then, then only when we love, we live.
William Congreve 1670-1729 (English dramatist)

I would like to follow the spiritual pathway, but I'm too fond of sex and booze.
(The author of this humorous little gem wishes to remain anonymous!)

Love is the
Law
Of life

10 Reincarnation

– Do we have more than one life?

I hold that when a person dies,
His soul returns again to earth;
Arrayed in some new flesh-disguise
Another mother gives him birth.
With sturdier limbs and brighter brain
The old soul takes the road again.
John Masefield 1878 – 1967 (Poet Laureate)

Reincarnation in its varied forms has been taught in the East and the Orient for thousands of years and is currently accepted by more than half the Earth's population. Although I would add that it is not exclusively a Hindu or Buddhist concept, it is also a doctrine known to Judaism, Islam and early Christianity. I say early, because in 553AD at the Council of Constantinople, the Byzantine Emperor Justinian and a tiny majority on the Council decided to ban the teachings from the scriptures – a gross historical blunder that plunged the Christian Church into the philosophical wilderness, where it has stayed ever since. Apparently, they didn't like the concept and thought it an anathema. This denied them plausible answers to life's traumas and tragedies, which were then explained as 'the will of God' or 'the works of the Devil!'

The Ancient Egyptians as well as the Greeks and Chinese were also well versed in the pre-existence of the soul. Reincarnation was also well known to many world cultures throughout history, including the Maoris, Aborigines, and the North and South American Indians. It was also taught to initiates in the Ancient Wisdom teachings.

I was fascinated why all of these religions, philosophies and cultures had embraced the doctrine of having more than one life when the vast majority of the Earth's population had only known poverty and hardship. Out of interest, I have asked numerous people if they would like to come back to this Earth in another lifetime. This produced many raised eyebrows and remarks like 'you must be joking' – or words to that effect! So if people are not too enamoured with life here and don't want to keep coming back, why is rebirth such a prominent doctrine? Could there have been a vast amount of evidence throughout history?

The Emperor Napoleon, Mahatma Gandhi, Plato, Socrates, Pythagoras, William Shakespeare, Oscar Wilde, the Dalai Lama, Winston Churchill, John Lennon, Yoko Ono, George Harrison, Henry Ford, H.G. Wells, Bernard Shaw,

David Lloyd George, Count Leo Tolstoy, Carl Jung, Ralph Waldo Emerson, William Blake, Alfred Lord Tennyson, John Masefield, Walt Whitman, Benjamin Franklin, J. B. Priestley, Dean William Inge, Lord Hugh Dowding, General George S. Patton and Shirley MacLaine are just a few of the famous people who accepted reincarnation and were convinced through personal experiences that they had lived before. Gautama the Buddha was reputed to have remembered hundreds of previous lives.

Investigation

Having investigated the life after death piece of the puzzle, I was intrigued by the doctrine of reincarnation, or rebirth, as it is also known, and felt that the subject was another important piece of life's puzzle worthy of investigation. By reincarnation, we mean the ability of the soul (consciousness, Overself or spirit if you prefer) to enter a body of flesh in a world of matter any number of times. That is to say, many births, lives and deaths.

On face value our materialistic world appears to chastise the good and reward the bad, with many complaining that 'life just isn't fair!' So, what if we *did* have more than one life? What if we had hundreds or even thousands of different lives on this planet – or any other for that matter? What if we had been male and female, rich and poor, killed and been killed, died young and old and lived in many countries – could that make a difference to our thinking about the fairness of life here?

If we had only *one* life, how would we explain or define the fairness or justice of the following?

- A stillborn baby.
- A baby born mentally or physically handicapped.
- A child of three or four years of age having a good knowledge of a subject it was never taught (mathematics, music, Egyptology or a foreign language for example).
- Children who continually talk of having lived previous lives.
- The death of a child (through accident, disease, murder or starvation, etc.).
- A child having wisdom well beyond its years (an old soul in a young body).
- Dying at, say, 20-years-of-age (from any cause).
- Living to be over 100-years-of-age.
- Born into poverty (in Africa for example).
- Born into wealth (in America for example).
- Killed by other's mistakes (medical negligence, car, train or plane crash, etc.).

- Disabled or disfigured by other's mistakes (medical negligence or accident, etc.).
- Wrongly imprisoned or executed (falsified evidence, etc.).
- Suffering a heavy financial loss due to someone's greed or negligence.
- An 'evil' minded or cruel person.
- A very kind, compassionate and loving person.
- All the pain, misery, bloodshed, heartache and suffering on this planet.

I personally accept reincarnation as a brick in my edifice,
for a variety of reasons. First and foremost, it 'makes sense'.
It enables one to account for lives terminated at birth, lives
spent as a hopeless cripple or a congenital idiot, criminal lives
where the poor child "never had a chance", and all those lives
which (to our eyes) could not be reconciled with Divine Justice
if they represented our sole appearance on this earthly stage.
Air Chief Marshall Lord Hugh Dowding G.C.B., G.C.V.O., C.M.G. 1882-1970
(The Dark Star)

Having pondered long and hard on such questions, I would add that during my years of research into the philosophy of life, no one, cleric or otherwise, in book form or to my face, has been able to give satisfactory answers that were not an insult to my intelligence. That is, other than what I am going to postulate here. There are, of course, those who would deny that there is an afterlife or a God, and say that life has no meaning or purpose so what does it matter that we suffer injustice, grief and pain and then die into oblivion? But I would again remind them that *criticism without investigation is the highest form of ignorance.*

If we consider the possibility of having more than one life, then we are into a whole new scenario and serious acceptable answers to the above enigmas can be contemplated. Fairness, unfairness, good luck, bad luck and life being the flick of a dice can now be deleted from the equation. If our soul can incarnate once, then by the same Law it could incarnate hundreds of times. So, let's have a look at what evidence we can find.

Regression Therapy

This is a particularly intriguing phenomenon where subjects are regressed under hypnosis to 'previous lives'. Some years ago I made the acquaintance of a very sprightly 80-year-old lady by the name of Margaret Robinson. Margaret, a retired nurse, had been practicing hypnotherapy for over 30 years and uses her knowledge to counsel people suffering from stress, phobias and other traumas of life.

During a session a few years ago, she regressed a patient back before birth in their present lifetime having felt that the problems encountered were deep rooted. To her surprise the patient spoke in a different dialect and was living a totally different lifestyle in a previous age. From then on Margaret made a study of reincarnation and decided to use 'past life' therapy to help patients with severe emotional problems. Keeping an open mind on the subject, Margaret is never concerned with proof or evidence of clients' 'previous lives'. She maintained that it is up to them to do their own research.

With her client's permission, provided his full name wasn't mentioned, Margaret tells the following story:

John H had a phobia about being in a car during heavy rain. It petrified him. One day, while driving home from work in the rain, he glanced out of the side window of his car and saw the wing and engine of a large turboprop aircraft. He looked away and then back again - it was still there. This happened several times on different occasions, which eventually prompted him to seek therapy, thinking he was on the verge of a nervous breakdown.

I put John under hypnosis and regressed him beyond his present birth. He immediately held his arms out in front with clenched fists around what could have been vertical handlebars. His hands and arms were shaking backwards and forwards repeatedly. He was looking around (with eyes still closed), up, down, left and right and appeared very nervous and frightened. When I asked him where he was and what he was doing, he said that he was the rear gunner in an American bomber and was encountering heavy flack in a raid over Nazi Germany during the Second World War.

When I realised that it was the heavy flack hitting the gun turret canopy that was frightening him, I knew why he was frightened of being in a car with heavy rain hitting the windscreen. Also, why it had triggered the vision of the wing and propeller when he had looked out of the side window of the car.

I asked John to go forward to his death in that life. Suddenly, he muttered: "We're hit, we've been hit, and we're going down." He slumped forward and there was total silence. As he lay motionless in the chair I realised that he had just died. Immediately, I asked him to go back a couple of years in that life and tell me his status.

John once again lent back in the chair and said that he was in the United States Air Force during the war; gave his name and rank and stated that he was stationed at a base in England. I asked him where, and he said that he wasn't sure but the name ended with ... ***ington****. I asked what he was doing at that moment, and he replied that he was in a pub a few miles from the base having a drink with some of his fellow aircrew. I asked him the name of the pub and where it was, to which he replied that he couldn't remember but he thought the* *village name ended in something like ...**worth**.*

I then asked John to recall a memorable event that happened on the base, and he mentioned a fire that destroyed one of the huts. He said that rumours suggested it was sabotage, but an official enquiry later established that it was an accident caused by two airmen playing around with a flare gun. Using the correct procedure, I decided that it was time to bring John back to his present life. He gradually opened his eyes and said how relaxed he felt.

*John later told me that he had done some research on the matter and had obtained a list of all the American Air Force bases in the UK during the last war. One he found of interest was RAF **Cheddington** in Buckinghamshire, home to the United States Air Force 36th Bombardment Squadron and nearby was the village of **Marsworth**. Despite living forty miles away, John decided to pay the area a visit. He drove to where the air base was listed but found that it was now an industrial estate. He recognised the area although he had never been there before in this life. He then drove to Marsworth to see if he could locate the pub, but after an hour he failed to recognise anything. Finally, John decided to call at one of the only two pubs he had managed to find and ask the landlord if there were any he had missed. He was told to take the next turning on the left, follow the lane until he passed the church and a pub called The Red Lion would be on the right hand side.*

*This he did, and immediately recognised the church **and** The Red Lion. But something was different about the pub that he couldn't account for. Once inside, John recognised the quaint and timbered interior. Speaking to the landlord he asked him if he had been there long and if he had done any alterations. The gentleman told him that he had stripped the ivy off the outside wall. **That** was what John remembered – the Ivy. He then asked the landlord if there used to be trees across the road opposite the pub and was informed that there used to be, but they had been cut down to build a car park. That was all John needed to know – he had definitely found the pub!*

When I showed an interest in his story, Margaret contacted John and we agreed to meet him one evening at The Red Lion in Marsworth. John was in his early forties, smartly dressed and apparently had a very busy and demanding job. This was what he told me in answer to my questions:

*I also made enquiries at Leighton Buzzard library and found a local author who had written about the wartime history of the Cheddington airbase. This revealed that a hut **had** been destroyed by fire; that it **was** originally thought to have been sabotage and an enquiry **had** found that two crewmembers had accidentally let off a flare gun in the hut. I also obtained a list of personnel who were stationed there during the war that confirmed the name and rank that I* *had given during regression.*

John mentioned that he had researched and found his 'past life' living relatives in America, and was considering going there to tell them his story but had second thoughts about the implications. 'How do you explain to someone that you are the reincarnation of one of his or her relatives who died during the war?' he said.

I asked John if this experience had convinced him of the possibility of reincarnation, and he said that he still had an open mind on the subject but confessed that his research had vindicated the regression and was good evidence for it. I also asked if this experience had changed his outlook on life and he admitted that he was more philosophical about it now. He also added that the phobia of rain on the car windscreen never returned once he came to terms with its possible cause.

Another of Margaret's regressions revealed a fascinating story that happened to Brian Mealing. Brian was taken back beyond his present birth and this is what he told me:

I became aware that my name was Robert and the year would be about 1780. I was an orphan, about 17-years-of-age, wandering the streets of London, begging and doing menial work for a pittance. I was wearing tattered clothes and was a bit backward due to lack of education. I was aware of cobbled streets and horse drawn carts when, suddenly, I heard a commotion. People were shouting and screaming and running everywhere. Then I heard a posh looking gentleman shout, "There he is, he did it – let's get him." Several pairs of hands grabbed me and dragged me in front of the gentleman. "That's him alright, I saw him do it," he said. I looked down and saw that a man had been fatally stabbed and was lying in a pool of blood.

Instinctively, I knew that the wealthy gentleman had murdered him and that I was the scapegoat. I said that I didn't do it and had never seen the victim before, but the crowd was looking for a culprit. The wealthy gentleman was whipping up their fury and insisted that I be arrested and thrown into prison. I was taken away by uniformed soldiers with rifles.

The next thing I remember was being in Newgate Prison with dozens of other people. There were young and old including crying children who were being comforted by their mothers. There was straw all over the stone floor and the stench of urine, excrement and body sweat was unbearable. I was hungry and thirsty, but I was scared because I was pronounced guilty at a farcical trial and was due to be hanged in a few days.

Margaret took me forward to the day of my execution and I was aware of standing on a scaffold and a rope being put round my neck. I couldn't see it because I had a cloth over my head, but I could feel it, and felt so alone and scared. Suddenly, I felt the boarding under my feet give way and had the feeling of falling. The rope pulled tight, then nothing – just blackness.

I tried to imagine why anyone would want to fantasise or invent such a pitiful and gruesome tale, and then Brian told me the amazing ending:

In my present life, ever since I can remember, I have always had a thing about wearing neckties – I hate them! The very act of tying them around my neck and pulling the knot tight made me feel uncomfortable. That's why I never liked formal occasions when I had to wear them, and just couldn't wait to get them off.

Brian's wife confirmed his necktie phobia, and added that he was a little easier about them since the regression, but I couldn't help noticing that he was wearing an open necked shirt! This story has the hallmarks of being a previous life experience, but it is difficult to check out because of the boy Robert's poverty and the sham trial. He felt the wealthy gentleman had bribed the 'legal' establishment of the day and that he was given a pauper's grave.

Sometime later, Margaret asked if I had ever been regressed. I said no, and although I had witnessed regressions, I had no desire to experience it myself. First, I wouldn't want to know if I had killed anyone in a previous life and, second, I never liked the thought of being hypnotised and under the 'control' of another person. 'If you're considering writing a book, don't you think it would be a good idea to experience it yourself?' asked Margaret in a rather persuasive voice.

I could feel myself going deeper and deeper as I counted backwards and followed Margaret's precise instructions. 'Go back to when you were five-years-old in this life,' I heard her say. I felt like a little child again and responded to her questions. 'Now go back to your birth in this life,' she instructed. I found myself in a dark, wet, warm and cosy environment, but I was struggling. Suddenly, I was forced into brightness and felt very uncomfortable. Several people gathered around as I was manhandled in various positions. I had breathing problems and they were extremely concerned (I was born at seven months and my birth weight was only 1.8 kg [4lb]. Although not a problem today, it was in 1938). I was put into an oxygen tent and not expected to live the night!

'Go back in time before this birth,' I heard Margaret say. I had a very relaxed feeling of travelling in darkness, when suddenly; I was riding a horse at full gallop across fields. I was in uniform, a sort of doublet, and could see and smell the steam coming from the horse and hear its thudding hooves as turf

and soil flew in all directions.
M.R: Where are you?
B.S: (I told her what I was experiencing).
M.R: Who are you and what year is it?
B.S: I'm Will Johnson; a captain in Cromwell's army. 'Tis 1646 – Civil War (I looked behind me and could see a dozen or more soldiers riding like the wind).
M.R: Why are you riding like that?
B.S: We're chasing traitors. They're on foot trying to hide.
M.R: What do you do with them when you catch them?
B.S: They're tried in a court and hung if found guilty.
M.R: Where is the court?
B.S: Devizes.
M.R: How old are you?
B.S: 'Tis 40 I be.
M.R: Go back to the age of 12. Where are you and what are you doing?

I was in a thatch-roofed timber building known as The Barn, in Everleigh in Wiltshire. I was with my mother and sister and was grooming horses – for which I was paid (I was later conscripted into an army because I could ride. I found 'favour' with the officers and was promoted to the rank of captain).
M.R: Go to a time when you were happiest.

It was my wedding day to Mary, I was 30, and we eventually had two children. I put my career before family and because of neglect one child died (cough problem) and Mary not long after. I didn't remember what happened to the other child.
M.R: Go towards your death in that life.

I had been wounded in the right thigh and walked with a limp. Because of this I was 'pensioned' out of the army after some of my men turned against me (didn't know why). I became very ill and was bedridden in a very basic stone-floored cottage.
M.R: What are you dying off?
B.S: Consumption (I was coughing; it was painful and had problems breathing). 'Tis a broken-hearted man I be. They have betrayed me – my own kind.
M.R: As you are dying, what are your thoughts on this life?
B.S: Who is right and who is wrong? Were they right (the traitors – Royalists) and I wrong, or were they wrong and I right? What was it all for? It was pointless. I lost my wife, my children and my health. I never questioned – I sold my soul to an army.
M.R: Is there anyone with you?
B.S: A man of the cloth. (I could see this very fat priest with a black rimmed

hat standing by the bed).
M.R: Come out of your body and describe yourself dying.

I felt myself floating away from my body and could see myself propped up in bed leaning against the wall for support and coughing up blood whilst gasping for breath. I was painfully thin and deathly pale with dark sunken eyes. I hadn't shaved for days, and was so cold and lonely. I was only 42-years-of-age but looked like a man of 80. I was a physical wreck. I saw my eyes close for the last time, my hand, grasping a blood stained cloth, fell to my lap and my head rolled sideways.

Margaret brought me back to the exact day and time of my present life and I felt very relaxed and refreshed. Although Patricia had been taking notes, much more took place than there is space for here. It was an extremely interesting experience and not at all like I imagined. I have an open mind on whether or not it was a previous life, but if it wasn't, I cannot think why I would have fantasised such a sad, waste-of-a-life story. I have never been interested in riding horses or joining the army, know nothing whatsoever about Oliver Cromwell or the Civil War and had never been to Devizes – until October 2009. Patricia and I were on holiday in Littlecote in Wiltshire and being only 20 miles or so away, decided to pay Devizes a visit.

What an amazing character town we found; full of historic medieval buildings steeped in Civil War history, with St John's and St James' churches still bearing the battle scars of canon and musket fire. The Civil War was fought in many phases from 1642 – 1651, and was between Oliver Cromwell's Roundhead Parliamentarians and the Cavalier Royalists of King Charles 1st. It ended with Cromwell's victory and Charles' defeat – the latter being executed in 1649. Any possible involvement on my part during that period is worthy of future investigation.

The Pond

Newspaper journalist Sarah Holmes shares her regression experience:

For some reason I have a feeling of dread and terror when I visit one of my local villages. 25 years ago I was driving from my then home town, through the village for a change of scenery. All was well until I reached the pond, and for reasons I cannot explain, I was overcome by a string of negative emotions and panic. I had never been to the village before (not in this life anyway) but I recognised it and felt I knew it well. For years, I never gave the odd experience another thought, but occasionally, due to my job, I have to visit this village, and I'm afraid to say that the feeling has not gone away.

Having recently read about past life regression, I decided to experience it for myself to see if it could throw some light on my déjà vu moments, as well as my deep-seated fear of water. I consequently met with regressionist, clairvoyant and author Brenda Harwood. Brenda told me that she was fascinated by regression, saying that it is proven that the subconscious cannot lie. And added that it could possibly explain why some people are obsessed with certain periods in history and cannot think why.

Open-minded, but nervous, I made myself comfy on the couch and closed my eyes. Brenda started to talk me through to my subconscious into a deep sense of relaxation and presented some doors in my mind's eye. I had to choose a door to walk through and chose a red one. Brenda asked if I could see the year above the door frame. Surprisingly, I could – it said 1861. Then an image or 'memory' started playing in my mind: I was a six-year-old girl and my name was Marg or Mary Stone. I say 'or' because after I'd said Marg, a 'y' kept popping into my head – all very strange. I had a pig-tail plaited hair, a dress and white apron and shoes with straps and buckles. I lived with my grandmother in Wiltshire and was happily playing in the garden.

Brenda then took me out of that door and back along the corridor to another. This time there was a green door with 1736 above it. I walked through, and sensed I was an eight-year-old boy. I was wearing shorts, boots and a brown jacket. My name was Jacob Arnold and I lived in Suffolk with my parents. I could see my dad was a carpenter and my mum was cooking. There were men on horseback riding past our house and I could see loads of apples on trees. My recollections grew weak and it was time to walk back.

Next, I walked up to a brown door with ivy growing around it. The year 1100 was above the door. I walked in, and there it was..... the pond. It was dark and I was filled with a terrible sense of dread. Rooted to the spot, I was unable to move, see or say anything. I sensed I was 23, female and wearing a brown dress and a white hat with my hair tucked up inside. I was too scared to say my name, but 'fl' sound came into my mind. For reasons unclear to me at the time, Brenda took me out of there pretty quickly and back to the present time.

She told me afterwards that my face was showing signs of deep distress, and I have no doubts that this was my déjà vu 'life' and that I probably drowned in the pond. Brenda said she sensed I was innocent but, thanks to today's education, we know that all women accused of witchcraft were.

Having an enquiring mind, I looked Marg or Mary Stone and Jacob Arnold up on the censuses for those years. To my surprise, both were listed under the areas I named! There was even a birth record of a Mary Stone born in 1855 in Alderbury, Wiltshire. There was also a death certificate, but I couldn't view it without payment to a find your ancestors' internet site – I decided not to delve further.

I could go to the village with the pond and look back to 1100 in the church records to see if anything jogs my memory. But, to be honest, going back to 1100 was far too scary and I've no intention of revisiting again – been there, seen it, done it!

The soul comes from without into the human body, as
into a temporary abode, and it goes out of it anew ... it
passes into other habitation, for the soul is immortal.
Ralph Waldo Emerson 1803 – 1882 (American poet and philosopher)

A Duel

At least once a week, for more than 20 years, I had a recurring dream. In vivid colour, I would be sword fighting with an angry and superior opponent. Judging by our clothing I put the time period in late 18th century France. The duel would last for a considerable time and I knew that I was fighting for my life. Eventually, when I tired and dropped my guard, my adversary would thrust his sword deep into my left side just under the rib cage. I would sink to my knees as he withdrew the sword, and feeling faint as my life-force drained from my body, I fall on my face thinking: 'So this is what it's like to die.' Then I would wake up.

From birth, I had a large pigmentation mark just under my left rib cage. In the mid 1970s I became very interested in metaphysical subjects and made a study of reincarnation and its implications. I then wondered if my dream and birthmark were connected. From that moment in time I never had the dream again and the birthmark gradually faded until it was no more.

Interestingly, as a child and early teenager I enjoyed playing mock sword fights with friends, and would thrust and parry with one hand behind my back in the most professional manner. Not one kid on the block could beat me! I was also very adept at making wooden swords in various styles for others and myself

Dedicated researchers like Helen Wambach, Ph.D., have regressed hundreds of people into 'previous lives' and documented their experiences. They were asked to describe their environment, clothing, type of food they consumed, what currency was in use and who the ruler was at the time. Some even spoke in dialects or languages spoken hundreds of years ago in various parts of the world. Many researchers had to delve into archives to prove the given facts and figures – archives that were unknown to the layperson. Past-life therapy has unveiled many anomalies and contradictions with current history which, when thoroughly investigated, have proven correct.

Many Lives Arjuna, you and I have lived,
I remember them all, but thou dost not.
Bhagavad-Gita (4:5)

Children's Memories

Numerous children have recalled a past life (or lives) when they were as young as three-years-of-age. This has surprised, or upset, a lot of parents who feel that their child is unique and shouldn't be talking about previous lives with different mothers and fathers. I feel it important for parents to listen carefully if their children spontaneously talk about previous lives since it could be excellent evidence for reincarnation. Researchers find that young minds have not been polluted with adult prejudices, neither would they have the knowledge of rebirth or the circumstances and events they claim to remember.

Professor Ian Stevenson of the University of Virginia is one of the foremost authorities on the subject and has travelled the world investigating stories of children remembering previous lives. For over 30 years he documented thousands of cases; hundreds of which stand up to meticulous scrutiny. In India, parents take the subject seriously and are honoured when their children talk of having lived before. In the Western world, parents have been inclined to dismiss such talk as the ramblings of childhood and tell their offspring not to be so silly. Today, particularly in America, they are becoming more tolerant of the subject.

It's most interesting when a child claims to have lived before in another town or city hundreds of miles away or even in another country. When taken there by investigators they remember the place, give directions to where they used to live, recall the names of their 'parents', 'brothers' and 'playmates', and often where and how they died in that life. Evidence is often forthcoming when the occupants of the house confirm the details, including dates and the name that the child remembers being called. There are also many recorded instances where children have birthmarks or other physical impediments that correspond to fatal wounds sustained in recalled previous lives. These have been verified when their cases have been investigated.

An intriguing book on childhood memories reminiscent of John H's reincarnation experience, as previously described, is *Soul Survivor* by Bruce and Andrea Leininger. It tells of their two-year-old son, James, having recurrent nightmares screaming about a plane on fire and not being able to get out. Their arduous search for answers over the following years, unearthed evidence that shocked their beliefs to the core. Young James was reliving the life of James Huston, an American fighter pilot shot down by the Japanese in the battle for Iwo Jima during the Second World War over 60 years ago.

As young James grew, he would draw and describe wartime aircraft, their controls and flying procedure that a child of his age couldn't possibly have known, as well as details concerning the life and fellow wartime comrades of pilot James Huston, who he had now become in this life.

If you are interested in children's rebirth experiences, *Children's Past Lives* by Carol Bowman, *Yesterday's Children* by Jenny Cockell, *Children Who Remember Previous Lives* by Professor Ian Stevenson and *Children Who Have Lived Before* by Trutz Hardo, are representative of the credible evidence available.

Roll Reversal

From thousands of worldwide accounts of children's past life memories, a pattern emerges indicating that roll reversal can take place. That is, in a previous life, the child could well have been the father, mother or grandparent of their present-day parents. For example; friend Fred was bouncing his four-year-old grandson on his knee, when he suddenly announced: 'Grandad, when we lived before, I used to do this to *you*.' 'What did you say?' asked a surprised Fred, who at this time was still a cleric. 'Don't you know, grandad,' continued his grandson, 'when we were alive before, I was *your* Grandad and used to bounce *you* on my knee.' Fred was flabbergasted when he heard this, but it later inspired him to study the subject when his life entered a new phase of enquiry.

Then we have David Walsh, who was talking to his three and a half-year-old son Charlie, saying: 'When I was a little boy we never had all these things (toys) that you have.' Charlie replied: 'I know daddy, but don't you remember when *you* were a little boy and *I* was the man?' David is convinced that Charlie is an 'old soul in a young body' as he often speaks with wisdom well beyond his years.

Child Prodigies

Without considering the reincarnation scenario, how does one account for the incredible knowledge and skills that some children from the age of two and upwards seem to be endowed with? Many have shown amazing musical aptitudes without being taught and, by the age of five or six, sometimes with the aid of a tutor, are playing the violin or piano like a maestro. Mozart (1756 - 1791) for example, was composing symphonies at the age of four without ever having been taught.

There are numerous accounts of young children having knowledge of advanced mathematics or physics that would do justice to any university student, and by the time they are in their mid teens they are classed as geniuses. There are child prodigies who show an aptitude for foreign languages and at the age of six can speak several fluently. On the practical side there are many young children that instinctively know how to drive a car or fly a light aircraft without ever having been taught. And when they eventually reach the age to do these things they drive or fly like a veteran.

Critics talk about inherited or genetic memory as an explanation for this phenomenon, but researchers dismiss this when family trees are studied and the relevant talent and abilities are not encountered. If a child has an aptitude for foreign languages, it's very easy to check for the foreign influence in the family particularly if the language is Russian, Chinese or Hindi for example. Generations of non-academics have been known to produce a genius.

There is, of course, a dilemma when an ancestor *did* have a special talent that manifests in a younger generation. 'Inherited memory', cry the critics. 'No,' say the researchers, 'the child is the reincarnation of that particular ancestor and has brought the gift with them!'

> Genius is experience. Some seem to think that it is a gift or talent, but it is the fruit of long experience in many lives. Some are older souls than others, and so they know more.
> *Henry Ford 1863 – 1947 (American motor manufacturer)*

Spirit Influence

Some people maintain that child prodigies are influenced by people from the spirit or astral worlds with talent that *they* had when they were on the Earth. Well, if spirit world talent could so easily influence us at such an early age, why do we need to go to school or university? If it was that easy to influence young children, then surely Doctors and Professors here on Earth would be able to teach them all to be geniuses!

Deja-vu Experiences

This phenomenon is applied to those who visit a place for the first time but feel they have been there before when everything feels strangely familiar. To some people, visiting a foreign country, for instance, and recognising buildings and streets with a memory as if they had once lived there can be a very uncanny experience. Some have been confused when expecting to see a particular landmark or building round the next corner they found it totally different. But, when intensive research revealed that what they expected to see *did* exist but was demolished 200 years previously, they have been even more perplexed!

Critics point out that these people could have read history books, seen old prints or watched historic films of the area. I am sure that most people having deja-vu experiences would know if that was the case or not. Many have had such experiences in the remotest parts of the world.

In October 2000, Patricia and I were driving in the Costa Brava area of Spain just north of Alicante, and decided to head for the hills to see some of the countryside. We eventually came across the quaint old village of Busot and decided to stop for a walk-about. The narrow streets and architecture were typically Spanish and we walked for an hour or so soaking up the atmosphere before heading back to the car.

I had been photographing so Patricia was way ahead of me. When I eventually caught up with her, I said, 'I've just had an overwhelming feeling that I've been here before, everything seems so hauntingly familiar.' In a surprised voice Patricia replied, 'That's incredible – I feel exactly the same about this place!' Neither of us had been to that part of Spain before or seen any books, photographs or films of the area.

I have been here before
But when or how I cannot tell,
I know the grass beyond the door
The sweet keen smell.
Dante Gabriel Rossetti 1828-1822 (English Poet)

Why Do We Need to Come Back?

The vast majority of the Earth's inhabitants are blown about by the 'winds' of life like leaves in an autumn gale. They have no idea who they really are or where they are going and have no set goals or aspirations other than to survive. Some philosophers have likened them to ships adrift in a storm without a rudder, compass or charts!

In the previous chapter, we saw how selfishness and greed have hampered our ability to comprehend the simplicity of the Spiritual Law of Unconditional Love. How much do you think our Mr and Mrs Average *really* learn about the Spiritual Laws and values of life in the 26,000 days, or less, that they spend on this Earth? Precious little, as you may have observed. And don't forget that 8,500 of those days are spent asleep! Many are so engrossed in the trivia of this materialistic and body-orientated world that they end their lives as spiritually ignorant as the day they were born.

Our more thoughtful people admit that by the time
they have learned something of life, it is time to die.
Prentice Mulford 1834 – 1891 (Thoughts Are Things)

Most of us go to school for at least 11 years to become 'educated' and hopefully gain some knowledge of the basic necessities of life. Our first year at a Junior School consists of elementary work, and from thereon we progress to higher classes where the work gets more involved and harder each year.

When the class ends we go home and return to class the next day for new lessons. Well, reincarnation or rebirth is very much like that. It is no more feasible to cram 11 years or more of knowledge and experience into the head of a five-year-old in one year, than it is to gain knowledge and experience of life's laws in one lifetime.

Let us think of one lifetime, however long or brief, as a term at school, and at the end of that term when our physical body is worn out or damaged beyond repair we go 'home' to one of the astral worlds. In Earthly schools some pupils are time-wasters and troublemakers, or just slower at learning lessons than others. And so it is with life and death – some will need more lives than others to learn the needed lessons.

For every problem that we cause here and fail to put right in this lifetime, then the Law of Karma kicks in and 'demands' that we put it right in the next life. 'Dying' doesn't absolve us of our duties, because they will be stored in our karmic bank account. Loving thoughts and deeds are plusses, and hateful thoughts and deeds are minuses – putting us in either credit or debit. Problems and injustices *caused* here are put *right* here – not in the spiritual worlds.

Reincarnation and Karma are Spiritual Laws. They are inseparable doctrines and compliment each other like pepper and salt. It is our Karma that will decide whether we need to come back here or whether we can stay in the spiritual worlds. I make no apology for repeating that it is simply the universal cosmic Law of Cause and Effect! What we sow, we will reap – in this life or the next!

Those who are cruel to their own kind, or animals, will pay the price of many lifetimes of self-inflicted suffering until the lesson of Love has been learnt, understood, put into practise and their debt cleared. In that respect, none of us should be too complacent, because we have probably all been guilty of such 'crimes' over many lifetimes! I have no doubt whatsoever that in past lives I abused my freewill and committed many atrocities. I would have killed countless numbers of times in various wars and isolated murders and probably died many horrendous deaths as a result. Hopefully, over many lifetimes, I have purged violence, in thought, word and deed, out of my system by realising how futile and meaningless it all is, and try to manifest love, peace and harmony in every aspect of my life – the emphasis being on the word *try*!

Only when our self-created grief and suffering has purged us of *every* gram of ego, anger, hatred, selfishness, greed and arrogance can we go on to better things and bid this training school Earth a fond and final farewell. At that stage we will have achieved some sort of 'diploma', but leaving this planet of trial and error is only part of our journey – not the end! Until the lessons of love, peace and harmony are learnt, our Overself will be drawn back to a body of flesh like steel is drawn to a magnet. Birth, suffering, learning and 'dying' ad infinitum! Or, as the Buddhists so aptly call it, 'The Wheel of Life'.

> To be born, to die, to be born again and
> to progress constantly, such is the law.
> *Allan Kardec (Tomb inscription)*

How, Where and When?

As we have seen from previous pieces of the puzzle, between earthly lives we live in the astral planes, and it is from there that our future lives are planned. The aim is to reach a higher astral plane each time we 'die', until we reach the higher spiritual worlds and are no longer tied to the karmic law of rebirth.

We have already seen that on all levels of the mid-astral planes and upwards there are highly evolved people who are always available for guidance on our spiritual welfare. It is they who will help us plan future rebirths on Earth, if and when it is necessary, according to the strengths and weaknesses in our character. Our spiritual mentors will discuss with us when and where we will be reborn. Our parents, country and conditions will be chosen according to our life review and the amount of karmic debt we accrued in previous lives.

Rebirth onto a physical world is not compulsory, but most of us will, at some time, be encouraged to 'enrol' for another course on Earth to further our spiritual education. For some there is almost instant rebirth, whilst others elect to stay until several generations of family have joined them. There are no set rules, but it appears that the higher the astral or spiritual plane we have reached the more right we have earned to plan our own progression. The length of stay in the higher worlds can therefore be from literally minutes to thousands of earthly years. It is, apparently, possible to progress from one spiritual plane to another, but it takes much longer than a few brief lifetimes on *this* planet!

To reincarnate here we have to 'die' in the astral worlds, since to go from one frequency to another we have to 'die' to the world we are living in at the time. This involves a sleep-like state when our Overself departs from our astral body in the astral world. Being of no further use our abandoned astral body will slowly disintegrate and its atoms will go into the cosmic recycling system ready for further use. The same thing happens to our abandoned physical body here when it is cremated or buried. The very bodies that we are 'wearing' now are made up of atoms that are billions of years old!

Having chosen our parents and future lifestyle, our Overself incarnates into a physical body at the moment of conception. It can be male or female, healthy or otherwise, whichever is fitting for the lessons that we and possibly others need to learn. For example, if we are born disabled or suffer disability in this life, then several possibilities present themselves.

Maybe we caused the disability of others in a previous life through acts of violence or negligence. Or, maybe we have chosen to be that way to clear any negative Karma quickly and save ourselves many lifetimes of further suffering. And it may well encourage those closest to us to manifest love and compassion by caring for us. It has been known for highly evolved souls to voluntarily incarnate here in physically disabled or mentally retarded bodies to fulfil that role.

If we are born to cruel or neglectful parents, perhaps we were the same to them in a previous life. What goes around comes around. Perhaps they don't know how to love and need to learn. It can be a vicious cycle that goes from life to life if not corrected. Maybe we can be in a position to change things when we get older and say to them, 'I love you and forgive you.'

We could have agreed to touch this world for a few brief hours or years as a baby or child to influence those that love us. This may encourage them to think deeper about the important values in life and help them to grow spiritually. By so doing, we will have helped both them and ourselves in the name of love. If we are born into deprivation, perhaps we abused wealth and people in a previous life and need to learn what it feels like so that we won't err again when given another chance. If we need to learn the lessons of patience and tolerance then – like wasps at a picnic – life will make sure that many aggravating so-and-sos cross our pathway. If we have been guilty of racism, then perhaps incarnating into the very race that we persecuted will make us understand their plight.

In whatever way we have tormented others or made their lives a misery in past incarnations, we will need to make amends or suffer the same torment and misery that we inflicted upon them. If we complain that life has caused us an injustice, perhaps we should reflect on how many times we could have done the same to others in this or previous lives.

As an observer of life I have winced many times when hearing or seeing people being cruel and unkind with words or actions, but have not been at all surprised when told of circumstances that caused *them* grief some time later. There is always karmic payback time and, as you are aware, we get away with nothing.

We can go far back into history and witness 'man's inhumanity to man'. So what fitting lessons would you recommend for those who have perpetrated cruel deeds? What suffering or 'community service' would you advise for them? Interesting subject isn't it!

We are all actors playing different roles on the world stage. It is our soul's evolving spiritual pathway, so it doesn't really matter how many lives we have, whether we are male or female, black or white, rich or poor, Queen or President, Arab or Jew, Native American Indian or Auntie Flo's Nephew from

Blackpool. And as our jigsaw is assembled we can appreciate that it's all about experiencing and understanding *Love* – and we will all get there in the end!

Divine souls, return ye into human bodies and therein undertake a fresh career. Behold here are the destinies that life offers. Choose freely, but remember that the choice is irrevocable, wherefore, if it be ill, accuse not God.
Plato [Republic] 428-347BC (Greek philosopher)

Summary

Cosmic Law is infallible, and is there to protect us as well as teach us lessons. All that happens to us in this life is the result of all our thoughts and actions over accumulated lifetimes. All the while we 'disobey' the Law of love, peace and harmony by behaving badly and entertaining negative emotions, such as anger, jealousy, lust, greed, envy and hatred we are, unfortunately, committing ourselves to rebirth time and again until we get the message. We will one day of course, and then we can stop asking, 'Why do these things keep happening to me?'

If reincarnation evidence, such as the philosophical reasons why it is necessary, the teachings of the great spiritual masters, children's and adult's memories, child prodigies, deja-vu and regression experiences were put to a jury, and the critics put their case – whatever it may be – then I feel that the jury would have to declare in favour.

If you can now accept the possibility that we could have many lives on this Earth as part of our spiritual education, then please accept another piece of the jigsaw. We can now continue our quest and investigate why so many want to stop the world and get off.

As a man casts off old clothes and puts on new ones, so the embodied self, casting off old bodies proceeds to other and new ones.
Bhagavad-Gita

You cannot die. It is only your body that dies. You had a body in an existence previous to this. That died as others died before it.
Prentice Mulford 1834 – 1891 (Thought Forces)

Reincarnation and Karma
are spiritual
Laws

11 Suicide – *Why Do They Do It?*

I take it that no man is educated who has
never dallied with the thought of suicide.
William James 1842 – 1910 (American Philosopher)

Scientists at the Life Extension Unit in Palm Springs, America, are experimenting with hormones to reverse the ageing process so that we can live for hundreds of years. And many international biologists claim to have identified the aging process and believe that in the future, moral and social consequences aside, we will be able to live on Earth forever. Good news? Well, not quite. According to the World Health Organisation (WHO), every year, worldwide, a million people commit suicide and 10 to 20 million attempt it because they see no point in *living*!

When we consider that there is an excellent life after 'death' system, featuring astral and spiritual worlds that have functioned perfectly well for millions of years, we might well ask why scientists would consider condemning us to this strife-ridden planet forever? Or, conversely, what drives us to terminating our lives here and cutting short our stay?

Over the years, I have come across numerous people who have reached the end of their tether and literally said to me, 'What the *hell* is life all about – do *you* know?' It's easy to laugh off such remarks with light-hearted replies or try to change the subject if it threatens our comfort zones. But if we wish to become serious students of life and not remain in ignorance, then it's advisable not to have comfort zones – Nature doesn't!

We should be prepared to comfort people who are stressed up to the eyeballs, depressed, see no meaning or purpose to their life and are feeling suicidal. And we will only be able to give them plausible answers if we have the knowledge and experience to do so. In that respect we can literally save a life! Let's look at it this way – what gives us the right to demand answers to life's puzzle if we are not prepared to give of our time and knowledge to help others who need reassuring words of comfort?

Four Attempts!

In the summer of 1976 I was asked to have a chat with a frail 77-year-old lady who had attempted suicide four times! At each attempt the hospital had pumped her stomach, brought her back to consciousness and taken her home. She confessed to being in a loveless marriage with an 80-year-old husband who spent most of their income on his obsession with betting on the horses. Not only that, he continually told her how pathetic and useless she was. After the fourth failed attempt to end her life with an overdose, he argued that she was so incompetent she couldn't even commit suicide properly, and offered to buy her a much stronger dose to guarantee success on her next attempt!

Needless to say, she portrayed her husband as a very callous man. She was dreadfully unhappy in that sort of atmosphere, and explained that she couldn't leave because she had no money and nowhere to go. This poor lady was suffering from mental abuse, depression, low self-esteem, loneliness, lack of security, feeling unloved, unwanted and a total failure. No wonder she saw life as meaningless and wanted to opt out!

I explained to her in simple terms much of what I knew about life after death, cosmic law and the futility of suicide. She was very interested, but how much she really understood I never knew. Maybe a few seeds were sown that day. I gave her healing, made her smile, left my telephone number and offered to see her again in a couple of weeks. On the way out I had a few words with her husband, but they fell on 'deaf' ears. I would have had more response from a brick wall! We met twice more and I was pleased to see her looking better and feeling stronger within herself. To the best of my knowledge a fifth attempt was never made.

Living never wore one out so much as the effort not to live.
Anais Nin 1903 – 1977 (American writer)

Hereditary?

I was introduced to a lady in her early 40s who was going through a rough patch. Her father had committed suicide when she was five-years-old and this had profoundly affected her ever since. She rang me whilst having a particularly bad day, and was sobbing and emotionally suicidal. She was convinced that because her father had taken his own life it was inherent in the genes and that it was to be her destiny also. I reassured her that there was no credible scientific evidence to support such thinking.

We talked for ages, and eventually I asked her if she would want to inflict the same emotional scars on her children that her father had inflicted upon her. She was horrified at such a thought, and suddenly realised that suicide was a selfish act that would cause years of suffering to other members of her family. I put the phone down only after she assured me that she was feeling much better for the conversation, particularly after having made her laugh at the world.

We eventually became good friends, and it is wonderful to see her happy and doing well in life. She now counsels others who suffer from low self-esteem. She is an excellent teacher because she has been where they are. Had she taken her own life she would have deprived hundreds of people she has since helped to lead more rewarding lives.

A Typical Cry for Help

Several years ago I had been working late on a design project, and after a long drive, arrived home two hours later than usual feeling mentally tired but looking forward to the evening meal. Patricia greeted me on the doorstep and explained that a distressed gentleman had telephoned saying that his wife was very depressed and kept talking about doing away with herself. He had asked if I could come and see her when I got home.

My meal was left in the oven and I went straight away. I stayed for a couple of hours, gave the middle-aged lady in question some healing to calm her down and talked about the meaning and purpose of life and death. She was extremely interested in the subject and kept asking how I knew about such things, did I really believe it all, and what reassurances could I give her that it was true. I explained that I had spent many years investigating as well as having personal experiences to back up the knowledge. She had mistakenly thought that death meant oblivion and would end her depression forever.

Before leaving I made the lady laugh – something that her husband hadn't seen her do for ages! Laughter is a wonderful stress buster and helps to disperse depression. She gave me a lovely hug goodbye and asked if I would see her again. It was 10 pm when I arrived back home, my meal had dried up and Patricia had seen little of me that evening, but it was a distress call that couldn't be ignored. I visited the lady several times over the coming months and saw gradual improvements in her condition as she responded to healing and reassuring answers to her questions.

Today she is fine, but thousands are not and want to stop the world and get off, some very early in their lives as the following UK statistics reveal:

- In 2009, 5,675 people committed suicide – 4,304 males and 1,371 females (ONS).

- More than 20,000 young people under the age of 21 attempt suicide every year – 3,000 of them succeed.

- Suicide is the biggest killer of young men in the UK today. In the 15 to 35 age range it accounts for 21 per cent of deaths (CALM report).

- NHS statistics reveal that more than 4,000 children aged under 14 attempted suicide in 2007.

- Eight 13-year-olds out of a class of 22 said they had attempted suicide (Samaritan, London Borough questionnaire). 17 out of those 22 felt *there was no point in living.*

- Out of a total of 17,000 children questioned, 1 in 8 (2,125) had attempted suicide. The most common reasons given were bullying at home and school, external problems, low self-esteem, *couldn't cope with life* and *seeing life as pointless.*

- 1 in 10 teenagers questioned had attempted suicide and 20 per cent of those said they had attempted it whilst still at primary school. In most cases the children concerned showed no outward signs of distress and seemed happy!

These are appalling statistics for a so-called 'civilised' and 'religious' society, and can only serve as indicators that we are not civilised and that organised religion and the society we have created are failing. How in this day and age can we justify children who cannot cope with life and see it as pointless? They are growing up faster these days and are thrust into a world full of adult pressures and problems. And if adults cannot cope with life then what hope is there for their children? Perhaps the time has come to re-evaluate their education both at home and at school. In most cases teachers and parents are sadly lacking in the knowledge and experience to give sensible and acceptable answers to children who are already seeing life as pointless.

Perhaps child and teenage suicides would be greatly reduced if their young trusting minds were taught about the astral body, karma, reincarnation, life after death, the astral planes, the Law of Love and the *truth* about the Absolute. This would surely give them a good reason for living and help them to see the point of life rather than confusing them with so much 'faith and belief' that many will reject when they reach adulthood!

Reasons

It isn't just youngsters who succumb to taking their own lives; many adults have either attempted or contemplated it for one or more of the following reasons:

- The death of a loved one(s).
- Bullying at home or workplace.

- Constant sexual abuse as a child: at home, school, church or care home.
- Depression and low self-esteem.
- The break-up of a marriage or other relationship.
- Acute loneliness.
- Severe debt problems.
- Being made redundant and unable to find work (particularly at middle-age).
- Drink or drugs addiction.
- Having a terminal and debilitating illness.
- Seeing life as meaningless and pointless.

We are looking at a serious and escalating problem, and none of us should feel complacent or judge those who decide to end their lives since we don't walk in their shoes. Especially when NHS studies highlight that *one-in-four* of us will suffer from a mental health problem at some time in our lives. This includes various stages of depression and suicidal tendencies.

I have stated many times and, will repeat yet again; this is not an easy planet to live on for the majority of people. And most of us, at some time or other, will undergo some form of emotional or physical trauma that will cause us, however brief, to question the futility of life. Ironically, it was at one of the lowest points in *my* life, early in 1981, that I received a telephone call from an acquaintance who, amidst her tears, informed me that because of a series of personal tragedies life seemed meaningless and that she was going to take an overdose. I spent over two hours giving good reasons why she shouldn't, and eventually managed to get a therapeutic laugh from her. All was well in the end, and the lady in question eventually regained a more positive attitude to life. I never mentioned that my wife had left me and that I was out of work – compared to my caller's trauma it didn't seem important!

Sometimes it's the last straw that breaks the camel's back, and this is when extremely sensitive people are most vulnerable to life's multiple traumas. With many, as in this last case, talk of doing it can simply be a cry for help and a way of attracting attention to their plight. It is those who bottle things up and do it on the spur of the moment that cause the most anguish to loved ones and friends.

The Samaritans are a marvellous organisation, and are never busier than during the Christmas and New Year periods when many contemplate suicide, mainly because they feel lonely when others are enjoying themselves. Speaking to a sympathetic ear on the end of a telephone can literally save the life of a lost and despairing soul.

Many of those with suicidal thoughts feel that they are alone in their problems, and cannot or will not, talk to others, either thinking they wouldn't understand or be unable to help. This is of great concern, because a problem shared is a problem halved, and under such circumstances a loving friend or relative is priceless.

Over the years, many have expressed their gratitude when they find that others feel as they do, and that their problems, fears and worries are far from unique and shared by millions of others. So in that respect, let's have a closer look at some of life's traumas that can plunge many into feelings of despair, often with thoughts of 'ending it all' as a means of escape.

The Death of a Loved One

This can be a tremendous shock to the nervous system of the bereaved, particularly if the death was sudden. Many grieving relatives find it hard to readjust and live without their loved one, especially when it plunges them into loneliness and depression. Whilst a few may briefly consider taking their own lives 'to be with their loved one', many can have a subconscious 'death wish' and commit slow suicide by not eating much and literally pine away with a 'broken heart'. This is all too common, particularly with the elderly once the will to live is lost, so I have covered many of the problems of 'losing' a loved one in the chapter *Just for You.*

Bullying: At School (harassment)

Any suicide is a sad and premature waste of life, but this is never more evident than when a youngster, for whatever reason, takes his or her own life. And one of the main reasons for attempted or actual suicide amongst youngsters is bullying at school.

As a victim of bullying in the late 1940s, I dreaded the thought of going to and from my Primary School. The bullies would pick on me, and others, in the playground and outside school. I never told my parents, thinking that they would just tell me to stand up for myself. This made early school life a misery, with constant fights, taunts and threats, but it has given me a great sympathy for victims ever since. Luckily, I never let it affect me in later years.

In the mid-1970s, one of our teenage sons suffered a spate of bullying at school and feigned sickness as an excuse not to go. We eventually suspected that bullying could be the problem. When this was mentioned he broke down in tears and informed us that bullies had, on several occasions, dismantled his bicycle, taken his packed lunch causing him to go without food, broken his pens and other personal equipment and continually ridiculed and taunted him.

We confronted the school, but merely got pathetic non-committal waffle from an incompetent Head teacher. It became evident that bullying was endemic in the school and that even teachers had been intimidated by pupils – hence a high staff turnover! Many parents had obviously complained and it took a change of Head teacher to finally sort the problem out – using a discipline sadly lacking today!

The inherent streak of cruelty in children can show itself at an early age, as many Nursery School teachers will confirm. And if it isn't corrected with love and attention, then bullying problems are sure to follow. This leaves the parents of such children asking, 'Where did we go wrong?' or declaring, 'I just can't do a thing with him', or 'her', as the case may be. Some parents refuse to believe that their offspring are bullies and can be as verbally abusive as their accused child when confronted by teaching staff – which usually proves a point!

Child bullies tend to be unhappy and frustrated children, often growing up in a negative environment, feeling unloved and unwanted. To bolster their own lack of self-esteem they torment and dominate others to make them more miserable than they are. They delight in pushing, punching, kicking, taunting and other spiteful tactics of mental and physical cruelty. Often the victims are of ethnic origin or are seen to be 'different' in other ways because they are tall, short, obese, clever or have ears or teeth that stick out. A physical or mental disability or not wearing 'street cred' clothes can also invite the wrath of the bully making their victims lives unbearable, often leaving them with emotional scars well into adulthood.

Although we touched on the subject in chapter 5 (*Religion*), other emotional scars, often with suicidal tendencies, are childhood incidents of sexual abuse by 'responsible' adults, be they tutors, carers or clerics. Such perverted bullying incidents are more prevalent in boarding institutions rather than day school.

Many children, particularly teenagers, are now addicted to online networking and this has handed the school cowards the subtle weapon of cyber-bullying to further terrorise their victims. It is estimated that, every year, over 10,000 children receive threatening messages on their computers and mobile phones. With children now spending so much time alone in their room with a computer, mobile phone or television for company, parents can get so engrossed in their own personal lives that they fail to notice the warning signs caused by their offspring's problems until it's too late. As a father and grandfather, I would always advise parents to keep a special eye on their son or daughter during the school years. Regular hugs and being told that they are loved very much is a wonderful tonic for all concerned.

The anti-bullying charity Kidscape regularly run 'ZAP' assertiveness training sessions regarding severe school bullying. Half of families who attend regularly report that their child attempted suicide or contemplated it.

At the time of writing I am on the board of governors of two local schools and can appreciate the concerns encountered by both staff and students when bullying incidents occur. Bullying, in a greater or lesser degree, is in *every* school – from primary to university. Every term, when older bullies leave, new ones arrive – a perpetual cycle!

If you know, or suspect, that your child is being bullied, in *any* way, notify the school immediately and ask them to investigate – 70 per cent of pupils will suffer bullying at some time or other. Never give in until you get satisfaction because the consequences can be fatal – as ChildLine are well aware, when every year, nearly 40,000 children ring for advice because of bullying!

Finally, for parents who are concerned about any bullying incidents affecting their child, I would recommend they read *Bullycide: death at playtime* by Neil Marr and Tim Field. This is an in-depth expose of child suicide caused by bullying.

Bullying: At Home (Domestic Violence)

This phenomenon is not new either, and can be traced back into history when many a wife and child had their lives turned into a living nightmare when a drunken husband regularly returned from the local inn or tavern and vented his frustration on them. The Equality and Human Rights Commission found that three million women a year were assaulted by husbands, boyfriends or partners; and every year nearly 480,000 women call the police to report being victims of violence – 100 of them die as a result! Thousands more don't call – they are too frightened!

In the 1960s my father witnessed the aftermath of many such attacks when beaten and bruised women came into his shop and broke down in tears whilst telling their stories. Countless times my father comforted and counselled these women. I am not aware of today's supermarkets offering this service!

For several years, an acquaintance was regularly physically abused by her husband *and* two adult sons. I frequently saw her with either a black eye or bruised arms and suggested that she report the matter to the police, but she was frightened of the reprisal threats from her 'family' if she did so. Being in her late 60s and unsteady on her feet it was not difficult for them to knock her to the ground. This poor soul suffered one beating too many and eventually took her own life with an overdose. It was upsetting to hear the news and, although I would never condone suicide, in this particular case I feel it was a blessed relief. She was in a living 'hell'' so 'What have I got to lose?' was probably her last thought.

Ironically, 20 per cent of domestic violence sufferers are now *men* and the problem is widespread. They receive abuse from female partners and often have to duck and weave when plates, vases and saucepans fly through the air – some are even viciously attacked whilst asleep! This sort of behaviour has now spawned a Battered Husbands Association! NSPCC figures show that more children are killed at the hands of their mothers than by their fathers. All of which goes to show that women can be just as violent as men!

According to Age Concern, 500,000 older people are believed to be abused at any one time in the UK, either at home or in Care Homes, and that twenty-five per cent of abusers are sons and daughters. Shocked? It gets worse! The National Society for the Prevention of Cruelty to Children (NSPCC) receives over 4,700 requests for help every month, and estimates that at least one child is killed each week by abuse from a parent or carer. The bottom line being, that 36,406 children were put on the 'At Risk' register in 2009!

Mental abuse by a partner or domineering parents can also be damaging, since emotional wounds take longer to heal – if ever. A child, husband or wife continually derided by being told how useless and inadequate they are over a period of time can have fatal consequences.

Whilst Chairing a County Council Community Services Committee, I was privileged to work closely with council officers, police officers and the Crown Prosecution Service dedicated to tackling domestic violence. One objective being to establish dozens of 'Safe Refuges' to house victims – including children – away from the perpetrators. The very nature of domestic violence is that it mostly takes place behind closed doors, and affects all ages, genders, races and religions. The message to get across is for victims not to be afraid of informing the police – they *will* be protected and the aggressor dealt with by a restraining order or prison.

Bullying: Adults with Learning Difficulties

In 2008, my Community Services Committee received a presentation given by a group of adults with learning difficulties. Many had speech impediments and others physical handicaps that impaired walking and hand movements. We found it a very moving experience, but what shocked and upset us was when we learnt of the amount of verbal abuse, ridicule and taunting that most of them were subjected to an a daily basis, whether they were on public transport or in the street. Much of the abuse came from ignorant youths who thought it great fun to mock and taunt those who couldn't stand up for themselves. Even to the extent of jeering and pulling faces through the windows of the Day Centre the group attended.

Speaking with some of the group afterwards, I was humbled to be in the presence of such lovely people who, understandably, found the continuous bullying from certain members of the public extremely depressing. But what impressed me, was when they said they felt very sorry for their tormentors and what sad people they must be.

Bullying: In the Workplace

Workplace bullies have been prevalent since at least Roman times – from the early mining pits to present day corporate companies, from the police force to prisons, from the armed forces to health services and from financial institutions to political establishments. Today, workplace bullying is *rife*, and it is estimated that one in eight workers suffer from it. Quite often racial abuse or sexual harassment is a feature of bullies who have destroyed the lives of many employees. Jealous colleagues can also ridicule and harass fellow workers who just want to get on with their jobs.

Those who rant and rave and torment others in the workplace are usually advertising themselves as incompetent at their jobs and lacking in people skills. That is why they resort to bullying tactics as a cover-up. I have personally never met anyone who is good at their job adopt such practices. Like all bullies, they tend to be unhappy people with unhappy home lives. Once again their victims are trapped in a stressful nightmare scenario, particularly, if due to their age, alternative employment is difficult. I have occasionally witnessed the aftermath of verbal bullying with women in tears and men close to it.

Physical threats or verbal abuse are bad enough, but mental is more subtle. Not only has cyber-bullying plagued online networking for students, a local survey of 1,043 office workers, found that over 50 per cent admitted to regularly receiving abusive and threatening e-mails, or 'flame-mails' as they are known. A further 84 per cent said they knew of colleagues who had also received 'flame-mails'. This is another example of widespread computer abuse that highlights how ignorant minds will find an 'evil' use for something that was designed for good.

I have a great trust in the laws of life, and have always found that bullies eventually get their comeuppance – what goes around comes around and what we sow we reap! The reason is simple. Bullying, in all its ugly forms, is a violation of the cosmic Law of Love, and a prime example of 'man's inhumanity to man', highlighting, once again, that we are a million miles from understanding Spiritual Truth!

Before we leave the subject of bullying in the workplace, if you are a victim of such abuse, you may be interested in two marvellous books on the subject. One is *Bully in Sight* by Tim Field. This tells how to predict, resist, challenge and combat workplace bullying. Tim is an expert on the subject, having suffered for years from sadistic workplace tyrants (see his anti-bullying website www.bullyonline.org).

The other is *Tame Your Terrible Office Tyrant* by Lynn Taylor. It's based on true stories and extensive research on the subject and helps employees to understand and cope with difficult, irritating, demanding, tyrannical bosses. It explains reasons for their childish bullying antics, mood swings and incessant criticisms. And, you'll love this – it likens them to troublesome toddlers and, with the aid of tried and tested solutions, explains the effective way to deal with them – and resume a sane, enjoyable work life, as is everyone's right!

Under Pressure at School

Throughout their school life, never before have children had so many tests and exams to sit. This can put them under extreme pressure to excel academically. Particularly if they are constantly told by well-meaning parents that good examination results are vital for a university place and future career prospects, and therefore expected of them. This can impart an enormous feeling of guilt and low self-esteem on a child should they be seen as a failure in the eyes of their parents and friends. If children are given plenty of love and encouragement and told just to do their best, then many a child tragedy could be avoided particularly if they are also a victim of bullying at crucial examination times.

According to social workers, many children are becoming depressed and turning to drink and drugs due to examination pressures and lack of parental contact, particularly where both parents go out to work. A study of 800 children by Affinity Healthcare found that one in five 11 to 19-year-olds admitted to self harm. The problem was greatest among girls. The mental health charity Sane stated that there were growing indications of a self-harm epidemic amongst the young. This is amplified by hundreds of Internet bulletin boards on self-harming.

Very few are born without *some* talent, and children who are not academically inclined very often show an aptitude for sport or working with their hands. This should be encouraged by parents and teachers so that their energies and enthusiasm can be channelled into a worthwhile future. This would help to alleviate many instances of anti-social behaviour that blight our society. Some children can be late developers and only blossom when they leave school so it is interesting to note that most millionaires neither did well in academic studies nor went to university. And even the eminent scientist Albert Einstein was considered a school duffer by his Head teacher!

Depression and Low Self-esteem

Government health statistics estimate that more than three million people in the UK suffer from mild to chronic depression, and that 80 million working hours are lost each year because of it. So should we be surprised that 34 million prescriptions are written for antidepressants (happy pills) every year to combat it. Depression invariably spawns low self-esteem and is a catch 22 illness that is now virtually an epidemic. Numerous people confided that they were depressed and didn't know why, or that they couldn't stop worrying about the problems of the world.

Many lose the will to do anything or go anywhere as lethargy and apathy take over with plenty of 'Nothing seems to go right in my life' phrases. It can be triggered by one traumatic event or a gradual build up of smaller occurrences until the recipient has a partial or complete nervous breakdown causing a 'can't cope with life' situation. Some are frightened of the future or can see no future for themselves. This is danger time, and well-meaning loved ones have been known to say: 'Come on, pull yourself together.' It's not that easy – if it was, they would do it!

It can be extremely difficult for many chronically depressed people to see a way out of their predicament other than taking their own lives, since in many cases they are not in a position to think rationally due to their feelings of isolation and loneliness. This is what 35-year-old 'Peter' has to say on the subject:

For many years I suffered a deep depression from which there seemed to be no escape. It was as though I was in a dark tunnel that had no light at the end of it. We never know where depression comes from or how it will affect us in our daily lives. The usual symptoms are fairly universal, such as tiredness, non-motivation, loneliness, and suicidal tendencies. One of the big problems is the varying level of depression from mild to manic.

My depression first started in my late teens and continued into my early twenties. During this time I was drinking heavily and losing friends fast. My feeling at that time was of floating on a black sea of despair in a small boat with no land in sight. This is similar to the tunnel syndrome. This was accompanied by feelings of dread, and the all-encompassing lack of a will to live in a world where I felt I didn't belong. I found myself in a vicious circle. Drinking to forget, forgetting what I was doing, and just wasting time sinking lower and lower. I was like a snowball building and building, waiting to hit something at the bottom of the mountain.

Five years ago I hit my wall when I succumbed to a nervous breakdown and ended up in a drink and drug rehabilitation centre. This was the culmination of years of living on the edge. After talking to doctors and a psychiatrist it was agreed that this was not the best place for me, and I came home to my family who I had never been so pleased to see. Something had changed. I now knew it was over, and mentally things felt different – the sun was shining again. I had my family around me – I was indeed a lucky man. I'm not saying that I don't have bad days, because I do suffer the odd day of mild depression, but nothing like what I used to feel.

I sometimes think that getting low and looking over the edge made me see what I nearly lost. I appreciate things for what they are now and live each day as it comes. I was lucky. I found light at the end of my tunnel and my little boat found dry land. I would always say to others that there is always ***hope****. Never give up or look back, and always give out what you would expect to receive – the rest will take care of itself.*

At the end of an evening of philosophical discussion, guests leaving our house found 'Peter' sitting on the doorstep with his head in his hands. It was at the time of his greatest despair. We invited him in and let him pour his heart out. He had heard that we held these evenings from time to time but was amazed to find that we understood his inner thoughts about life.

As well as being a deep thinker, 'Peter' is a very kind and sensitive person and, like so many, found it difficult to relate to a world where fear, violence, greed, selfishness and other negative factors are portrayed in the media on a daily basis. He thought he was unique in his thinking and different from others – no wonder he felt lonely and depressed.

The tragedy of life is what dies inside a man while he lives.
Albert Einstein 1879 – 1955 (Physicist)

Mirror, Mirror on the Wall

Because we live in a body and image obsessed society, women often experience negative emotions and depression when they reach the menopausal stage of life. They feel that youth is fast ebbing away and that they are no longer attractive when fat, cellulite, grey hair, 'granny whiskers' and wrinkles seem to appear from nowhere every time they look in the mirror. This often creates an urge to try every fad diet, exercise gadget, 'natural' hair dye and anti-wrinkle cream that comes onto the market. Airbrushed magazine photographs of young 'perfect' female models only exasperate the situation!

With men, it's termed 'having a mid-life crisis', but the symptoms and emotions can be the same when the mirror makes them aware of thinning or grey hair, a developing 'beer-belly' or double chin. Instead of anti-wrinkle creams, there can be an urge to wear a medallion and purchase a fast motorbike or sports car, hoping that this will revitalise their 'lost' youth. And airbrushed magazine photographs of young studs with 'six-packs' are an anathema!

The 'I'm not getting any younger' and 'what's it all about?' period in peoples' lives is when many, perhaps for the first time, question life in depth and feel a need to rearrange their priorities – particularly lifestyles.

It's worth bearing in mind that The Absolute and Spiritual Hierarchy are not in the *least* bit concerned about our ego and whether we consider ourselves to be attractive or not. Neither are they interested in whether we are short, tall, obese or thin, nor whether we have wrinkles, dark hair, grey hair or no hair! All these are facets of our temporary, disposable physical body. It's the amount of *unconditional love, kindness and compassion* that we are capable of giving that matters.

We are now informed that young people are going through a 'quarter-life' crisis where statistics show that many suffer loneliness, apathy and depression. This is brought on by a multitude of concerns, including the state of the world, lack of job prospects, and little or no money – in fact, they can see no hope for the foreseeable future!

In some cases psychological factors are not the prime cause of depression, which can simply be an under-active thyroid gland or an inappropriate lifestyle causing vitamin and mineral deficiencies and a depleted immune system. Depression causes tiredness and burns up vital vitamins and minerals renowned for their synergistic effect on the nervous system. Health and nutrition practitioners often recommend physical exercise and a regular dose of laughter. Unlike medically prescribed anti-depressants that sedate over 30 per cent of the UK population, laughter addiction is a brilliant therapy!

Many confess that they feel like skittles; no sooner do they get on their feet than something comes along and knocks them down again. So in the end they become exhausted and depressed and just feel like lying down and not bothering to get up. This is the saga of life and, in reality, there are only two things we can do – give in and go under, or get up and do something positive about the situation.

As long as you live, keep learning how to live.
Lucius Annaeus Seneca 4BC – 65AD (Roman Statesman and philosopher)

Human Givens

When it comes to the understanding and counselling of depression sufferers, I have been extremely impressed by a professional therapy system that has a remarkable success record. The nationally acclaimed Human Givens Institute understands depression and how to lift it naturally without pills and potions. They offer help for anxiety, stress, panic attacks, depression, anger problems, addictions, phobias, relationship problems, low self-esteem, sleep problems and lack of concentration. Having a wide understanding that such issues invariably result in worry – a major cause of depression – with many sufferers losing the will to live, is one of the keys to the Human Givens' success. Testimonials speak for themselves when clients kiss their depression goodbye, regain their sense of purpose as well as their sense of humour and happiness! One of their many excellent books is *How To Lift Depression – Fast* by Joe Griffin and Ivan Tyrrell (see *Bibliography* and *Useful Contact Details*).

The charity Resolution has also proven the Human Givens therapy for treating armed forces veterans suffering from Post Traumatic Stress Disorder (PTSD). Many service veterans experience combat stress caused by the mental anguish of warfare with all its brutalities, flashbacks and nightmares, often leading to depression, anger, violence and drug and alcohol abuse – the worst scenario being family breakdown and even suicide. According to Resolution statistics, over 300 Falklands veterans have committed suicide – more than were killed in the conflict in 1982. And 20,000 ex-servicemen are currently in jail or on probation.

> The message is clear. It is not circumstances that lead to
> depression but how you respond to them that matters.
> *Joe Griffin and Ivan Tyrrell (Human Givens)*

The Break-up of a Marriage or Other Relationship

The two words 'I do' can turn out to be the most emotionally and financially expensive words ever uttered! Current UK statistics reveal that 40 per cent of all marriages will end in divorce, despite every bride and groom hoping that theirs will last 'forever' and that they will never leave each other. The statistics for cohabiting couples are even worse.

Apart from arguments about sex, money or the children, most couples in this situation have invariably grown apart over the years rather than growing closer together – particularly when domestic violence occurs. Taking each other for granted and lack of communication play a big part in marital breakdowns, when the inability to talk to each other about needs and problems can build up in both partners. When love flies out of the window, criticism, arguments and depression can set in with both parties living separate lives.

It's almost inevitable that such marriage's will eventually fall apart, particularly if another person 'arrives' on the scene in the form of an affair causing one of the partners to leave home because of it. This can be devastating, particularly if it was sudden and without any apparent warning signs. Emotionally it's similar to bereavement, since a partner has as good as 'died' in the sense that one is now left on their own.

The reasons why partners split up or get divorced are manifold, but the pain and heartaches are nearly always the same. Many go through the emotions of disbelief, hurt, anger, resentment, hatred, revenge, guilt, rejection, loneliness and depression, often with suicidal thoughts running through their mind. As we have previously discussed, such negative emotions, if harboured, can invite mental or physical health problems due to disharmony within the individual. Emotions are generally compounded where young children are involved.

Because separation and divorce are so traumatic and life-changing, I will touch on the issue again in the chapter *Just for You*.

Those who do not know how to weep with their
whole heart, don't know how to laugh either.
Golda Meir 1898 – 1978 (Israeli Prime Minister)

Redundant and Unable to Find Work

Being out of work at any age, through redundancy or any other cause, is extremely distressing for the vast majority of people. Particularly when it happens at that 'middle-age' time in someone's life or during a recession period when jobs are not easy to find. I have been in that position several times, looking at an uncertain future when engineering contracts became virtually non-existent. It's very easy to let apathy and depression creep in and stop logical thinking, but understanding how the laws of the Universe operate, I found that positive and optimistic attitudes *always* pay dividends in the long run. If you recall – it's our thoughts that attract to us that which we give out.

We are living in times of rapid industrial and commercial change on a global scale with few promises of a job for life or a steady career. We witness companies going into liquidation and industries closing or being taken over. Often with the emphasis on short-term profits by downsizing, asset stripping, closing departments and divisions and making workers redundant – often those with the most experience – a recipe for disaster that I have witnessed many times!

Life isn't always a bowl of cherries, and there are times that try and test us to the utmost – but we should never *ever* give in, no matter how hopeless the situation appears. Some of the greatest success stories started from desperate situations, spawning statements like: 'being made redundant was the best thing that ever happened to me'. I have known many who changed – or life 'forced' them to change – their daily work routine to something entirely different, and found themselves much happier and financially better off, particularly when something suddenly came out of the blue. Some pursue a hobby, turning it into a profitable business, whilst others turn their hand to writing a novel or teaching a sport in which they excel.

The Internet, for example, has opened up a whole new world and totally changed the working environment giving good incomes to people who thought their working life had hit the rocks. It pays to look carefully at all opportunities as they can quite often be a stepping stone to something much better.

My advice to anyone finding it difficult to regain employment, is to keep their CV updated, consider any retraining options and look at the situation as a potential new chapter in their working life, not the end of it. And remain optimistic with no regrets about the past – it's happened. Do all that can be done to earn honest money, be *very* patient, keep an open mind and, above all, *trust in the laws of life.*

The greatest discovery of any generation is that a
human being can alter his life by altering his attitude.
William James 1842 – 1910 (American philosopher)

Debt Problems

Many have lived beyond their means for a considerable period of time and incurred huge debts on credit cards and other loans. When economies decline due to global recessions, the inevitable insolvencies and bankruptcies happen, whilst debt collectors hover like vultures over a carcass. The Citizens Advice Bureau is inundated by those who feel stressed and suicidal due to personal debt problems, compounded by redundancies, house repossessions and the inevitable strain on relationships. Many of which lead to separation, divorce and the sad break-up of families.

In 1998, Patricia and I made an overseas property investment using a large proportion of our capital. It was a disaster, and we realised that we had been conned with little chance of getting our money back. Our financial outlook, retirement prospects and the future looked extremely bleak. Taking full responsibility for the decision, I apologised to Patricia stating that it was entirely my fault and that I was terribly sorry.

Patricia put things in perspective when she replied: 'It's only money. I love you very much and don't care if we live in a wooden shed so long as we are together.' She was right, it *was* only money, and our love for each other *was* stronger and *much* more important than any financial disaster. We hugged each other and tears ran down our cheeks. As our despair lifted, we sent out a big thank you to the Universe for helping to get our priorities right and bringing us even closer together – we also asked for guidance as to our future direction.

Within days, 'coincidences' happened whereby numerous people crossed our pathway and imparted information that, over a period of time, enabled us to get our money back. I also used the information and experience to help many other victims of the same professional scam to retrieve *their* lost investments. When couples take the marriage vows of 'for better or for worse – for richer or for poorer' it saddens us to hear of broken relationships caused by money problems. But perhaps they were just the last straw.

Some may argue that we cannot live on love alone. True – but genuine unconditional love between couples and families is an amazing bond that can make all the difference between feeling isolated, depressed and suicidal, and that of working together with moral support to overcome the problem.

Feeling Lonely and Unloved

There are many reasons why people of all ages can feel lonely, particularly with the hectic pace of modern life which has escalated the problem and prompted remarks such as 'Nobody seems to have the time for each other any-more'. Loneliness feelings are often coupled with depression, unhappiness and other negative factors. Even in a crowded place it's possible to feel alone as the throngs go about their business or appear to be having fun. Some people prefer their own company and don't have a problem being independent, but many elderly people, having 'lost' a loving partner after many years of marriage find the loneliness and loss of physical contact unbearable. But, as we have discussed, this is where a pet can be invaluable.

Thousands of children call the charity Kidscape every year to complain of boredom, loneliness and isolation, mainly due to non-caring parents. Some roam the streets and join gangs to feel wanted and part of a 'family', often obtaining alcohol and drugs to blot out their inner loneliness. Having sat on committees devoted to child welfare and talked to youngsters accused of anti-social behaviour, I have been surprised at the number of parents or carers who give their teenage children a pack of cider or lager and tell them to get lost for an evening. Eventually, many such children are taken into care, never really knowing what it's like to feel loved and wanted.

One of the laws of life is that to receive we must first give, since we can never get more out of life than we put into it – to *receive* love we must learn to *give* it. Giving love and affection is the quickest way to attract like-minded genuine friends. If we find it difficult to show love and affection to people, then there is no reason why we can't show it to the animals, birds, trees and flowers, because all living things thrive on love – as I hope you are beginning to appreciate.

Did you know that most sensitive people have felt insecure, lonely or unloved at some time in their lives? This is where belonging to a religion, joining a social or sports club, gymnasium or any other activity where people get together can give a sense of belonging and purpose. One of life's lessons is learning to cultivate an inner strength, and one way of achieving this is to realise that we are more than just flesh and blood. We are never truly alone or unloved, since those from the spirit worlds of love and light have our interests and spiritual development at heart – if we are aware of it, and *trust them*!

Life is not so much what each individual makes of it,
but what we make of it for each other.
Helen Keller 1880 – 1968 (American writer – blind and deaf from 19-months-old)

Back So Soon?

I would like to recount an incident that happened to my medium friend Derek Markwell in 1975. At the time, Derek was working at a farming research centre. One day, whilst busy with his work, a strong intuition came to him to go and have words with his colleague Arthur who was working on the same site. He ignored the thoughts and continued working. 'Go and speak to Arthur', came the impressionable words in Derek's mind. Again he ignored them and decided to do it later when he had finished his task.

Moments later, another colleague rushed up to Derek and informed him that Arthur had strung himself up in one of the barns. Derek was shattered at the news, and felt guilt and a deep regret at not having obeyed his 'inner voice'. He went home feeling depressed with a big 'if only' on his mind.

That evening, as it happened, was the regular night of Derek's Psychic Development Group. Derek wanted to cancel the meeting because he was too upset at what had happened at work, but Eileen, his wife, insisted they went ahead as normal as if nothing had happened. Within minutes, Victor, who was sitting opposite me, started to speak. 'Derek, I have a spirit gentleman here by the name of Arthur who would like to speak to you.' He paused a while before continuing, 'I can't 'see' him, but he wants to say that whatever you would have said to him would have made no difference.' Again a pause, 'Does that make sense to you?' Victor asked. 'It most certainly does,' replied Derek in a relieved voice.

At that instant, I clearly 'saw' the head and shoulders of a man appear in front of me. When I described the face in detail, an elated Derek announced that it was a perfect description of the gentleman in question and that he would reveal all after the meeting.

An hour later we heard the full story of Derek's traumatic day at work. He had deliberately not said anything in case any evidence came through that evening, and it had. Victor had 'heard' Arthur and I had 'seen' him. What surprised us all was the fact that Arthur had taken his own life that very afternoon, and four hours later he came back to give evidence of his survival and put Derek's mind at ease!

Where Do Suicides Go?

We have seen in the chapter *Invisible Worlds*, that there are numerous astral worlds from the lower frequencies to the higher, and it depends entirely on a person's state of mind at the moment of 'death' that determines their immediate abode. Since most people who take their own life are depressed with an unbalanced or confused mind at the time, this is the state in which many will find themselves when reawakening on the next frequency. Imagine their surprise when they find that they are still alive (in their astral body) and that destroying their earthly physical body has solved nothing.

Initially, most will find themselves in one of the mid-astral planes – often called 'Summerland' – and be counselled and nursed by one of the many volunteer workers in hospices constructed for such purposes. Luckily for most, their stay will be brief, and 'Guides' from the higher frequency worlds will come to their aid and explain their predicament. Since freewill is respected on all levels of existence they will only be taken to a suitable astral world if they so wish. There they will be able to meet, and be looked after by relatives and friends who left the Earth Plane ('died') before them.

Summary

Once again we have a chapter revolving around love – the lack of it! Love is harmony, and all the reasons why people feel depressed and suicidal can be put down to lack of harmony. The likes of bullying, relationship problems, the 'death' of a partner, being out of work, debt problems or severe stress can create the negative emotions of despair, fear and anxiety – which is disharmony – lack of love. And when harmony is missing from our lives then life can often seem futile.

If you have thought about or tried ending your life because of tragic circumstances or because you are depressed and feel that you can take no more from an 'insane' world, then I would urge you to seriously think again. It will solve ***nothing***, and only cause untold suffering to loved ones. You will die once, but they will 'die' a thousand times in their grief for the rest of their earthly life. Is that what you would wish to inflict upon them? Suicide is a futile act because you cannot die – your spirit is immortal! Oblivion doesn't exist, there *is* only life – this is one of Nature's little jokes. Once this is appreciated, you will laugh at the stupidity of human pettiness and probably be appalled at its greed, selfishness and ignorance of the laws governing life and death.

You have enrolled as a student in the University of Life. So please don't think about quitting or resigning, because the bad news is that you will only have to come back and learn the lessons all over again. I *know* it's tough, and you may well be at the end of your tether due to circumstances that have deeply affected you, but *no one* escapes the lessons of life by playing truant. Unfortunately, as I have said many times, most of us only ever question life when it smacks us about a bit.

It takes more courage to live than die. You have that courage. How do I know that? Because you had the courage to read this book – some will not. They will unfortunately prefer to wallow in their own misery and reject all forms of help. But you are made of stronger stuff than you realise. You are a spiritual being here and now and, despite the harsh lessons that you may be experiencing, the ***Absolute loves you more than you will ever know***, and in the great scheme of things you ***are*** very important. If you can come through this dark cloud, the sun ***will*** shine for you again – but it will take time.

Even if you cannot understand now why things have happened, please don't despair. Have confidence in yourself, ride it out and you will emerge a stronger and better person – trust me. Once life's lessons are learnt they rarely repeat themselves!

Please do two things for me. First, I would like you to talk about your situation to someone you think will be understanding and sympathetic. Please don't think that no one will understand your predicament – there is ***always*** someone. And when you find them I would like you to talk and talk and talk. Cry as well if you feel the need, but talk! It is lack of communication that has caused you to bottle things up and exaggerate them in your own mind. If you find this hard then please contact the Samaritans or other organisations (see *Depression* in *Useful Contact Details*), they will always have an understanding and sympathetic ear for you any time of the day or night.

Second, I would ask you to pray. Why? Because you are about as low as you are ever going to get – you have plumbed the depths so you will have nothing to lose, and you will be speaking from humility – which ***always*** rings The Absolute's bell. As the next chapter will reveal, the simplest prayer in the world is, 'Dear God, please help me'. Take heart from the words of the spirit guide and teacher Silver Birch:

It is not possible to be able to comfort the mourners, to help the troubled, the perplexed and the problem-stricken ones unless you yourself have plumbed the depths of sorrow and sadness, till your own soul has been so touched by your own experiences that you are fit to teach others.

What he is saying is that you are now 'qualified' to help others who are walking in a dense fog of despair and can see no meaning or purpose to life.

You can literally save lives! Why? Because you have been there, done it, seen the film, read the book and got the tee shirt!

During my years as a clairvoyant medium, I met several people from the astral dimensions who had taken their own lives when they lived on Earth. Most were accompanied back here by spirit guides. As they stood by my side to be recognised and described to loved ones in the audience, their remorse and guilt for what their selfish act had inflicted on their relatives was indescribable.

They used phrases like, 'I'm so dreadfully sorry. Please forgive me for what I have caused you – I love you very much.' It is the forgiveness from loved ones that eases the pain of the suicide and helps them to recover so that they can lead a normal life in the higher astral worlds with relatives and friends already residing there. Such reunions are always emotional. Many mediums confess that they have been through the same tearful but rewarding drama numerous times.

When life is not to our choosing, it's very easy to feel sorry for ourselves and become unhappy, depressed or suicidal. Every day, throughout the world, hundreds of thousands of people suffer dreadful calamities, but they pick up the pieces and carry on as best they know how, putting any thoughts of doing away with themselves out of their head. This is always the wisest policy and the most rewarding, especially when so many of them go on to lead meaningful and happy lives as well as helping and comforting others who are experiencing trauma for the first time. And, as we have already observed, happiness comes through helping and caring about others.

If you can now accept that suicide is futile and solves nothing, then another piece of the puzzle can be put into place. We can now move on and see if prayer and meditation can help us on life's journey.

Guns aren't lawful;
Nooses give;
Gas smells awful;
You might as well live.
Dorothy Parker 1893 – 1967
(American critic and humorist)

Resiliency is an important factor in living. The winds of life may bend us, but if we have resilience of spirit they cannot break us. To courageously straighten again after our heads have been bowed by defeat, disappointment and suffering, is the supreme test of character.
Anon

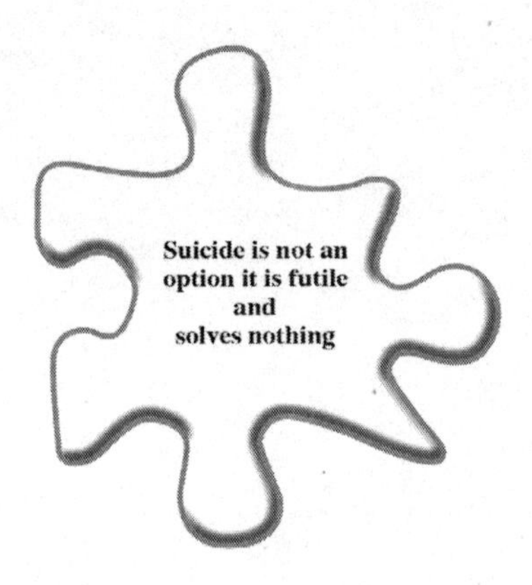
Suicide is not an
option it is futile
and
solves nothing

12 *Prayer and Meditation*
– What Are They?

The greatest revelation is stillness.
Lao – Tzu 6th century BC (Chinese philosopher)

'What's the point of praying if there is no personal God?' 'My prayers are never answered, so praying is just a waste of time and pointless.' 'I'm not religious so I don't see the need to pray.' 'Prayer is asking God to do something that you can't do for yourself, isn't it?' 'Isn't meditation something they do in caves in India?' 'Meditation is for weird people who have nothing better to do.' 'Meditation – isn't that sitting for hours on end doing nothing?'

From a layman's point of view these are perfectly logical questions and statements. Although some will find it amusing, when those who think prayer and meditation are a waste of time or pointless, will themselves sit for hours, night after night, staring at a screen in the corner of a room.

Since they are an important part of our puzzle, let's throw some light on both of these subjects.

Prayer

In desert wilds, in midnight gloom;
In grateful joy, in trying pain;
In laughing youth, so nigh the tomb;
Oh! When is prayer unheard or vain?
Eliza Cook 1818 – 1889 (English poet)

I am sure that at some time you have felt the need to pray, particularly when the storm clouds of life hovered above your head and the mists of gloom and despondency surrounded you. In all probability you felt helpless and inwardly alone regarding your predicament. You may well have uttered the simplest of prayers, such as: 'Dear God, please *help* me,' or maybe your cry for help was for a loved one.

They say there is no such thing as an atheist on a sinking ship, and that even the hardest of men will utter a prayerful call for help from a Deity when all is lost and they can see no hope for life. I would also expect atheists to suddenly become an extinct species during a massive earthquake or hurricane. I have known macho truck drivers burst into tears and resort to prayer when a child becomes terminally ill, which was something that probably wouldn't have entered their heads when life was good. There is something inherent in the human race that under certain life threatening conditions, manifests itself in a degree of humility as a plea for help from an 'invisible intelligence' far greater than itself. For many it can be a last act of self-preservation before impending doom strikes. For others it can be an unselfish desire to see a 'Divine intervention' in the sorry state of human affairs.

There are many and diverse reasons why, at times, we feel a need to beg for mercy from the Absolute, yet show very little of the same to our own kind or the animals to which we are so cruel. Some people, who have prayed 'parrot fashion' all their life, suddenly lose their 'faith' and stop altogether when they blame God for a personal tragedy that has hit them hard. Knowledge of what prayer really is and how it works would save many from such torment.

The childish interpretation of prayer is asking or demanding a favour of a 'humanised' invisible God who sits on a golden throne surrounded by angels in a realm called 'Heaven' somewhere up in the sky. Some people are encouraged to pray to the Saints or other enlightened beings that they are told dwell in this heaven world. If only 25 per cent of the world's seven billion population all prayed at the same time then these deities would certainly have their work cut out. One could imagine the prayer-lines jammed with requests!

'Welcome to God's Prayer-Line. If you are a believer, press *one*. If you are an agnostic, press *two*. If you are an atheist, press *three*. I'm sorry, but all our Prayer-Lines are busy right now. Your call is important to us so please hold the line. You are number 1,531,642,347 in a queuing system' (followed by distorted harp music). Perhaps that's why so many feel their prayers don't get answered!

Now that we have moved on from the notion of a personal God, you may well ask to whom or what do we pray, how do we pray and what is the point of prayer? First, as a gentle exercise in thought, try to grasp the realisation of a Universe that is programmed to respond to certain commands, rather like an enormous computer. Think of it in a similar fashion to our personal computers (PCs). If we don't enter the right password or commands then we are denied access to the programme. In other words, only those who have the right authority are allowed access to the information or 'game plan'. Why? Because it is Cosmic Law (rules). We have already discussed how Spiritual Law governs every aspect of our individual lives and prayer is no exception.

To Whom or What Do I Pray?

In reality, prayer *is* asking favours of a living Cosmic Principle of Love – God, The Absolute. That is because it is the primary cause of all life throughout the cosmos, and without it, nothing could or would exist. As we have seen from previous chapters our link with the Absolute is inside us. We are literally walking around with a communication 'device' within us – rather like a mobile phone – that can receive and transmit thought impulses from the Spiritual Intelligence from which we emanated in simple form billions of years ago. This 'device' has been known down the centuries as our spirit, soul, Higher Self, or 'Overself' as it is known in many esoteric teachings. So it is to our *Overself* that we should pray!

How Should I Pray?

Talk normally and say what is in your heart and how you feel. We are living in the twenty-first century now, so it isn't necessary to use medieval language such as 'thee', 'thy', 'thine' or 'thou knowest'. It won't cut any ice with the powers that be or make it any more 'official'. Talk – or think, if you wish – in modern everyday language in a simple down to earth sort of way in a natural tone of voice just as if you were confiding in your best friend. And in many ways, your Overself (soul) *is* your best friend – it's been with you for a *very* long time.

Shouting or constant repetition of a prayer is also unnecessary and a waste of breath since the Absolute is neither deaf nor does 'It' have a bad memory. Prayers chanted 'parrot fashion' from a textbook or memory will have about as much sincerity as a politician's speech and be about as useful and effective as a flat battery. The only exception to this rule is the repetition of a mantra during meditation – which will be explained later in the chapter.

Praise and flattery will also be ignored by the powers that be. The Absolute *knows* how great 'It' is and doesn't have to be continually told. It is we less than humble humans with our inflated egos that thrive on praise and flattery. So let us talk with love and humility to a loving Spiritual presence that knows us better than we know ourselves, loves us more than we will ever know, and knows exactly what we are going to say before the thoughts leave our minds and the words leave our lips.

It is our *Overself* that will respond to the prayer, and if it thinks our request is in our best interest then it will grant us access to the 'cosmic programme' and help will automatically be given in one way or another. Thus our prayer *will* have been answered – but *not* necessarily in the way that we think or expect! Let me give you a tongue in cheek example that I trust will make the point. I love my family dearly, and there isn't anything that I wouldn't do for them if I thought it in their best interest. But, 'Oi Dad, can you lend me a fiver for a pint and a packet of cigarettes?' would definitely not get the same response as, 'Dad, I've got a problem. I'm at my wits end and don't know which way to turn. Can you help me – please?' Cosmic Law is very much like that and responds to sincerity and humility.

A word of caution, if I may. Do you recall in the chapter *Love – The Law of Life*, we considered the power of thought, especially regarding the effects it had on Masaru Emoto's water experiments? Well, if prayers can be voiced by just thinking as well as speaking, then that makes *every* thought a prayer doesn't it? So if our thoughts are negative, then perhaps we shouldn't complain if nature answers our prayers by causing negative circumstances to happen in our lives. More food for thought!

What is the Point of Prayer?

I have been asked a few times if I have ever personally felt the need to pray in private. The answer to that is yes – many times. Apart from childhood prayers, the first time I felt the need to open my heart to a 'higher power' was in the April of 1971. At the time, I knew nothing of the laws governing the Universe, the spirit worlds or the Absolute. I suppose I was a typical agnostic. The country was in the grip of yet another recession and once more engineering was suffering badly. I was a freelance designer and couldn't find work anywhere, having been in contact with numerous companies and agencies only to be told the same tales of misery. With a young family to support and a mortgage to pay it was the typical ball and chain around my ankle. At the time we were struggling financially just to keep our heads above water.

Being self-employed I didn't qualify for unemployment benefits for several weeks, and was too proud to ask my parents for a loan. I was desperate, and in a moment of despair and utter humility, I sat with my head in my hands and, with tears trickling down my cheeks, uttered: 'Please dear God, help me. I don't know what to do. I have tried everything I can think of to get work. *Please* help me.' I had no idea as to whether I would get a response, but at least I had got it off my chest.

Foolishly, I had let the worry of being out of work deplete me, resulting in a severe mouth and gum infection that made eating extremely painful. On visiting the doctor, he prescribed antibiotics and casually asked my line of work. I explained and mentioned that I was out of work. He looked at me deeply and asked if I had an Accident and Sickness insurance. 'Yes I have,' I replied. 'I'll sign you off for a couple of weeks,' he said with a glint in his eye, 'come and see me then and we'll take it from there.'

I received reimbursement from the NHS and, combined with my insurance money, I was financially comfortable. The doctor signed me off for another two weeks until the infection had gone, and on the last day of the month an agent telephoned to offer me an engineering contract. I had spent a month at home with my wife and children, and it was the sunniest April for many years enabling us to go for long walks together. I said a big thank you to the powers that be. Was it a coincidence or an answer to my prayer for help?

Why do we need to pray? When life hits hard and all seems lost, why not – what have we got to lose? I have proved it many times, and when the pressures of life seem unbearable, it is sincerity and humility that connect with the Absolute's 'Prayer-Line'.

When life knocks you to your knees – well, that's
the best position in which to pray, isn't it?
Ethel Barrymore 1879 – 1959 (Actress and writer)

Who Should We Pray For?

There is no reason why we shouldn't pray for ourselves if we have a problem that we have genuinely and sincerely tried to solve at a physical level without avail. Sick and suffering animals also need our thoughts of love – which are prayers. And prayers said for others in need are very effective when said from the heart. Many times a silent blessing has been offered for a complete stranger that I have observed suffering from trauma, anxiety or having mobility problems. It could be in the High Street, a shop, or even a television documentary or newspaper article. The beauty of this is that they don't even know that they have been prayed for. It is a selfless act of love for a fellow human being, and that is probably the best prayer we can ever offer to the Absolute.

Let me leave you with two very different styles of prayer but said with great simplicity from the heart and both equally as effective. The first is from Suzanne Green who, for eighteen months, suffered from severe depression and a constant fear that something negative might happen to her two children. Suzanne's health was also deteriorating and eventually she reached the end of her tether. These are her words:

I was so low and depressed, and constantly thinking that life was meaningless. During my worst moments of despair I would think, "This life is crap – what's it all about? I just don't want to be here." I have, ever since I can remember, been an agnostic, and often wondered if there was something out there. Because of my problems, I felt the need to do something, and one day whilst in utter despair, I just closed my eyes and said the first thing that came into my mind: "Oh hello – it's me. I don't really know what to say, or who I'm talking to, but if you can hear me, thank you for keeping my girls safe for another day. I don't want to ask for anything – just to say thank you."

I did feel more comfortable not having to mention Jesus or God, and shortly afterwards an urge to meditate came over me. This I did many times, and ever since then I have felt more in control with a lovely sense of inner peace and calm. Sometimes while meditating I feel so charged with energy that it's like being plugged into the mains. That's the only way I can explain it. My life has now changed out of all recognition and I recently started a job teaching autistic children, which gives me great satisfaction and a new value for living.

Suzanne is a very sensitive person and, like countless others of such nature, could not relate to the selfish, greedy, violent and artificial world of materialism that she could see around her. Consequently her thinking became negative, with fears and anxieties causing her to become depressed and unable to cope with life. Suzanne probably hadn't realised that life was giving her *exactly* what she was thinking (praying) about. Fear and anxiety! Her prayers had been answered!

In a mood of total despair, Suzanne unknowingly made a positive move by talking to her Overself (soul) which, as we have previously discussed, has direct links with the Absolute. Notice also that she didn't *ask* for anything, she merely said thank you – a positive act of love and humility. Her Overself then impressed upon her the need to meditate, which automatically brings peace and calm and dissolves negativity.

Finally, from the wisdom of a race that fully understood the meaning and power of humble prayer:

O' Great Spirit,

Whose voice I hear in the winds, and
whose breath gives life to all the world,
hear me. I am small and weak, I need
your strength and wisdom.

Let me walk in beauty, and make my eyes
ever behold the red and purple sunset.

Make my hands respect the things you have
made and my ears sharp to hear your voice.

Make me wise so that I may understand
the things you have taught my people.

Let me learn the lessons you have
hidden in every leaf and rock.

I seek strength, not to be greater than my brother,
but to fight my greatest enemy – myself.

Make me always ready to come to you
with clean hands and straight eyes.

So when life fades, as the fading sunset,
my spirit may come to you without shame.
Native American Indian prayer

Meditation

Meditation is the withdrawal from the appearance of the outer scene to the inner harvest. At one and the same time it is the 'Divine Awakening'. Through its application comes inner knowledge – and a direct knowing through Divine Direction.
Michael Gardner-Jones 1920 – 1990 (Healer, medium and spiritual teacher)

In the Western world meditation is a much misunderstood and maligned discipline, but it is really an essential subject for the student of life to understand and practise if answers to life are desired. First and foremost, let me clarify that it is not in any way connected with religion. Some religions may have adopted it over the centuries, but meditation was practised in the East and the Orient by all cultures long before the advent of organised religion. In its highest form (Raja Yoga) it is a universal spiritual practice that is at least 4,000-years-old, and is mentioned in the ancient writings of the Indian Vedas and the Bhagavad-Gita.

So, for the novice, what is meditation? In a nutshell it's a change of consciousness. Rather like the state of mind when we are awakening from a night's sleep – we are neither fully awake nor asleep – it's that in-between stage. But we are *aware* that we are neither awake nor asleep. It is a serene and peaceful state in which we could willingly stay for hours. That is the meditative state, and it has profound mental, physical and spiritual benefits. Practised regularly we will develop a constant state of peace and tranquility that will enable us to cope better with the 'trials and tribulations' of everyday life.

Every moment of our waking life our five physical (body) senses are picking up 'information' about our physical world, because that is their primary function. And whilst these physical senses are functioning we are 'deaf' and 'blind' to the non-physical information that is all around us. Now, if we temporarily shut these physical senses down, then we become more receptive to the natural spiritual frequencies of love, peace and harmony that permeate the Universe.

As previously discussed, the minds of our Mr and Mrs Average are in a constant state of turmoil and starved of inner peace. Minds that are constantly working overtime due to incessant negative thinking, with thoughts of fear, worry and anxiety, causing stress, loss of sleep and a constant feeling of tiredness. If this habit is maintained, it will inevitably lead to mental or physical ill health. Our mind is either *constructive* or *destructive* according to our thinking.

Meditation offers the opportunity to calm an overactive and unruly mind and still the incessant flow of uncontrolled thinking. It is the natural process of the mind to think, and that is precisely what it does all the time if it is not trained otherwise. Meditation is to the mind what food is to the body. If we feed our body with junk food and drink or drugs then it will not be able to maintain good health, so sickness and disease will be the inevitable result. Similarly if we feed our mind junk (negative) thoughts, then it will not be able to transmit harmonious and wellbeing instructions to the cells in our body. Therefore dis-ease of the mind in the form of apathy and depression often follows.

Meditation is the transformation of this constant chatter of the mind – which can even hold conversations with itself – into a state of harmony. Do you think it impossible to control your thoughts? If you have been engrossed in this book then you have been meditating. Your mind (attention) has been focussed on the book and hopefully you will not have been aware of a ticking clock, that dripping tap or the neighbour's dog barking! The artist engrossed in painting, the musician composing or playing, the inventor or designer with their project, the gymnast in an event, are all meditating on their allotted tasks. They cannot afford to let their minds wander from what they are doing. They know that total and utter mind absorption in what they are doing will bring success. Do you imagine that a high wire walker without a safety net would entertain some trivial thought of yesterday? Unlikely – unless he or she had a death-wish!

Accidents happen because people let their minds wander from what that are doing at that precise moment. It's called not paying attention! How many drivers apply 100 per cent concentration on their driving? Very few I would wager. Many let their minds wander to other things and are consequently badly shaken, injured or killed when their vehicle collides with another or runs off the road.

Water and Breath

Many moons ago, a Chinese Emperor had a court adviser who complained that he found it impossible to control his thoughts and stop his mind from wandering. The Emperor immediately ordered a full bowl of water to be placed on the adviser's head, and instructed him to walk round the palace grounds. But, should he spill just one drop of water he would be put to death. Many hours later, the adviser made his way, very precariously, back to the Emperor. 'Has this man spilled any water?' asked the Emperor. 'Not a drop,' said a palace official. 'Good. Now what were you thinking about whilst you were walking the grounds?' asked the Emperor of his adviser. 'The water sire, the water,' replied a nervous adviser. 'There you are,' said the Emperor, 'you *can* control your thoughts.'

Now, if we substitute the breath for the bowl of water, then we have the same principle. Just for a moment, assuming that you are in reasonable health, do not have a heart or breathing problem and are not reading this book on a crowded bus or train, you may like to try this little exercise. Sitting comfortably upright with hands on thighs – palms uppermost – close your eyes and, concentrating on your breath at all times, gently breathe in through your nostrils to the count of six. Hold the breath for three seconds and then slowly breathe out through the nostrils to the count of six. Hold the breath out for three seconds and then repeat twice more. Now open your eyes and breathe normally.

If you have never meditated before and you managed this simple exercise without thinking of anything else but the flowing of your breath, then please congratulate yourself. You have just mastered the basic technique of meditation. But don't get *too* carried away because you have only learnt that one plus one makes two! Ideally, you will need an experienced teacher and at least six months under your belt before you are able to grasp the lasting benefits of training the mind to enter the 'no thoughts zone' for set periods of time.

Living in the Now

If you are sincerely interested in learning the basics of meditation, choose a place that is quiet and where you will not be disturbed. If you are in a class then this will automatically be provided. 15 minutes twice a day (morning and evening) will be ample at first, and you could try the simple breath concentration technique. One of the 'secrets' of life is to live in the moment of *now*. What happened 30 seconds ago is history, and what is going to happen in the next few minutes, hours, days or months is the future. There is only *now*. Right this split second is the only thing that should concern a meditator. The problems of yesterday or tomorrow's busy schedule should not be allowed to intrude. If your mind wanders – and it *will* – to either 'history' or 'future' thoughts, then let them go and bring your mind back to the '*now*' breath. Do this every time it wanders. Eventually, after much patience and constant practise, it will get the message and be under your control. It's rather like training a disobedient dog. 'Sit! – I said *sit!*'

Another meditation technique is visualisation, where the teacher guides students through a preset imaginary scene such as a walk across a meadow and around a beautiful lake for example. Most students find this very rewarding and feel as if they are physically in the scene that they see within their mind.

Other meditations are based on the repetition of a mantra. This centres the mind on a particular word or phrase. It can be something quite simple like, 'God is love', or 'Love I breathe in, peace I breathe out'. One of the more popular mantras is the OM (AUM) meditation. The sound Om has ancient Tibetan mystical connotations in that it represents the sum total of all the vibrations of the Universe and, when chanted correctly, can be very powerful and uplifting, particularly so when done within a group. Another well-known mantra is OM MANI PADME HUM and means 'OM, the jewel in the lotus'.

> The sound of Brahman [God] is OM. At the end of OM is silence.
> It is a silence of joy.
> *Maitri Upanishad (6:23)*

Raja Yoga Meditation and the Chakra System

Raja Yoga, sometimes known as Kundalini Yoga, is probably the oldest and most profound of all the meditations and, when studied seriously with strict discipline, can give the student evidence and proof of the existence of the Absolute. Raja Yoga is highly spiritual in its application and, simply put, is the raising of spiritual energy from the base of the spine up through the chakras. Chakras are spiritual energy centres that have been known to mystics and sages for thousands of years and feature in their esoteric teachings (see fig. 3). For the reader's interest, the Sanskrit names are also given.

There are seven main chakras in the human body running in line with the spine. Each one when fully opened energises various glands and organs in the body via meridian lines (these are the lines where acupuncture therapists place their needles when treating health problems). They also play a part in our emotional and physical wellbeing as well as our psychic and spiritual development. Both in the past, and the present day, many Oriental and Western mystics and psychics have seen and described these chakras as vortexes of energy, likening them to lotus petals.

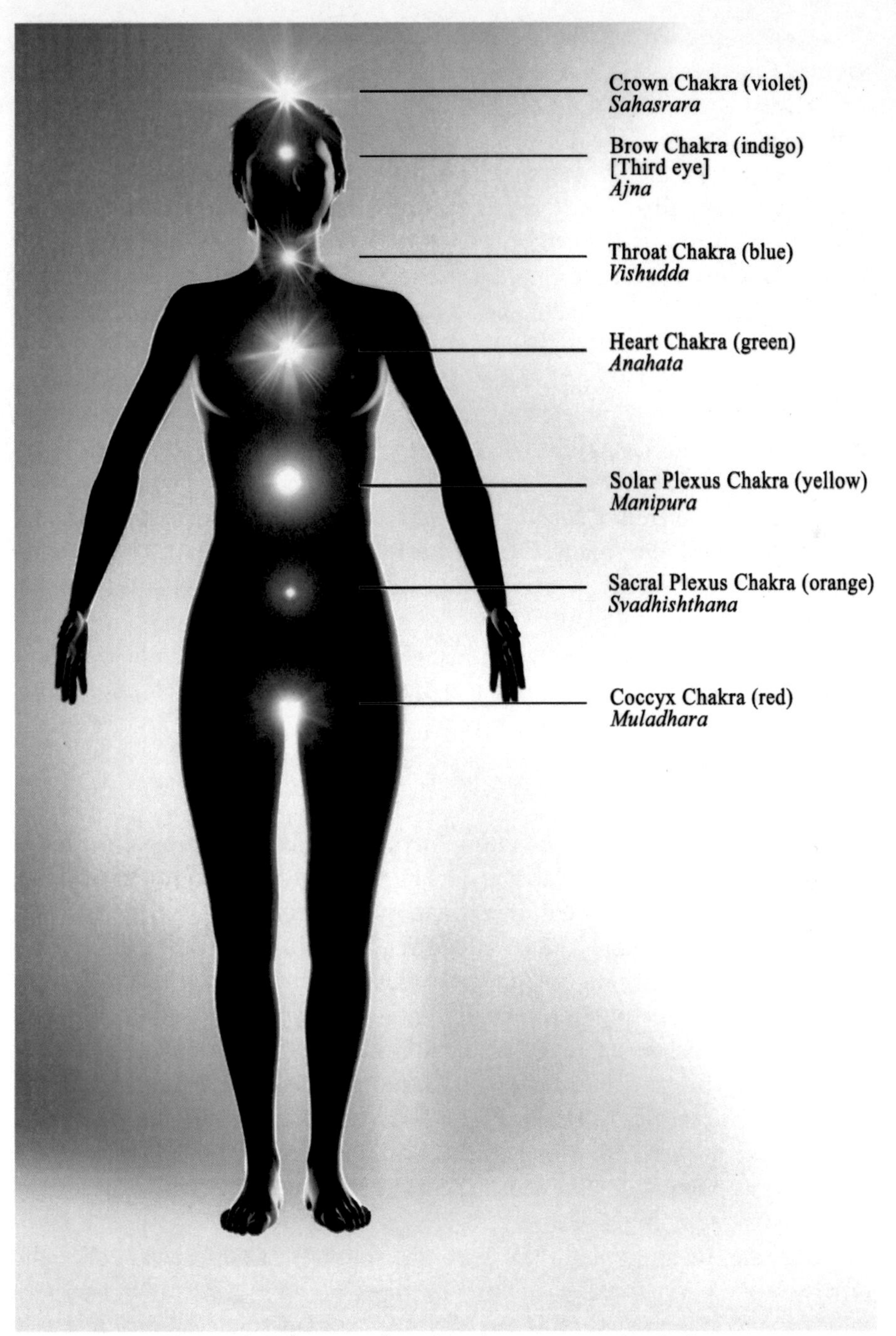

Figure 3. Diagram showing the seven main chakras

The first, or Coccyx Chakra, is at the base of the spine. The second, or Sacrum Chakra, is just above the sexual organs. The third, or Solar Plexus Chakra, is just above the navel. The fourth, or Heart Chakra, is at the heart centre. The fifth, or Throat Chakra, is situated by the larynx. The sixth, or Brow Chakra, is located just above the nose in the centre of the forehead. This is also known as the Third Eye and has often been associated with psychic or clairvoyant vision. The seventh, or Crown Chakra, is situated at the top of the head. When this and all the other chakras are fully open and operational, total enlightenment (all knowledge and wisdom) and union with the Absolute is possible.

As a student of Raja Yoga Meditation back in 1973, it was the opening of my third eye chakra that stimulated my psychic faculties into 'seeing' into some of the other dimensions of the Universe (spirit worlds). At the time, I was sidetracked by becoming fascinated with this phenomenon and wanted to study it in greater detail from a scientific standpoint. And, as you are now aware, I did just that, and over many years proved for myself the reality of life after death. But meditation on higher levels of consciousness is still the main interest in my quest for Truth.

We will not be dwelling on the philosophy of the chakra system here as there are many informative books on the subject (See *Bibliography – Meditation and Chakras*).

Summary

After years of devoted meditation, many students find that their mind is stilled to such a degree that they can achieve a state of serenity, love, peace and harmony that they would never have thought possible. They will still be aware of sitting in a chair or cross-legged on the floor, but will experience a different state of consciousness to the 'normal' everyday thinking and talking that we call 'wide awake'. Eventually they will be able to meditate on their own with confidence, and enter a near blissful state from which they will not wish to be disturbed. It is the mastery of shutting out the five physical senses, stemming the ceaseless chatter of the mind, and understanding the process of 'going within' to find and make contact with their real self – their very soul – the Overself. They will have found their true spiritual centre and experienced the oneness and unity of all life.

Prayer and meditation are based on the Spiritual Law of Love, Peace and Harmony and compliment each other like pepper and salt. Prayer is talking to the Absolute and meditation is the Absolute 'talking' to us. It's just a simple two-way communication system with our spiritual 'Parent'. When our ego has been silenced, our Overself can make contact with the Absolute! That is how the Absolute 'speaks' to us – in the *silence* of meditation! All the while we are *noisy* and, via our five physical senses, become preoccupied with the trappings of materialism, we will 'hear' and experience *nothing!*

When we read of spiritual masters, gurus, mystics or prophets of old going out into the 'wilderness' or into the mountains to pray and meditate, they did so for a very good reason – to find peace and quiet away from crowds and the distractions of noise and turmoil so that they could be alone with their God. God's universal language is the 'bliss' of unimaginable, unconditional Love – *in silence*. This is one of life's most profound 'secrets' and fundamental *spiritual* Truths practised by devout Buddhists, Hindus, Sikhs, Sufis, and all who teach enlightenment (God Consciousness) through meditation.

If this chapter has given you food for thought, or even encouraged you to pray or learn meditation, then another piece of the puzzle can be fitted. We can now continue our quest and investigate the phenomenon of healing.

Peace is the most important thing in our life. Meditation not only provides you peace, but also lets you be in touch with your inner self. The purpose of life for human beings is not just to pursue one's 'worldly' life but to realise one's True Self. It is for us to evolve from 'ego' existence to Self-Awakened human beings. It is not a difficult task to achieve once we learn meditation.

Buddha Maitreya (Koji Takeuchi)

13 Healing – Does It Work?

This is the great error of our day in the treatment of the human body, that physicians first separate the soul from the body.
Plato 429 – 348 BC (Greek philosopher)

How can a complete stranger place their hands on or over a sick person and see them recover? That was the question that baffled me. In 1968, my mother's sixtieth year, her hip was x–rayed and the joint found to be virtually non-existent due to the corrosive action of osteoarthritis. At that time replacement artificial hip joints were in their infancy and, according to her doctor, were 'more kill than cure'. My mother was a very strong and active lady, who had been in business most of her working life, could do simple car and house D.I.Y, garden all day, dance all night and still have energy to spare. But the one thing she couldn't cope with was the pain in her hip that reduced her to tears from time to time.

One such occasion found her in excruciating pain, trying to hide the tears whilst serving a customer in the village shop that she and my father owned. 'What's the matter Elsie?' asked the customer, 'You don't look too good.' 'I don't know where to put myself with this pain,' mother replied, 'the doctor can't do anything for me, the painkillers aren't very effective and the hospital physiotherapy just makes it worse. I'm at my wits end.' 'Have you ever thought about Spiritual Healing?' asked the customer. 'No,' mother replied, 'but I'll try anything to get rid of this pain.'

The customer gave details of a healer in Watford who had healed her and many of her friends of complaints, that according to doctors, they would 'just have to live with'. The following evening my parents set off on the half-hour drive to Watford to keep an appointment with John the healer.

John was a middle-aged gentleman with a regular daytime job. He had no medical knowledge whatsoever and gave healing in the evenings and weekends. He was not unduly concerned with the 'complaint' and simply talked about life in general whilst putting his hands over my mother's hip.

Six visits later, my mother was completely free of pain and only suffered slight twinges if she over-did the dancing or gardening. I ribbed her that it must have been auto-suggestion. 'John never suggested anything; he talked mostly about gardening and holidays; *and* he never charged, so we took him and his wife some tea and coffee.' 'Did he ask you to have faith?' I asked. 'No he didn't – I went because I was desperate!' was the reply.

For the next 10 years my mother remained free of pain and it was only the trauma and grief of my father's death in 1978 that caused it to partially return. In 1981 she had an artificial hip replacement, as it was by then a routine operation.

Healing Apprenticeship

As previously mentioned; in 1973, I joined the Healing Sanctuary of Michael and Vera Gardner-Jones for training in the 'laying on of hands', or Spiritual Healing as it was commonly known. We were taught to place our hands about 2.5cm (one inch) over a volunteer patient's head and gently scan the body using them like a metal detector, but instead of searching for metal we were searching for cold emanations or 'icy blasts' as Mike called them. This was where the *problem* was, he explained, not necessarily where the *pain* was. An aching knee, for example, could be the result of lower back problems, and it was impressed upon us that healing treated the *cause* not the *effect* (symptoms).

Whilst detecting cold emanations on volunteers we were instructed to leave our hands in that particular area until the emanations diminished or ceased. The patient would often feel tremendous heat from our hands, which was usually accompanied by a 'pins and needles' tingling sensation in our fingertips. This confirmed that the healing energies were being absorbed. Most volunteers reported that their discomfort had gone, which gave us confidence to learn more and not doubt our ability. 'Go home and practise on the cat,' Mike would joke. 'They don't put up mental barriers like humans do.' We didn't have a cat, but I did practise on our dog and, much to their amusement, the rest of the family!

I have given healing a chapter in its own right, not just because it played a big part in my life, but because healing with the hands is based on love and compassion – the principle Law of Life. This is *natural* healing and many a mother has healed her child with her hands and not realised. By touching fellow human beings or animals in that way we are imparting love, which channels the natural healing energies of the Universe into a sick person or animal, thereby stimulating and kick-starting the patient's immune system and psychic energy centres (chakras).

These energies have been known by many cultures. To the Indians they are known as Prana and to the Orientals as Chi. The history of hands-on healing goes back at least 4,000 years and was practiced by most of the ancient cultures in places like China, India, Tibet, Egypt and Greece. The Native American Indians were also well aware of its potential centuries ago. In the Western world, many people are denied the experience because of naïve attitudes and misconceptions. Many think it is weird and freaky, mainly because they have been conditioned into believing that being cut with a scalpel or dosed up on prescription drugs is natural.

The Universe is sustained and energised by countless frequencies of harmonious energy patterns emanating from a single source – *The Absolute*. When we live in peace and harmony with ourselves and Nature we receive these energies automatically, thereby remaining healthy and full of energy. But if we become anxious, fearful, stressed, angry, or adopt other negative lifestyles, then we cut ourselves off from these energy fields. We become 'out-of-sorts', run down, tired and depleted with the inevitable danger to our mental and physical health. Dis-ease (disharmony) of the mind eventually leads to disease of the body, which will be accelerated if a poor diet is part of our lifestyle.

Many times I have read in the media of healers referring to their 'powers'. A healer has no power any more than a light bulb has. A light bulb shines when plugged into a power source. Healing energies should flow *through* a healer and not *from* them if they are connected to the 'Power Source'. If healers channel their own magnetic energy then they will become depleted as well as absorbing the patient's symptoms, all of which can have dire consequences for the healer. Many an inexperienced healer has been temporarily laid low through this costly mistake.

The terminology of healing can seem confusing when some call it faith healing and others psychic, holistic or spiritual healing. Love, peace and harmony heal, and are therefore spiritual in essence, so my personal preference is the term spiritual healing. In all my years of involvement I have never known faith come into the equation. How does one ask a sick baby, child or animal to have faith? If faith was required, then babies, animals, agnostics and atheists wouldn't be healed – and numerous numbers are. Some people are so sick they have lost faith in everyone and everything – God, doctors and even life itself – and visiting a healer is often a last resort.

Orthodox Medicine

I have questioned many who turned to alternative healing methods as to why they did so. Their answers were invariably the same:

- Hospital waiting times can be too long for serious medical treatment, thereby causing anxiety, additional suffering and sometimes the premature death of many patients.
- Unnecessary stress is put on sick people who have had their operations cancelled at the last minute due to a shortage of beds and other factors. Many have been sent home after making an effort to get to the hospital.

- The side effects from certain prescription drugs seem to be worse than the illness.
- Patients require additional drugs to counteract the side effects of the original drugs.
- They have become addicted to their prescription drugs and want to get off them.
- They feel that they are guinea pigs for testing new drugs.
- They suspect that the prescription drug industry is more money orientated than patient orientated, and that the drug industry is only interested in alleviating symptoms rather than curing, because a *cured* customer is a *lost* customer.
- The medical profession can do nothing for their illness or complaint and have been told that they will just have to live with it or been given a short time to live.
- Being treated for the wrong illness due to a wrong diagnosis.
- Their medical treatment has made the condition worse.
- Many elderly patients feel that they are given a low priority rating for treatment (age discrimination).

It is always advisable to consult a doctor for *any* health problem before visiting a healer or considering other alternative therapies. From personal experience, I have nothing but praise for my local GPs. They are dedicated, wonderful people, and I have got to know many of them whilst sitting on Health related committees, working together for the wellbeing of the town. And in many of the hospitals I have visited, nurses have shown care and devotion beyond the call of duty. But the problems facing many of them seem to be unacceptable 'Targets' and the typical inadequacies of a system creaking at the seams, leaving them overworked, understaffed, underpaid and having to cope in outdated and unhygienic buildings.

Many alternative therapies, including spiritual healing, have been frequently criticised by the medical profession for being unregulated or denounced as 'quackery'. But spiritual healing does have the regulating bodies of The National Federation of Spiritual Healers, The Harry Edwards HEHS Certification *and* a proven track record over thousands of years.

The National Health Service (NHS) has itself been the subject of intense media criticism over the past decade. Hospital hygiene infringements causing the deaths of thousands of patients infected with MRSA and C difficile; patients dying from adverse reactions to prescribed drugs and the inhumane treatment of many elderly hospital patients – who often die of neglect – have topped a long inexcusable list. Is it any wonder that legal claims for medical negligence are at an all time high?

> We are told that we have the brightest and the best trained doctors in the world looking after us. So why is Western health care now the third leading cause of death in our nations today?
> *Phillip Day (Health Wars)*

To be fair, such criticisms could equally apply to many hospitals throughout the world – private or otherwise. Private hospitals have also been sued for medical negligence.

Perhaps it is because they are seeing the inadequacies of the present health system, or maybe they are becoming more open-minded, but many GPs are now referring patients to Spiritual and Reiki Healers. Some hospitals are also allowing registered healers to attend patients in the wards. This would be in the best interests of the National Health Service as it would speed patient recovery and, in many cases, avoid surgery or drugs, thus saving much needed funds.

Most sick people don't care who they go to as long as they get prompt attention, are treated like human beings and not a commodity, the diagnosis is correct, the treatment works without side effects and they are cured. But, having said that, wouldn't it be better to investigate the *reasons* why people become sick in the first place and try to eradicate the *cause* rather than the *effect* (symptoms)? We all recognise that prevention is better and cheaper than cure, so it would seem logical to eradicate the 'permitted' and *known* dangerous and carcinogenic chemicals and other toxic substances in our food chain, cosmetics, teeth fillings and cleaning products. Wouldn't this be more practical and common sense rather than spending billions on research to cure the diseases that these chemicals and toxins cause? Now is that too easy – or am I missing the point somewhere?

A Public Appearance

In May 1973 Mike received an invitation to attend a healing demonstration at Maidenhead Town Hall that was to be given by one of the greatest spiritual healers of our time – Harry Edwards. Mike, who had known Harry for many years, asked if I would like to accompany him as a guest healer on the stage with Harry.

After the war, Harry Edwards became world renowned for his spiritual healing and treated tens of thousands of patients, including members of the royal family and prominent members of the government. He appeared on television, wrote books and put spiritual healing on the map, making it acceptable and accessible to vast numbers of people. It was also in May 1973 that 5,000 people packed the Royal Albert Hall in London to witness the world's largest public healing demonstration given by Harry Edwards to celebrate his 80th birthday. That was why I was honoured and humbled to be on the same stage with such a marvellous man.

On that memorable evening Maidenhead Town Hall was packed to capacity. Mike and I were among the dozen healers sitting at the back of the large stage behind Harry Edwards, and St. John's Ambulance personnel were in attendance to escort various patients onto the stage. Harry had particularly asked for volunteers that had visible handicaps or impediments so that any healing would be evident to witnesses.

There were handicapped people in wheelchairs that had not walked for years, as well as the deaf, the blind and arthritic. One by one they were assisted onto the stage. Some had to be carried and placed on the chair in front of Harry. He attuned himself with his spirit helpers and placed his hands on or over the patients, often moving their locked arms or legs within a minute of commencement. Many who walked on crutches left the stage unaided without them. The totally blind could count the number of fingers held in front of them, the totally deaf could hear faint sounds and those with arthritis could walk without pain. Many of the patients and their loved ones were crying tears of joy.

We were asked to raise our hands to the 'surrender' position during the demonstrations to project healing energies to the patient. To our surprise, an intense burning sensation emanated from the centre of our palms together with a 'pins and needles' sensation in our fingers. When the healing stopped, so did these sensations. The moment Harry put his hands on another patient the energies once again emanated from our palms and fingers.

That evening, we were privileged to witness many wonderful and almost instantaneous healings. There was no mass hysteria, no shouting of 'Alleluias' or 'Praise the Lord'. No mass hypnotism with patients falling over and convulsing on the ground. No autosuggestion or fake 'patients' primed beforehand. No ego-orientated healer in an expensive suit, bedecked with a gold watch, bracelets or large crucifix. Just a humble old man working with rolled up shirtsleeves in an incredible silent atmosphere of love and compassion that will live with me for the rest of my life.

The evening was not without humour. As assistant healers we had been asked to wear white coats. So not owning any, I asked a friend who worked for Express Dairies if we could borrow some. This was duly organised, but we noticed that the initials E D were embroidered on the top pockets. After the demonstrations, and still wearing the white coats, we were walking towards the exit when a gentleman who had been sitting in the audience stopped us and asked what the initials E D stood for. Quick as a flash, Mike replied, 'Etheric Doctor'. We collapsed with laughter, but the gentleman, unfortunately, and understandably, didn't appreciate the joke and replied in all seriousness, 'Oh I see. Thank you very much.'

My Healing

During the summer of 1973, I lifted a heavy slab of concrete from the top of a coalbunker and felt a searing pain shoot up the left side of my body. I dropped the slab and tried to make my way to the bungalow but found I could hardly put one foot in front of the other without excruciating pain in my torso. I realised I had done something foolish and shuffled precariously to the doorway. My wife Sheila helped me indoors and immediately rang for the doctor. He arrived an hour later to find me laying on the floor in agony. Having pressed and prodded me in various places he diagnosed severely strained muscles and tendons on my left side.

The doctor advised that I take painkillers and give it a week to sort itself out. The thought of having to endure the pain for a few days didn't appeal to me. 'Why don't we go to the Sanctuary and see if we can get you some healing?' announced Sheila. Brilliant, why didn't I think of that? So with great effort and still in pain, I managed to get into the car and was driven the couple of miles to the Sanctuary.

'Sit sideways on that chair and relax as best you can,' said Steve, an ex-policeman and one of the resident healers. Relax? It felt as if a Samurai sword had been plunged into my side and twisted! Steve scanned my torso with one hand in the front and the other at my back. 'There it is,' he said, 'I've got it.' His hands were directly over the painful area and the heat coming from them was incredible. Suddenly, it felt as if a hand had gone inside me and moved some of my internal bits and pieces. The pain and nausea feeling went immediately, just as Steve remarked, 'That's shifted it.'

What a blessed relief that was. Within half an hour of entering the Sanctuary we were saying goodbye to Steve. I walked to the car unaided and totally free of pain. The next day I went to work as usual. As a freelance designer I couldn't afford to lose the time or money. During the next few days the left side of my torso came out in the most horrendous bruise I had ever seen. Thankfully, the pain and discomfort never returned. That was my first experience of receiving healing, and it was good that I had been on the receiving end for a change because it taught me its benefits of removing or alleviating pain.

Tears

From then on there was no turning back. I visited the Sanctuary to help with the healing whenever I could and some of the results were extremely humbling. It was the first time I had seen so many terminally ill patients who had been given just months to live and, unfortunately, not all could be helped. Many times the sick and suffering that came to the Sanctuary brought tears to my eyes. At the time, I couldn't relate to a God that 'allowed' such grief. Mike informed me that I would be no good as a healer if I let my emotions control me. 'If doctors and nurses behaved like you they would be emotional wrecks within a few months,' he said. He was right, but it made me determined to try and understand why we, particularly in the western world, suffered from such serious health issues.

The New Sanctuary

The Sanctuary garden was very picturesque with its meandering trout stream and little bridge dominating the scene. Mike had long had this dream of building a new Meditation and Healing Sanctuary overlooking the stream. He had recently purchased an old prefab – one of those temporary buildings put up after the war to house bombed-out families. For what he had envisaged it was perfect – but there was a stumbling block. The local council had twice refused planning permission on the grounds that it 'would not be in keeping with the area'.

As a design engineer, drawing plans was my forte, so after reconnaissance of the area new plans were drawn and resubmitted with a letter. It simply stated that I did not understand what they meant by 'would not be in keeping with the area', when diagonally opposite the sanctuary, behind some trees, was a sewage treatment plant and 300 metres up the road was the corporation 'rubbish tip'. It was made clear that 'it would probably be the only thing of beauty in the area.' Planning permission was soon granted!

Volunteers erected the new building – which looked just the part. Its main room, which seated 60 people, would be used for seminars and workshops. There was also a small kitchen and a healing and meditation room. On a beautiful sunny day on the 12th April 1975, Harry Edwards officially dedicated the new Healing and Meditation Sanctuary.

A Friend is Healed

At the time, I was technical director of an engineering design company in Watford, and one of my fellow directors, Ray Gaines, mentioned that he had a potentially serious ear problem necessitating an imminent operation. Ray knew of my involvement at the sanctuary, so I suggested that he might consider having healing on the offending ear. Here are Ray's words:

I had suffered from an ear infection for several years and was given drops as medication whenever it flared up. Eventually, the severity was such that I was in excruciating pain. Upon visiting my doctor he simply prescribed antibiotics and more drops. The pain became so severe that I returned to my local surgery prior to my next appointment. The doctor took one look at my ear and sent me to the hospital.

The Ear, Nose and Throat (ENT) consultant diagnosed a mastoid and booked me in for an operation. He told me that there was a high probability of losing my hearing in that ear. I know much worse things happen to people, but I found the prospect of being totally deaf in one ear quite alarming.

It was at this time, in 1974, that Brian suggested I visit Michael Gardner-Jones' Healing Sanctuary in Chesham, so with nothing to lose, I went. Michael was not what I perceived to be a typical healer or man of God, but a lovely man none-the-less and totally dedicated to his cause. After a few hilarious jokes, Michael placed his hands on my head and neck and told me that although I would 'go under the knife' I would definitely ***not*** *lose my hearing. From then on I cheered up and fully believed that I would be OK and went to the sanctuary a few more times for healing from Michael and Brian prior to surgery.*

After the operation, and with my head heavily bandaged, I put the telephone to my ear and heard the dialing tone. This meant that despite having only half an eardrum, my hearing was working normally. During a routine examination a few days later, the junior doctor called the surgeon, and both were amazed to see how quickly it had healed, allowing the stitches to be removed.

It was extremely pleasing to see Ray's hearing back to normal and heal so quickly. To this day he has had no more ear trouble. He is also proud to mention his father's healing experience many years before:

As a child, I often remember my dad lying on the settee perspiring profusely with a serious migraine headache and mum applying a cold flannel to his forehead. Despite the misery of having several migraines in a week, nothing cured them, and taking as many as fifty strong painkillers over the same period, all he could expect was a slight numbing of his nervous system.

At the time, dad implied that he was an agnostic, and when it was suggested that he went to a spiritual healer he dismissed the idea. Eventually, an aunt persuaded him to go to a sanctuary. He, like many others, decided to go on the basis that he had nothing to lose – but with some trepidation. Dad went to see a Mr and Mrs Worjer at Cheam, who were advertising in the Psychic News and were practicing healers in the early 1960s. On his first visit he was told that he would be cured but would require a total of six visits, which incurred the traditional laying on of hands and prayers.

From that period, until he died at the age of 82 in 1997, he never suffered another migraine. He was no longer an agnostic and would pray nightly to the power that cured him of that terrible pain.

Some Natural Healers

The months rolled by and I finally came to terms with sickness and disease in the world and its manifold causes, such as chemical toxins, junk food diets, smoking, prolonged negative emotions and other lifestyle habits outlined in Chapter 2 *(Health – A Precious Gem).*

As my name spread on the 'grapevine', healing became a big part of my life. Assisting Mike when he visited patients in their homes was also humbling, seeing many of them improve or recover over the weeks. There were, of course, the inevitable few who never seemed to get much benefit. This caused me some sleepless nights until Mike, in his infinite wisdom, stressed that we shouldn't be too concerned with who is healed and who is not. 'Just put your hands on them,' he used to say, 'and leave it to God and consequence.'

Many patients that have been healed often become healers themselves and tend to pursue spiritual pastimes such as meditation. It was noticeable with some that healing raised their consciousness to a spiritual level, often developing within them a love and compassion that they had never before experienced. They felt the desire to give back to life because life had given to them, and helping fellow sufferers gave this opportunity.

Virtually all of us have the healing ability in one degree or another. Like clairvoyance it is a part of Nature. Anyone with an inkling of love and compassion has the ability to lay their hands upon the sick and see improvement. And I have no doubt that you also have that ability, because you would have put this book down long ago if you didn't have a loving and compassionate nature. Let me give you some examples of natural healing ability and you will see what I mean. Let's take the case of Eve O'Sullivan who came into healing through tragedy:

It was a lovely summer's day on June 12th 1969, and I had just started to walk away from my house when a neighbor – whose 13-year-old son had recently been knocked down and killed – confronted me. Unbeknown to me, his intense grief had caused him to be mentally unbalanced, and he said he was going to kill me because my 13-year-old son was still alive and his was dead.

He was brandishing a large cane that he raised into the air and brought crashing down onto my head. The blow knocked me to the ground and dazed me and, as I looked up, he hit me again and again, each time on the right side of my head. I could feel my life-force ebbing away. Suddenly, a voice, very loud and clear in my head, said, 'Grab the stick, if it comes down again you will die.'

I was covered in blood and could hardly see, but somehow I managed to roll away on my right side, and as the stick came down again I grabbed it and pulled myself up. By this time others were on the scene and apprehended my neighbour.

I had to have intensive hospital treatment, but unfortunately I was left with a very bad memory and severe migraines that the doctors could do nothing for. A year later, in June 1970, a friend told me that a healer and medium by the name of Michael Gardner- Jones was appearing at the Queensway Hall in Hemel Hempstead. And it was there that Michael laid his hands on my head. I had an instant healing, and from that day onward I had no more memory problems or migraines.

Michael told me that I was a potential healer. I went to his sanctuary in Chesham and over the years I became involved in some wondrous healings. I am so humbled to say that I developed an understanding and compassion for others, and that is the true meaning of healing – the greatest of all love.

It was at the Chesham sanctuary in 1973 where I met Eve and witnessed her wonderful healing ability. And since her own remarkable healing in 1970, with love, compassion and humility, despite a personal life of hardship and suffering, Eve always put the needs of others first. Indeed, a truly remarkable and spiritual lady who deserves a standing ovation when she eventually returns to the spiritual planes.

In 1976, I was working in an engineering company near Aylesbury, and one morning a colleague, Joan Double, came into my office extremely upset. Upon enquiring why, she informed me that her Basset hound 'Buck' was very ill with Distemper, and according to the vet, not expected to live much longer. Joan was a very loving and compassionate person, so I knew that she would be a good healer. I explained that when she got home she could put her hands on 'Buck' and ask for healing in the name of love. Joan continues the story:

Brian advised that at 6pm every evening I should stroke 'Buck' downwards from the direction of his head for 10 minutes. Whilst stroking, I was not to allow my hand to touch his coat but hover above it. This I did each evening for a week. At the start of the healing our poor dog just lay there, and as I stroked him I could feel my hand getting hotter and hotter until it was burning up. In my 'agony' I wanted to snatch it away, but Brian had warned me of this heat sensation so I persevered.

On the second day after I had completed the healing, 'Buck' lifted his head and seemed to give me a grateful look. That evening he drank a full dish of milk. From then on 'Buck' proceeded to progress in his recovery and by the end of the week was again wagging his tail and running around the house!

On the Friday of the same week I had an appointment with the vet in Wendover who had told me to expect the worst, but if the dog was still alive to bring him to the surgery. The vet just couldn't believe that it was the same dog he had seen the previous week. He hastily checked his notes to make sure his original diagnosis was correct. All the symptoms proved that 'Buck' had indeed contracted Distemper.

The vet was astonished (apparently Beagles don't usually recover from Distemper) and called his colleague for a second opinion. He confirmed that 'Buck' was cleared of Distemper and had been restored to his former inquisitive self and that he had no explanation for the recovery. I told him that I had and informed him what had transpired. He was very impressed and said that he had heard of these 'miracle cures' and congratulated me on the success of 'Buck's' recovery.

I would also add that Brian's trust in me gave me the confidence to carry out what he advised me to do, and I know that at 6 o'clock every evening for a week, he was linked in with me in healing prayer. To the joy of our family, 'Buck' lived for another three years, and to this day I still recount the story of our little 'miracle'.

This is an excellent example of a natural healer who, for the first time, healed a very sick animal. It was certainly not a question of faith on the part of the dog. Joan put her hands over him because she knew that 'Buck' would have died if she hadn't. Unfortunately, Joan never pursued her healing gift.

My Father's Illness

In the summer of 1977, my father was diagnosed as having an 'inoperable tumour' on one of his lungs. 'A typical smoker's cancer' according to the surgeon, and there was nothing they could do about it. My mother was heartbroken when she was told that my father had about 18 months to live. Emotionally, it didn't do my father any favours either. The news came like a bolt out of the blue when I received the early morning telephone call. Strangely enough I was not unduly concerned as I felt that the condition would respond to healing in the early stages. My father and I were very close and I loved him dearly. Although he never looked 69-years-of-age, apart from the lung problem, he was extremely fit, so the thought of him going into one of the spirit worlds prematurely never entered my head.

For the past four years I had been laying my hands on sick people and, in the majority of cases, seeing excellent results, so I naively thought that The Absolute (God) owed me a 'favour'. Looking back, I realise how ignorant I was trying to curry favour with the powers that be for purely selfish reasons.

Over the weeks my father received healing at every available opportunity, either from Mike and others at the sanctuary, from healers at Hitchin Spiritualist Church or myself. On one occasion, with my hands placed either side of my father's rib cage, I clearly saw the Zulu warrior that Fred had seen during our first meeting at the Sanctuary. Although I had previously seen the Zulu, even long enough to sketch him, this time, words were communicated. 'I am Mubutu and will help with the healing' he said, fading from my vision. Rightly or wrongly I interpreted this to be a good omen.

Although my father received regular hospital checkups they were surprised that he didn't need prescribed painkillers. But twelve months after the original diagnosis, still free of pain, my father had got noticeably thinner, and when he could no longer keep food down we suspected the worst. He eventually resembled a living skeleton and was now half his original bodyweight of 102 kg (16 stone) and encountering breathing difficulties. Due to the brittle bone phase of the disease, the final indignation was breaking an arm whilst trying to get out of bed.

My father had paid a terrible price for being addicted to a notorious and lethal drug that kills millions every year and yet is openly on sale to the public – cigarettes. And the irony is, that almost one in every two smokers is willing to risk this style of dying. It's neither pleasant for the sufferer nor their loved ones who have to watch. On the 14th December 1978, Dad's heart gave out and he 'died' in mum's arms. She was devastated, and I felt that the spirit world and The Absolute had let us down. I was hurt and angry, and from that moment, decided that I would do no more healing.

In accordance with mother's wishes, Mike took my father's funeral service at the local Crematorium, and we later scattered the ashes in the crematorium rose gardens. To this day, thanks to numerous experiences and subsequent knowledge, I have never felt the need to revisit the site.

It was now the spring of 1979 and, against the wishes of Mike and Vera, I still abstained from healing sessions. As a committee member of Chesham Spiritualist Church I felt obliged to put in an appearance from time to time. The following Sunday evening the medium was Clive Daniels, and not having seen him before I was extremely impressed with his 'survival' evidence. The opportunity to converse with him afterwards never occurred, so I decided to arrange a private sitting and subsequently obtained his telephone number from the booking secretary.

The appointment was made for the following week at Kenton Spiritualist Church near Harrow where Clive was president – the booking being in my first name only. 'You're Brian I presume?' asked Clive, as I walked through the door, 'take a seat and place your hands on the table.' I did as he asked, whereupon he sat opposite and placed his hands on top of mine. Closing his eyes and taking a deep breath he said, 'You don't need evidence of a life after death, you have the clairvoyant ability.' This was followed by another deep breath. 'I have a very tall Zulu here who wishes to speak with you,' continued Clive, and I knew straight away that it was Mubutu. 'Why are you not doing the healing?' he asked, in a strange voice. 'Well you should know,' I replied, in a sarcastic tone.

This immediately invoked a stern reply. 'Who are *you* to play God? Who are *you* to decide who lives and who dies? Do you think that no *other* has lost a loved one from your world?' And in a reassuring manner, Mubutu added, 'do not concern yourself – all is well with your Earth Father.' I took that to mean that dad was OK in his new abode. The voice continued in a much softer tone, 'You have many questions – that is good – but you must first *earn* the answers.' There was a long pause, then, in a reassuring manner, Mubutu added, 'It is our wish that you continue with the healing – there is much work to do. Our love is always with you. Do not fear and strive to be at peace within yourself.'

There was an even longer pause, and I quite expected Clive to continue, but he gave another big sigh, opened his eyes and said, 'That's all young man. There's no charge, but if you would like to make a donation the plate is over there.' I sat and stared for a few seconds, and can remember thinking, 'So that's it then? No direct message from my father, just a five-minute ear-bashing from a Zulu!'

The 40-minute journey home gave me much food for thought. At the time, I was only thinking of my father, and in no way did I expect Mubutu the Zulu healer, of whom only Fred and I were aware. But what hit home was the message. Mubutu was right, I so wanted my father to live, and instead of remaining detached with the healing and leaving it to 'God and consequence'. I had been personally and emotionally involved with a patient. A patient whose time on Earth was due to expire and the healing was purely to alleviate his pain. As many healers have since told me, it's a hard and painful lesson to learn. But I still wondered if my hurt would allow me to return to healing?

Healed By a Dog

Weeks later, whilst taking our dog for a walk, a lady walking towards me suddenly stopped and said, 'Brian? – Brian Sadler?' 'Yes,' I replied, 'do I know you?' 'Several years ago you gave me healing at Chesham Spiritualist Church,' she replied. And then came the crunch question! 'Do you still give healing?' she asked. I was taken aback, and about to say no, when she continued, 'I was wondering if you would give my dog some healing. She's crippled with arthritis in her rear legs and can hardly walk. It would break my heart to have her put down.' Her request took the wind out of my sails. How on Earth could I have refused an animal in distress, especially a dog? I love them to bits! Without realising, I agreed to see the dog that same week!

On the evening in question I was shown into the lounge, and lying on the floor by the fireside was a beautiful golden-haired Retriever. She attempted to get up as I approached but abandoned the idea when it hurt. 'Let Brian give you some healing,' said the owner as she patted the dog. I knelt by the side of this lovely, elderly animal and asked Mubutu to guide my hands in the name of love. As I scanned her body near her hind quarters, the dog lifted its head and gave me the most amazing eye to eye contact, just as words came into my head that said, 'Welcome back to healing – we knew you would never refuse an animal.' Tears rolled down my cheeks as I felt the emotional hurt and anger drain away. I had gone to give an endearing animal healing – but she had healed me!

I visited the Retriever twice more in the coming weeks and, thankfully, the healing relieved most of her pain. So much so, that she was once more, able to go for short walks with her owner. It was the best that could be done for her as, unfortunately, healing cannot alleviate old age.

A Golden Light

In 1979 I visited Kathy, an 80-year-old acquaintance who was in hospital awaiting an operation for a diagnosed stomach tumour. Kathy was a devout Roman Catholic and had been psychic since childhood. She had asked if I would give her some healing prior to the operation as she was extremely concerned about having major surgery at her age.

Sitting at her bedside, I asked her to close her eyes and meditate on peace and love. Placing my hands just above her stomach – which was swollen to the size of a heavily pregnant woman – I asked for healing in the name of love and light.

Almost immediately, a brilliant pulsing golden light enveloped us both, with an energy of love that was virtually indescribable. My hands were burning as if they were on fire, coupled with the feeling that we were floating into the air – bed and all. How long this lasted I cannot recall, but as the golden light faded and we 'floated' back down again, I knew that everything was going to be OK. 'That was the most amazing thing I have ever experienced,' said Kathy. 'I feel so calm and peaceful now,' she added, 'and everything's going to be all right, isn't it?' She then went on to describe how she felt she was floating in the air in a golden mist vibrating with love energy!

Kathy had the operation the next day, and the surgeons removed a tumour the size of a rugby ball from her stomach. It was sent away for biopsy and, thankfully, found to be benign. Within a few days she was sent home and managed to walk a little with the aid of a frame. One week later the scar had virtually healed and she could walk around the block with the aid of a stick. Her surgeon was amazed at her progress and, to be honest, so was I!

A New Beginning

Over the next few months, if you recall, my personal life fell apart when Sheila admitted that she had met someone else and would leave in the January of 1981. This was another body blow that emotionally put me on my knees, but this time it didn't stop me from giving healing – it was just a different type of hurt.

By the beginning of February 1981 I had met Patricia, who was very much into healing and meditation, which gave us an immediate rapport. Over the months our friendship blossomed.

In the Hands of God and Consequence

Previously, I mentioned that Patricia had an ongoing intermittent health problem, but for obvious reasons I have reserved the outcome for this chapter. For several months prior to our meeting, Patricia had been plagued with bouts of nausea and stomach pain that had baffled her doctor. He thought it was Hepatitis and treated her accordingly.

In May 1981 Patricia collapsed and was rushed to hospital where they diagnosed a gallstone problem. This they eased, put her on a waiting list for an operation and sent her home. Luckily, the company for whom Patricia was working had an employee's medical scheme. Within a couple of weeks she was in a private hospital having surgery for gallstones that had lodged in her main bile duct. Unfortunately, serious complications arose due to medical negligence causing bile from the bile duct to leak into the lungs. This caused her excruciating pain and severe breathing difficulties.

An early morning telephone call from the hospital requested my presence due to the seriousness of the problem. When I arrived, Patricia was screaming with pain and being continually shouted at by the doctor to *'breathe'*. I was informed that the situation was not good and that the next twenty-four hours would be crucial. It really was a matter of life and death. I literally called upon all my known spirit helpers to assist if they could. I didn't want to lose Patricia having just found her.

I stayed for the rest of the day and waited by her bedside as she drifted in and out of consciousness making the most frightening sounds whilst trying to breathe. She whispered to me in between gasps saying that she couldn't stand the pain any longer and asked why they weren't doing something? The doctor had given her the maximum allowable painkillers and could do no more. Trying to remain emotionally detached whilst scanning her lung area with my hands was very hard for me, but I realised that I must remain detached if healing energies were to be effective.

Not being a relative, I wasn't allowed to sleep in the hospital and had to go home, but was assured I would be contacted if the situation worsened. That evening I telephoned several friends and asked them if they would send absent (distant) healing thoughts to Patricia at a given time. I could only do my best and really had to leave it in the hands of 'God and consequence' this time. I had learnt my lesson over the death of my father.

Early the next morning I telephoned the hospital for a report and, to my amazement, and theirs, Patricia was sitting up in bed having eaten a little breakfast. They informed me that she was free of pain, in good spirits and breathing normally. Apparently the doctor and nurses were amazed at her rapid recovery, but I was pretty sure I knew the source of the power behind it and said thank you in the right quarters.

I could ill afford more time off work but Patricia's health was more important, and upon arriving at the hospital I was elated to see a smiling Patricia sitting up in bed. 'I have something wonderful to tell you,' she said. Here are her words:

In unbelievable pain I was drifting in and out of sleep all night, but in the early hours I awoke to find myself enveloped in what looked like a swirling blue mist. Within this mist were numerous pairs of hands – too many to count – hovering over me. I felt a tremendous wave of peace, love and wellbeing come over me, and watched in amazement as the hands interacted and moved about my body. The pain and discomfort seemed to melt away, and as the mist and hands dissolved into thin air, I drifted back to sleep. It was daylight when I finally awoke and realised that I was totally free of pain and feeling quite hungry.

I eventually fell in love with, and married, "the guy with the hot hands". I have been privileged to have received healing many times since when the need arose, but the healing experience in the hospital will always be special and I am eternally grateful.

Patricia made a remarkably quick and permanent recovery, and the experience brought us even closer together. Healing has been an intricate part of our lives ever since.

Distance or Absent Healing

Although Patricia's experience could be classed as 'absent healing', I will endeavor to explain the technique. Absent healing is a method of mentally channeling the healing energies to a sick person where the healer is absent and unable to be with the patient. In reality, they are being prayed for in the name of love. The request can be spoken or thought. Distance is not a problem since the energies will automatically go to the patient, even if they are on the other side of the globe. Most healers have a list of names of people and animals requiring distance healing. Friends or relatives of the sick and suffering usually donate these.

Let me give a hypothetical example. Suppose a Mary Smith is ill and on our list then, during a quiet moment, we focus our thoughts on her and say something like, 'In the name of love and light, I (we) ask that Mary Smith be blessed and receive healing.' Then, just leave it to 'God and consequence'. If our list has dozens of names, then all we need do is hold it in our hands and ask of the powers of love and light that healing energies be given to all.

Jeff Watts had this experience when he sent absent healing to his sick brother:

In 1999 my brother was confined to bed having been diagnosed with glandular fever. The doctor told him that he would be ill for at least eight weeks. My brother and I were still living with our parents at the time, so I sat with him for a while. He was very ill and totally depleted in energy. Upon returning to my bedroom, I sat in a meditative state and visualised myself in his room giving him healing. I could feel the love and spiritual energy flowing from me as I surrounded him with it. This experience lasted for about twenty minutes, and when I came back to myself I was totally charged up and refreshed.

My brother slept through the night, and in the morning he got up unaided and walked about. There was no trace of the glandular fever and he appeared to be his usual self, although he did suffer from slight tiredness for a few weeks.

Battery Healing

This is achieved when several people form a linked 'horseshoe' profile with the two end persons touching the patient, thereby completing a circle. This channels the healing energies through the group giving the patient a mega-dose of spiritual energy. This is what happened to June Ives:

About 10 years ago I had made arrangements to visit an Ashram in India, but because I had acute bronchitis at the time, my doctor refused to give me the necessary vaccinations. Over the weeks I tried everything to get rid of the persistent chesty cough, including antibiotics, but nothing seemed to work. I was beginning to despair of ever getting to India because the travel date was fast approaching. It was at that time that Brian and Patricia invited me to one of their philosophical discussion evenings. Because of my annoying cough, I wondered if I should attend, but my hosts offered to put me up for the night so I accepted.

Midway through the evening the discussion got around to spiritual healing, and it was then that Brian suggested that the group try 'battery healing' on me to see if it would alleviate my cough. They formed a partial circle and Brian and Patricia closed it by putting their hands on my head and upper chest. A request for healing in the name of love and the Absolute was then made, and almost immediately an incredible heat permeated my entire body. The peace and tranquility that I felt was just amazing. The healing session lasted for about 15 minutes.

The following Sunday morning I felt a little easier but the cough was still there, so after breakfast I bade Brian and Patricia farewell and drove home. On the Monday morning when I awoke, the cough and chestiness had completely gone – I was delighted. The doctor consequently gave me my jabs and I was able to go to India.

Healing Experiments

Some years ago I made the acquaintance of 70-year-old American parapsychologist and Chemist, Professor Douglas Dean, from Princeton University. He had come to England to attend a healing seminar. A mutual friend brought him to our house and he accepted the invitation to stay the night. We sat up until the early hours listening to Dean's experiences regarding years of research into metaphysics and paranormal subjects.

Apart from life after death, Dean was extremely interested in healing, and had done experiments with world-renowned spiritual healers. One such healer was the late Rose Gladden, whom I had the pleasure of meeting back in the early 1970s. Under laboratory conditions, Dean had asked Gladden to give healing to bottles of ordinary tap water. At random, she held half of the bottles for about 15 minutes at a time and ignored the remainder. The bottles were then numbered, but only Dean knew the 'healed' water samples.

When the 'healed' water samples were tested it was found that the atomic structure of the water was totally different to the untouched water samples. Also, when the samples were used to irrigate potted plants, it was noted that the plants that had received the 'healed' water grew far more profusely than the ones that received the untouched tap water.

On a similar theme, casting our minds back to Chapter 9 (*Love – The Law of Life)*, in his book *The Hidden Messages in Water,* you will recall the remarkable experiments of Dr. Masaru Emoto. He repeatedly noticed that ice crystals formed perfectly when pre-frozen water samples were subjected to love, peace and harmony by way of thoughts, words and music. But when the same water was subjected to thoughts and words of hatred and discordant music, the resulting ice crystals were deformed and almost unrecognizable.

When we consider that our bodies are at least 70 per cent water, we can appreciate what effect negative thoughts, words and actions have upon us compared to those of love, peace and harmony. And absent healing or, with the hands, is simply the channeling of energies of love, peace and harmony into a body made up of 70 per cent water!

Reiki Healing

Reiki healing is another hands-on healing system that channels the Universal life force (Prana, Chi or Ki) into the Chakras, the psychic energy centres of the body. This energy flows through the hands of the healer and balances the Chakras, thus helping to restore natural healing via the immune system. I have also been a recipient of this very relaxing form of healing and discussed its benefits and similarities to spiritual healing with Reiki Masters.

Reiki (*Rei* means universal, and *ki* means life force) was rediscovered and so named by a Japanese teacher Dr Usui over 100 years ago. The Reiki principle is timeless and its history can also be found in the esoteric teachings of ancient Egypt and Tibet.

Psychic Surgery

This form of healing, although rare in the UK, is often practiced in many countries – notably those in South America and the Philippines. Psychic surgery is so named because it entails, in many cases, 'cutting' open the body either, with a knife or a pass of the healer's finger or hand. The hands are then placed inside the body and the offending tumour or growth removed, often with the sight of blood. This may sound gory and incredible, but scientists and doctors from around the globe have studied such healers. Once the fakes have been accounted for, the genuine healers have had amazing testified results.

One of the most famous was the late Jose Pedro de Freitas, the Brazilian healer known internationally as Arigo. For 20 years, prior to his death in 1971, Arigo often treated over 300 people a day in his little wooden shack, accurately diagnosing their symptoms – many terminal – and 'operating' accordingly with an ordinary knife. Virtually all his patients survived. He would even do eye surgery with amazing results. Quite often the 'wounds' healed almost instantaneously with no visible scar tissue. Those he didn't treat were sympathetically told that their time had come and dismissed with a blessing. Arigo, never charged, had no medical knowledge and claimed that he was guided by the voice of a discarnate doctor.

The Philippines has also produced many psychic healers, both fake and genuine, who have also been investigated by international doctors, scientists and researchers. It was from there that two healers came to England to demonstrate their techniques. Michael Collins tells his experience:

In 1979 I was invited to Stansted Hall in Essex to meet Helen and David Elizalde who were Filipino Psychic Surgeons. I witnessed many of their operations over a six-week period. On one occasion I saw David Elizalde wave his hand in the air over a patient's legs and watch the man's hip open up. Clots were extracted, and a metal plate was exposed which the healer took out and held in the air. He then reattached the plate in the hip, and as he took his hand away the opening closed. He wiped it with some cotton wool leaving just a tiny scar. The man later told me that he had found great improvement for his condition.

When it was my turn for 'surgery', David made a cutting motion in the air and my groin opened up in two places either side of my stomach. It felt as if I had been cut with a razor blade even though there wasn't one in his hand. He extracted two large clots of blood, which were placed in a screw-top jar for me to keep, but within half an hour they had totally vanished from the sealed container. The procedure hurt like hell – so if they had been fakes it wouldn't have hurt. The wounds healed with just a hint of a scar. I felt fine and much better for having had the 'operation' for my bowel problem.

There were the usual accusations of fakery thrown at them by the media and the BMA, but I know what I witnessed and experienced was genuine. The Filipinos helped 75 people a day for six weeks for just their expenses.

Why Are Some Healed and Others Not?

This initially caused me concern. After years of observation and talking to other healers, the reasons why became a lot clearer. First and foremost, the patient must *want* to be healed, and I am being serious here. It's quite noticeable that a few sick people subconsciously *love* their illness and continually play the 'sympathy card'. They are never 'happier' than when they are talking about their predicament. Never have they had so much attention, so much sympathy and so many people at their beck and call looking after their every need. They have, in reality, surrendered to their illness, making it difficult for healing energies to do their job!

Some come for healing when they have a short time to live and hope for a miracle – although it can often relieve pain or discomfort. Others expect healing to restore youth to age-related problems. The causes of sickness and disease are manifold, and if long term negative lifestyles and emotions such as anger, frustration, fear and stress are still present, then complete healing will be virtually impossible. With many, healing is so therapeutic that a spiritual change of consciousness takes place, allowing healing to take effect causing their old lifestyles to become obsolete and dissolve naturally.

Summary

The knowledge and experiences discussed in this book are not for a privileged few, they are for any sincere seeker with the right attitude. Healing is no exception, and I have given a brief insight into my early years of using healing energies – the rest is history as they say. If you have never contemplated or received healing by the laying on of hands, I hope this chapter has given you some insight into its simplicity and natural function. Perhaps it has encouraged you to consider having healing or even becoming a healer yourself (see Healing in Useful Contact Details). You can always practise on the cat! I jest, but you could try scanning your hands over sympathetic friends and relatives whilst mentally asking for healing in the name of love and light – it really is that simple.

Healing is not ego, arrogance, shouting or 'show-biz' tactics and it is not the copyright of any religion, sect or group. Over the years, all the genuine healers that I ever had the pleasure and privilege to meet had an abundance of love, compassion and humility. These are the only qualities required for the healing energies to flow from the healer to the patient – because healing is LOVE. The Absolute is LOVE – therefore all genuine healing emanates from the Absolute.

Healing with the hands is as natural as breathing, is 'Love in Action', and gives us another piece of life's jigsaw. We can now investigate the enigma of good and evil.

I believe, too, that it is a misnomer to call spiritual healing,
faith healing, for it is very often those who are most sceptical
who receive the most benefit.

Charles A Simpson 1882 –1958 (Healer and founder of The Seekers Trust)

Spiritual healing is the result of law-governed healing forces that induce change.
Harry Edwards 1893 –1976 (Spiritual healer and writer)

14 Good and Evil - *Why the Conflict?*

Only one principle will give you courage, that is the principle
that no evil lasts forever nor indeed for very long.
Epicurus 341 – 271 BC (Greek philosopher)

There have been few promises of an easy ride in this book, since the aim is to encourage you to think deeper about the philosophy behind life and death. Hence you have been presented with some profound questions from time to time. Numerous people have commented after lectures and seminars that they had never thought of life in this or that way before, but that it made perfect sense when explained in a simplistic manner. This has been my approach, particularly with this chapter, as the subject in question has caused many a barrier to Truth seekers who find it difficult to comprehend where 'evil' fits into a Cosmos based on Love.

It is such a pity that it takes a disaster, or an 'evil' event, if you like, to make most people reflect on life. So why do we not live in a world where only nice things happen? Why do we have the fear of 'evil' hanging over our heads all the time? Perhaps it is a case of not being able to see the wood for the trees, so let us look at the good and evil scenario from a different perspective and see if it makes more sense.

Suppose we witness a colony of ants attacking a doomed beetle, while in the same garden a bird kills an 'innocent' worm by pulling it from beneath the soil. Would we call these acts of evil? Moments later our neighbour's cat attacks and kills the bird. Is *that* evil? Or is it evil when two stags fight to the death over their territory, or when a tiger stalks and kills an 'innocent' antelope? 'That's nature – it's the law of the jungle' we would say, simply because our level of consciousness is superior to theirs, hence we see things differently to what they do.

But, are we not cruel to animals? We incarcerate and torture them in our laboratories in the name of science and progress. We kill them in the name of sport, incarcerate them in 'battery' farms, ship them to slaughterhouses and cook and eat them in the name of gourmet food. Like us, do these animals not sense fear and feel pain? And similarly, do they not have families and feel the need for love and affection? It's interesting to ponder how we would feel if a 'superior' race treated *us* in this fashion, and whether we would call *them* evil!

We have enslaved the rest of the animal creation, and have treated our
distant cousins in fur and feathers so badly that beyond doubt, if they were
able to formulate a religion, they would depict the Devil in human form.
William Ralph Inge 1860 – 1954 (Dean of St Paul's 1934 – 1937)

We willingly swat a fly or a wasp, or tread on a spider just because they are there. And we have it within our 'power' to take their life or spare these little creatures when they have strayed into our home. So are we saying that they have no right to live just because we don't like them, because they are smaller than we are or they just happen to be in the 'wrong' place at the 'wrong' time? If we magnify that attitude a thousand fold, then could we be guilty of doing the same thing to our own kind?

When one human being attacks and takes the life of another we call it 'evil', and want to see justice done by having the perpetrator put to death or imprisoned for life. Why? Because the 'evil' act was committed by one of our own species. Is it 'evil' when we call it murder - or is it permissible when we call it war?

I am not condoning the taking of a life in any shape or form, but let me put this to you. If insects and animals killing each other is nature's law of the jungle, would a life form *far* superior in wisdom and intelligence to us human 'animals', consider our torturing and killing each other just another fact of nature in our concrete jungles? If so, what *is* evil or a sin in the *Absolute's* 'eyes'? Perhaps Moliere (Jean-Baptiste Poquelin 1622 – 1673) was right when he said, *'...my mind is no more shocked at seeing a man a rogue, unjust, or selfish, than at seeing vultures eager for prey, mischievous apes, or fury-lashed wolves.'*

We apply the term 'evil' to individuals or organisations that deliberately cause untold misery, suffering and death to fellow human beings. In other words, the negative and destructive element in society. But as we have already discussed, when *Nature* unleashes destructive elements causing us untold misery, suffering and death, we call it an 'Act of God!'

'Evil' is only the absence of good, just as darkness is only the absence of light. But where does darkness end and light begin? To limited levels, 'evil' is 'permitted' here as an aid to our spiritual progression. Just as tiny seeds struggle through the darkness of the soil to reach the light, we need resistance to grow spiritually – it is all a matter of contrasts. Would we recognise or appreciate good if we never experienced the bad, or warmth if we had never experienced cold? Love and hate, right and wrong, good and evil are but a thread apart.

In order for the light to shine so brightly, the darkness must be present.
Francis Bacon 1561 – 1626 (Philosopher and Statesman)

Tyrants

Tyrants have plagued this tiny planet for centuries, and used every conceivable form of violence to achieve their aims and, as a consequence, have changed the course of history. These perpetrators of 'evil' have consisted of dictators, emperors, monarchs, presidents, politicians, warlords, generals, tsars, popes and business tycoons. Their lust for power and wealth has caused untold cruelty and suffering.

We have suffered the likes of Nero, Attila the Hun, Genghis Khan, Thomas de Torquemanda (Spanish Inquisition), Vlad Dracula, Ivan the Terrible, Joseph Stalin, Adolf Hitler, Augusto Pinochet, Idi Amin, Pol Pot (Khmer Rouge), Nicolae Ceausescu (Romania), Saddam Hussein, Robert Mugabe and Colonel Muammar Gaddafi to name but a few in a vast rogues gallery. They come and go, but in their day were held responsible for wars, genocide, ethnic cleansing, murder torture, persecution and incarceration. Many were hailed as heroes when they first came to power but their deeds simply proved that 'absolute power corrupts absolutely' when they condemned their subjects to lives of misery.

There are many 'evil' tyrants active today and there will be many more in the future. Why? Because this planet is an ideal breeding ground for such kind. Mainly because the masses are easily influenced and manipulated by rostrum thumping, air punching power-seekers who rise to 'glory' on the promise of a utopia.

As we discussed in Chapter 11 *(Suicide)*, we can observe 'little tyrants' in everyday life at school or work when they bully, threaten or cajole others. We also have the mindless anti-social behavior of drug and alcohol-fueled thugs who terrorise our villages, towns and cities, making life intolerable for law-abiding citizens. Given positions of power, this is the same mentality as the 'evil' regimes that wouldn't hesitate to cause untold suffering, death and destruction to further their inhumane agendas.

By nature, all tyrants are control freaks, and many who have been brave enough to oppose them have usually paid the price. That is why history abounds with persecuted individuals who merely told the *Truth*. Tyrants and Truth don't sit comfortably together on this planet! Thankfully, we have also seen the likes of Abraham Lincoln, Mahatma Gandhi, Martin Luther King Junior and the Dalai Lama, who have been motivated by the spiritual nature of wisdom, Truth, love and compassion.

It is only necessary for good men to do nothing for evil to flourish.
Edmund Burke 1729 –1797 (Politician)

The Evil of War

For centuries, war has brought untold misery and suffering to countless millions, and has been one of the greatest 'evils' ever to inflict this planet. But war can bring out both the worst and the best in human nature. The worst is the ability to hate, wantonly kill and destroy, and often ethnically cleanse the 'enemy' (murder), with torture and rape frequently on the agenda. The best of human nature during war often brings out love and compassion, with self-sacrifice, comradeship and a more sympathetic understanding of human suffering. War often gives us good reason to ponder the futility of life, whether there is a life after death or a God that could allow such things to happen.

Barely had I set foot on this planet when all hell broke loose – World War II started! I was soon indoctrinated into the evil of war when my early childhood and schooling were spent in air-raid shelters during bombing raids. The sound of air-raid sirens, wearing my gas mask, the drone of the German V1 rockets ('Doodlebugs'), hearing their engines cut out and watching them drop on shops and houses are still haunting memories.

Many-a-night, cuddled up in fear, mother, myself and baby brother slept in the Morrison shelter erected in our lounge. She brought us up in the role of a single parent for five frightening and uncertain years whilst my father was in the army. Most of that time food and other essentials were rationed, so she had to cope as best she could.

Nearby houses had their windows blown in and tiles blown off their roofs by bomb blasts. They were the lucky ones – I used to play in the rubble of the houses that weren't! Every night, thousands never knew whether they would live to see daybreak. Mother sent me to school not knowing if I would come home alive, and father prayed he would have a family to come home to when the war ended. The war taught people to live for the day, because the tomorrows didn't bear thinking about!

Teachers taught classes of over 40 children in shelters that were cold, damp, badly lit and smelled of stale air. Fire crews, ambulance personnel and air-raid wardens worked tirelessly round the clock night after night, dragging the wounded, dying and dead from blazing houses. The hospitals that had not been bombed coped as best they could with continuous streams of casualties.

Today, I hear people complain that they have had a stressful day, they are bored or have problems coping with everyday life!

Peace is the happy, natural state of man.
War is corruption – his disgrace.
James Thomson 1700 – 1748 (Scottish poet)

'Entertainment?'

We watch films and TV programmes showing actors committing murder, portraying violence and other fictional atrocities. The more blood, gore, obscenities, brutalities, vulgar language, high body-counts and explosions the better the effects. And to add to this negative scenario we play computer games that are virtually sadistic. We call this 'entertainment', but when the same events happen in everyday life we are shocked and horrified, call the perpetrators 'evil', demand tough justice and wonder why such things can happen in a 'civilised' society. Do I detect double standards or am I just getting old and cynical? Is 'evil' acceptable when it's glamorised and called 'entertainment?'

One might question why we write, act or watch such violence when all we are doing is polluting our minds, making people depressed, desensitising society and violating the Cosmic Law of Love, peace and harmony. And what of the actors who play violent roles, swear or speak hateful words? Apart from being dreadful role models for society they are creating harmful negative vibrations in our homes and cinemas as well as their own bodies when they portray such anger and violence. Little do they realise that negative emotions wreak havoc with our mental, physical and spiritual wellbeing, as evidenced in Chapter 9 *(Love)*, when we reviewed the remarkable experiments of Dr. Masaru Emoto in his book *The True Power of Water*, where he demonstrated the negative effects of violent thoughts, words and actions on water samples.

Ignorance

We reason that all human beings should think and act alike, and that if one person can be good all their life then so can others. In philosophical and metaphysical terms it doesn't quite work like that. We are spiritual beings 'trapped' in physical bodies who are evolving by experience to higher levels of consciousness and, as previously discussed, we will eventually merge back into the ultimate consciousness – The Absolute. We can only achieve this by having an indeterminate number of lives in various planes of existence.

Many young and immature souls in human form for the first time will tend to be more 'animalistic' by nature, and are inevitably going to abuse the 'system' and make dreadful mistakes. So it would be grossly unfair to compare them with the more mature souls that have probably had hundreds of earthly lives to achieve their level of wisdom and understanding. It is an observable fact that all forms of life, from primitive to advanced, only learn and evolve by making mistakes.

So perhaps we should replace the word 'evil' with the word 'ignorance', as all those who commit offences that we would deem 'evil' are spiritually immature and ignorant of the Universal Law of Love, Peace and Harmony. Because they know no better they should be pitied not hated. It is highly probable that even the best of us have been called 'evil' at some time during our soul's evolution from one life to another.

> For the cause of evil always look for ignorance, and for the cause of good, seek for the knowledge that brought it about.
> *Arthur Findlay MBE, JP 1883-1964 (The Curse of Ignorance)*

The human race is a very mixed bag when it comes to progression from 'evil' to good, or more apt, from *ignorance to enlightenment*, so let me give a few examples and you will see what I mean. They have been segregated into two groups purely for convenience, but in reality it is not quite so cut and dried. Although we should never judge another's spiritual credentials it will give you some idea of what to expect at various levels of spiritual awareness.

Immature Souls – Lower (body) nature predominant.

These come from all walks of life and all nationalities and usually have some or all of the following characteristics:

- Lack of forgiveness, love and compassion (nasty natured).
- The use of violence as a first means rather than dialogue.
- A tendency to act in an irrational and irresponsible manner.
- Grossly materialistic with a love of money, power and control (megalomania).
- An abundance of anger, hatred, jealousy, lust and greed (robbery, rape, mugging, etc.).
- A tendency towards gang culture.
- A tendency to ridicule, torment (bully) and torture.
- A tendency to carry an offensive weapon.
- Adult, child or animal abuse (cruelty).
- Verbal abuse, obscene language, obscenities, insincerity and lies.
- Domineering, antagonistic, arrogant, argumentative, prejudiced and racist.
- A lust for physical stimulation with excesses in food, sex, drugs and alcohol.
- The enjoyment of malicious gossip.
- Self-centred (selfish) with a 'What's in it for me?' attitude.
- Destructive tendency (vandalism, graffiti, litter, etc.).
- Negative attitude to life (whinging and moaning).
- Egotistical (conceited and vane).
- Have eyes that are sullen and soulless.

Down the centuries, most of the world's tyrants and troublemakers could be observed as having many of these characteristics when they wreaked havoc and committed the vilest of atrocities, especially so when involved in politics and religion.

For most, forgiveness, compassion and love are rarely seen, except the love of self-gratification, money, power and control. Such ignorance and violation of Cosmic Law will create a personal 'bank account' of negative Karma that will have to be paid back over numerous lifetimes. Sometime, somehow, somewhere; life will demand its 'pound of flesh' before we become aware of our conscience and thus guided by spiritual values.

All life manifests from The Great Spirit – The Absolute, which means that we are, whatever colour of skin, *all* spiritual brothers and sisters linked by the great Cosmic family tree. As we discussed in Chapter 10 *(Reincarnation)* most of us will have done things in our soul's history that we are not proud of, so it would be wiser for us to make allowances for those who are now doing what we probably did in the past when we were less enlightened.

As we have already seen, the Absolute gives equal and unconditional love to all – it has no favourites – just as the sun and the rain never differentiate between flowers and weeds. So what right do we have to hate our less spiritually evolved brethren? It may be hard to forgive, especially if 'evil' deeds have affected us personally, but once we comprehend the jigsaw of life we will realise that forgiveness and love will serve us better than hatred and revenge. But, for those who do seek revenge it would be advisable to dig *two* graves!

Let's have a look at the characteristics that we would expect to see in the 'older' souls that have had many lifetimes of experience – those who have been round the block a few times!

The More Enlightened Souls – Higher (spiritual) nature predominant.

These also come from all walks of life and all nationalities and usually have some or all of the following characteristics:

- An abhorrence of verbal and physical violence (confrontation).
- An abundance of unconditional love and compassion.
- Humility (lack of vanity and conceit).
- Guided by conscience and intuition.
- Genuinely happy and prone to smiling or laughing.
- Consider the needs of others before self (unselfish).
- Innate wisdom and the ability to think rationally.
- Derives great pleasure from being creative and constructive (building, designing, composing, painting, writing, teaching, etc.).

- Healing ability with words or hands (homeopaths, osteopaths, chiropractors, doctors, nurses, healers, reflexologists, aromatherapists, etc.).
- Positive attitude to life.
- Love and respect for people and all living things.
- Love of beauty (Nature), peace and quiet, art, music, poetry, literature, gardening, spiritual philosophy, meditation, yoga, T'ai Chi, etc.
- Have compassionate eyes.
- Are more aware of their spiritual heritage (Divine nature).

These are characteristics of those who care and who generally live lives of peace and love, showing kindness and compassion to all. Many are the volunteers and unsung heroes of society. Even if they are unaware, they are truly spiritually inspired and sadly missed when they depart this Earth.

Since the Second World War, we have seen an abundance of the more enlightened souls incarnate on Earth. They give me hope for the future of the human race and it is always a pleasure to meet them. Many of today's children are extremely sensitive, and show a wisdom and understanding far beyond their earthly years. These are the ones who will shape the future for the better. As adults, great numbers of them are working tirelessly behind the scenes to uplift the hopes and moral thinking of this backward planet, or the 'Dark Star', as Air Chief Marshall Lord Dowding so aptly called it.

Obviously we are not so neatly categorised as the examples quoted, since they represent the worst and the best characteristics within the human psyche. Our Mr and Mrs Average are neither all good nor bad and can be quite a mixture of each in one degree or another. This can give some of us a Jekyll and Hyde character - a strange mixture of good and not so good - when our higher (soul) nature is in conflict with our lower (body) nature. There is very often a little bit of good in the worst of us, and a little bit of bad in the best of us. Even some of the worst villains in history had a soft spot somewhere; either for a pet or their dear old mum!

Love and compassion show in the eyes, and it has often been said that the eyes are the windows of the soul (Overself). The eyes never lie – mouths do! So if you don't like what you see in another's eyes, then be *very* wary.

However evil a man apparently becomes,
that which is divine in him is never touched.
Dr. Paul Brunton 1898 – 1981 (Discover Yourself)

The Devil

I have never subscribed to the childish notion that a God of love sits on a throne in a 'Heaven' and idly watches 'His' creation being influenced and tormented by a devil that is solely responsible for all the 'evil' on this tiny planet – a mere speck of dust in such a vast Universe. Hopefully, the human race will eventually be mature enough to take full responsibility for its own negative actions, listen to its conscience and stop blaming a negative entity.

All I am prepared to tell you for now, is that there is no single negative 'power' in opposition to the Absolute (God). The Devil as such, was an invention of ancient priest-craft to subjugate the uneducated masses of the day. The scenario of the Devil versus God is known as dualism and is rife in the history of religion. I know of no Guru, mystic or philosopher, past or present, who has had personal experience of oneness with the Absolute that accepts a god of 'evil'.

> Does the Devil exist? If there is only one existence which is omnipresent and omniscient, then where is the place for the existence of the devil? Those who are religiously sick believe in the existence of the devil by forgetting the existence of God. A negative mind is the greatest devil that resides within the human being. .... Fear of the devil is a phobia that needs to be eradicated from the human mind.
>
> *Swami Rama (Living with the Himalayan Masters)*

Neither is there a hell of fire and brimstone full of 'evil' humans being barbecued for eternity for their sins. The hellfire doctrine is another outrageous and outdated religious invention that has no place in a modern thinking society. This doctrine was used to create fear and blind obedience amongst illiterate people, and is the very antithesis of a loving and compassionate God. We create our own 'heaven' or 'hell' according to our *thoughts and actions*. Although many who have suffered dreadfully think this Earth is as near to a 'hell' as we will ever get!

There are, throughout the Universe, tremendous cosmic forces (energies) that can be used for either good or evil purposes. These energies are neutral in operation and it is their use that determines whether they are classified as 'good' or 'evil'. When used for 'evil' they are known as 'black magic' or 'forces of darkness' and have been collectively called by such names as The Negative Powers, Satan, the Devil, Beelzebub or Arihman. When used for good they are known as 'white magic' or 'forces of light' and have been called by such names as 'Buddha Consciousness', 'Krishna Consciousness', 'The Christ Light' or 'The God force'.

For thousands of years these forces, or energies, have been termed as occult forces. The word occult simply means 'secret' or 'hidden' knowledge and is nothing to be frightened of if studied seriously with high morals and integrity.

Centuries ago, only Spiritual Masters and teachers of ancient wisdom understood occult laws and forces which, when rightly understood, divulge the Truth about the Absolute (God), good and evil and the 'mysteries' of life and death. They were carefully guarded secrets taught only by word of mouth to initiates of the highest order, and were 'hidden' from the masses lest such knowledge should fall into the hands of unscrupulous fanatics. But the inevitable eventually happened. And guess what? They used it for 'evil' purposes, power and control. No surprises there then!

It has often been said that money is the root of all evil. But as we know, it is frequently used for humanitarian purposes. Money is a neutral commodity and it is only the greed for it and its abuse that makes it 'evil' and gives it bad press. If it were not money it would be gold, diamonds, oil, drugs or any other substance that appeals to the lower and materialistic nature of humans. Those amongst us who are devoid of love and compassion and intoxicated by greed and corruption, will use and abuse technology, politics, religion, finance or occult knowledge to cheat, swindle, dominate, kill, maim or torture their fellow human beings to satisfy their lust for sex, wealth, power and status. Such is the lower nature of Homo sapiens – not the Absolute, nor an invented devil!

'Evil' exists only in the minds of the human race, and we have a freewill choice to follow the pathways of either 'good' or 'evil'. Most of us *instinctively* know the difference between right and wrong when the Overself (soul) speaks through our conscience. But some of us deliberately choose the latter when we are dominated by our lower, greedy and selfish materialistic nature – the prime cause of what we call 'evil'.

A belief in a supernatural source of evil is not necessary;
men alone are quite capable of every wickedness.
Joseph Conrad 1857 – 1924 (Novelist)

Astral Influences

Many question the role of the astral worlds in their influence for good or 'evil' upon this Earth. As we know from this world, like minds attract like minds. In this respect nothing changes after 'death'. Since the lower astral frequencies are very close to the Earth's, the depraved types in the lower astral regions can latch on to and influence depraved minds here on Earth. These 'evil' entities, or malevolent spirits have, throughout history, been known as devils and demons or, in Arab literature, as Jinns, and constitute part of the 'forces of darkness'. They encourage weak, like-minded individuals to murder, abuse children, push and take drugs and every other 'evil' and vile act that depraved individuals can commit. When caught, many have stated in their defence that they 'heard voices' telling them to kill or do harm. They have been classed as 'criminally insane' and given 'life' sentences!

Some lower astral entities can, and do, enter the physical bodies of low moral individuals. This is known as possession and, unfortunately, is a fact that has been known for thousands of years. It is mentioned frequently in many philosophical and religious writings including the Bible. Often, vile expletives come from the mouths of their 'victims'. This can be remedied by successful exorcisms but it is not a job for the squeamish, as many experienced mediums know only too well. Dr Carl Wickland wrote of such experiences in his renowned book *Thirty Years Among the Dead.*

In the summer of 1973, I attended a venue with meditation teacher Michael Gardner-Jones. It was there that I overheard one man telling another that, hours before, he had punched some guy who had bad-mouthed him, knocking him to the ground. He then told him to clear off in equally foul-mouthed language. On hearing this, I kept my distance from the abuser and sat the other side of the room.

Momentarily, our eyes met and, in that instant, a tall black hooded figure came out of him and made its way slowly across the room towards me. As it got nearer I became paralysed with indescribable fear and found myself unable to move a limb or utter any cry for help. I knew that if this 'creature' reached me I could be in deep trouble. As it got nearer, the most foul and evil obscenities and anti-God thoughts poured from it into *my* mind. It was like something from a horror movie!

At that moment, Mike entered the room and approached me. With every ounce of willpower, I managed to move my right arm and touch him. Instantly, with a piercing scream, the 'creature' shot back into the man it had left moments before, causing him to jump in his seat as if he had been stung. Instantly, the paralysis left my body. Mike was unaware of all this, but mentioned that the man in question was of dubious character and could flip from being extremely nice to downright nasty, and had obviously attracted an 'evil' possessing entity that, for some reason, saw me as a threat. Having no knowledge of the 'dark forces' at the time, it was, to say the least, a most unpleasant experience.

Two years later, a middle-aged lady suffering from depression and possible Multiple Sclerosis symptoms came to my house to receive healing. My friend Fred was staying with us at the time so I asked him if he would like to assist. He willingly obliged and sat next to me. I leant forward, asked the lady to hold my hands and said a prayer in the name of love and light. As soon as I had finished the prayer, six black-hooded figures came out of her shrieking and screaming obscenities. Immediately, a pulsating blue mist enveloped all of us, and from behind me a Native American Indian and an Arab guide rushed forward saying: 'Do not fear, we will handle this.' They wrapped the screaming entities in the blue mist using it like a huge blanket and escorted them towards the 'spiritual light' where they would try to help them. An unenviable task, but it was typical of the cooperation between the two worlds.

There was no fear on my part, only a feeling of love and compassion for the lady who, afterwards, said that her depression had gone and how much better she felt. She also confessed that she suffered constant domestic violence from her husband whom she described as 'an evil man'. I had, unwittingly, done an exorcism on a lady who had been possessed by her husband's 'evil' entities. But the interesting thing was that Fred also heard the commotion and saw the released possessing entities as well as the blue mist – but *not* the guides. 'What on earth was that all about?' he exclaimed! Even as a seasoned clergyman he had never experienced anything like it before.

Let me stress, that those with integrity and a kind and loving disposition should have no fear of possession. Fortunately, there are highly evolved beings of light from the higher spiritual worlds that have a benevolent interest in our welfare. They can often influence us for good when they come close and try to encourage like-minded individuals to lead lives based on unconditional love, compassion and service to others. As mentioned in Chapter 9 *(Love)*, these wonderful souls, known as guides, teachers, guardian angels or benevolent Jinns, often show themselves to those sensitive enough to 'see' or 'hear' them.

> I would impress upon you again most strongly that the dark forces can only influence and endanger those in whom they can find some affinity to their own nature.
> Fear nothing. There is no power in the Cosmos, no destructive force, however malignant, that can touch the man who, by a deliberate act of choice unites himself with the Divine Will.
> *H. K. Challoner 1890 – 1980 (The Wheel of Rebirth)*

Good Vs Evil

Life here is a continual battle between the 'forces of light' and the 'forces of darkness'. That is the 'resistance' that will help us to evolve our spiritual nature. The forces of darkness try to divert the human race from seeking the Truth about life and death and discovering its spiritual heritage. They are 'nourished' by the negative energies of lies, greed, corruption, sexual depravities, war and other self-inflicted violence. They prey on human weaknesses, and it is in their interest to create as *much* confusion, turmoil, mayhem and havoc as possible to maximise fear and anxiety amongst the masses. Therefore, those of us who are violent in thoughts, words or actions are, knowingly or otherwise, aiding and abetting the 'evil' schemes of these dark forces.

'Evil' thrives on *fear*, which is extreme anxiety, and feeds on it as a glutton does food. 'Evil' *needs* fear to survive, and any person or institution that *deliberately* creates fear is aiding and abetting 'evil!' The human race has *always* been 'controlled' by fear in one form or another. Fear of God, fear of a devil, fear of nuclear war, fear of terrorism, fear of ill health, fear of aging, fear of death, fear of poverty, fear of unemployment, fear of crime and fear of the unknown. In other words – fear of life itself! And why are people such easy prey to anxiety and fear? *Ignorance*! Ignorance of the Laws governing life and death. Constant fear destroys health and happiness.

Those who begin to understand life's Laws and the *true* nature of the Absolute are regarded as having elevated consciousness levels, or more 'enlightened' minds. And enlightened minds are not affected by human-created fears. Why should they be when they *know* that they are part of the Great Spirit – the Absolute?

If there is one comforting message I would convey to the fear and anxiety ridden minds of our Mr and Mrs Average it would be this: 'FEAR HAS NO PLACE IN THE ENLIGHTENED MIND.'

No passion so effectively robs the mind of all its powers of
acting and reasoning as fear.
Edmund Burke 1729 – 1797 (Politician)

Why So Much Evil Now?

Vast numbers are voicing concern at the present state of the world and the increasing levels of crime and violence in all walks of life as they observe declining morals and witness criminals receiving lenient sentences and their victims treated like criminals. Conspiracy theories abound, sex scandals, lies, spin, sleaze, corruption, incompetence and cover-ups at establishment levels are exposed and fill the tabloids, whilst murder, anarchy, indiscriminate wars, suicide-bombings and other terrorist atrocities form the back-drop to an insane world. This causes many to question as to whether the inmates really *are* running the asylum or whether there are hidden agendas to such chaos and confusion. Hence, globally, governments have never been so distrusted or come under so much suspicion and scrutiny.

Many state that they fear for the future of their children and grandchildren and see events escalating out of control and going from bad to worse with 'evil' seemingly having the upper hand. Yes, things do appear that way and it's encouraging that so many have noticed, want to do something about it and have made their voices heard. Could it be that Mr and Mrs Average are at last waking up?

To put things in perspective, there never have been 'good times'. We can go far back into recorded history and find instances of violent skirmishes and wars. Such is the legacy of our suffering planet. Long before rape and pillage raids on our shores, no village or town was safe from invasion. Even in Victorian and Edwardian times it wasn't safe to walk city streets at night. And up to the beginning of the last century the life span of many children was cut short due to poverty and disease.

As we saw in Chapter 8 *(Is There a God of Love?)*, the Old Testament carnage inflicted on towns and villages by violent people several thousand years ago, must have, even then, made individuals question their own and their family's future! It was literally continuous massacres with one tribe or kingdom fighting another. And as for climate change; Nature's been doing that for millions of years as our fragile Earth's crust moves and sunspots flare giving long periods of hot and cold. Pollution? Well, Nature's pretty good at that as well when volcanoes erupt and pump some pretty obnoxious filth into the atmosphere, or via drought instigated forest fires causing fossil fuel burning on a colossal scale.

If we really want children, and feel that we would make good parents, then the time to have them is always the right time. How do we know that they are not going to grow up and be of great benefit to the human race? Right now, for every child born that will grow up to create havoc and destroy lives, there are thousands born that will give hope and inspiration to future generations.

In occult terminology, we are now in what is called 'The Age of Kali Yuga' or the age of 'transformation'. This is the time when 'evil' appears to show its ugly head to all and sundry. The rotten elements are now coming to the surface like scum on the top of liquid ready to be skimmed off. Things *will* get worse before they get better, but on a note of optimism, everything in the Universe works in accordance with the Cosmic Law of harmony and, when the scales of life tip too far one way they must eventually rebalance.

We live in a constantly changing and evolving world where nothing stays the same forever. Repressive regimes that have restricted physical and spiritual freedom, along with old and outdated systems that have suppressed the Truth and kept the human race in ignorance will, as we are now witnessing, decay and fall apart. In many cases this is hastened by greed, corruption and internal power struggles, plus the inevitable fact that they have had their day and must make way for something better. It may seem like chaos, but skilled builders will confirm that before anything can be rebuilt there is always a lot of preparation work and dust and rubble to be cleared.

When the dust of change begins to settle on this planet we will be able to see and feel the new and more vibrant earth-energies that are affecting each and every one of us. These are coming from the deeper regions of the Cosmos, making us more sensitive to spiritual values and the need to question and speak out against injustices, violence and suffering.

Today, more people than ever before are ready to experience and understand the profound truths of spiritual philosophy and the finer qualities of life that money cannot buy. They are now searching for peace and harmony in their lives, having realised that confrontation and violence are outdated and futile and that cooperation and love are the formulas for health and happiness.

Evil is unspectacular and always human,
and shares our bed and eats at our own table.
W. H. Auden 1907 – 1973 (English poet)

Reminder Time

This would, perhaps, seem an opportune moment to remind you of the task I set you in Chapter 1 *(Life)*. I asked for, say, one month, if you would be an impartial observer of people and life in general, with no judgments, prejudices or opinions. But that doesn't mean that we should accept ignorance or not stand up for ourselves when necessary.

You will no doubt have observed immature attitude problems (often called throwing toys out of the pram!) including body language – which can speak volumes! Rudeness, lack of respect, arrogance, greed and selfishness in all aspects of life should not have escaped your observations. This will have been compensated by the love, compassion and helpfulness that brought tears to your eyes and a lump to the throat when you witnessed such unselfish and spiritual acts of kindness – often by complete strangers.

Again, on the other side of the coin, perhaps you have been a victim of car theft, mugging or burglary; or come across those who knowingly steal from their employers, con the public and fiddle their state benefits, the taxman and their expenses. And how many amongst us have been known to spread malicious gossip, lie, cheat, commit fraud, forgery or shoplift. Oh, and don't forget the avoidance of fines, car tax and insurance, television licences and train and bus fares. And perhaps we could add 'road-rage' and bitter neighbourly disputes to further prove a point!

Let's not dwell on the more depraved aspects of human nature such as murder, rape, torture, looting, bullying, domestic violence and child abuse as we have covered those in previous chapters. All these, and numerous others, are observable facets of 'evil' in a greater or lesser degree, and are violations of Cosmic Law.

Tomorrow, we can go out into the big wide world and be as kind or unkind as we wish; be selfish or generous; indulge in malicious gossip or say kind words; give physical abuse or an embrace of love; whinge and moan or volunteer for a worthy cause. In every case we are either taking from life or giving something back – the choice is ours.

Now, I bet you thought I had forgotten. How did you get on being an observer of yourself – observing your own thoughts, words and actions? Shocked? Well, most truthful people are, particularly when it comes to negative thinking – worry, fear, anxiety or criticism of others. The object of the exercise is to make us more aware of our own strengths and weaknesses so that we can build on our strengths and correct our weaknesses. The way to a better world is better people, and that always begins with ourselves!

One should look long and carefully at oneself before one considers judging others.
Moliere [Jean-Baptiste Poquelin] 1622 – 1673 (French playwright)

Summary

At its best, the human race can compose and perform musical masterpieces, paint wonderful pictures, write profound poetry and literature, perform amazing medical feats, design and build awe-inspiring structures, spend a lifetime volunteering to help the deprived, sick and suffering and live lives of love, peace and compassion embracing all living things. Conversely, at its worst, it can sink to levels of unimaginable depravity.

Most humans, at some time or other, will suffer from lack of self-control and be tempted to do something dishonest if they think they can get away with it. We may think that nobody will see or hear us, but our *Overself* will see and hear us – *it* will know. Like a minute silicon chip, our Overself records *everything* that we think, say and do. As pieces of the puzzle have shown, Karmic Laws were put into place to maintain Universal Justice. If we wish to abuse our freewill, then we must be prepared to pay the price – sometime, somewhere, somehow – 'as we sow so shall we reap'.

It is virtually impossible for us to understand the concept of what is 'good' and what is 'evil' until we become aware of the Great Cosmic Plan. What is evil in the eyes of one, might not be so in the eyes of another and, under the Law of Karma, it is always the *motive* behind our thoughts and deeds that define them as 'good' or 'evil'. Very often 'good' can come from an act of 'evil' when it stimulates people to change things for the better. In this way 'evil' becomes the catalyst for 'good'.

We have brought 'evil' upon ourselves by our greed, anger, hatred and aggression over the centuries, but it is always self-defeating and ultimately brings about its own self-destruction because the Cosmos is based on Love. 'Evil' cannot exist where there is Love. Although we need the experience of both, it will, hopefully, grant us the humility and compassion necessary for our spiritual and moral growth, for it is only through our own tears that we can recognize the suffering in another's eyes.

Understanding that 'evil' is merely spiritual ignorance, presents us with another piece of the jigsaw. In the next chapter, I would like to talk at a more personal level about some of the traumas and tragedies of life that cause us so much grief.

Man evolves through suffering. As light requires the dark to realise illumination, so divine Law decrees that good should be tempered by evil.
W. Raymond Drake 1913-1989 (Gods and Spacemen in the Ancient East)

The ultimate good is for one human being to love another.
The ultimate evil is for one human being to hate another.

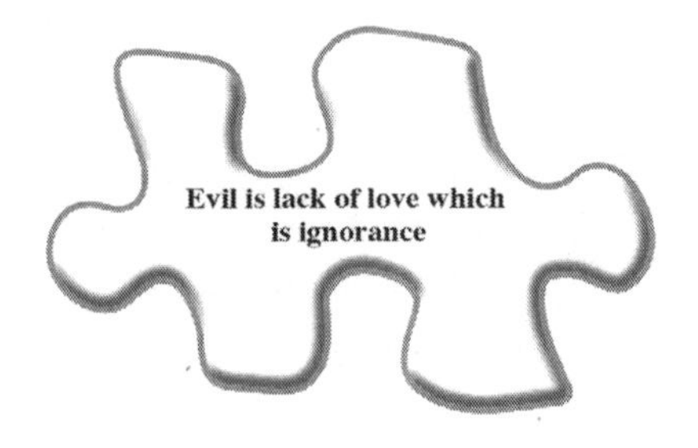

15 Just for You

– A Personal Message

From the greatest sorrow comes the greatest knowledge.
It is though you had learned a great many languages, for you
can now understand all whom you meet. Comfort as a rule can
only come from him who has himself been comforted. No man
who has never wept can wipe away the tears of his fellows.
Adrienne Sarti (Writer and philosopher)

When life hits hard, it can suddenly seem cruel, lonely and devoid of any meaning and purpose. 'Why has this happened to us, we've done nothing wrong?' And, 'What have I done to deserve this?' are often repeated questions. On the roller-coaster journey of life the highs of the enjoyable moments are easy to cope with, but the lows of despair, in most cases are not.

I am taking the liberty of assuming that some personal trauma, or series of traumas, has hit you hard in the past or quite recently, and caused you some degree of mental anguish or suffering when your world collapsed around you. And also that you are trying to pick up the pieces, come to terms with life and get back to some form of 'normality'.

Over the years, often with hugs amidst the tears, I have tried to comfort some of those who have been devastated by personal traumas and tragedies, particularly when they struck suddenly. Many cannot believe what has happened let alone try to understand. Often there is an open disbelief in a God of love because of their grief, whilst others feel they are being punished by God or a devil, for one reason or another.

Love and compassion will compel us to put a comforting arm around the shoulders of those who are suffering trauma or grief, and try to dry their tears and answer their questions with some form of wisdom and logic that they can grasp. They may well be a loved one, neighbour, friend, acquaintance or even a complete stranger. The Absolute works through compassionate people – that is the true meaning of unconditional Love.

So, let's have a look at, and try to comprehend, some of the many traumas of life that can cause havoc with our emotions:

- The collapse of a business and financial ruin.
- The death of a loved one, husband or wife, mother or father, son or daughter (baby, child or teenager) from any cause.
- The death of a much loved pet.
- Giving birth to a stillborn baby.

- Giving birth to a handicapped baby.
- Having a child mentally or physically crippled by a virus or an accident.
- Suffering physical violence.
- Being raped.
- Suffering sexual abuse as a child.
- Having one's home broken into, burgled and vandalised.
- Having the marital problems of unfaithfulness or divorce.
- Being left paralysed or disfigured after an accident or stroke.
- Being diagnosed with a terminal or debilitating illness.
- Having a loved one go missing.
- Having one's home and family devastated by a hurricane, tsunami, flood, earthquake or war.

Many have more than one of such traumas and tragedies devastate them within a short period of time. Needless to say they become changed people and, whilst some are scarred for life by their experiences, the fortunate ones see it as a purging effect to rearrange their priorities. Most never see life from the same perspective again and mundane material problems no longer seem important. What does it matter if the washing machine leaks or the garden fence is broken? And that argument with the neighbours last week seems so childish and pointless now.

Time *is* a great healer, and most do come through these dark periods, often with regrets and many an 'if only', but life, as we know, must, and does, carry on. The rest of the world goes about its business whilst we wallow in our own misery and grief. Eventually, the vast majority do pick up the threads of some normality again and find that acceptance of the situation and a good dose of TLC from family and friends are two of the best recipes towards recovery.

Many find that the circumstances leave them with a greater degree of inner strength, wisdom, sensitivity and humility than before, thereby enabling them to help and counsel others in a similar predicament. Having said all that, let me put a consoling arm around your shoulder, trusting that the assembled pieces of our jigsaw have helped you to understand that life and, particularly death, are *not* pointless in the great scheme of things. I would like to talk to you now about some of the most traumatic and emotional circumstances in life's rich tapestry.

The Death of a Partner

If you have lost a loving partner, particularly after many years together, and are trying to come to terms with coping and living on your own, then you will have suffered one of life's most traumatic experiences that very few of us will escape from. It is a sad fact of life that with most couples who stay together, one partner will eventually attend the funeral of the other. 'Until death us do part' is an oft-repeated phrase, but to the majority it can be shattering when it happens. The surviving partner will be plunged into an alien world. Women are left to sort out the finances of bank accounts and insurance policies and the chores of house and car maintenance. Men, on the other hand, try to cope with shopping, cooking, washing, ironing and housework, and in some cases bringing up children on their own.

An emotional minefield is sorting through a partner's personal belongings – something best done with the help of a relative or good friend – unless you feel strong enough by yourself. Clothes will inevitably bring back memories of special occasions, but if you put yourself in their position you will be inspired to do the right thing and find them a useful home with either, family, friends or a charity shop. It can be a harsh reminder that we take no material objects with us when we enter the 'next world' – only our personality.

If you nursed your partner through a long debilitating illness then you may feel that 'death' was a blessed relief. If you did the best you could, then have no regrets. There are no dress rehearsals in this life and we can only do what we think is right at the time. If your partner 'died' when you were not with them, then the shock, disbelief, grief and loss will be especially difficult to cope with because you feel you were unable to say goodbye. Since few of us will be aware of our 'death' day, please don't chastise yourself. Because there is no 'death', your partner will still be very much alive and aware of you - albeit from a different dimension – so you can still say your goodbyes.

As we touched on in a previous chapter, loneliness is another obstacle to overcome, especially if you are now on your own in the house with no one to confide in. This is where close family or pet can be a blessing. Coming home to an empty house can be distressing as can sleeping alone after years of sharing a bed. It is perfectly natural to miss the physical presence of a loved one when hugs and kisses and those little mannerisms that made them so human and loveable will no longer be a part of everyday life. Because of this you may well feel that half of you is missing. It's also quite natural and, not surprising, how many mention that they expected to see their loved one walk through the door at any given moment.

The hardest times will be anniversaries and Christmas. So why not toast them with a glass of wine or fruit juice and wish them a happy birthday or Christmas, just as if they were in the room. My experience has been that they probably will be, especially on such occasions – I could put it no simpler than the following verse:

Death is nothing at all. I have only slipped away into the next room.
I am I and you are you. Whatever we were to each other, that we are
still. Call me by my old familiar name, speak to me in the easy way
which you always used. Put no difference into your tone; wear no forced
air of solemnity or sorrow. Laugh as we always laughed at the little jokes
we enjoyed together. Play, smile, think of me, pray for me. Let my name
be ever the household word that it always was. Let it be spoken without
effort, without the trace of a shadow on it. Life means all that it ever
meant. It is the same as it ever was; there is absolutely unbroken
continuity. What is death but a negligible accident? Why should I be out
of your mind because I am out of your sight? I am but waiting for you,
for an interval, somewhere very near, just round the corner.
All is well.
Henry Scott Holland 1847 – 1918 (Canon of St Pauls Cathedral)

One of the hardest lessons from this experience is learning to be strong, stand on one's own two feet and start a new chapter in a life that will never be the same again. It won't happen overnight but, as close friends who have gone through this dark period have proved; with a positive effort it can be done. At the time, none of them could possibly see how they would get through it and see the brighter side of life again.

If you still have children at home then they will be your priority and the best reason to get out of bed in the mornings. They will be grieving as well – you have 'lost' a partner and they have 'lost' a parent', so you will need each other more than ever. With the help of others who have gone through the grieving process, here is a list of some things you could do to focus your mind on positive issues. I do appreciate that it is easier said than done, but only *you* can make the effort.

- First and foremost, *accept* what has happened. This is essential to regain any sense of normality in your life. Remember, 'death' is perfectly natural at *any* age. It is going to happen to us *all* at some time or other.
- Mentally ask your partner if they would want you to be miserable and sit at home grieving. You *know* what the answer would be, so continue with your life as they would want you to.
- When you are on your own, talk to your partner as if they were still with you on Earth. They will be 'around' you for a while because they will be concerned for you, and will be able to see and hear you when you talk. They are still *alive* – more so than us if the truth be known – but they are living in another dimension.
- Try not to grieve for any longer than you need as it will only upset your partner. *They* will be OK; it is *you* who will need to get your act together.

- Try to get out of the house more often by going for walks (particularly if you have a dog), swimming, shopping or the cinema for example. Why not go with family or friends, it will make it more interesting.
- Find a friend or friends to go on holiday with.
- Try to show love and be positive in everything that you do (remember that positive thoughts attract positive results). Never become one of life's whingers or you will lose what friends you have and isolate yourself from your family.
- See more of family and friends. You will appreciate them even more now.
- Try to get a part time job if you are not already working or retired.
- Join a club or start a group of your own. U3A have over 60 different interests to choose from in some areas (see *Useful Contact Details*).
- Volunteer for work in a local charity shop or organisation.
- Baby-sit for family and friends or even acquaintances. Spread the word around, you could be in business here!
- Do crosswords, read, play cards or start a hobby if you haven't got one already. In fact, anything that keeps the brain ticking over.
- Visit your local library and choose some good books. You could even sit there and read them; it would make a change of scenery for you now and again. And, who knows, you might even make new friends who are in the same position as you.
- Join a yoga class. You're never too old, and it's one of the best mind and body therapies that I know of.
- Join an amateur dramatic society (help behind the scenes if you don't fancy acting).
- Enrol for an interesting evening class at your local school or college such as pottery, art, languages, etc. Once again, you could make new friends (you can get details of classes from your library).
- Absorb yourself in the garden if you have one. If not, maybe friends or family could do with some extra help in theirs.
- Use your predicament to help and comfort others who are in a similar position.

How's that for starters? The last one is particularly important, because when we help others we tend to forget our own problems and self-pity.

Yes, time does heal, but with the 'death' of a loving partner, particularly in the latter stage of one's life, many find there is no total healing, as part of the survivor also 'dies' with the loved one. As I have mentioned many times, Nature is no respecter of persons, and she can plunge us back into loneliness and fending for ourselves again at any time in our lives. And not just in those twilight years when we are a little unsteady on our feet, slightly hard of hearing, not always remembering what day it is, where we left our glasses or wondering what we went upstairs for.

So, if this is your predicament, then our jigsaw will have shown you that 'death' is the 'great illusion'. The human personality, or life force, lives on in its astral body in another dimension when the physical 'spacesuit' has been discarded at 'death'. The bond between a loving husband and wife, or any other loving partnership, is still the same whether one is in the physical body and the other out of it. If there was love between you, then you *will* meet again when your time comes to depart this Earth. Meanwhile, enjoy and learn from what life you have got left here – it is precious.

Let me leave you with some words of comfort from my friend Keith Hagar, whose dear wife Jean left this Earth to further her 'education' in one of the many spirit worlds:

After almost 50 years of a very happy, loving and fruitful marriage my darling wife Jean was 'taken' from me in an instant, dying in my arms with no chance to say goodbye. At our age we had discussed the inevitable happening, but such discussions could not bring home or prepare one for the actual shock of the emptiness, the loneliness and the heart wrenching pain of such a parting.

For many years we had both believed, and indeed investigated, the possibility that life after death does exist, and that our soul, memory banks and personality continue in another state or world that co-exists with our own world but in an unseen higher state of vibration.

My first confirmation that this is true came within 48 hours of Jean's passing. My eldest son Julian and I were sitting in the lounge waiting for the start of the six o'clock news, when I was suddenly enveloped in an intense and overpowering smell of flowers. After about 10 seconds I asked Julian if he could smell anything. He replied that he could faintly smell flowers, and as he said this, the smell left me and became overpoweringly intense for him. We then realised that Jean was making her presence felt – she loved nothing better than the sight and smell of flowers. The following evening the experience was repeated, but of slightly less intensity.

The day after Jean's funeral – feeling despondent and very low in spirit – I telephoned my dear friend, the author of this book, to ask him if he knew of a Spiritualist Church near me. Within the hour he had located one that was holding a meeting that very evening some 12 miles from my home.

The meeting was in a room at the town hall, and on my arrival I found it was packed, with only two vacant seats in the front row, one of which I self-consciously occupied.

I felt much better after the service commenced, and enjoyed the readings and singing. The visiting medium was good, but no messages for me. I was disappointed but not upset. At the end of the meeting I was walking towards the exit when a lady stepped out of the audience, touched my arm, and said, "Please wait a moment, I have something to tell you." She then asked, "Did you know that a grey-haired lady in bulky clothing has been sitting next to you all evening? She is upset that you are so distressed, but wants you to know that she is alright and wants you to be happy." After thanking her I made to move off, when she said: "Just a moment, she is telling me that she had difficulty in walking just before she passed over."

I felt that a great burden had been lifted from me. This description was Jean who, at 71 had grey hair – not white like mine. She was wearing a bulky Fair-isle cardigan when she passed over, and in the last few weeks had to use a zimmer frame because the steroids she was using made it difficult for her to walk. I was gob-smacked. This was spontaneous information and evidence from an independent source that did not know me or my circumstances. Jean and I had always agreed that whoever went first would try to make contact.

I have subsequently attended other meetings at this venue and found the people to be very friendly and supportive. A recent visiting medium described Jean's character to the letter whilst giving a message of love and guidance, all of which was confirmed by two friends that I had taken along with me. They too, incidentally, received excellent evidence from their departed loved ones – including a description of their recently deceased pet dog.

I do feel that death should be renamed "transition", because it is definitely not the end. Love does pierce the veil to the other world, and you ***will*** *be with your loved ones again. God loves us all!*

Keith has come through this bravely, and was determined that he was going to obtain evidence of Jean's survival and not just sit at home feeling sorry for himself. He is now an ardent seeker of Truth, and in a very short time has already proved to himself that love does not end at the grave.

If I should die and leave you here a while,
be not like others, sore undone, who keep
long vigils by the silent dust, and weep.
For my sake turn again to life and smile,
nerving thy heart and trembling hand to do
something to comfort other hearts than thine.
Complete these dear unfinished tasks of mine,
and I, perchance may therein comfort you.
Mary Lee Hall (Turn Again to Life)

The Death of a Parent

Most of us will suffer bereavement and grieve for a much-loved mother or father. And when a parent 'dies' it is the end of an era, leaving us with photographs or DVD memories to remind us that they were once with us. If this is your plight, now or in the recent past, especially if the love link between you and your parent was very close, please understand that you have only lost their physical presence for a brief while.

Your immediate concern will be for the parent who is left on their own, as they will need an abundance of love and support. You have 'lost' a parent and they have 'lost' a partner, so it is inevitable that from now on life will change for you both. With an elderly parent many experience role reversal as time goes by, and find *themselves* being the 'parent'. This is where tact, diplomacy and oodles of patience are required to ensure that dignity is maintained.

Keeping a discrete eye on your remaining parent to see how they are coping will be a wise move. The activity suggestions listed under *'The Death of a Partner'* may prove helpful here.

If you have recently suffered the 'death' of your remaining parent then it really is the end of an era. It's a time of great sadness and will require an inner strength, especially if your parent's house and personal belongings need to be sorted out and disposed of in one way or another. I have been down that path, and it can be emotionally draining deciding what to do with the little knick-knacks and ornaments that have been collected over the years. But it's all part of life's rich tapestry and a big learning curve.

If your parent(s) was blessed with even a modicum of love and compassion in this dreary old world then they will not be disappointed with their new life in the next frequency. Where there is a bond of love, then you *will* all meet again. Nature always rewards those who give love – sometime, somewhere. That is the Law.

The Death of a Son or Daughter

Few of us are ever prepared for the trauma of arranging and attending the funeral of a beloved son or daughter. If, as a parent, this is your burden of grief, either now or in the distant past, then there are no words that can adequately describe your sense of 'loss' and despair. Whatever their age or cause of 'death,' there will no doubt be emotions of anger and frustration with life and a God that you probably don't understand, or find difficult to believe in, but still blamed for the 'senseless' taking of a young life from you. You will probably have lost count of the number of times you cried yourself to sleep or said the word 'why'? Or 'Why my (or our) child'? And wonder if you will ever pick up the threads of your shattered life again and find a happiness and meaning to it all. It has probably given you a sense of insecurity and shaken your confidence in a life that will never be the same again.

Like all close bereavements, the normal life that you knew suddenly ended, and probably left you struggling to lift your head off the pillow and get out of bed each morning to face a new day. But taking each day as it comes and doing what you have to do will in time bring about a new 'normal'. You will have good and bad days, but step by step things will gradually get better. Do you think your loved one would want you to destroy the rest of your life by grief?

If you are married, or have a partner, then I hope your tragedy has brought you closer together as a result of your shared grief and not driven you apart. So many couples find it hard to share their grief with each other. Each can grieve in different ways – there are no set rules. Life may seem to take from us at times, but I have always found that if we adopt the right attitude it compensates in one way or another.

You may feel that nothing can compensate you for your 'loss', but I would ask you to please let the 'Laws of Life' be the judge of that. If you can, try to put your experience to good use by helping and comforting others in the same predicament. If you have done this already, I salute you. Many loving souls who have suffered the most appalling tragedies in life have used their experience as a force for good. It proves time and again that only by suffering can we grow in love, strength and wisdom, and that 'Before we can dry another's eye, we too must have cried'.

We expect our children to grow old with dignity, as we would wish of our parents and ourselves. But, as I hope I have shown you and trust you have understood, life is not like that. Babies can touch this earth for but a few brief minutes or hours, whilst children can return to the worlds of spirit at any time for a hundred different reasons. Nothing can or will bring your son or daughter back to this Earth. It was meant to be or it would not have happened.

It is an oddity when we say 'my son' or 'my daughter', for in reality we own no one. We may have helped to provide the physical vehicle for our offspring, but their soul (Overself) is a free spirit. Its purpose on Earth and what it had to learn may have been entirely different from ours. It is the 'age' of the soul that is important not the age of the physical body. Hence we can have 'old souls' in young bodies that can come and go of their own choosing!

Please take what comfort you can from the knowledge that your son or daughter is now more 'alive' than you are and simply living in another and better world that is 'invisible' to our earthly eyes. And in the name of love *you will meet them again*. They will be well attended by friends or relatives on the 'other side'. So, *just for you*, here are words of comfort from Margaret Prentice who, with her husband Roy, suffered the 'loss' of two of their three children at different times and through different reasons:

When my son Richard died in 1988, he was only 10-years-old. At the age of eight he was diagnosed as having Acute Lymphoblastic Leukaemia (ALL). What a shock it was to be told he only had 18 months to live if he didn't respond to chemotherapy. Roy and I were living in a nightmare from that moment on, and we both fought our emotions to keep this dreaded secret from him. We loved him so much, and we soon became aware that many other people loved him too.

People from all over the country got in touch with us to try and give us comfort. They offered money to help with my train fares and accommodation expenses when he was in hospital having chemotherapy, and also kindness and words of assurance that we were not alone in our worry. At the time all I could think about was my pain and sorrow at what was going on, in and around Richard.

Nothing anyone said or did could comfort me. I was absolutely enveloped in my own misery. The fear and shock that our little boy might die in fear and pain was almost unbearable. He thought his mum had everything under control as usual, and nothing could harm him while she was around to protect him. What a burden that is for a mother to carry. No one, not even loving parents can save their child from dying if that is the way it has got to be.

We know the doctors tried everything they could to save Richard, but he died – he actually died! How could he die when he was loved so much by so many? To try to make sense of his life and death I went on a search for some answers. I went to the Spiritualist Church to get a basic knowledge of 'life after death' and evidence that it really did exist.

Richard apparently had the same idea in his 'world'. He was evidently trying to get in touch with loved ones he had left behind on the Earth plane. Soon my broken heart was mending as Richard gradually managed to make his presence known. He gave us proof of his continued existence in the most amazing ways. He gave us wonderful messages through mediums about things that only he and us knew.

Simon died all alone one night in April 1994 at the age of 29. He was drinking and taking drugs. The coroner told us that he probably didn't know that he had taken too many pills as he had also taken some pain-killers for the constant pain in his leg due to a motorbike accident a few years earlier.

Not long after Simon's death, he too soon made us aware that he was around. He once appeared briefly to Roy, which made him question his 'When you're dead you're dead' belief. To comfort myself and lift me out of my depths of despair, I always reach for a book written by someone who has had evidence from his or her loved ones in the spirit worlds. I have found that it is the only way to get me through a bad patch of longing and grief.

Yes, I say grief, because I am still grieving after all these years, and no doubt I will be grieving until the day I die. Grief is the same as love – it goes on and on. There is one difference though – love is everlasting. Even when we die we go on loving our loved ones, but our grief ends with our death, because as I now know, we are eventually united with them. The only thing to grieve about is the lost years we have missed since our precious one 'left' us

In Dr Ian Pearce's book called One Man's Odyssey, his daughter spoke to him through a medium and she told him what to say when he prayed. This is the prayer: "I thank thee Father for the blessings of my joys. But I thank thee even more for the blessings of my sorrows, for out of them has come an illumination that has enriched my soul."

If I hadn't had the sorrow of losing our sons I wouldn't have searched for them after they died, and I would never have gained all that wonderful knowledge about life and the spirit worlds. After sorrow has come happiness through knowledge. Without knowledge life is shallow and pointless, so if your loved one has 'died', my advice is learn all you can about their life and world they are now living in. Would you move to another country that you didn't know anything about? Millions of people do just that. Knowing one day that they are going to die, they never bother to find out anything about the new world they are eventually going to pass into.

Margaret now spends her time lecturing and comforting other grieving parents, and has also written a book *Richard, Spirit and I.* In so doing, she has turned from inner grief to outwardly helping others.

> Very many parents have tragically lost a child to an illness,
> accident or suicide (surely one of the most emotionally painful
> experiences a human can undergo) yet have managed, after
> a natural period of grieving, to pick up their lives again.
> *Joe Griffin and Ivan Tyrrell (How to Lift Depression [...fast])*

Because the 'death' of a child is one of the most devastating of human experiences, I have included another touching story in the hope that it may help you to further understand your own as well as others' emotional grief. This is the personal story of Angela and Charlie Savage and, although different from the previous one, it brings it home to us all how the 'death' of a child, of any age and from whatever cause, can affect us:

In September 1997 we said goodbye to our 23-year-old son Jamie as he and his friends left for a holiday in Ibiza. Seven days later we were disturbed late at night by a loud knock on our front door. It was a policeman who had come to tell us that something had happened to Jamie. We immediately thought it was something trivial like a lost passport or tickets, but nothing prepared us for the shattering news that we were told. Jamie had been found dead in the street at the foot of a wall and the Spanish police were mystified as to the cause.

Our family was devastated. Charlie was still grieving from the sudden death of his 76-year-old mother only five weeks previously, and now we had lost Jamie. Charlie was torn apart and plunged into the depths of despair and depression. He was very close to Jamie, they were like best friends and used to do many things together – football, darts, go-karting. I was also numb with grief and felt as if all my limbs had been cut off and my soul ripped out. Charlie said he felt as if he had been taken apart and put back together with bits missing. We both cried a lot.

Our other son, Christopher, who is now 40, was also totally devastated. He now suffers from depression and is angry and bitter inside with grief. His brother's death completely confused and unsettled him. Jamie's best friends, who were with him in Ibiza, were also devastated and distraught. They will never get over it, and had the emotional trauma of bringing his luggage home with them. This hit us hard, and it tore me apart sorting through Jamie's clothing.

It took two weeks of phone calls and paperwork to get Jamie's body flown back to England. This compounded our grief, particularly as we never saw his body before it was put into the coffin. Because of this, we still find it difficult to accept that he has gone, and often think that it was all a mistake and that he will one day walk in the door. Jamie was a fit and healthy sporting lad and the verdict given was death by misadventure, as we were told he had slipped and fallen badly from the wall.

There isn't one day when we don't think about Jamie as so many things remind us of him. I get very emotional when I see lads of his age playing football or spot someone who looks like him. We still have our depressed days, but luckily Charlie and I are not down together. We somehow manage to comfort each other despite difficulty in talking about our feelings. Charlie bottles things up and is reluctant to talk, but I am convinced his pent-up emotions have resulted in his now severe health problems.

It was also very strange and hurtful, that many friends and acquaintances tended to ignore us. We felt that they just didn't know what to say. We also get emotional when strangers ask us how many children we have. If we say two, but one died, they seem lost for words. And if we just say one, then we feel we are pretending that Jamie never existed. It is very sad when people don't know how to respond to our predicament.

Jamie's death has profoundly changed the way we look at life now, and we feel deeply for other people's grief and suffering. It has also put things in perspective, as we are no longer interested in material things or the petty trivia that seems to bother so many people and rule their lives. We also get upset when people are nasty and hateful to each other, particularly when it's portrayed on television as popular "entertainment". Don't they understand that love and happiness are the most important things in our very brief lifetimes?

On the brighter side, I visited a recommended medium with a sympathetic friend. She immediately gave a perfect description of Jamie and said that he was standing by my side. She said he was concerned over my worry about the way that he had died in another country, but I mustn't because it was very quick. The medium also informed me that Jamie was with his best friend in the spirit world, and that his friend had died in a car crash soon after Jamie's passing and that he was younger than Jamie.

I had never met the lady before and there was no way that she could have known these facts. The medium finally mentioned that Jamie and his friend were doing good work in the astral worlds by comforting and helping suicides to mentally readjust so that they could take them to higher spiritual levels. I had to take her word on that of course, but knowing Jamie and his best friend it's the sort of thing they would have loved to do. They were both so kind, thoughtful and loving when they were on this Earth and nothing was too much trouble.

Angela, Charlie and Christopher gradually came to terms with Jamie's passing, but have said that grief is not like a broken arm or leg – it never completely heals. But, in their grief, they experienced a new-found love and compassion for all life.

Grief can be the garden of compassion. If you keep your
heart open through everything; your pain can become
your greatest ally in life's search for love and wisdom.
Jalalu L-Din Rumi 1207 – 1273 (Sufi mystic)

The Death of a Pet

If you have recently 'lost' your pet through an accident or had it 'put to sleep' out of kindness due to a debilitating condition, then you are entitled to grieve as you would with a human life. Over one million pets die each year in the UK and that's a lot of grief and sadness for their owners. Animals have distinct personalities and are characters in their own right with their little ways and idiosyncrasies. Most of the domesticated ones, particularly cats and dogs, give an abundance of unconditional love and affection, and especially for people living on their own, companionship and loyalty. To many, they are very much part of the family and seem to understand virtually every spoken word and even read our thoughts. They are extremely trusting, and I have noticed that dogs in particular always give eye to eye contact when spoken to – and I love the way they tilt their heads in response.

Sometimes a child's first experience of death is when a family pet dies. And many a child has cried itself to sleep over the 'death' of its hamster, rabbit or guinea pig. I have lost count of the number of adults who confessed to crying buckets of tears when their cat or dog 'passed away'. And I'm not too proud to admit that, even with my knowledge of life after death, tears ran down my cheeks when we had our 14-year-old Jack Russell put to sleep when old-age and kidney failure finally caught up with him. It's the price we pay for being softies and forming attachments to them.

Bless them all, they have as much right to be here as we have. In fact they were on this planet millions of years before we were. And, many show a wisdom and intelligence far greater than some of our own species!

Just as humans survive bodily 'death' so do animals. They too have an astral counterpart that lives on in the astral dimensions. There are countless stories of children playing with spirit animals as well as spirit children. Once again, where there is love there will eventually be a happy reunion. As with humans, it is love that bridges the gap between the two worlds. When domesticated pets 'pass over', relatives or other spirit helpers care for them until they are reunited with their earthly owners. What would life be like in any world without their company?

Over the years, I have described many spirit animals sitting or walking with their earthly owners. In the chapter *Death and Dying*, I mentioned my grandmother 'seeing' her departed pet dog Macky just before she herself 'died'. There is an abundance of documented and scientific evidence for animal survival just as there is for humans.

The Christian Church has, unfortunately, never accepted that birds and animals have souls and therefore don't survive physical death. But, it's interesting to note that the Church didn't consider *women* worthy of having souls until a vote was passed by a majority of three at the Council of Trent (1545 – 1563)! Can you imagine the spirit worlds only populated with *men* – no women, birds or animals – just *men*? What a dull afterlife this 'heaven' would be. About as boring as watching paint dry I would think!

I think I could turn and live with animals,
They are so placid and self contained,
I stand and look at them long and long.
They do not sweat and whine about their condition,
They do not lay awake in the dark and weep for their sins.

They do not make me sick discussing their duty to God;
Not one is dissatisfied, not one is demented
with the mania of owning things.
Not one kneels to another, nor to his kind
that lived thousands of years ago,
Not one is respectable or unhappy over the whole earth.
Walt Whitman 1819 – 1892 (American poet)

Giving Birth to a Handicapped Baby

If you have a baby or child so affected, please take comfort from the fact that a loving soul chose that body for a specific purpose and chose you as the proud parents. It can be very hard work with concern for the future, but many have stated that by giving lots of TLC they are compensated by an abundance of love from their very special child.

In the UK, on average, 45,000 babies a year are born with some form of handicap (1 in 16). These numbers have risen 50 per cent in the past few years, prompting The Birth Defects Foundation to caution women trying for a baby to reappraise their lifestyles such as refraining from smoking, alcohol, junk food and the taking of hard drugs. They also recommend consulting a doctor regarding prescription drug dosages. Hereditary factors can also come into the equation.

Take encouragement from Maureen Kay who tells her optimistic and uplifting story:

As I lay in the delivery suite two hours after our daughter was born, she opened her eyes for the first time and immediately I knew something was wrong. My overwhelming love for our daughter increased but it was also mixed with fear. Fear ***for*** *her but not* ***of*** *her. I wanted to be told I was wrong, but I knew I wasn't. My husband Philip assured me that all was well and that he could see nothing to worry about – but I was not convinced.*

Phil went home to put our elder son to bed whilst my sister came to visit. I asked her if she could see anything wrong with our baby daughter, and she agreed. I knew it. I didn't want anybody to agree with me, but they had. We decided to call the midwife and ask her opinion but she was very evasive. Then, a paediatrician with a medical team arrived at my bedside and insisted that Phil be called back.

Phil returned shortly after and was a little angry that I had pursued a subject that he had dismissed. Until then the words had not been mentioned, but the doctors confirmed that they were sure our baby daughter had Down's Syndrome and that a blood test would confirm this. Even so, I still felt a faint hope that they were wrong or God would change his mind overnight.

I had an underlying fear throughout the pregnancy that something was wrong, but Phil's positive attitude had kept this suppressed. Now those fears had become a reality. How would the world treat our little girl? Would people be kind to her or single her out? We were still to find out!

The next day the four grandparents were due to visit. I could deal with our daughter but not with everyone else. I needed Phil's help on this and wanted him to be there when they arrived. This is where we differed. My problem was not the diagnosis, but people's reaction to our little girl. Phil's was the diagnosis not people's reaction. Thankfully all the grandparents reacted in a positive manner and have never ceased to give us or our new daughter the utmost love and devotion.

Over the following days, although he needed time on his own with his thoughts, Phil was wonderful with our little girl. He even thanked me for giving him a beautiful daughter. He took it hard, but soon came to terms with the situation and decided that it didn't matter what the outside world thought or did. For me, I loved our little girl and wanted to protect her, and people's reactions did matter.

More tests were carried out including a heart scan. When I looked at our little daughter I sometimes wondered what we had done to her and what sort of life she would lead. But Phil was quick to set me straight and reassure me that it wasn't our fault. I felt that if our son was ill we could take him to the doctor and get him sorted out, but for our daughter there was nothing we could do to put things right. As her mother, this weighed heavily on my mind. I worried whether she would have acceptance in society as well as our son, because his sister was different from other brothers and sisters.

The days in the hospital were pleasant, and everyone was kind to Ashleigh as we had now called her, although I realised I was still living in a false environment. We had lots of visitors, but even this I questioned. Why did everyone want to see Ashleigh when they hadn't rushed to see Elliot our son? Were they showing their support as Phil had said, or did they just want to see what Ashleigh looked like? My protective barriers had risen!

We came home, and a few close friends who knew the situation visited and were very supportive. It was our wish that people would only be told of Ashleigh's condition as and when they met her. Other than that, why should they know? They wouldn't get to know this innocent baby, and this proved to be true. Word eventually got around and a few people visited as though there had been a death in the family and not a joyous birth. They seemed totally unable to relate to the fact that we were proud of our newborn daughter and loved her dearly. We didn't know what the future would hold so we decided to cross each bridge as and when we came to it! After all, she was a baby first that happened to have Downs Syndrome, not a condition first as some people treated her.

Our first outing was to a shopping centre, and we stopped to feed Ashleigh in a coffee shop. The young lady clearing the tables had Downs Syndrome and tears welled up in my eyes. We wondered if this was the life we had condemned our daughter to, but quickly realised that it didn't have to be that way because we didn't even know how our son Elliot's life would turn out.

Ashleigh is now12-years-old and goes to mainstream school. She may grow up to live independently or even get married. All we know is that she is very much a loving personality in her own right, and makes her presence felt wherever she goes. She is very independent and a great communicator even though she is lacking in vocabulary. Ashleigh and her brother Elliot love each other very much and we will be right behind her in all that she wants to do with love, support and encouragement. We feel sorry for people who can't accept her or who have trouble in doing so because they miss out on such a wonderful experience. So far these have been relatively few, and we hope this continues for Ashleigh's sake and others like her.

Ashleigh is now 13-years-of-age, an intelligent and delightful young lady, full of fun and confidence. Far from being handicapped, she gives such a lot of love and is a credit and a blessing to all. At a party, one guest remarked: 'If everyone in the world was as loving as Ashleigh we would all be living in a paradise.'

[NB: To put things in perspective, most of the population are suffering from some form of handicap, whether it is arthritis, diabetes, breathing difficulties, poor hearing or eyesight, heart problems, digestive, bowel or bladder problems, migraines, fatigue, poor memories and numerous other debilitating health problems known to medical science.]

> The Law of life is this – that the strong souls take upon themselves the heaviest burdens, whether burdens of physical disabilities or suffering in its many forms. So remember that if you are having a difficult life today this illustrates you are a strong soul and one who has endeavoured to learn some of life's harder lessons.
>
> *Adrienne Sarti (Writer and philosopher)*

Physical Violence (Grievous Bodily Harm)

If this has befallen you, then it could well have left you feeling insecure, shaken your trust in humanity and caused emotional scars – if not physical. Yes, there are those out there who are violent and we did discuss this in previous chapters – particularly domestic violence – and you may well be wondering why they picked on you or what you had done to deserve it. Answers to questions like that, as with many of life's tragedies, can often be rooted in previous lives, if the answers are not forthcoming in this one. If you have found the doctrine of rebirth, or reincarnation, hard to accept, then please try to understand that *no one is in the wrong place at the wrong time* – all is in accordance with Cosmic Law.

Such perpetrators act in ignorance, and the spiritual law of forgiveness will serve your emotional health better than any negative thoughts of hatred or revenge. You may never *forget* the incident but you will grow stronger spiritually if you can learn to forgive. Universal Justice will more than settle the debt should you do so.

'Sophie', a 36-year-old ex policewoman shares this experience with you:

During the early hours of a dull winter morning in January 1993, I was on uniformed patrol with a male and female colleague in a marked police car. We had decided to complete a final tour of the area before having our refreshment break. Our attention was drawn to two young men in a deserted street. We noticed that one of them was carrying a radio cassette player and a large bottle of alcohol, whilst the other hid behind a parked car as we approached. That was reason enough for us to investigate.

As we got out of the car the hidden man attempted to run away. We caught him and a struggle ensued. We managed to restrain him on the ground with his hands behind his back, and were about to handcuff him when I became acutely aware of the presence of the other man with the bottle standing behind us and getting very agitated.

Leaving my colleagues to finish the job – which I thought was under control – I took the bottle away from this man and went to place it on the pavement, but was caught off guard by a punch in the face. Instinctively knowing I was in big trouble with him being the stronger person, my instant reaction was to stall him until my colleagues were in a position to help. Never having faced this scenario before, I decided to opt for the restraining approach by clinging to him for dear life.

The kicks and blows came raining down as I felt my strength ebbing away, but I refused to give up. The situation was further complicated when the first man managed not only to free himself, but also to produce a knife with which he stabbed my male colleague. Hearing all this over my personal radio and knowing that the "cavalry" were on their way, strengthened my resolve. As we both saw the bloodstained knife appear on the pavement in front of us, a strange calmness came over me as I mentally prepared myself for the end. I knew he wanted the knife and I couldn't hold on much longer. I was just about to give up when our backup arrived and saved the day.

Both men were arrested and subsequently convicted. My injured colleague was rushed to hospital, and although he sustained a horrific assault totalling 12 stab wounds, miraculously managed, not only to survive, but also to recover sufficiently to resume active duty. I sustained neck and back injuries that incapacitated me for six months. Physiotherapy over a three-year period eventually restored most of my mobility, but not enough to return to active duty. This resulted in my medical retirement.

That battle, surprisingly, proved to be the least of my problems. Nothing in my 26 years on this planet had prepared me for the ferocity of my attack upon myself. I was engulfed by a torrent of negative emotions such as guilt, self-recrimination, fear, anxiety, vulnerability, failure, anger, self-doubt and depression. All my negative traits were magnified as I sank deeper into a pit of despair. I became a recluse who was weak and out of control and I hated myself for it.

A combination of prescription drugs, alcohol, and therapy from psychologists, psychiatrists, psychotherapists and counsellors failed to reach me. I was labelled with "Post Traumatic Stress Disorder"! When my marriage fell apart and my mother died, I was left with two choices – to live or to commit suicide. I opted for the former.

Knowing I needed to get my head sorted out, I joined a meditation class. All the professionals had previously told me that our thoughts dictate our feelings, but I had not been taught how to master this art – until now. The metamorphosis was gradual but permanent. This also led to my attending a Hatha Yoga class that taught me to love my body as well as myself. The lesson I learnt the hard way was that you cannot find the answers you need unless you look deep within yourself. No one can do this for you.

I was amazed by what I found and who I really was – it gave my life a new meaning and purpose. I feel I am growing into a much better person and have been given the tools I need to achieve it. I still have my bad days, but I accept them as part of me and move on. The more I practise the more I realise that every day is a blessing.

Knowing that only she could make that decision to pull back from the depths of despair, 'Sophie' brought her life under control through self-realisation, utilising the spiritual tools of meditation and yoga.

Non-violence leads to the highest ethics which is the goal of all evolution.
Until we stop harming all other living beings we are still savages.
Thomas Alva Edison 1847 – 1931 (American inventor)

Sexual Abuse as a Child

The sexual abuse of children is more of a problem than society is willing to admit. And the shocking truth is that much abuse comes from someone the child knows or trusts, be it a teacher, priest, carer or relative. It is a disease that seems prevalent in so-called 'civilised' societies and is rife across the class barrier. Those who perpetrate such abuse have yet to develop a conscience, integrity or morals and understand the meaning of love and affection.

If you have been a 'victim', then you may well feel that you have been mentally and emotionally scarred for life by harbouring feelings of guilt or shame or finding it difficult to form relationships or trust people again. This is a heavy and unnecessary 'baggage' to carry and really needs to be dumped rather than let the past spoil the present moment and the future. 'Rosemary', a 50-year-old mother of two relates her story:

When a male neighbour began to be verbally aggressive towards me I started to experience a deep anxiety. I was overcome with fear, felt suicidal and became hysterical at the slightest provocation. I realised this was an over reaction, but that didn't change the feelings. Although my doctor prescribed antidepressants, I didn't take the medication and was fortunate enough to be recommended to a good homeopath who was also a healer and counsellor.

My therapy revealed that the neighbour's behaviour had triggered a reaction to the three years of sexual abuse I had suffered from the age of 13 at the hands of an uncle. All the fear, confusion and revulsion of being violated by a trusted adult was now pouring out. I had feelings of shame, guilt and disgust at myself as the responsibility for keeping the 'secret' for 28 years was released. When I realised that the abuse had had such a profound effect on virtually every aspect of my teenage and adult life, I experienced intense anger.

The therapy also allowed me to grieve for my father who had committed suicide when I was five-years-old. I had suppressed this grief for 35 years and it had caused me great distress. I had come across his suicide note when I was 14-years-of-age, which was during the period of my sexual abuse.

After six months of counselling and spiritual healing there was a marked improvement in my mental wellbeing, but an unexpected encounter with my abuser set me back, and once more my emotional instability surfaced. By this time I had been encouraged to take up Hatha yoga and found it to be beneficial both mentally and physically. After many months of yoga practise and the study of its philosophy, I felt that meditation was a natural progression, and under the guidance of a teacher, found it very therapeutic. I meditated every spare moment and asked the eternal question, "Who am I?" and asked for guidance on healing myself. It brought me a great spiritual awareness.

Over the next month or so, remarkable things occurred. People came into my life who guided and helped me. During meditation I received insights into how I could move forward, and on occasions saw images of people who would later support me. I learnt to trust my own instincts and have the courage to act upon them. When this experience proved successful, it gave me feelings of enormous strength, courage and power over my own destiny – something that I had never felt before.

A major step in my healing occurred when I 'woke up' to the knowledge that my spirit was separate from my mind and body, and no matter what damage was inflicted on my mind and body, nobody could touch or harm my spirit. I knew that my body was for this world only, and that my spirit was eternal and a source of peace, love and happiness. This allowed me to forgive, though not condone the actions of my abuser, which was something that I had thought impossible. I had been set free. Truly a miracle had happened.

Shortly afterwards, I felt spiritually guided to confront my abuser – a man of whom I had previously been terrified. In a dignified and controlled way I told him of the damage that he had done to me and that in future he must stay out of my life.

The above story illustrates, once more how, by using the spiritual approach, negative emotional baggage can be dissolved, and hatred and fear of the abuser replaced by pity and forgiveness. It doesn't take away the fact that these things happened, but it proves the fact that people like 'Rosemary', and you, have the power to change things for the better by letting the past hurts go and living for the peace of the *now*.

Nothing can bring you peace but yourself.
Ralph Waldo Emerson 1803 – 1882 (American philosopher and poet)

Marital Problems of Unfaithfulness or Divorce

I have previously highlighted this problem in the chapter on suicide, simply because many feel suicidal when it happens to them. Because divorce is ranked second to bereavement as one of the most traumatic and stressful experiences, I will touch briefly on it again. If this is your predicament, whether you are the one who left or has been left, feelings of hurt, loneliness and a dozen other volatile reactions will create emotional havoc. It doesn't mean to say that there is something wrong with you or that you are a failure – although many in such circumstances quite naturally feel that way.

At whatever age it happens, starting a new life is always something to see as a challenge and not an obstacle. How do you know that life hasn't got someone or something better for you? If you have children to look after then they are your first priority, as they will probably be more confused, unsettled and insecure than you, so give each other lots of love and cuddles. It's very therapeutic, will work wonders and pay dividends in the long term.

I have been where you are now and, as countless others have found, it can be extremely painful. But life can often take a turn for the better with no desire to put the clock back. It can make us look at life from a different perspective and rearrange our priorities. In my case it gave me more love and affection than I could ever have dreamed of, and was the beginning of a new spiritual phase in my life. It can be one in yours also. Let the past go, look forward to the future and let life unfold for the better – it will if you really want it to! Here are the words of Janet, a 62-year-old mother of three grown-up girls:

I have been a seeker of truth since my teenage years, and now reflect on my life as one big rollercoaster ride with its ups and downs and twists and turns. Life has taught me well, even though some of the lessons have been hard. But nothing could have prepared me for my hardest lesson yet to come.

My marriage developed problems soon after we decided to move house and prepare for retirement. I didn't really want to move and found it difficult to leave friends, sell our furniture and move to a place where we didn't know anyone. Change is something many of us are apprehensive about and I faced it as a new chapter in my life. But, unbeknown to me, my husband had planned a different agenda – one that didn't include me!

After severe emotional pressure and a series of difficult circumstances I couldn't take much more, and decided that divorce was the only way out. We discussed divorce, but he still stayed in the house and was determined to make things as difficult for me as he could. At the time, I was looking after an elderly sick relative who was staying with us. This and the stress of the last year had affected my family badly, especially me. My husband, who was not working, started to lay guilt and blame on me – everything was my fault. Day in day out his bullying verbal abuse never stopped as he belittled and insulted the family and me.

One day, my elderly relative collapsed on the floor. I was crying and begged him to leave, as I was not coping very well with the situation. He refused, and said the courts would decide. I was now on a pathway I didn't want to be on. I don't like confrontation but he left me no choice – it was going to be a bitter fight through the courts. The pressure became immense and, broken and confused, I left the house and stayed with one of my daughters. I had lost the plot and didn't know what he was up to. After receiving medication and advice from my doctor, I returned to the house to collect my youngest daughter, elderly relative and dog.

Depression set in, and as the days passed I became more isolated within myself. I couldn't believe this was happening to me and found it difficult to raise my spirits. I felt alone, disconnected, unbelievable sadness, emotionally bereft and physically exhausted. I couldn't eat, sleep or think. It felt as though a thick fog had descended around me and I couldn't see, hear or feel anything.

At the time, I had an assortment of painkillers and various medications needed by my elderly relative who was still dependant upon me. Suicidal thoughts crossed my mind as I wondered if these painkillers would end ***my*** *pain – permanently. Then I thought of the consequences for my daughters, as ripples of their grief would go on forever and destroy their lives.*

With tears streaming down my face, I prayed to God to help me through this darkness and despair, as I could feel a nervous breakdown looming and couldn't hold on much longer. It was then that I fell into a deep sleep. For how long, I didn't know, but when I awoke, something was different. For the next two days I realised that the fog was lifting and things were starting to become clearer. It was then that I opened a magazine and found the poem 'Footprints' and just cried. They were tears of relief, knowing my darkest hour was now over and that I hadn't been alone at all! I moved back into my home with a new-found confidence, clarity and strength.

My husband moved out – to live with "the other woman". The mental and financial battle continued, but I could handle it. Every day I was thankful as my heart opened up and filled with love. This enabled me to learn forgiveness and I felt very sorry for my husband that he had behaved in such an underhand and nasty way. I was determined to put this chapter in my life behind me and move on.

I have learnt that choice and responsibility ***are*** *mine, and mine alone, as I now have the freedom to be me – and understand the* ***real*** *me that was waiting to emerge from being dominated and manipulated. This lesson has been harsh, but I now realise that I have a 'silent army' by my side that is giving me love, strength and encouragement as a new chapter opens before me. Where will I go, what will I do? Who knows? I just know that I will not do it alone – and I find that exciting!*

This is but a part of Janet's divorce drama that was ongoing for two years, during which she was taken to breaking point when love turned to premeditated hatred and abuse. It is interesting to note that, at her lowest ebb, Janet turned to prayer. Listening to her now, not once did I hear talk of revenge or hatred on her part for the man she once loved and trusted – just compassion. Janet is a lovely person who has still retained her sense of humour, and one might argue that she didn't deserve to suffer such a trauma. But if she was being tried and tested spiritually to see what she was made of then, as far as I am concerned, she passed the test with honours!

> We must always realise that the particular set of circumstances in which we find ourselves – the events and the happenings that take place in our life from time to time – are the best and most suitable for the character teaching, and the character testing and the character formation, that we could have in order to learn the lessons needed at that particular time and to attain a further advance in our spiritual progression.
>
> *Adrienne Sarti (Writer and philosopher)*

Paralysed or Disabled after an Accident or Stroke

If this is your plight, then you will have had good cause to seriously reflect on life, especially if your disablement was due to an accident caused by someone else's mistake. People can, and do, overcome severe injuries and strokes through sheer determination that they are not going to let it beat them. Willpower, or mind power if you like, can heal and work apparent miracles. I have met many people who have recovered to lead normal lives again despite being told otherwise by doctors.

Here are encouraging and inspiring words from Lin McLoughlin who, at the age of 37, was badly injured in a car crash in November 1997:

I don't remember being cut out of the wreckage or the journey to the hospital in Yorkshire, but I do remember regaining consciousness in a hospital in Leeds. Apparently they had taken my neck brace off without being aware of the severity of my injuries. This resulted in a stroke that put me into a coma for four days, hence the transfer to a more suitable hospital. I was paralysed from the neck down, and the doctors told my husband that I probably wouldn't survive and, if I did, would never walk again and probably be a "vegetable".

After a couple of weeks I started to regain partial movement of my left side, and had to wait a few more weeks before my right side responded. I couldn't speak because my brain was still affected by the stroke, my nose had been broken, my cheekbone smashed and my jaw wouldn't move properly. Although I had tubes coming out of every orifice, I became aware of a non-physical person with me all the time. I wasn't at all frightened, and instinctively knew that they were giving me healing, whoever they were.

Several times, whilst lying in bed, I would see a bright ball of light about 60 centimetres (two feet) in diameter hovering in front of me. When it hit me I would feel a warm glow inside and a tremendous feeling of love and well-being. I knew that I was being healed and it seemed to give me a great humility and an inner knowing of the Spiritual Laws of life, coupled with a love and compassion for all living things. [This is reminiscent of the God Consciousness experiences discussed in Chapter 8 – Author].

On another occasion, I saw, quite clearly, my ex-boss standing at the foot of the bed. He was smiling at me and looked extremely happy. At that exact moment, I once more, intuitively knew that I was going to get better. I didn't know it then, but I was later told that he had died of cancer soon after my accident. I was in hospital for a total of six months – and I ***did*** *make a remarkable recovery.*

I had only been out of hospital for a couple of months when my 62-year-old mother had a massive stroke and was put on a life support machine. The situation was hopeless, and it was a unanimous family decision to have the machine turned off. Within minutes of it happening I saw a vision of my smiling mother standing in the doorway of my father's house where I was staying at the time. It was at least 10 miles from the hospital.

By now, I was seeing spirit people frequently, and would even wake up in the night and find them wanting to chat with me. They were very nice people and I wasn't in the least bit frightened, but I began to regard it as an invasion of my privacy and a disruption to my sleep pattern.

I was, by then, convinced that my accident had somehow awoken psychic and spiritual faculties within me, and realised that life-threatening incidents can change people's awareness factor. I was ***determined*** *to get better and I am convinced that I had help from people in other dimensions. I have never been interested in dogmatic religion, but I am now seriously drawn towards meditation, yoga and metaphysical subjects.*

Despite her appalling injuries and severe stroke, Lin has, through healing and shear determination, made an incredible recovery. There is not a scar on her face or any other visible impediment with her body.

I first met Lin at a yoga class, but it was months later after a meditation session that she told me of her frustration of constantly seeing spirit people. I realised that she was an open psychic and told her how to 'close down' by firmly, but politely, telling them to please go away and not bother her, mentally flick a switch to 'off' and symbolically 'zip' herself up from head to toe. This she did that same night and has not had a problem since. Lin explained that she would like to be a healer to help others just as she has been helped. She has the necessary qualities and the right attitude – love, compassion, humility and dedication.

This is an example of how traumatic events quite often change the direction of our lives onto pathways that we might not have otherwise ventured!

It is possible to lose one's job or a limb, to break one's spine, contract polio or an incurable disease, and still rise above it, to make the most of what is left, and even to use it to spur one on to greater heights. History is full of stories whose achievements were negligible till they were struck down. Only when faced with an interminable future of uselessness or immobility did they determine to prove they would not be beaten.

David Brandon-Jones 1936 - 1986 (Practical Palmistry)

Diagnosed with a Terminal or Debilitating Illness

Over the years I have come into contact with numerous people in this situation, and most have borne it bravely. 'Why me?' or 'What did I do to get this?' as well as the negative emotions of anger, fear and resentment are perfectly natural human responses. Most have found that acceptance of the problem and the dumping of negative factors was the first and best requirement to allow any form of healing to take place.

'OK, I have it, so what can I do about it?' and, 'I'm not going to let this beat me,' are often voiced positive statements. A positive attitude is an extremely powerful immune system booster.

Coping with a debilitating illness isn't easy, and it can put a terrible strain on relationships until all concerned come to terms with it and learn to cope as best they can. Let me introduce you to Anne B, a mother of three:

I can still remember the day the symptoms started, pushing my six-month-old baby along an alleyway next to a local supermarket. And I'll never forget the moment I got the diagnosis. "How do you feel?" asked the neurologist. "Great," I said. "No you don't," he replied, "we found something wrong." The "something wrong" was brain lesions, and the diagnosis was multiple sclerosis. From that moment my health started on a downward spiral.

It may sound strange, but this was what I had always dreaded. I have no idea why – I didn't know anyone with it and had always been fit and well. But once over the initial shock I resumed a normal life. It wasn't painful or debilitating and it wasn't obvious. In fact, it wasn't a problem.

Perhaps I was too complacent, because in March 1999, six years after the first symptoms, I suddenly went downhill – rapidly. Coincidentally, I had just had all my amalgam teeth fillings removed and I am certain there was a connection. Within a month my balance had practically gone; my right arm wasn't working and I was dragging my right foot having to hang on to walls and furniture to get around. I could no longer take or collect the children from school. After 40 years, I found I couldn't take my body for granted any more.

Even my personality started to change and I accused my husband of not being able to understand. It put a terrible strain on our marriage and brought us to the brink of divorce. Suddenly, the marriage vows of 'In sickness and in health' hit home. We went to counselling and talked our problems through with each other. Gradually, we put our lives back together.

Even at the height of my despair I knew it wouldn't last, despite what the neurologists told me. I just know the human body isn't meant to be permanently ill, and it didn't take me long to get into alternative health. It's an obvious step when faced with an illness that baffles the medical profession. Is it something we are born with? What causes or triggers it? And most baffling of all, what cures it? Since my diagnosis I have done a lot of research and written articles on alternative medicines and therapies regarding MS. Drugs are thrown at it, but they only work for some people. Many mock alternative treatment but there is no doubt that it works for many.

I thought I was a weak person, but MS has taught me that I am far from that. It has also made me think deeper about life, and it amazes me how much more understanding, knowledge and empathy I now have. I can't deny that I would rather have had these things without having to suffer a major health setback in the process, but then, would I really have had them without that experience?

This is an interesting story in that Anne contracted the very disease that she had continually feared, highlighting once more the power of thought for good or ill. I have come to admire Anne's sense of humour and positive attitude towards her MS, and how she sees it as a challenge rather than an insurmountable problem. She also confessed that in many ways her illness has made her a much better person.

> We need to be careful of what we think and talk. Because thought runs in currents as real as those of air and water. Of what we think and talk we attract to us a like current of thought. This acts on mind and body for good or ill.
> *Prentice Mulford 1834 – 1891(Thoughts are Things)*

Summary

The stories you have just read, painful though they have been to the ones affected, have been emotional and encouraging, and are but a fraction of the life-changing traumas of everyday life. On a global scale the list can be lengthy, and virtually all of us will experience at least one of these in our lifetime – even those who think that such traumas only happen to 'other people'. Once experienced, it is noticeable how many rearrange their priorities and no longer view material objects and trivial concerns as important. The arguing, bickering, violence, tittle-tattle, selfishness and greed that are so prevalent in society become abhorrent to them.

I make no apologies for repeating that the tragedy of life is that few ever sincerely question or search for any meaning and purpose to life until tragedy strikes. It reinforces the truism that life *is* the best teacher.

Some of the kindest and the most compassionate and humble of people that I have ever had the pleasure to meet have experienced tragic situations in their lives. Most have triumphed over adversity – and so can you. All it needs is your permission to do so! My heart goes out to all who have suffered such emotional trauma. But my sincerest wish is that out of your suffering you may experience a new-found awakening of wisdom and spiritual growth so that you will see the world in a different light.

Understanding that grief, pain and suffering can be character and soul building gives us another piece of life's puzzle. Hopefully, this book will have inspired you to ask many questions on the philosophy of life, so in the next chapter I will endeavour to answer some of the ones most commonly asked.

You are in this world to face problems and difficulties and to learn the lessons from them so that your spirit grows and evolves as the result. It is only through meeting with handicaps, obstacles, problems, and sufferings, and facing them constructively that your spirit can thrive. Otherwise you would be spineless mentally and you would be weaklings spiritually.
Silver Birch (Spirit Guide and teacher)

Do you not see how necessary a world of pain and suffering is to school an intelligence and make it a soul.
John Keats 1795 –1821(Poet)

16 Questions and Answers

I never learn anything talking. I only learn things when I ask questions.
Lou Holtz (American football coach and writer)

There are no foolish questions and no man becomes
a fool until he has stopped asking questions.
Saul Steinberg 1914 – 1999 (American artist)

If we are thoughtful enough to ask a serious question then we deserve to get a serious answer. If the person you ask doesn't know, or can't give you a satisfactory answer, then move on and ask someone else who can – being wary of flippant answers that can sometimes mask ignorance.

When setting out on the quest for Truth I questioned everything, almost to the point of being a pest, and was never satisfied until the answers were confirmed by at least three independent sources, that it made sense and intuitively felt right. There are four principle ways of gaining this knowledge and, that is, by reading books, attending lectures, asking questions and having direct personal experiences.

If we don't read books or ask questions then we will remain ignorant and, as previously stated, ***criticism without investigation is the highest form of ignorance***. As humans, we are unique in having the ability to question, so if we don't, then we are no better than the plants and animals. For *almost* every question the human mind can ask there is *always* an answer – somehow, somewhere. Quite often, a question answered can invite even more questions.

So bearing that in mind, I have compiled a list of typical and often asked questions. No doubt you will find many more to ask. Some have been covered in previous chapters, but you may find it helpful to have them in this format.

1 Life

Q: Why isn't everyone interested in the philosophy of life?

A: Many people are simply not interested or don't have the awareness to question such things. There are also those who think it's mumbo jumbo, evil, dabbling with the occult or only for weird people – that is, until tragedy strikes in their life. We should also respect that many have very restrictive comfort zones and prefer the 'ignorance is bliss' philosophy, particularly if they are frightened of such subjects. Nature is still the best teacher and she will, sooner or later, cause every one of us to question life – even if it's on our deathbed.

Q: Why isn't this knowledge taught in schools?

A: A question many ask. If this knowledge was understood at an early age and put into practice in everyday life. We would certainly have a much happier and peaceful world, with less violence, selfishness and greed. It would also enable many to understand life's purpose and perhaps save some from taking their own lives when life feels unbearable.

Q: Is this philosophy called New Age Teachings?
A: Some might call it that, but such knowledge is ages-old and hasn't changed for thousands of years. How can it if it's the Truth? It was better known as the Ancient Wisdom Teachings in the East and Orient and was taught and practised by the Chinese, Egyptians, Tibetans, Native American Indians and the Greek philosophers as well as dozens of other ancient races and cultures. Some of the early religions picked up on the spiritual and mystical aspects but, down the centuries, what truths they contained became virtually lost due to misinterpretations, mistranslations and interpolations. In reality, we are dealing with the fundamental laws of life that govern the Universe. It is simply the science of mathematics and physics that the Greek mathematician and philosopher Pythagoras taught 2,500 years ago – known today as quantum physics.

Q: How can we have a better and more caring world?
A: By becoming better and more caring people. We have tried violence for thousands of years and proved it doesn't work. Unfortunately, many amongst us haven't learned that lesson yet. If we make an effort to change ourselves for the better and see that our children are brought up with love, affection and security, then within a few generations we will have a less violent, less corrupt, less greedy and more caring world. Study Native American Indian philosophy – it worked for thousands of years.

2 Health

Q: Why is there so much sickness and disease if there is a God of love?
A: Harbouring negative emotions such as anger, fear, worry and anxiety, and generally abusing our bodies has lowered our immunity to disease and altered our genetic structure. The problem is now amplified due to all the junk food and drink on the market, much of which is a lethal cocktail of chemical additives. Add to this, drugs and large doses of alcohol and we have a recipe for disaster.

Our health is our own personal responsibility – not an impersonal God's – so we have the freewill choice to wreck our bodies with self-destructive habits if we so wish. And because there is no 'death', all it will do is prematurely put us into one of the astral planes.

Q: Why do domestic animals get sick and die of degenerative diseases?
A: Because we feed them on processed foods laced with chemicals and other rubbish foods that they would never eat in their natural state. We also over-feed them, particularly with sugary 'tit-bits' and 'treats' that can lead to obesity, arthritis and cancer – we can literally kill our pets with 'kindness'. When we feed animals with unnatural foods they become sick – just like humans! Many are also cooped up in houses or back yards all day and never given adequate exercise to keep them healthy. Chemical foods and cramped conditions are the main reasons why battery-farmed animals get sick and have to be pumped full of antibiotics and steroids – which we ingest if we eat them!

3 Happiness

Q: Why is it so difficult to find real happiness?
A: As a race we are selfish and greedy. All the while we continue to think of self with our materialistic needs and wants we will be unhappy – because we are *taking* from life. When we practise the spiritual Laws governing life and death and, care about others and all living things, we will find real and lasting happiness – because we will be *giving* to life. In a nutshell, takers are unhappy and givers are happy.

Q: I often get depressed; will I be happier in the spirit worlds?
A: No. Happiness is *now*, and has to be experienced here first. You will be exactly like you were at the moment of death and take your unhappiness with you – nothing changes. We have incarnated on this planet to learn valuable lessons for our spiritual progress. Getting our priorities right by cultivating happiness for the right reasons is but one of them.

4 Religion

Q: Why do we have so many diverse religions and cults?
A: Simply the differing interpretations and opinions of the scriptures. People must find their own pathways in life, and many have found great comfort in a religious faith and belief system. If it is a religion based on love and compassion and helps us to lead better lives then it is fulfilling a useful purpose. If it divides the human race instead of uniting it, then it is not.

Q: Don't we need religion to give society moral guidance?
A: That should have been its purpose but it has failed miserably. Many see

religion as outdated, intolerant, corrupt, hypocritical and divisive. It needs to get its own house in order if it's going to survive or give any form of moral guidance. In the past, and even in our supposedly more 'enlightened' age, unimaginable atrocities have been committed in the name of religion.

Most of us instinctively know the difference between right and wrong, and parents or carers are in the best position to be good role models for their children. We don't need to belong to a religion to understand and live a life based on unconditional love, peace and harmony – it's plain common sense!

Q: Isn't the human race inherently religious?
A: No, it's inherently spiritual, with a natural desire to love and be loved.

Q: What is the difference between religion and spirituality?
A: Religions are organised institutions where followers accept set dogmas, creeds and rituals that they must believe in. They are also encouraged to have blind faith and belief without questioning – any literature to the contrary being generally discouraged. This becomes a veritable ball and chain for the mind. Being informed that we are miserable sinners who must confess and repent or go to 'an everlasting fiery hell' when we die, could be considered laughable from institutions and clerics that, over the centuries, have themselves been far from spiritual.

A person is called spiritual if they have a natural abundance of unconditional love and compassion for others, irrespective of their religion or beliefs. There are numerous very 'spiritual' self-confessed atheists who are the kindest and most compassionate of people.

Q: Should we just have blind faith in a God and not question?
A: If there is a God then we have a right to question the enigma of life; that's what we have a mind for – to think and question. Faith is often an excuse for lack of answers, knowledge and experience. Doesn't the Christian religion say 'Seek and ye shall find'? How can we do that without questioning? We each have a mind and the knowledge is out there.

Q: What is your opinion of agnostics and atheists?
A: The vast majority of those I have met over the years have been very nice people. Taking the world on face value and the hypocrisy and sham of religion, I wouldn't blame them. It's not my policy to convince or convert, but if they ask sincere questions about the philosophy of life then I will respond based on knowledge and experience. I was an agnostic until I investigated.

5 Life After Death

Q: Do you believe in a life after death and why?
A: I more than believe – I *know* there is life after death, because of serious investigation and countless personal experiences, as well as proven research by some of the world's most renowned scientists.

Q: How do you know that it's not wishful thinking or self-delusion?
A: I'm not a wishful thinker. I set out with an open mind to prove a life after death one way or the other. Just as I did with engineering design projects – if it didn't work then I abandoned the idea. Similarly if I had proved to myself that there was no such thing as life after death – just oblivion – then I would have abandoned the project years ago. Life's too short to waste it on meaningless 'airy-fairy' beliefs of my own making.

Q: What do you say to sceptics and debunkers who don't accept a life after death?
A: Very little, except to advise them to read some of the hundreds of books and reports written by eminent scientists and researchers who thoroughly investigated the subject. I try not to waste time and energy with people who are not interested in researching a fact that is under their very noses. Despite satellite evidence, it would be like arguing with the Flat Earth Society. Evidence is readily available to the numerous open-minded ones who seriously want to know.

Q: What is your opinion of fraudulent mediums?
A: The same as I think of bogus and incompetent doctors, corrupt and rotten policemen and paedophile vicars and priests. They are the dregs of humanity that abuse a position of trust and take advantage of people at a vulnerable time in their life. They give the majority a bad name that, unfortunately, gets tarred with the same brush.

Q: Does it bother you that some people think mediums are weird because they claim they can communicate with the dead?
A: No. Over the last century thousands of mediums have been investigated by prominent scientists and proven genuine. On the other hand, some people believe that on an indefinable 'judgement day' trumpets will sound and the dead will rise up from the graves and take possession of the Earth. I'm not aware of any scientists that have investigated and proven that theory.

In 1937, The Archbishop of Canterbury, Dr Cosmo Lang, and the Archbishop of York, Dr William Temple, appointed the Church of England to form a committee to investigate Spiritualism. In 1939, two years after intensive investigation, the report was suppressed when found to be in favour of Spiritualism offering genuine evidence of life after death. It was officially released into the public domain 40 years later.

Q: Should we believe everything that we are told by mediums?
A: No, any more than you should believe what you are told by anybody. Even genuine mediums can get it wrong or have off-days and, even the best are never 100 per cent accurate. Be guided by your own intuition and if it feels right at the time then accept it. No two mediums work the same and many work at different levels of consciousness.

The main objective of a medium should be to give evidence by way of physical descriptions, personality or voice contact that our 'deceased' loved ones live on in another dimension. If people only wish to hear whether they are going to be lucky in love or get a better job then they must take what comes whether it be true or false.

Q: Can anyone be taught how to see and hear people in the spirit worlds?
A: Yes, most people can, but it's best done through a competent and experienced teacher not a DIY book on the subject. It requires dedication and discipline combined with love and humility. The human race is inherently psychic, which is Nature's way of proving to us that there is no death. This fact has been known for thousands of years in all cultures until vested interests interfered with this knowledge.

Many children are naturally psychic and often play with spirit children and animals that reside in the normally unseen universe. Unfortunately, many of them lose the ability as they grow up due to the pressures of this materialistic world and parental ignorance of the subject. Children can give excellent evidence of life after death. It's also fascinating when a cat or dog follows a spirit person across a room with their eyes. Our feline and canine friends are very good mediums which, to them, is perfectly natural.

Teaching people to be clairvoyant is only bringing out latent psychic faculties. If we can sense atmospheres in buildings and places then we are naturally psychic. Indigenous tribes that live close to nature naturally see the spirit worlds and it's no big deal to them. It is we in the Western world that freak out and make such a fuss about a perfectly natural phenomenon.

Q: Is it true that our loved ones in the spirit worlds are always with us and will protect us?
A: I doubt it. They may pop back from time to time to see how we are getting

on, for special anniversaries or when we have a problem, but they also have lives of their own in their new environment and must move on to learn and progress. Coming back here every five minutes is not going to do them any favours.

Those in the spirit worlds, who are endowed with the most love and compassion, will be in a better position to offer protection to their loved ones. The more highly evolved spirit guides are better served because of their additional knowledge and experience. Many a person has been saved from tragedy by spirit warnings, either visual or vocal.

Q: Is it evil to talk to the dead?

A: Is it evil to talk to the 'living'? Of course not, so how can it be evil to talk to them when they are 'dead'? They are still people. My parents and other loved ones are in the spirit worlds and were lovely people when they were on earth, so who says they are now evil or that it's evil to talk to them? What an insult to our intelligence!

This myth originated from orthodox religion, so if they really believe it, why do so many clergy have private consultations with mediums? Some clerics quote the Bible where it says 'Thou shalt not consult mediums', but rarely quote the contradiction (1 Corinthians 12:10) where Paul talks about 'spiritual gifts' and is credited with saying '… To another the discerning of spirits'. The Bible also tells us to test the spirits to see if they be of God. If the truth be known, we are *all* spirits and we are *all* of God, whatever dimension, planet or galaxy we inhabit.

All praise to the late Rt. Reverend Mervyn Stockwood, former Bishop of Southwark who, with evidence and proof, fully accepted life after death and spoke to many of his 'deceased' loved ones through mediums. And, unlike many of his contemporaries, he wasn't frightened to speak on the subject. He even wrote the introduction to the book *Ena Twigg: Medium.*

Q: The Earth's population is growing at the rate of 100 million a year, so if we have souls or spirits, where are they all coming from?

A: It is rather naïve of us to think that our tiny Earth has the only life forms in a Cosmos billions of light years across. The Absolute (God) continually manifests life in myriads of forms throughout this vast arena. Consciousness (souls), in every species – minerals, plants, trees, insects and animals – will, over millions of years, take on human form to continue to evolve and learn by experiencing.

Q: Did you see spirit people all the time when you where a medium?

A: No, thank goodness, and I have never met a working medium who wants to. To see people in the astral worlds we have to switch on and tune in, rather like a radio or television receiver. Would you want to keep telephoning your family and friends all day and all night? Probably not, because they wouldn't thank you for it and, *you* wouldn't get much done here either. Our families and friends in the spiritual worlds feel exactly the same. They have their lives to live and we have ours – but chatting now and again is fine.

Q: When you see spirit people how clear are they?
A: It varies. Sometimes they are as clear as looking at people on Earth. When they are not so clear, it's like seeing them through frosted glass. Sometimes they can't be seen, but sensed (clairsentience), enough to give a description. It depends on atmosphere and the recipient's positive or negative attitude.

6 Death and Dying

Q: Why are so many people afraid of death?
A: Ignorance, due to lack of knowledge and personal experience. One has only to witness the hysteria of the masses around the world when death scenes have taken place to see that they don't understand. Talk of God, heaven and a 'life hereafter' is cheap and rolls off the tongues of priests the world over, but it means nothing to our Mr and Mrs Average, hence their fear, anger and hysterics when it happens. I have even met clerics who didn't believe in a life after death, so what hope have they got of comforting the dying and bereaved?

Q: Why is death such a taboo subject for the majority of people?
A: Fear, and the thought of the inevitable. Knowledge and experience will dissolve the fear. Death has been part of life for millions of years. How strange that we should still be so ignorant of it in the 21st century!

Q: What is death?
A: When our astral body leaves our physical body for good – a permanent astral projection. Once the physical body becomes too old, diseased or damaged beyond repair then the astral body can no longer operate it. The astral cord – the lifeline with the physical – disintegrates, and the astral body leaves the physical to be cremated or decay and thus 'recycled' under the law of Nature.

Q: Is death and dying painful?
A: The physical process of 'dying' can be painful depending on the circumstances of the 'death'. The physical body can only stand so much pain

before it loses consciousness. Pain ceases once the astral body is free of its physical counterpart, as those who have had out-of-the-body or near-death experiences and lived to tell the tale, will confirm.

Q: My six-year-old daughter is obsessed with death and dying since my mother passed away and keeps asking where her nanny has gone. I tell her she has gone to heaven but she wants to know where heaven is, what it's like and if we are all going to die and go there. What can I say to reassure her?

A: This is a common predicament for many parents, particularly when we tend to underestimate the intelligence and understanding of young children. You could say something like: 'Although we have a physical body that can die because of sickness or an accident, everyone also has an invisible body [called the astral body (optional)] that *doesn't* die. It will continue to live in an invisible world surrounding our Earth. It is known as *Heaven* and is full of love, beautiful flowers, trees, animals, birds and people. Nanny will be there with lots of our loved ones who went before her.' Most children will understand the word 'invisible' because it is widely used in their play themes, books and films. The words can be varied to suit the age and understanding of the child.

Q: Spiritually, does it make any difference whether we are buried or cremated?

A: No difference whatsoever. The physical body is only a worn out garment that has no further use once the spirit has abandoned it. The type of funeral we have is our own personal choice. Many areas of the world are running out of land to bury their dead, leaving cremation as the only option. Many now feel that the 'dead' should not take up the land of the living. Personally, I have no hesitation in having my physical body cremated when I have no further use for it.

Q: Does it matter whether we have a grave and headstone or our ashes scattered in the sea, a river or on a garden?

A: No, once again it is personal choice. Graves can, and do, help people to grieve over the 'loss' of their loved ones, and many feel that they are making contact with them whenever they visit the cemetery. Please bear in mind that graves and headstones do need constant upkeep and are a regular commitment for relatives to undertake for the rest of their lives. Most graves deteriorate after the second generation and tend to become overgrown and forgotten. If headstones lean or collapse, councils try to trace relatives who can then be liable for maintenance costs, otherwise tax payers foot the bill.

Q: Why do children have to die?
A: Very few ever consider that they may have to bury their children. It is a sad fact of life that thousands of parents the world over have to do just that every day. We call our children our own when we say 'my son' or 'my daughter' but, in reality, we own no one, even though we may have been the vehicle for the production of their physical body. We expect everyone to live to a ripe old age, but why can't we come and go when we like? In the great scheme of things we can never die, we merely shed a body to enter the next dimension of existence. We are *still* alive!

Q: Does it matter how we die?
A: No, the end result is still the same, whether our physical body is shot, blown up, suffocated, burnt, drowned, poisoned, crushed, strangled or succumbs to a disease or illness. The astral body is free to go into the frequency that it has 'earned' in its Earthly life.

Q: When tens of thousands of people are killed in an earthquake or tsunami, are they all meant to die at the same time on that particular day?
A: Yes. Hundreds of thousands of men women and children 'die' every day on this planet through every conceivable cause. Mass entries into the astral and spirit worlds on a daily basis are not a problem and are perfectly natural. Humans exterminate hundreds of thousands of animals every day to satisfy their appetites, sending them back to the astral worlds en mass. Consciousness can never 'die', so in the great scheme of things it makes no difference which frequency species live.

Q: I have never been christened; will I go to Hell when I die?
A: No, because there is no Hell. There are dreadful lower astral regions where the 'undesirables' within humanity finish up when they 'die', but I presume you are a nice person with a fair degree of love and compassion so you should have nothing to worry about. It matters not one jot or tittle whether we have been christened, it is ***how we live our life*** that is important. In other words, how many people have we helped and how much love and compassion have we shown?

7 Invisible worlds

Q: Where are the astral planes and spirit worlds?
A: As close as the nose on your face – they interpenetrate our world. We live in a multi-dimensional universe – quite literally, worlds within worlds. The only difference being frequency rates (vibration of atoms), which means that

they can co-exist within the same space without interfering with each other. This is no different to the thousands of radio and television channels that occupy the same space using different frequencies.

Q: If we destroyed this Earth with nuclear or chemical weapons, or all life died as a result of a virus, global pollution or an asteroid strike, what would happen to us all?
A: Exactly the same as if we had 'died' through any cause. We would all be plunged back into the Earth's astral worlds, which would still exist, and would continue to live our lives there until another suitable planet in our wonderful Cosmos was allocated for our future education in physical forms. All planets throughout the solar system have astral worlds and, according to esoteric teachings, they interact with each other, thus we can travel the Cosmos in our astral bodies.

The Universe had a 'birth' – astrophysicists currently estimate it to be about 13 billion years old (give or take a day or two!) – and it will eventually have a 'death'. Solar systems, stars and planets are continually being 'born', having life-spans of billions of years and then 'dying' (imploding or exploding), ready to be recycled throughout the Cosmos. Inside each and every one of us is a miniature universe – a microcosm of the macrocosm – in which billions of cells in our bodies are experiencing such a scenario on a minute scale

Q: What determines which astral or spirit world we go to after death?
A: Quite simply, the amount of love that we have shown in our earthly life. When we give unconditional love, kindness and compassion to others – including animals – the atoms in our astral body vibrate faster. Love speeds them up and hatred slows them down. Hence, at the moment of our 'death', we automatically go to the spirit world that is vibrating at our personal frequency. Therefore all the people, trees and houses in that world will appear solid to us because they are vibrating on a similar frequency.

Conversely, those whom we call 'evil' that cause so many problems here and show no mercy, love or compassion, will have astral bodies that vibrate at very low frequencies. They will have condemned *themselves* to a low frequency astral world and will be with others of like minds – which will literally be a living 'hell' for them. We grade ourselves after 'death' by the way we live our earthly lives. The higher the frequency, the more love – the lower the frequency, the less love. Brilliant – and yet *so* simple!

Q: Do we become wiser and more knowledgeable when we get to the spirit world?
A: Not immediately. We will be as we are here, warts and all. If we are of an

arrogant and argumentative nature, then that's what we will be when we get to the 'other side'. 'Death' doesn't suddenly change our personalities or give us immediate knowledge and wisdom. So don't expect Uncle Joe and Auntie Flo to suddenly know everything when they get into the astral planes.

Once the newly arrived have purged their minds of the earthly trivia they have left behind, they will find there are plenty of opportunities for learning and the furtherance of knowledge in the finer worlds.

Q: What is it like in the astral and spirit worlds?

A: The astral and spirit worlds consist of thousands of interpenetrating frequencies, and all of them contain human life at varying degrees of consciousness levels. And, with the exception of the lower levels, animals, birds and plant life as well.

The higher frequency worlds are permeated with incredible energies of love, and have the most beautiful landscapes of lakes and mountains, with the most exquisite smells coming from exotic flowers the likes of which we have never seen on Earth.

Many of these worlds have cities, houses and streets similar to Earth's but without the need for transport – travel being achieved purely by thought. People merely think of a place and they are instantly there – including return trips to this Earth plane to see loved ones. Hobbies and pastimes once enjoyed on Earth can also be pursued in these other dimensions – assuming they were not violent, of course. Universities, libraries and concert halls are there for the furtherance of knowledge and cover a vast array of subjects. The quest for knowledge and learning never ceases.

Those who led lives of violence, selfishness, greed and corruption on Earth will qualify themselves for the dense lower astral regions, where they will stay until they have seen the error of their ways – encouraged by helpers from the higher spiritual realms. Their *own* state of mind will be the 'ball and chain' that keeps them there.

Q: How do we *know* what the spirit worlds look like?

A: From varied sources. Firstly, there are the descriptions given by spiritual masters, gurus, mystics, prophets, seers, sages, philosophers and mediums down the ages. There are also thousands of contemporary documented cases from all over the world, of people who clinically 'died' and experienced floating out of their bodies and going down a long dark tunnel into a world of incredible love and light (near-death experience). There they conversed with 'dead' relatives who showed them what life was like in these realms.

Many of these experiences are virtually identical, and have also happened to agnostics and atheists who had no preconceived ideas about a 'heaven' or 'spirit world', and yet they gave similar descriptions of the terrain.

Since the early 1950s we have had the scientific breakthrough of communicating with the mid-astral planes via electronic instruments and have now established picture contact via computer monitors and other devices – known as Instrumental Transcommunication (ITC). The scientists and researchers that dwell there have given very precise descriptions of the life and terrain at these levels.

Q: What is the difference between the astral and spirit worlds?

A: Frequencies, but what's in a name? The Native American Indians call them the Happy Hunting Grounds. Some people like to call the after-death frequencies astral planes and others call them spirit worlds. Strictly speaking this Earth is a spirit world because *we* are spirits wearing 'space suits' called physical bodies. The lower frequency worlds are generally called 'astral planes' and the higher ones 'spiritual worlds' or 'celestial planes'.

Q: Do people eat food in the spirit worlds?

A: Yes, if they want to, although there is no need because they have no biological physical body to sustain. Eating is one of the necessities and great pleasures of this Earth and many wish to continue the habit when they first arrive in the spirit worlds. We are informed that there are fruit trees of every description with the most succulent fruits, and that meat is not considered a food because it represents the act of taking the life of a living creature, which is not conducive to the spiritual values of the people residing there. You will appreciate such values should you ever visit a slaughterhouse (abattoir).

Q: Do people have sex in the astral and spiritual worlds?

A: Not as we know it here, where its primary function is for propagating the species and providing physical bodies for souls to temporarily 'inhabit'. Our astral body doesn't need to reproduce. It is *love* not *lust* in the higher spiritual worlds, and sex for physical gratification is not seen as a requirement any more than is alcohol or other substances. People living in spiritual worlds of incredible beauty with atmospheres of ecstatic love inform us that earthly pleasures and physical stimulation are superfluous and pale into insignificance by comparison. To many, this may seem hard to comprehend, but once we have tasted even a sip of absolute spiritual bliss, then such statements become perfectly understandable.

Here on Earth, sex, drugs and alcohol are addictions that dominate many people's lives. When undisciplined and excessive physical desires get out of control, the resulting human misery is a minefield of countless affairs, broken marriages, sexual diseases, rape, unwanted pregnancies, abortions and untold numbers of drug addicts and alcoholics.

Many will still have excessive sexual urges and cravings for drugs, alcohol and other earthly stimulants when they arrive in the astral worlds. This will initially stunt their progress, but with the help and guidance of spiritual mentors, they will see that the 'Love and Light' is infinitely more rewarding!

Q: Is there any form of government or politics in the spiritual worlds?
A: Not as we know it here – thank goodness! There are over-lords and other hierarchical beings who are responsible for 'managing' the various astral planes and spirit worlds. It is they who guide and counsel individuals residing there in their spiritual education and evolvement. Those who have had near-death experiences (NDE's) have been lucky enough to meet some of these highly evolved souls when they are informed that their time has not come and that they must go back. Many of them wear the white robes of a Spiritual Master and talk the most loving and reassuring words of wisdom. I have been honoured to have 'seen' some of them and felt humbled just to stand in their presence – such was the emanation of their love.

Q: I married again after my husband died, which one will I be with in the spiritual worlds?
A: Whichever one you want to be with, or with whichever one you had the greatest love and affinity with. Or, both if you want to – assuming you are all spiritually compatible.

Q: I married again after a divorce so which partner will I be with when we pass over?
A: The one where there is the greatest love, which is presumably your present partner.

Q: When I die will I definitely meet my loved ones in the next world?
A: Yes, most definitely if there was a loving bond between you. Love will automatically reunite you, that is Spiritual Law.

Q: Do animals go to the spirit worlds and will I meet my pets again when I die?
A: Yes they do. They too have souls (consciousness) therefore they will live on in the spirit worlds. Once again the law of love will reunite you after you leave this Earth.

Q: Will my loved ones meet me the moment I die?
A: Yes, no one dies alone. A mother, father or other close relative such as a son or daughter will come from the spirit worlds to meet and accompany you to your new abode. If you have lived a good life by giving a lot of kindness, love and compassion, then a spirit guide may also be at your 'death' to greet you.

Q: Are our death dates known to our loved ones in the spirit worlds?
A: In the vast majority of cases yes. They can access that information if they enquire at the libraries or educational establishments in the spirit worlds. That is why many relatives in the spirit worlds tell their loved ones who have near death experiences (NDE's) that as they still have valuable work to do on Earth, their time is not yet, and they must go back.

Q: Do we visit the astral planes and spirit worlds in our sleep?
A: Yes, quite often, but not every time. We live in many worlds simultaneously – this world during the day and the astral planes at night. When the physical body is resting and repairing itself, our astral body is free to roam into other dimensions. In many cases we can chat to our loved ones who reside there. Sometimes we remember our visits and sometimes we don't.

Q: I have a physical disability, so will I still be this way on the 'other side'?
A: For your peace of mind the answer is *no*. Whether we have lost an arm, a leg, our sight, or are badly scarred or in a wheelchair due to an accident, illness or birth incident, our astral body is *not* affected by disabilities to our physical body. Whilst giving clairvoyance, I had to describe those from the astral worlds with the disabilities they had on Earth, otherwise they would not have been recognised by their loved ones. But all assured me that they were not that way now and in perfect health.

Q: My wife is much more spiritual than I am, will we be together in the after-life?
A: Not necessarily. If you *assume* that to be the case, she could well be in a higher frequency than yourself. It is very difficult to categorise people in terms of spirituality, but if there was love between you then you will meet again. It could be in a neutral frequency, often called 'Summerland', suitable for you to meet at frequent intervals. We segregate ourselves in the afterlife according to how we have lived our life *here*.

Q: Can we progress in the spirit worlds without having to come back to this Earth?

A: Yes, apparently, but it takes much longer to progress to the next higher spirit world by this method because the basic lessons to be learnt and the shedding of negative emotions such as anger, lust, jealousy and greed are ideally learnt on this Earth where the problems originated. Any problems we have personally created *here* necessitate our coming back. Politicians please note!

Q: What is the difference between a ghost and a spirit?
A: These terms are often confusing to many who tend to call all spirit phenomena ghosts. Scientifically speaking, ghosts are atmospheric recordings of traumatic events or happenings rather like a film and have no awareness of us. We cannot communicate with them any more than we can with a film. Many researchers think that murders or battle scenes somehow record themselves in the atmosphere and under certain conditions, replay over and over again. Numerous sensitive people have witnessed such events – hence, haunted houses, castles and sites.

On the other hand, those we call spirits have intelligence. They are aware of our presence and can communicate with us in various ways. In a nutshell, a ghost is an atmospheric recording and a spirit is a real person living in another dimension.

Q: Will people meet the likes of Jesus, Buddha, Krishna and Mohammed in the spirit worlds when they die?
A: The devout Christian, Buddhist, Hindu and Muslim would expect to see their spiritual mentors, so that is whom they might see. The spirit worlds are thought worlds and as the inhabitants think so it is formed. We all survive the death of the physical body whether we call ourselves religious or not. It is the amount of love, compassion and kindness we have shown on Earth that counts in the after-life not our religion.

Q: Do spirit people influence our lives here on Earth?
A: Yes, more than we think. The more enlightened ones from the higher frequencies try to inspire us to live good lives by living in accordance with Spiritual Law and showing kindness, respect and compassion whenever we can. Those who are resident in the lowest frequencies try to influence those with similar minds to commit murder and other atrocities to satisfy their own depraved desires. Once again, it is a question of like minds attracting like minds!

Q: Will we be able to meet famous people when we get to the 'other side'?
A: More than likely. But famous people on Earth will not necessarily be famous

in the spirit worlds. Earthly rank counts for nothing there; it is a totally different set of values. Money is the currency on Earth and love is the currency in the higher worlds. So if we haven't got much love '*here*' then we are going to be bankrupt when we get *'there'* – irrespective of earthly rank or fame.

Q: My father died at the age of 35. I am now 76-years-of-age. How will we appear to each other in the spiritual worlds when I die?
A: Providing you and your father are spiritually compatible and qualify for the same frequency of spirit world, then you will see him as you last remembered him and he will see you as you are at the moment of your 'death'. Age is not the same as it is here, and spirit people tend to 'mature' upwards or downwards to a common age of between 40 and 50. During 15 years of mediumship on public platforms, unless mentioned, it was always difficult to guess the age of spirit people who showed themselves to me.

Q: In what regions do spirit guides live on the 'other side'?
A: Again, it depends on their level of advancement. Most of them reside in the higher frequencies of the spiritual worlds where love and wisdom manifest in abundance. They have earned the right to live there because of the spirituality they have accumulated over hundreds of Earth lives. They too have learnt through making mistakes and suffering grief and hardships the same as us. That is why they have such compassion for like-minded souls here who are struggling to understand spiritual truth and life's purpose.

Q: Why do so many guides seem to be Native American Indians and Chinese?
A: I cannot think of a more spiritual race than the Native American Indians or a more profound and philosophical one than the ancient Chinese. Guides, or spiritual social workers as many call them, represent *all* nationalities. I have personally experienced Chinese, Native American Indians, Indians, Tibetans, Egyptians and Arab guides. All of them have given love, guidance and inspiration on my quest for Truth.

Throughout history there have been enlightened thinkers and spiritual philosophers of great wisdom from all countries. These loving souls from the higher realms of the spirit worlds *volunteer* to come back to this dense Earth realm to help those who choose to walk the spiritual pathway in life. And many of them in their humility wish to remain anonymous. Many choose the body of their favourite incarnation to do this service and, perhaps, they could have been Joe Soap the plumber in their last incarnation here!

8 Is There a God of Love?

Q: Is there a God of love and how do you know?

A: Yes, there is a 'God' of love, and I know by personal experience *not* by what I have read or believe. I cannot prove it to you, but you can prove it for *yourself* if you *really* have a desire to know and you are prepared to understand life's laws and live by them. Some call it God's Grace or touching one's own Overself, which is part of the Absolute.

Q: Who or what is God?

A: God is not describable – God is a 'Cosmic Experience'. God is not a 'He' or human being somewhere up in the sky. God is neither male nor female. If you like, 'It' is the 'mother-father' principle of the cosmos. God is the all-pervading, creative and governing spiritual intelligence of pure consciousness behind the whole of life, in worlds visible and invisible. There is nowhere that God *isn't* – we are literally living in the 'Infinite Mind of God'. God vibrates on the frequency of love – *total unconditional love*. If we tune our finite minds to that frequency we can experience fleeting moments of absolute bliss.

Q: Does God work in mysterious ways?

A: Only to those who need a mystery. Once investigated, knowledge and experience of the laws governing life and death dissolves any mystery. Life is really quite simple – it is we who make it complicated and mysterious. What could be simpler than a Universe based on *Love*? At our stage of spiritual evolution we can never fully understand God.

Q: Does God forgive our sins?

A: Most emphatically no! The Absolute does *not* interfere in our personal lives – 'It' has no need to. The Absolute 'programmed' the cosmic principle of Love and, if we break that law in either thoughts, words or actions, then we *automatically* bring into operation what is known as karmic retribution or '*Universal Justice*'. If we work with the Law it will work with us.

Q: Can a priest forgive our sins if we confess?

A: If God is non-judgemental, then on whose authority does mankind forgive? Those who break Spiritual Laws have to put things right *themselves.* No amount of 'Hail Mary's' or 'conscience money' in a box will change a thing. If confessing our sins to another human being only eases our conscience then what does that solve? A realisation that we have done something wrong in harming another human being, or animal, is the first step to putting things right and not repeating the mistake. Making amends by genuinely saying sorry or apologising to others is a good start and *may* lessen the 'pound of flesh' that life will demand of us. If we could only live our lives totally by the Laws of Love, peace and harmony then our sufferings and guilt would eventually cease.

Q: Is there more than one God?
A: Yes. There are numerous lesser 'gods', but there is only *one* GOD – The Absolute, Allah, The Great Spirit – or whatever name we understand. Try to imagine a large corporate company that has a chairman, a dozen or so directors, dozens of managers and assistant managers, accountants, secretaries, et al, all helping to run the company. The Universe is very much like that. Every Universe, galaxy, and planet, as well as all the countless billions of astral and spirit worlds, has a spiritual hierarchy to oversee the whole vast and incredible scenario. Guides, Archangels and angels also come into that category. Many NDE survivors have been privileged to have met some of them.

Q: When we die and go to the spirit worlds, will we meet God?
A: We don't have to 'die' to 'meet' God – we are *already* living in the *Mind* of God, and God Consciousness experiences are the ultimate proof to the individual. The more love and compassion that we have the more we will understand this phenomenon. Most of us have too many faults and failings to understand the full meaning of what God is. The only people that I know of who have walked this Earth and understood the True nature of God are the genuine spiritual masters and highly enlightened seers, sages, prophets, avatars, gurus and mystics who return (reincarnate) from time to time to teach the human race the error of its ways.

Q: How is communication with God possible?
A: Through *silence* via the *soul* (Overself). That is why initiates were taught meditation thousands of years ago so that God Consciousness (Nirvana, Enlightenment) could be attained. The knowledge gained formulated early teachings such as the Indian Vedas, Upanishads and Bhagavad-Gita.

Gautama the Buddha achieved Enlightenment through meditating in remote forests and plains. The Master Jesus chose desert wilderness and mountain areas to commune with God. The Prophet Mohamed meditated in caves and desert wilderness before contact with spiritual hierarchy and eventual Enlightenment. The Sufis also teach God Consciousness through meditation. The Native American Indians communicated with The Great Spirit (Wakantanka) in the Pine forests and remote plains.

The same applies today. It is with love, peace, harmony and *silence* that God (Allah, The Great Spirit, Universal Mind) can make itself known with an 'all knowing' and ecstatic infusion of Love to all who seek in sincerity and humility.

Q: I am a gay man and very devout in my religious matters, but I am concerned about my relationship with God. Is this just a mental barrier?
A: More than likely. God, The Absolute, does *not* discriminate or judge. It is a non-personal Universal Intelligence that radiates energies of love throughout the Universe. All the gay people I have ever met have been kind, loving, compassionate and respectful – truly wonderful people. That is what spirituality is all about.

9 Love – The Law of Life

Q: How do you know that love is the law of life and not hate?
A: Because love heals, love unites and love gives a meaning and purpose to life. If love was taken away from our lives and replaced with hate, then life would seem pointless. Life only exists because of harmony, which is love. Nature exists because of harmony. All the laws in the physical world exist because of harmony. All the atoms and molecules that are the building blocks of life vibrate because of harmony. If there was only hatred (evil) then there would be chaos, and if there was only chaos, then nothing could be. Love is the 'glue' that holds the Universe together.

Q: Why do nice people have to suffer?
A: Many nice people have fears and anxieties, which are negative emotions. These can cause ill health and tragic personal consequences. They can literally attract to themselves the very fears and anxieties that they worried about. Cosmic Law is impartial and *very* obliging, since it always gives back to us what we give out in thought, word or deed – whether we are deemed nice or otherwise. It could also be that such people have elected to pay off multiple karmic debts accrued in previous lives.

Spiritually speaking there is no such thing as an innocent person. No one is ever in the wrong place at the wrong time, or suffers for anything that they have not brought upon themselves at sometime. I cannot repeat enough times – violation of the Law of Love sets in motion the Law of Karma and causes people to utter things like, 'If only I hadn't taken the wrong turning, I wouldn't have had the accident'. And 'Why did they have to be there just as the bomb went off?' Or, 'It's unbelievable that they had to be in that particular hotel when the earthquake struck'. Or, 'If only they hadn't missed that last bus home', and ad infinitum. Put your hand up if you have *never* uttered an 'if only'.

Q: Is it true that the good always die young?
A: No. It only seems that way because nice people are always missed. Are you

intimating that nice people *have* to live to a ripe old age? This world is *not* our real home, it is a 'transit camp', and from the moment we are born we can leave it at any time for a hundred different reasons.

Q: What is the definition of Karma?
A: It is the general term for Spiritual Law and derives from Buddhism. In ancient China it was known as the Tao, or the way, and refers to the energy patterns that pervade the Universe. It is also known as the law of 'Cause and Effect' or 'Sowing and Reaping'. What we 'sow' today we will 'reap' tomorrow, next week, next year or the next life. Hence the term Karma is intrinsically linked with reincarnation. The accruing of negative Karma continually draws us back to this Earth to learn from our mistakes.

Q: What is the difference between Soul, Spirit and Mind?
A: Down the centuries Soul, Spirit and Mind have been regarded as one and the same entity, and recognised as the moral and emotional aspect of our being. In other words it is our spiritual self that identifies love and compassion as essential attributes for living. And because it is part of The Absolute (God) it is immortal and can never die. The spirit worlds have also been known as soul worlds. It is Mind that causes us to think and reason and operates the body's computer – the physical brain.

Q: At what stage does the Soul (Spirit) enter the foetus in the womb?
A: The consensus of opinion is that it is at the moment of conception, or soon after.

Q: If we have a soul, where is it situated in the body?
A: According to ancient esoteric teachings, it is an atom that has infinite life and is situated in the heart chakra. This apt verse from the Indian Katha Upanishad states: *Concealed in the hearts of all beings is the Atman* [Soul]*, the Spirit, the Self; smaller than the smallest atom, greater than the vast spaces* (Ch: 2, V: 20). Some have likened it to a spiritual 'micro-chip' that has infinite life and records everything that we think, say and do over numerous lifetimes.

10 Reincarnation

Q: What evidence is there for reincarnation?

A: Thousands of testimonials going back generations, where men, women and children have remembered living on Earth before; often recalling how and where they died with vivid recollections of events, including names and nicknames, both of themselves and relatives. And when investigated these proved factually correct in every detail. There are many documented and evidential cases where children have returned to the same bereaved parents a year or so after their first 'death'. Over half the world's population (4 billion people) accept reincarnation.

Many past life regressions have also given excellent evidence that people have lived before in many different countries and at various times in Earth's history. Volumes have been written on the subject and invite interesting reading.

Q: Why do we need to reincarnate?

A: One life is not long enough to learn the needed lessons for our spiritual growth and progression. If we take our hypothetical Mr and Mrs Average once more, we can observe that from cradle to grave that they learn very little about the important values in life, particularly *unconditional* love and compassion for *all* living things. We witness selfish and materialistic attitudes and minds clogged with petty and meaningless trivia.

If we have caused harm, in any way whatsoever, to another human being, then we will be advised to reincarnate with them to put matters right. If we only had one life on Earth, how would you explain all the inequalities and tragedies that inflict the human race? We are a very mixed bunch; from downright 'evil' to the highest epitome of love, and it is having this contrast here that enables us to learn more quickly.

Q: Why can't we remember previous lives?

A: Many can, particularly children, but for the majority of us each new Earth life is a fresh beginning. It might not be particularly pleasant to know that we have committed terrible atrocities in the past, which is why for most of us a veil is drawn across our memory, just as we forget a dream when we wake up unless a chance remark during the day reminds us. We start each earthly life with a new brain, but the soul remembers.

Q: It doesn't seem fair to be punished for something that we can't remember doing.

A: Our soul (Overself) remembers, and that's good enough. It's that spark of pure consciousness (part of the Absolute) that accompanies us from life to life, and is literally recording everything that we think, say and do. What we sow we will reap, that is Karmic Law. We get away with *nothing*. That's something worth thinking about, and it would probably be wise for us to act appropriately.

Q: If our soul is recording everything that we think, say and do, doesn't that sound like George Orwell's 1984 'Big Brother' tactics of being spied on?
A: To many people, probably. But it's done in the name of Love and for our long term 'reward' of eventually merging back with the God – The Absolute – and not to control or dominate as 'Big Brother' is interpreted.

Q: Is it fair that we have to suffer for what we did in a previous life?
A: One could well ask, 'Why do we have to suffer for what we did yesterday?' Our previous lives are but the yesterdays in our spiritual evolution. If we accept the pleasures and rewards in this life for the good things that we did in previous lives, then we must be prepared to accept similar mental or physical suffering if that is what we inflicted upon others in the past.

The law of Karma is very precise and irrevocable. It is the Universal Justice that I have alluded to many times. If I commit a crime and then die, does that mean I am pardoned? 'Death' in this world doesn't absolve us from any of our karmic debts; they are simply accrued and carried over into the next life. Some of our 'evil' debts are so massive that it could be virtually impossible pay them back in one lifetime or, if we tried, our suffering would be intolerable.

In this life many people put themselves in debt by borrowing huge sums of money and agree to pay it back over 25 years (one third of their lifetime) because they cannot envisage paying it back any quicker. Karmic debts are the same, only they are spread over many lifetimes.

Q: On average, how many lives do we have?
A: How long is a piece of string? We have enrolled in the school of life and it all depends how long it takes us to learn the necessary lessons. We go from nursery school to college, or university, in the course of our education here. But some learn quicker than others. And so it is with our spiritual growth, some of us take hundreds of lives and others take literally thousands to accomplish the same result.

Q: How long do we spend in the spirit worlds before reincarnating?
A: Once again it depends on the individual. No one is ever forced to do anything in the spiritual worlds, and that goes for returning to Earth in another body. Unlike this Earth, unconditional love is the motivating factor for everything there. It is with love and guidance that we are encouraged to further our spiritual education by returning to this planet of suffering to learn the lessons that we struggled over when we were last here.

Some people elect to spend the equivalent of a 1,000 Earth years or more enjoying the peace and tranquillity of the higher realms of spirit life, whilst others choose of their own freewill to enter a new body of flesh within a few months of their Earth passing. This enables them to be back on Earth at the right time and place to meet the right people for their 'new' lessons. Time as we know it here doesn't exist in the higher frequency worlds, so what is a few thousand years?

Q: Will my loved ones have reincarnated by the time I get over to the spirit worlds?

A: To the best of my knowledge and, in the vast majority of cases, no. But please bear in mind that no two cases are ever the same, which is why reincarnation is a complex but fascinating subject. Most of us elect to stay in the spirit worlds until the majority of our immediate loved ones have joined us.

Q: Do we have an equal number of lives as male and female?

A: Yes, give or take a life or two, to experience the qualities of both. The female is generally more loving and maternal and, dare I say it – more spiritual (sorry chaps), whilst the male is more forceful and aggressive. It is advisable that we have an equal balance of the male and female energies (Yin and Yang).

Q: Could my mother have been my son, or my father my brother in a previous life?

A: More than likely, or any combination of relatives. The soul takes on many different garbs in each lifetime to learn the experiences necessary for its growth and spiritual education. It's similar to an actor playing many parts in different plays or films. We are all one big family, including our animal, insect and plant relatives. Everything is linked – we came from the same source and to that we will eventually return.

In the highest known spiritual worlds we become pure spirit without form, so the title of mother, father, brother etc., becomes superfluous. It's just one of the many earthly labels that we give each other.

Q: Who or what decides into which country, race and time period we are born?

A: The sum total of all our thoughts and actions over previous lives is automatically recorded by our Overself (soul) and helps to decide our future lives. After a previous life review and the advice and guidance of mentors from the higher spiritual worlds we will be born into a country, race and time that will enable us to learn the spiritual attributes in which we are lacking. If we lack patience, tolerance, compassion and love for example, then we will need to live a life (or many) that exemplifies those attributes until learnt – be it painful or otherwise!

11 Suicides

Q: What happens after death to people who commit suicide?

A: It greatly depends on their state of mind at the moment of 'death'. If they have acute depression and, many have, then they will probably go to one of the lower astral regions until they realise what they have done. Many are hoping for oblivion because they imagine it will end their problems. But they may well be confused upon finding themselves still alive in another dimension and witness the grief their futile act has caused to loved ones.

If those who take their own life have any degree of love in them and, most have, then relatives or helpers from the higher astral worlds will escort them to a more harmonious frequency and take care of them until they have a more balanced frame of mind.

Q: Does committing suicide solve earthly problems?

A: No. We incarnate on this planet to learn certain lessons. If we opt out and don't learn them now, then we are only going to get them again. There is no cheating the system.

12 Prayer and Meditation

Q: What is prayer and is it necessary?

A: Prayer is concentrated unselfish thought echoed by our own soul (Overself) to the Great Universal Soul – God, The Absolute. It is often a cry for help to a power far greater than our own. All the while we remain imperfect we will have a need to pray for ourselves. As we progress we will learn to pray for others.

Q: Does prayer really work?

A: Yes, if said in humility from the heart.

Q: What is meditation, and why the need for it?

A: Meditation is an inward change of consciousness. It is the shutting down of the five physical senses and the ceaseless chatter of the mind to allow a spiritual serenity to take over and put us in touch with our real self – our soul (Overself). It is the process of going within to find our true spiritual centre and has distinct physical, mental and spiritual benefits.

If practised regularly and sincerely you will lose fear, anxiety and other forms of stress. In return you will gain peace of mind, inner strength and better health. If practised at deeper levels (Raja Yoga) it is one of the pathways to God Consciousness. It needs to be experienced to be fully understood.

Q: Is meditation anything to do with religion?
A: No, it is a way of life and was practised in the East and the Orient thousands of years before organised religions evolved. Many religions adopted the practice as a means to God Consciousness (Enlightenment). The Buddhist, Hindu and Sufi religions are good examples.

13 Healing

Q: How does healing with the hands work and can anyone learn to be a healer?
A: It is the channelling of the universal energy Prana, or Chi, into the aura and body of a sick or diseased person or animal. Healing energies flow through those that have love and compassion for the sick and suffering, not the arrogant or ego motivated.

Q: Is it autosuggestion or mind over matter?
A: If it was that easy anyone could cure the sick and diseased. How do you 'autosuggest' anything to an animal or a baby? I am convinced that the emotional mind, whether full of fear, worry, anxiety, stress or happiness, plays a big part in destroying or curing the body.

Q: Do we have to have faith to be healed?
A: Once again, how do you ask a sick baby or diseased animal to have faith? I have not met many agnostics or atheists who would claim any faith in it. Most people go for healing because they have either, lost faith in orthodox medicine, been told they will have to live with their problem or been given a short time to live. Healing is often a last resort when they realise that they have nothing to lose.

Q: Are all forms of healing with the hands the same?
A: In essence yes. Spiritual healing, psychic healing, Reiki healing and Chi Gong are all names for channelling healing energies into sick people. I have personally experienced these healings and spoken to various practitioners.

Q: Some churches maintain that healing must be in the name of Jesus or it is the work of the Devil, is this true?
A: Since when has this 'Devil' been renowned for healing the sick? Does this mean 'he' has changed his ways? Healing is *love* and it can work through *anyone* who has love and compassion for the sick and suffering, both human

and animal. Children have even been healed whilst swimming with dolphins!

Healing with the hands has a history going back long before organised religion and is the most natural thing in the world. Many a loving mother has healed her sick child just by cuddling it; without even realising what she has done. There is no reason whatsoever why a healer shouldn't call upon the name of Jesus to help with the healing if that is their preference. Jesus represents love and that's good enough for me. Anyway, if your question was true, where does that leave thousands of Buddhist, Muslim, Jewish and Hindu healers?

Q: Does Distance or Absent Healing work and, if so, how?
A: Yes, it does work and can be very effective. It is still the same healing energies that are used with the hands except they are now channelled to the sick person or animal in the form of a spoken prayer or thought. Thoughts are living energies.

Q: Do spirit people have an influence over the healing?
A: From my experience and, in numerous cases, yes. Many a spirit healer has helped to channel the energies into a patient, and I have frequently felt their hands guide mine. Some healers are completely taken over in trance by spirit doctors who carry out very complex procedures on the patient. Think about all the thousands of medical doctors who are now in the spirit worlds and have no sick bodies to deal with. What do you think would give them the most satisfaction for their talents? They volunteer to assist healers in this world so that they can continue with their work. Many hospital surgeons have had their hands guided and thoughts put into their heads during difficult operations – although they might not admit it in public.

There are also multiple nationalities and ethnic groups of healing guides including Native American Indians, Arabs, Chinese, Egyptians, South American Indians and African tribal doctors. There have also been instances of nuns, monks and other clerics from the spiritual worlds assisting with healings.

As I have stated many times, and will continue to say it until I am blue in the face, it doesn't matter which 'world' we live in, visible or invisible, we are still people and we are all spiritual brothers and sisters with the same *'Parent'*, so why shouldn't we help one another? To heal the sick and comfort the bereaved is one of the finest services we can give to the Great Spirit, whether we are known as healers, doctors, counsellors or spirit guides!

Q: If we are ill should we go to a healer first or a doctor?
A: There is certainly no harm in seeing a healer first in many cases, but I would ***always*** advise that you see a medical practitioner as soon as possible. Most of

us, at some time or other, particularly as we get older, will need the services of the medical profession. Healing is *not* guaranteed and no promises should ever be given by a healer any more than they should by a doctor.

Q: What are doctor's attitudes towards healers?

A: Unfortunately, some still think that *anyone* who practises 'unorthodox' methods of healing is a quack or a charlatan. The more enlightened amongst them often refer their patients to recognised healers. I personally know several of my local GPs who simply exude love, compassion and humility – truly wonderful people. They would make excellent healers. By arrangement, some hospitals and doctors allow healers into wards to offer their services.

All sick people want to do is get better by being treated as quickly and humanely as possible, without catching a hospital virus, having drug side-effects or suffering medical negligence. Although healing with the hands is not good news for the drug industry, the ideal surgery or clinic of the future, for any civilised society, should incorporate *all* forms of proven healing – orthodox or unorthodox.

14 Good and Evil

Q: Is there a Devil?

A: Not unless you *want* to believe in one. The Devil, as such, was an invention of ancient priest-craft to subjugate the people of the day. Fear was the motivating factor. There are however, evil and hellish entities in the lower astral planes that can have an influence over evil-minded human beings. It is the law of like-minds attracting like-minds.

Q: Is there such a place as Hell?

A: Not the traditional fire and brimstone abode. The lower frequency astral planes are a living 'hell' to their inhabitants. These are the dark and dismal places where the Earth's troublemakers go to when they 'die'. Due to Nature's ferocity and human stupidity, this Earth can also be a living hell from time to time for many of its inhabitants.

Q: Is there a Heaven and, if so, where is it?

A: Heaven, Paradise, Nirvana – what do they mean? Some imagine it to be a place up in the sky, full of angels and continuous love, peace and happiness – absolute bliss? Well, the higher frequency spiritual worlds that interpenetrate this Earth come very close to that description. They radiate the tranquillity of love, peace and harmony, and are inhabited by people who have earned the right to be there due to the quality of their Earthly lives.

Q: Why is there so much evil on this Earth?
A: 'Evil' is purely of our own making due to ignorance of the Law of Love – and now we have the audacity to complain about it. Over the centuries, we have lived lives of cruelty, arrogance, prejudice, selfishness and greed, with a total disregard for the feelings of our fellow human beings and animals. We continually violate cosmic law and pay a price for doing so. Unconditional love will dissolve all 'evil'. It is *that* simple!

This Earth is a kinder-garden school, and immature souls generally tend to abuse their freewill using violence; much like bullies in the playground. We call it 'evil', but to the Absolute we are still 'children' that have yet to grow up and mature. After many lives of self-induced suffering we will eventually learn that love, peace and harmony create happiness – which is the true way to live. We will all go through this stage in our spiritual evolution, so we should have sympathy for those who don't yet understand the laws of life.

Q: Are some people born evil or do they become evil?
A: Another often asked question. People classified as 'evil' in previous lives, will take numerous incarnations before callous and brutal behaviour is gradually replaced by respect, love and compassion. This is when morality and conscience develops (soul awareness).

Yale University experiments with babies, found that more than 70 percent showed a high morality, and those who didn't exhibited selfishness and other negative tendencies. Interestingly, tests and scans on psychopathic cold-blooded killers found that *all* were missing a gene known as MAOA. Many police officers are convinced that there is such a thing as a 'criminal face', where certain facial features are common-place on violent people. The eyes are the windows of the soul – all this is there to see!

Q: Spiritually speaking, which is the most advanced; the most loving and loyal dog or the most vile and evil human being?
A: The most loving and loyal dog. It is better to be at the top of a lower evolutionary group than at the bottom of a higher one. We can observe animals giving total and unconditional love, and humans who don't know the meaning of it. Soul evolution sorts it all out.

15 Just For You

Q: We have a mentally and physically disabled son of 25, and have had to sacrifice those years of our lives to look after him. He can do nothing for himself and is a pitiful sight to behold. We have cried many tears over him. We are not young and get very tired. If there is a God, what have we all

done to deserve this?

A: The reasons for such circumstances in our lives run deep, and can be the result of many causes and many effects from previous lives under Karmic Law. God is not the cause of your dilemma. God is a neutral force of unconditional love and does not interfere in personal problems of our own making. Hard though it is, the lessons you are learning are crucial for your spiritual development or you would not be experiencing them.

What has your son taught you in this life – unselfish sacrifice, or total unconditional love and compassion for another soul that has chosen you for his parents? Perhaps it is a debt being repaid, and in a previous life he looked after you when *you* were incapable. Think deeply about what lessons you are learning and ask yourself if you would have learned them if things had been different. If you continue to pray for strength and guidance, those from the higher spiritual planes will assist you. You are not alone in your sacrifice. Look upon it as an honour.

17 The Meaning and Purpose of Life

Q: I have been very interested in metaphysical subjects for years and have had many psychic and mystical experiences, but my husband continually ridicules me. How can I convince him otherwise without arguments?

A: You are not alone! As numerous women will testify, many men are frightened of the subject and any talk of spirits and reincarnation, etc., is well out of their comfort zone. Hence the closed mind attitude of denial and ridicule comes into play! Never try to convince anyone about a subject they have never bothered to investigate. You could always mention one of my favourite sayings: *'Criticism without investigation is the highest form of ignorance'*.

Q: Are our lives predestined or do we have freewill?

A: Both. With each incarnation we elect to learn various lessons that are lacking in our character (karma), and with the help of mentors (guides, etc) a plan of action is drawn up whilst in the spiritual worlds. How we learn these lessons is up to us (freewill), but we will have to pass certain milestones on route (destiny), such as where we live, whom we meet and how. Our thoughts and actions can either accelerate or retard the plan.

Q: Where do UFOs fit in with this philosophy?

A: At least two per cent of flying objects observed invading the world's airspace remain unidentified. That's a lot of hardware! UFOs have been tracked countless times on radar over the decades and are a well-documented phenomenon in both military and civilian archives. They represent another piece of the jigsaw puzzle of life that readers may wish to investigate. We would be tiny-minded and arrogant if we thought our little planet had the only living creatures in the Universe. I have no doubt whatsoever that there are 'beings' on other planets in galaxies that are thousands of years ahead of us in evolution and technology.

Numerous people in many countries are convinced that UFOs have landed here in past history and are still doing so today. We will do the same when we have the technology to traverse the vast regions of space, and probably terraform life on other planets as some of our space scientists are already planning.

It would appear that many UFOs have the ability to change frequency (dematerialise) and hence suddenly disappear, as many military pilots have observed. It has been speculated that some UFOs travel through the astral dimensions in this fashion and then change their frequency back to ours (materialise). Hence they have been tracked on radar travelling at tens of thousands of miles an hour.

For open-minded readers new to the subject, *ABOVE TOP SECRET – The Worldwide UFO Cover-up* by Timothy Good (Sidgwick & Jackson 1987) is very informative in its evidence for military involvement with UFOs. The Foreword is written by former Admiral of the Fleet, Lord Hill-Norton, GCB, Chief of Defence Staff (1971 – 1973).

Q: Why is there life at all instead of nothing – just oblivion?
A: Once we begin to understand the jigsaw of life and, hopefully, have some wonderful experiences such as being at one with the Universe with indescribable frequencies of love, we will know why there is life (consciousness). Conscious never dies; it evolves to unimaginable spiritual heights. It is an amazing and exiting journey.

Q: Do you know everything there is to know?
A: No. I'm totally baffled as to why I have a drawer full of odd socks. I have asked God for an answer, but apparently 'He' has the same problem!

A touch of humour to end the chapter, but hopefully it will have given you an insight into the sort of questions that are being asked. And for every question that you receive an answer, you will no doubt find dozens more to ask. Who? What? Why? When? Where? How? These will always guide you to pieces of the jigsaw. So please be my guest and fit this piece of the puzzle. In the next chapter we will assemble some of our jigsaw and look at the emerging picture of the meaning and purpose of life.

The important thing is not to stop questioning.
Curiosity has its own reason for existing.
Albert Einstein 1879 – 1955 (Physicist)

17 The Meaning and Purpose of Life – The Jigsaw

We are caught in the contradiction of finding life a rather
perplexing puzzle which causes us a lot of misery, and at
the same time being dimly aware of the boundless, limitless
nature of life. So we begin looking for an answer to the puzzle.
Charlotte Joko Beck 1917 – 2011 (Zen teacher and writer)

We have now reached that stage in our quest for Truth whereby we can begin to assemble pieces of the puzzle. We have looked at some of the formerly isolated areas of the enigma of life and death and, hopefully, it will have given you a clearer understanding of both. I will summarise the meaning and purpose of life as it has been given to me over years of searching via direct personal experiences and by enlightened beings from both this world and the next.

At this stage of our quest, many will have been comforted to know that we are *not* alone on a God-forsaken ball of rock, hurtling blindly through space in a God-forsaken Universe. Neither are we a freak, billion to one chance of Nature – knowing that there is an intelligent cosmic meaning and purpose behind it all. So, does this mean that there is a life after death? If there is, where do we go and what is it like? Does a God of love exist? If so, why is there so much dreadful suffering in the world – particularly to children? Such questions have occupied the minds of some of our greatest thinkers from ancient times to the present day.

It's the rollercoaster ride of life with its highs and lows of happiness and despair that cause many to seek for answers. But in our greatest moments of despair there is one word that, irrespective of any belief system, can sustain us, and that is *hope*. Hope that our suffering is not all in vain or will last for long. Hope that the inmates are *not* in charge of the asylum; and hope that some benign cosmic super-intelligence has everything under control!

The first port of call for many seekers is often religion. Many seek through choice or curiosity, whilst for others it is virtually mandatory from birth with no choice depending upon country and culture. When compulsory from birth it becomes indoctrination with freedom of thought and enquiry 'discouraged'. Orthodox religion thereby becomes an organised, dogmatic faith and belief system.

Investigation reveals that much of religious history is based on plagiarised myths and legends which, over the centuries, have often been embroidered and translated into fact, with precious little of whatever truth was evident at the inception now remaining. This opens the door to diverse opinions and interpretations regarding ancient scriptures, hence the endless problem of conflict between the different faith and belief religions which have seemingly lost the plot and spawned numerous cults, extremists and devout atheists as a result.

It's not a question of replacing orthodox religion with another dogmatic system. There will *always* be the need for a basic religion for the masses to find solace during distressful times. It's more a question of *outgrowing* a religion when it ceases to truthfully answer meaningful questions or solve the problems of life and death with satisfactory evidence. This leads to a gradual and natural migration from blind faith and belief to the search for something more tangible. Just as a caterpillar transforms into a butterfly, giving it more freedom of movement, so faith and belief can transform into knowledge and experience giving the mind freedom to expand into undreamed of consciousness levels. Thus faith becomes a *trust* based upon knowledge and proven Universal Truths.

So, despite their fundamental differences, what is the key element that should be uniting genuine religions? An omnipotent, omniscient *Universal God of Love,* one would expect! But whilst religions continue to pray to, *and* preach, a fictional, humanised, *personal* God with the negative human traits of anger, jealousy, revenge, favouritism and multiple prejudices, then global peace and the enigma of existence will continue to elude them.

> Prayer is addressed to the personal God, not because he is personal indeed, I know for certain that he is not personal, because personality is limitation, while God is unlimited.
> *Leo Tolstoy 1828 – 1910 (Russian novelist)*

In a solar system billions of light years across, and our galaxy being just one of a 100 billion or so others in this vast realm of space, the renowned British physicist, Sir James Jeans, stated: *'The more we learn about the universe the more it appears to be the product of a single great thought.'* From around the world, enlightened scientists are now seeing the Universe as a vast intelligent field of energy, a grid system or web that connects all things. And what has astounded physicists, is that this cosmic web of energy responds to human thought. Here is what Chief Seattle (1786 – 1866) of the Suquamish Tribe had to say on the subject: '*Man did not weave the web of life, he is merely a strand in it. Whatever he does to the web, he does to himself. This we know; the Earth does not belong to man, man belongs to the Earth. All things are connected. This we know. All things are connected.'*

Profound words from a native American Indian, when he echoed what philosophers and mystics have known for thousands of years when they refer to this vast web of energy that permeates and connects the entire universe as 'The Mind of the Universe' – hence the term Universal Mind. It is also known as the 'Unifying Ocean of Love' and is recognised as being of *unimaginable* love and intelligence from whence everything is continually manifested. For our jigsaw and the sake of argument, we will stick with God, or The Absolute.

Identified with this 'Cosmic Intelligence' is Universal Law which, by definition, applies to every living thing, including our own planetary law of Nature. Hence it is impersonal *not* personal. We live in a *law-governed Universe* – which is good news for optimists and bad news for doom and gloom pessimists. Astrophysicists confirm that the Universe works with clockwork precision, it being a marvel of celestial mechanics enabling them to calculate the exact position of stars and planets throughout the solar system well into the future as well as the past.

Down the ages, untold millions have experienced a spontaneous merging of their minds with this Universal Mind. Or, if you like, their consciousness merging with God's consciousness – the ultimate experience! This becomes proof to the individual that God exists and is the font of all knowledge. So powerful is this energy of love that the western writer and philosopher, Paul Brunton, wrote – with great humility: *'In the still presence of that mighty power the soul walks on tip-toe.'* And I would add that he earned the right to pen those words.

The key to understanding the existence of such a loving 'Universal Power' is in the words love, compassion, kindness, forgiveness and humility. These wonderful human qualities have been evident throughout my years of investigation in those who sincerely respect all living creatures, be they plant, insect, bird, animal or fellow beings.

For centuries, throughout the east and the orient, direct proof of the existence of God was taught by spiritual masters using the discipline of meditation, the technique of stilling the mind by slowing the breath and turning the attention inwards. This has the effect of distracting the five physical senses from the material world, and connecting our finite consciousness with that of the Infinite Consciousness within us known as the soul or Overself. Or as Indian Masters lovingly refer to it, the *'Spark of the Divine'*.

Our soul, therefore, is our direct link with God – the Absolute. We can *pray* to it, silent or spoken; ask for guidance, help or healing for ourselves and others, as well as wisdom, understanding, guidance, inspiration and intuition. And, if asked with humility and for the right reasons, then such requests *may* be granted under Universal Law. Many have called the soul our conscience – it is that which prompts us to do the right thing, makes us feel guilty if we don't, and warns us with uneasy feelings if we are in danger or about to do something foolish.

So, having stated that we are not alone on a godforsaken planet in a godless universe, we may well reason that life is futile if it ends in oblivion in the inevitable grave that beckons us all. It is personal tragedies that cause many to question if there is a life after death, and, unable to accept bland unproven statements that loved ones are 'in heaven with God' they embark on a quest for evidence and proof.

Nature has planted in our minds an insatiable longing to see the truth.
Cicero 106 – 34BC (Roman politician, philosopher and poet)

Avoiding time wasters, the ego orientated, the grief-charlatans and the deluded, the evidence for a meaningful life after death is in abundance – much of it substantiated by eminent scientists from around the globe. It has also been verified by untold numbers of sensitive people over the centuries when they have subjectively and objectively 'seen' departed loved ones. In many cases, the fully materialised physical form of a mother, father, son or daughter, often with the added bonuses of hugs, kisses and meaningful conversations.

During the last 100 years or so, we have documented evidence of photographs of departed relatives, friends and colleagues, as well as hearing their recorded voices on tape recorders and more modern electronic devices. Again, much of this has been subjected to rigorous scientific scrutiny before being pronounced genuine. There is also abundant evidence for domestic pets and other living creatures being seen and photographed after they 'died'. Volumes continue to be written regarding factual evidence for life continuing after the earthly grave.

The more we read and experience the more we realise that death is a perfectly natural phenomena and nothing to be feared. Millions have undergone a Near-Death-Experience (NDE) and proven this for themselves, having 'floated' out of their bodies and witnessed events and conversations whilst being pronounced clinically dead on the operating table or hospital bed. Often with overpowering feelings of indescribable peace and love, as well as 'knowing' that death is not the end. The icing on the cake for many, is floating down a tunnel into a world of brilliant light and unimaginable beauty whilst being greeted by highly evolved spiritual beings and departed loved ones, friends and pets. They hugged and conversed, often being given information that they were not privy to on Earth which, after full recovery, was proven correct.

Countless numbers have had an out-of-the-body experience (OBE) when they found themselves floating above or standing beside their physical body.

This phenomenon is known as astral projection when the astral – or spirit body – disengages from the physical. This too, is often accompanied by feelings of love and peace, and is again proof to the individual that consciousness (soul or spirit) can exist independently from the earthly body. It's interesting to note that in nearly all reported cases of NDEs and OBEs the fear of death and dying is eradicated, with many stating that they look forward to it when their time comes.

It has been voiced numerous times by those who have experienced separation from their physical body, that if they can think, reason and have a conscious memory whilst out of the body, then it's not their physical brain that is operating. All of these faculties must therefore reside within the astral body.

Having established that 'death' is not the end of life, many ask: 'Where do we go?' 'Are there such places as Heaven and Hell?' 'What is the afterlife like and where is it?' As an answer to such questions, scientists are now confirming what esoteric teachings have taught for thousands of years, particularly amongst advanced ancient races having knowledge of mathematics. That is, that we live in a multi-dimensional universe – worlds within worlds. Each world operating on a different vibrational frequency, hence they can co-exist within the same space.

> Today we realise that God, the Absolute, is dreaming
> into existence countless finite, ever-recurring universes
> in many parallel dimensions, worlds co-exist spatially
> in different frequencies of matter, all mirrored by
> complimentary universes of anti-matter; there may possibly
> be other manifestations of Creation beyond our cognisance.
> *W. Raymond Drake 1913 - 1989 (Gods and Spacemen in the Ancient East)*

Such worlds have been called different names by different cultures, with belief system religions designating a paradisiacal 'Heaven' for believers and doers of good deeds, and an everlasting tormenting 'Hell' for unbelievers (atheists) and doers of bad deeds (sinners). This of course, prompts the awkward question: 'Where do we go if we confess to being a believer but do bad deeds or are a confessed atheist who does good deeds?'

Well, The Absolute didn't have to phone a friend or ask the audience to sort that one out. The Universe is 'programmed' to respond to unconditional love, peace and harmony and those who fail to live in accordance with that Law in *thought, word or deed* will automatically reap the consequences – sometime, somewhere, somehow. The Law of Karma, or to put it simplistically, what we sow we will reap, applies not just to our earthly life but to where our astral body goes in the afterlife.

Thousands of 'invisible' worlds, vibrating on different frequencies, surround this Earth and every other celestial body in the Universe, and all are linked. The higher the frequency the greater the atmosphere of love and light, and the lower the frequency the denser the atmosphere. The astral body atoms respond to the Universal Law of Love and vibrate accordingly. Thus, the more love, kindness and compassion that we give to life, the higher the vibrational frequency of our astral body. Hence, it makes sense that when we 'die', our astral body is automatically attracted to an astral world that it is compatible with (in vibrational harmony).

Despite the fact that we are a mixed bunch on this beautiful, violence-weary planet, we can now appreciate that it is not *belief*, but *Love* that determines our position in the afterlife. Hence we have the lower astral frequencies populated by the gross and 'evil' aspects of humanity, through to the higher celestial spheres of the spiritual worlds, where the wisest, kindest and most humble and compassionate of beings dwell. The latter having an atmosphere so vibrant in love, peace and harmony as to defy description in earthly words. There is a place for each and every one of us after 'death' and it will be no more, or no less, than what we have earned according to the way we have lived our life on Earth.

Many question that because we can 'die' when we are just a few hours old, or even still-born, what experience of life will we have had to determine which astral world we will go to? No life, however brief, is wasted. Another piece of the jigsaw fits nicely here, and that incorporates the cosmic Laws of Reincarnation and Karma. Even if we lived to be a 100-years-of-age or more, one lifetime is not enough to experience and learn from every given human emotion under every conceivable earthly condition. Common sense apart, fairness and justice would dictate that we have more than one chance at passing our earthly 'exam' in the University of Life to finally obtain our first class honours degree in Unconditional Love.

Throughout all ancient cultures, the doctrine of reincarnation teaches the process of having multiple earthly lives to experience, learn, understand and partake in the spiritual meaning to the Universe. Life is not learnt merely by reading books or listening to teachers, it is learnt by personal experiences and learning from mistakes – by enjoying, suffering, laughing, crying, grieving, hating, and finally, by giving unconditional love to all. Just as God – The Absolute, doesn't discriminate and emanates unconditional Love throughout the Universe, so we, during our spiritual evolution, will progress from ignorance to enlightenment. It is the progression from ego orientated, violence, confrontation, hatred, selfishness, prejudice, envy, lust, greed and attachment, to selflessness, unconditional love, kindness, forgiveness, compassion, cooperation, healing and non-attachment over numerous lifetimes.

The ancient Egyptians fully understood the natural Laws governing the Universe and the meaning to life and death, especially the soul's journey through time and space over many lifetimes. As an example, here are brief extracts from the Papyrus Anana, written by the Chief Scribe to Pharaoh Jentle Leti II and dated C1320BC:

'Men do not live once only to depart hence forever. They live many times in many places, though not only in this world.'

'Our religion teaches us that we live on eternally. Now eternity, having no end, can have no beginning; it is a circle. Therefore, if the one be true, namely that we live on forever, it would seem that the other must be true also. Namely, that we have always lived.'

'Man comes into being many times, yet knows nothing of his past lives, except occasionally some daydream or thought carries him back to some circumstance of a previous incarnation. He cannot, however, determine in his mind when or where the circumstances occurred, only that it is something familiar. In the end, however, all of his past lives will reveal themselves.'

'The spirits or souls of one incarnation, possibly, may meet again in another incarnation, and may be drawn together as if by a magnet, but for what cause neither knows.'

'All gods send their gift of love upon this earth, without which it would cease to be. My faith teaches me more clearly, perhaps, than yours, that life does not end with death, and therefore that love being life's soul, must endure for all eternity.'

It's interesting that the Scribe wrote: *'They live many times in many places though not only in this world.'* The notion of humans living in a multi-dimensional universe – and even on other planets – was part of the esoteric knowledge taught in the mystery schools in the east and the orient as part of the 'jigsaw of life.' And yet in today's western society we are just beginning to understand and grasp these teachings. Although many refer to them as New Age Teachings, in reality, there is nothing new about them.

For example, from the civilisation that gave us science, medicine, mathematics and the basis of democracy, Socrates, the Greek philosopher, walked the streets of Athens, nearly 2,500 years ago, discussing spiritual philosophy and giving clairvoyant evidence of life after death to passersby.

This went down like a lead balloon with certain members of the local establishment, so they had him convicted on the grounds of 'impiety and corrupting the youth'. He was sentenced under the Athenian death penalty and chose to die by drinking hemlock. Unafraid of dying, and as a defying gesture to his accusers, he described his death stage by stage as the poison gradually took its toll.

One of Socrates' firm convictions was that we should never cease to question life. He argued that if we don't question then we will get no answers and shouldn't complain if we continue to suffer in ignorance. He maintained that understanding universal (Karmic) laws would cushion us against the harsh realities of life.

Life's journey, or quest, is not easy for the vast majority, and many will fall by the wayside especially when traumas come thick and fast and hit hard. As the ego orientated trap of materialism bites even harder causing unemployment, debt, broken relationships, stress, illness, anger, bullying, unhappiness, insecurity, low self-esteem and depression, vast numbers will succumb to taking their own life when at their lowest ebb. Many, thankfully, fail or are saved just in time. Numerous others succeed; causing loved ones grief, distress and lifelong mental scars.

There is something radically and fundamentally wrong with our society when suicide statistics, especially amongst our youth, are staggering. Until we make an effort to understand the meaning and purpose of life and its Laws, this needless loss by self-destruction will continue. There are those who have been saved using 'lifebelts' offered by faith and belief systems, but the majority of lost souls that I have encountered have found no acceptable answers to life's multiple tragedies from such institutions. This is amplified when clerics question or lose their faith, especially when they have no answers to an 'Act of God' natural disaster that can claim tens of thousands of 'innocent' lives in one hit.

When explained in simplistic terms, I have not known the universal philosophy, as outlined in our jigsaw, fail to offer an acceptable meaning and purpose to those who have attempted, or considered, taking their own lives. Suicide is futile and serves no useful purpose for the victim or for those who have to pick up the pieces in the aftermath. Because the 'death' of the physical body is not the end of our lives, what we don't learn in this life will only have to be learnt in another. In the meantime, all we can do is be aware of the traumas and multiple problems that can cause loved ones and friends to reach such lows.

It is not my intention to enter any moral debate or offer an opinion regarding assisted suicides prompted by the severe health difficulties of a loved one. It is a strictly personal matter, and until we are in such a position ourselves we will never fully understand such anguish. Suffice to say that observation teaches us, often dramatically, that health is a precious gem that, once lost, can be difficult to find again.

We are born onto this Earth with a physical biological body that has to last us a lifetime – however long or brief that may be – so is it not in our best interest to look after it and treat it with respect? I know of no one who likes visiting hospitals, and yet, according to our unhealthy lifestyle statistics, it would seem that many of us can't wait to become a patient in one and go under a surgeon's knife! That is, assuming that being dosed with synthetic prescription drugs for some complaint or other has failed to cure us.

Apparently, much of our health damage is caused by putting incompatible chemically laden, high fat, sweetened, processed food and drink into our mouths, often in huge quantities. This has been likened to committing slow suicide – which in the long term, helps to make the pharmaceutical industry huge profits! Treating the adult epidemic of degenerative diseases is alarming enough, but nutritionists and healthcare professionals now fear for the health of our children as they pile on the pounds through consuming 'junk' food and drink.

Sickness and disease is *not* a natural state for the human body. But, since we consume painkillers and prescription drugs by the truckload, it would seem that every other person is suffering from some health condition, whether it is headaches, arthritis, high blood pressure, diabetes, heart problems or any number of afflictions mentioned in medical dictionaries. Since we seem determined to wreck our only line of defense – our immune system – with cigarettes, drugs, excess alcohol, fear, stress and needless anxieties, et al, then poor health will continue to dog our lives and threaten to destroy any happiness that we are entitled to.

> Look to your health; and if you have it, value it next to a good conscience; for health is the second blessing that we mortals are capable of; a blessing that money cannot buy.
> *Izaak Walton 1593 – 1683 (English writer)*

A natural alternative that many now seek for debilitating health conditions is Spiritual Healing. It is called 'spiritual' primarily because it is based on the universal laws of love, peace, harmony and compassion. This is a centuries old treatment where a sensitive person (the healer) channels natural healing energies (Life force; Prana; Chi) through and around the patient. This helps to restore the imbalance present in a body that is not in harmony with itself (dis-ease) and, in many cases, revitalises the patient's Chakras and immune system so that the body can heal itself. Much has been discussed in the healing part of our quest, but suffice to say that Spiritual Healing is love in action, aiding both our wellbeing and attendant happiness.

On special occasions, we wish each other good health and happiness, since the two are intrinsically linked and, like health, happiness is the natural state of wellbeing. We have previously considered diverse factors that can keep that elusive happiness at bay, but there is one *vital* overriding factor that needs to be addressed at this stage in life's jigsaw. True and *lasting* inner happiness can *only* come through the spiritual attributes of love, peace and harmony. Why? Because that is the natural state of the soul (Overself) – which is an intricate part of God. Those who have experienced God Consciousness – however fleeting – will appreciate the ecstatic state of bliss, love, peace, harmony, knowledge, security and *unbelievable* happiness that this brings.

That is why, those who have gone through the spiritual distraction and trappings of materialism – which panders to the ego, with all its fears, worries, vanities, jealousies, greed, wants and 'must have' mentalities – seek for that which money can rarely buy. The silence of Nature in all its serenity, a starry night or a breathtaking scenic view, giving and receiving unconditional love, meditating in the peace and quiet, listening to soul stirring music, reading inspiring and uplifting literature, and just being with like-minded loving, peaceful, kind and humble friends, are just some of the soul's happiness quotas.

> The ideals which have lighted my way.... have been kindness,
> beauty and truth. The trite subjects of human efforts – possessions,
> outward success, luxury – have always seemed to me contemptible.
> *Albert Einstein 1879 – 1955 (Physicist)*

This is the true pathway to lasting happiness. It is spiritual, and that is the food of the soul. Once tasted, there is no going back. Knowledge and experience of God, The Absolute, is the only true and lasting happiness that one will find whilst on this planet of blood, sweat and tears.

And talking of blood sweat and tears, in *Just for You*, we looked at touching stories of the trials and tribulations that can affect any of us at any time on the pathway of life. They are typical examples of how the human spirit can overcome or learn to cope with the testing times of grief and despair. None of us are immune, and it can be a stark reminder that we are enrolled in the 'School of Hard Knocks' – or as some have quipped – a Boot Camp! It's a stark reminder that, in a Law-governed Universe, nothing happens to us that we have not brought upon ourselves by our thoughts, words and actions, either in this life or previous ones. Such times can test us to breaking point, but the way in which we handle any given situation determines our rate of soul growth –

or spiritual progression. That is why we should always caution against arrogance and look upon humility as a spiritual strength, not a weakness.

Genuine humility is always accompanied by an open mind free from prejudices and opinions. This can be a breath of fresh air and far removed from the suffocating negative atmosphere of the biased, arrogant, argumentative and opinionated amongst us. An alien observer would use reams of paper recording our appalling irresponsible behavior, and observe our breaking of almost every spiritual law in the Universe as we continue to perpetrate atrocities on ourselves, the animal kingdom and our fragile planet. Many of them executed in the name of high finance, politics and religion – fuelled by the human weaknesses of selfishness, greed, sexual perversion and promiscuity.

This causes many to question the presence of evil and a devil, and doubt the existence of a benign force of good. There is no 'Devil', only the interplay of positive and negative cosmic forces that interact with human thought causing us to think and act in accordance with our level of spiritual growth. The 'D'evil' is our lower human nature that debases us lower than the beasts – that which impels us to rob, lie, cheat, wantonly destroy, sexually abuse, bully, dominate, torture and murder our own kind.

'Evil' can always be overcome (dissolved) by good (love). Difficult though it may be at times, if we look for the good in all then we will *almost* always find something, even if it is a minute spark rather than a flame. The eyes are said to be the windows of the soul, so let us try to catch that spark of the Divine in the briefest of smiles. But in our rogues' gallery of tyrants and cold-blooded psychopathic killers, that may well prove extremely difficult!

In the Drama of Life, we are all actors on the earthly stage playing a role that befits our 'script' for each individual life. In some lives we play the good guy and in others we are the 'evil' villain. The worst that can happen to us is that we are 'killed off' and have to leave the stage. Because we can never die, merely returning to the astral planes in our astral body after each lifetime, then in the long term, it doesn't really matter how many times we enter the plot and are shot, blown up, strangled, drowned or 'die' of a disease. The Buddhists call it The Wheel of Life – birth, death, birth, death, ad infinitum. Only the scenery, props and costumes change.

Many ask how we, as individuals, get off this continual Wheel of Life. Gautama the Buddha informed us that it is by striving to become a better person, and letting love, peace, harmony, compassion and forgiveness become a way of life. That way we can all subtly and gradually change the world for the better. Our lives are too short for anything else!

A person's life is just a moment in infinity.
Leonardo da Vinci 1452 – 1519 (Italian painter, sculptor, architect and engineer)

Since under universal law we have freewill – within the boundaries of what we need to learn – to think and act as we please, it is the wise ones who understand that every thought and every action on our part is a force for either good or evil. It is the human race, not God or a 'devil,' that is responsible for so-called 'evil' on this planet. For 'evil' we should substitute 'ignorance' – ignorance of the laws governing life and death. And it is ignorance of such laws that cause our hypothetical Mr and Mrs Average to worry, fear and long for peace and security.

We seek for security in a world of continuous change that, as well as giving, can take from us in an instant. Where shall we put our money – in a pension, stocks and shares or a financial institution or business that could collapse? We look for security in a job until redundancy threatens. We rely on other people who can let us down, leave us or 'die.' We buy property, but have to hand the keys back to the bank when we default on the payments – that is if nature doesn't destroy it in a fire, flood, mudslide, hurricane or earthquake. And we will all live to be at least a 100-years-of-age with guaranteed full health – won't we?

After many lifetimes, much deliberation, countless questions, priceless experiences with attendant spiritual knowledge, understanding and Truth under our belts, we will be drawn to two inevitable conclusions. Conclusions that have been reached by all enlightened beings, spiritual masters, seers, sages, mystics, philosophers and seekers of Truth since the dawn of time.

The first conclusion is that there *is* no lasting outer peace or security in this world, but you can find it within *yourself.* Whatever turmoil exists in the outer world, calm and stillness exists in your inner world. That world is the real *you* – not the birth name that your physical body was given – the *real* you that is your soul – or if you prefer, Overself or spirit. It is the very seat of consciousness within each and every one of us – the immortal essence of God. Thus it is possible during meditation to go within and make contact with that very source of consciousness.

The second conclusion is that the only *unchanging* security in a changing Universe is the very Intelligence that brought everything into being in the first place – God, The Absolute. The Absolute's love for us and all living creatures is immeasurable, but there will be no Divine intervention in our earthly affairs. We must learn by our own mistakes, since that is the only way to learn – although it is the wise ones who learn from the mistakes of others!

Having said that, there are highly evolved spiritual beings – guides, guardian angels, or whatever name we wish to call them – even deceased loved ones that, under certain conditions, can inspire, encourage, warn, heal or protect from danger, individuals who are psychically or spiritually attuned to their wavelength.

> Once we push the gate of the mind slightly ajar and let the light stream in, the meaning of life becomes silently revealed to us.
> *Paul Brunton 1898 – 1981 (The Secret Path)*

Every single piece of the jigsaw will eventually lead us to a recognisable but continually evolving picture, in that life is not a series of fragmented meaningless happenings that bear no resemblance to each other, but rather they are all linked and form part of a wonderful Spiritual Plan. Just as a wiper blade, steering wheel, tyre, spark plug, brake cylinder and headlight bulb may seem meaningless unconnected objects, but connect them together with 3,000 or so other components and we have a motor vehicle.

Over the decades, I have met many people who called themselves atheists and would have no truck with organised religion. In fact, so much so, that most refused to discuss the subject. Even the words, soul, spirit, spiritual and God were an anathema to them. I have previously stated that I am not in the convincing or converting game, but, when the names were changed to the Overself and The Absolute, the Power Source, etc., and the word 'science' mentioned, then great interest would be shown. Especially so when sub-atomic particles, frequencies, people living in other dimensions (multi-dimensional Universe) entered the conversation, with 'spiritual' being defined as having a loving, compassionate and forgiving nature.

Once we become aware of our spiritual heritage, money and ambition are no longer the driving force. A new and more vibrant force takes control. Why? Because we are in possession of a priceless 'jewel' that transcends the pseudo-wealth of this materialistic world of false values that merely serve to distract us from our true goal.

As the false values of the material world change and institutions crumble to make way for the new and better, we witness the greed and corruption within political and the financial institutions and the weakness and failings of organised religion to bring security and comfort to the masses. Comfort zones are shattered as many question life's meaning and purpose and where they fit in to such change.

The meaning of life is Love – ***Unconditional Love***. Without it, life has no meaning neither does it make sense. The purpose of life – or objective, if you like – is ***Soul Growth***. It is the process of our soul (Overself) evolving over eons of time via the simplest life forms to the complex nature of humanity and beyond. We learn through trial and error on our magnificent cosmic journey towards enlightenment. Culminating in the indescribable bliss of the merging of our 'individual' consciousness with the Supreme Consciousness of the Universe – that which we call God, The Absolute, The Infinite, Universal Mind or whatever name we feel comfortable with. From that moment, we will have arrived 'Home'. Then the *real* journey begins as we join highly enlightened spiritual Minds in co-partnership with the Absolute as the great Cosmic Plan continues to unfold before us. Fantasy? Why not investigate and prove it for yourself!

> If it is true that man has an immortal soul, and that his true task in life is refining and growth of that soul, then the only important thing in life is how we treat each other as humans.
> *Anonymous*

Finally, let me leave you with the following often quoted verse, which aptly sums up the Meaning and Purpose of Life and the soul's cyclic journey through the cosmos.

MY LAW

The sun may be clouded, yet ever the sun
Will sweep on its course till the Cycle is run.
And when into chaos the system is hurled
Again shall the Builder reshape a new world.

Your path may be clouded, uncertain your goal;
Move on – for your orbit is fixed to your soul.
And though it may lead into darkness of night
The torch of the Builder shall give it new light.

You were. You will be! Know this while you are;
Your spirit has travelled both long and afar.
It came from the source, to the source it returns –
The Spark which was lighted eternally burns.

It slept in a jewel. It leapt in a wave.
It roamed in the forest. It rose from the grave.
It took on strange garbs for long eons of years
And now in the soul of yourself it appears.

From body to body your spirit speeds on
It seeks a new form when the old one has gone
And the form that it finds is the fabric you wrought
On the loom of the Mind from the fibre of Thought.
As dew is drawn upwards, in rain to descend
Your thoughts drift away and in Destiny blend.
You cannot escape them, for petty or great,
Or evil or noble, they fashion your Fate.

Somewhere on some planet, sometime and somehow
Your life will reflect your thoughts of your Now.
My Law is unerring, no blood can atone –
The structure you built you will live in – alone.
From cycle to cycle, through time and through space
Your lives with your longings will ever keep pace
And all that you ask for, and all you desire
Must come at your bidding, as flame out of fire.

Once list' to that Voice and all tumult is done –
Your life is the life of the Infinite One.
In the hurrying race you are conscious of pause
With love for the purpose, and love for the Cause.
You are your own Devil, you are your own God
You fashioned the paths your footsteps have trod.
And no one can save you from Error or Sin
Until you have hark'd to the Spirit within.
Attributed to a Maori (Tieme Ranpari)

If you feel that you now have a better understanding of the meaning and purpose of life and death, then I offer you this major piece of the puzzle. We can now turn to the final chapter which offers advice on the 'Do's' and 'Don'ts' should you wish to continue your philosophical studies.

I died as a mineral and became a plant,
I died as a plant and rose to animal,
I died as animal and I was a man.
Why should I fear? When was I less by dying?
Jalalu 'd Din Rumi 1207 – 1273 (Sufi mystic and poet)

The great and glorious masterpiece of humanity is to
know how to live with a purpose.
Michel Eyquem de Montaigne 1533 – 1592 (French writer and moralist)

The unsolved mysteries which we seem to delight in
printing over and over again are not mysteries at all. The
only real mystery is why we have not solved them before!
David Wood (GENISIS: The First Book of Revelations)

18 What Do I Do Now?

All men by nature desire knowledge.
Aristotle 384 – 322BC (Greek philosopher and scientist)

A closed mind is a dying mind.
Edna Ferber 1885 – 1968 (American writer)

We have now come to the end of our quest for some of the pieces to life's puzzle. I have enjoyed the journey with you and hope you have also. I have given you the basic pieces of the puzzle hoping that you will see the promise of an evolving picture, but have refrained from giving you more of the puzzle for the following reasons:

a) I had to stop somewhere or I would still be writing.

b) I have to fit more pieces myself, although I have fitted many more than have been offered to you. I once had a glimpse of the evolving picture and *know* that all is well and that the picture is a masterpiece in the making – I have all eternity to fit the pieces. It is the most satisfying and rewarding project that I have ever had the pleasure of being involved with.

c) Hopefully, you have been encouraged this far, but it is now time for you to find some of the additional pieces for yourself – if you wish to do so of course. Throughout the book there have been subtle hints regarding other areas of investigation that will reveal further intriguing pieces of the puzzle.

Should you wish to further your knowledge on the subjects covered in this book and beyond, you may well be asking 'What do I do now?' or 'Where do I go from here, and what advice would you give?' Equally so, you may be quite content to accept what you have read as a possibility and leave it at that. That is entirely your prerogative. My policy has always been to help those who ask, so based on my own experiences, here is some advice that I would offer to any seeker of Truth.

- First and foremost you must have a deeply rooted and sincere desire for this knowledge, and if you truly seek it with an open mind, unconditional love in your heart and humility in your soul, you will eventually succeed. Be an observer of life and of yourself. Strive to be happy by pursuing what is good, refrain from hurting others in thoughts, words and actions, and respect *all* life. Discard preconceived ideas and prejudices about life and death, see the world for what it is, but don't take it too seriously.

- This pathway is not for the feint or half-hearted, so you will need patience, determination and dedication. You will get results *exactly* in accordance with the amount of effort you put into your quest. Take comfort from the fact that the ignorant, arrogant and egotistical amongst us never find anything except confusion, lies and fraud. That's the way Nature protects her secrets from such kind, and that's the way I like it.

- Read, read and read, and question, question and question. Never accept anything that you read or are told unless it feels right by your intuition or personal experience. That applies to every person and every book – *including* this one.

- Many will offer you advice and guidance for 'the pathway', but be wary and learn to distinguish the genuine from the deluded. The lunatic fringe and time wasters are easy to spot if you look them in the eyes and observe the way they speak and behave. If you don't like what you see or hear, bid them farewell and move on.

- Never, *never* argue with others about this philosophy. Discuss, yes. Argue, *no*. Those who truly understand life's philosophy never argue. Argument is always based on opinions and opinions are not Truth. Experience will teach you that it is invariably those with little or no knowledge on such subjects who argue. There are, of course, those who love to argue for the sake of arguing, and will swear that black is white and that two plus two equals five just to get a reaction. Don't be drawn, avoid ignorance whenever possible. Change the subject, or find someone with wisdom and knowledge to talk to – you will find it much more refreshing.

- Never, and I repeat, *never* try to convert others to your way of thinking. And *never* tell others that their way is wrong and yours is right. People will believe what they want to believe. So please respect that we should all have the freedom to choose our own 'pathways' in life, whether they lead us to ignorance or enlightenment. Years of observation has proven that those who try to convert others to their 'pathway', sect or religion are often insecure and are invariably the blind leading the blind.

- Never let others put you off or deflect you from your quest. You could get various diatribes like, 'you are doing the work of the devil' or, 'you are dabbling with the occult', or my favourite, 'you don't believe in that rubbish do you?' My advice, once again, is to look them in the eyes. The eyes will tell you everything! You will become aware that those who say such things are unhappy and lost souls themselves, often talking from ignorance and well out of their comfort zone with this philosophy. Again, *never* argue, especially with time wasters. Life is short and time is precious – it can never be recouped.

- When you first understand this knowledge you will have a natural desire to tell the world. *Don't!* I fell into this trap and learnt the hard way that not everyone is interested or can handle it. Many live in a make-believe world and are out of their comfort zones when such subject matter is discussed in front of them. Please respect that, and only talk to like-minded people or those who *want* to know if it crops up during conversation. Never pretend or imply that you know all the answers – nobody does! If you can't answer a question tell the inquirer that you will find out and get back to them as soon as possible.

- Don't spend too many years absorbed with the psychic aspect of life – I made this error. Fascinating though it may be, it is only a part of the puzzle. By all means observe, learn and experience it, but I would advise that you also investigate the higher spiritual philosophies. In that respect, the works of Paul Brunton are highly recommended (see Bibliography). Learn to meditate if you are not doing so already. It will open up your consciousness levels and enable you to go within and find your Overself – the *real* you. You will prove to *yourself* that you are a spiritual being and part of the Absolute.

- This knowledge, when *rightly understood and lived*, will give you peace of mind, better health, and an understanding that many don't have. This Truth *will* set you free – free from the fear, anxiety and suffocating complacency that afflicts the minds of so many. Treat it wisely with great respect, and *never abuse it.* Keep your ego under control at all times. An inflated ego will destroy humility, send you down false trails, stunt your spiritual growth and deflect you from your goal.

- You are a student in 'The University of Life', so never let grass grow under your feet. Read, ask, and learn. When the pupil is ready the Master will call! Never be afraid to move on when you cease to learn and don't let people or institutions put a ball and chain of ignorance around your ankle.

As one door shuts so another will open. Life is a series of stepping-stones of experience towards enlightenment. Go for it!

- Truth does not have a label or dog-tag, so no one can own it or claim it as their own. It has stood the test of time for millions of years and cannot be added to or embellished – despite attempts to do so down the centuries. Truth is not always where you expect to find it, so be prepared for surprises and disappointments – be aware that all that glistens is not gold! Truth is not noise, dogma, pomp or ceremony, and no amount of alleluias and hand clapping will necessarily bring it to you. It's not fancy buildings or the worshipping of icons. Truth is *spiritual*. It is in Nature, silence, and unconditional love and compassion for *all* living things. This is true wisdom and it can only be *experienced* – it is priceless!

- Be wary of placing people, past or present, on pedestals – whatever 'truth' they have proffered. Eventually, many will fall off of their own accord or be pushed. Again, I learnt the hard way as many do. I know of no genuine guru, master, mentor or writer of Spiritual Truth who wished to be worshipped in any shape or form. They have always encouraged us to find the God within ourselves. There have been many enlightened souls, both on Earth and in the spirit worlds whom I greatly admire, and in the name of love they have been my mentors and guiding light. To them I owe a debt of gratitude, and can only hope that I have helped others in a similar way to repay that debt.

- Sometimes during your quest you may feel that you are not making progress or that you are not worthy of such knowledge. Some students feel that they are experiencing the 'dark night of the soul'. This is when they feel that they have been cut-off from all spiritual knowledge and experiences, or that they are being 'ignored' by the Absolute. Don't worry; all that set foot on the spiritual pathway go through this phase. Numerous esoteric and philosophical writings state that it is par for the course – a time for reflection and consolidation. Be patient, it will eventually pass and all will be well.

- Gaining this knowledge will not excuse you from life's responsibilities, so be prepared to *give* to life, despite problems, traumas and tragedies of your own, and life will give back to you in one way or another. The more love and compassion, help and advice that you give to others will be more than repaid in kind. Sometimes when we have been hurt the most an opportunity will arise to help another. That is one of the spiritual tests by which we will rise or fall. Giving of our time to someone *genuinely* in need can be priceless. The way I see it is this. By what right do we ask for help if we turn our back on others?

Well, that's probably enough advice for one day. So what do you do now if you wish to further your knowledge and experience? Firstly, you could visit your local library and look under 'Philosophy', 'Metaphysics', 'Mind, Body and Spirit' or 'New Age' sections. You will find books on life after death, reincarnation, healing, astral projection, meditation, etc. If they are not in stock, try ordering titles listed in the Bibliography. Many of the older ones are out of print but can often be acquired second-hand in charity shops for example. Many book shops offer a 'book search' service, as does the internet.

Reading such books will keep you out of mischief for many months and are essential groundwork for the knowledge they contain. If this philosophy is meant for you, you will soak it up like a sponge. Eventually, you will intuitively know which books are for you. Sometimes, well-organised Psychic Fairs can yield good mediums, books and lectures and worth a visit. Scour the local newspapers or look in your library for information.

In the early days you might wish to arrange a sitting with a medium. If you do, *always* choose a recommended one, and if in doubt contact The Spiritualist Association of Great Britain or The College of Psychic Studies (see Useful Contact Details). A local Spiritualist venue will also give you the opportunity to observe mediums and the evidence they offer. Don't be put off by poor 'messages' – the good ones are worth waiting for! Steer clear of telephone 'Psychic Hotlines'. Most are money orientated and offer little or no help. Horror stories abound in that respect!

Consider forming a philosophical discussion group with open-minded and like-minded friends and acquaintances and meet, say, once a month in each other's houses. Make a social evening of it and talk on different subjects, people's experiences and various books that the group has read. You can have fun and companionship as well as gaining knowledge and helping others to search for the jigsaw pieces in the puzzle of life. More people than you perhaps realise have had psychic and spiritual experiences and would love to talk about such subjects but don't know who to talk to or where to go.

Why not join a yoga or meditation class? This will help you physically, mentally and spiritually. Ask at your local library or contact the British Wheel of Yoga for classes near you. If you are interested in receiving or giving Reiki or Spiritual Healing, see Healing in *Useful Contact Details*.

Finally, I would ask you to please remember that the truly great and genuine masters, seers, sages, Rishis, philosophers, mystics, deep thinkers and many of the world's greatest scientists have, down the centuries, known and expounded the simple truths written in this book. I did not write the song – I am merely another singer who has proven these things for himself. I offer them to you as food for thought.

This is merely a part of my story. If I have given you hope for the future, a better reason for living, a meaning and purpose to life and death, a greater sense of personal responsibility, a quest for better health, a modicum of enlightenment and a desire to know more, then this book will not have been written in vain.

My love and blessings

Om Shanti Brian

In the spiritual life every person is his or her own discoverer, and you need not grieve if your discoveries are not believed in by others. It is not your business to argue or prove them to others. It is your business to push on, find more and increase your own individual happiness.
Prentice Mulford 1834 – 1891 (Thoughts are Things)

We are all seekers in the quest for Truth.
Ken Alexander, MSP, FNCP (Hon), MNCH (Acc), FRC,
(Editor: The Seeker Publications)

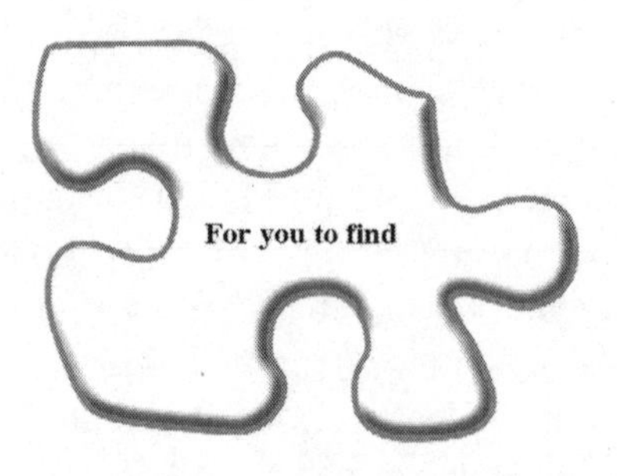

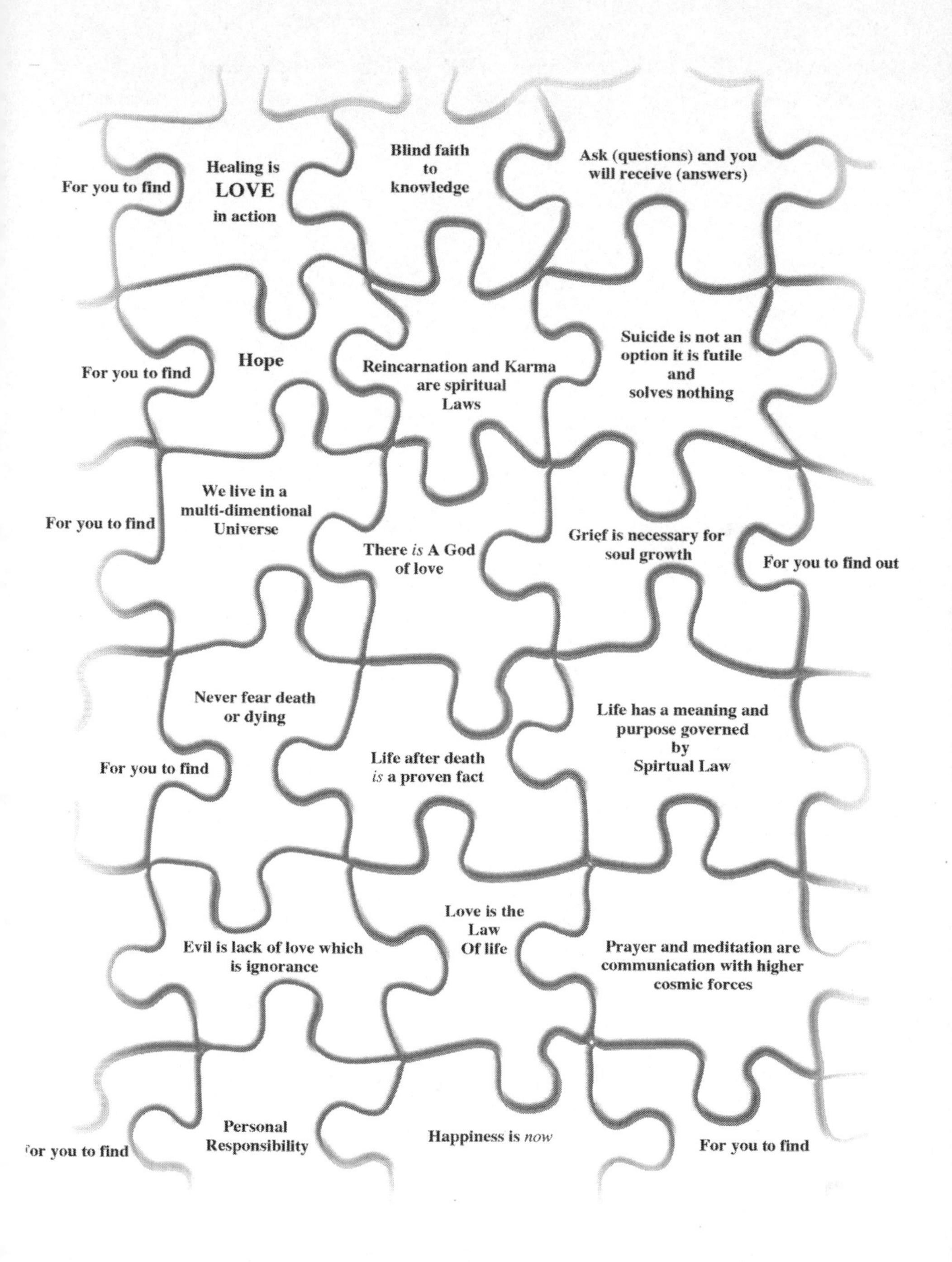

Figure 4. Some assembled pieces of the jigsaw of life

Glossary

Akashic Records: The memory bank of the universe where everything that happens is recorded.
Astral Body: The counterpart of our physical body that vibrates on a harmonic frequency. It is the 'vehicle' that enables us to leave the physical body.
Astral Cord: The silver coloured cord that attaches our astral body to our physical body.
Astral Projection: Coming out of our physical body – an out-of-body experience (OBE).
Astral Worlds: Other dimensions (or frequencies) interpenetrating the Earth where most of the Earth's inhabitants go after 'death'.
Aura: The electromagnetic energy field or life force surrounding the physical and astral body. This is made up of various colours within the spectrum depending upon our mental and spiritual development and bodily health.
Automatic Writing: The process whereby people living in other frequencies can communicate with us by guiding a pen or pencil on a blank sheet of paper.
Chakras: The seven main spiritual energy centres situated along the spine.
Clairaudience: (French) meaning clear hearing. Hearing beyond the normal.
Clairsentience: (French) meaning clear sensing. Sensing beyond the normal.
Clairvoyance: (French) meaning clear sight. Seeing beyond the normal.
Cosmos: The whole Universe seen as an ordered and organised system.
Cosmic Consciousness Experience (CCE): The experience of being at one with the Universe – an all-knowing – an awareness of being immortal and merging with God, The Absolute.
Death: When our consciousness (Soul) leaves the physical body to enter the next frequency of existence – a permanent astral projection.
Earthbound: People who are bound to existence between the Earth and astral frequencies after 'death' because of unsatisfied materialistic or sensual desires (often confused with ghosts).
Ectoplasm: The substance emanated by physical mediums to enable spirit world people to appear solid to us.
Electronic Voice Phenomena (EVP): The receiving of spirit voices via the telephone, tape recorder, or other recording devices (See also ITC).
Enlightenment: The merging of the human finite mind with the infinite Universal Mind – God. A state of absolute bliss – love, peace, happiness, knowledge and wisdom.
Etheric Body: The sheath that interacts between the astral body and the physical body – often described as the aura by psychics.

Ghosts: Magnetic recordings in the atmosphere of past traumatic events – murders, battles, etc. Sometimes seen by sensitive (psychic) people.
God: The Infinite Spirit of love and light that energises and sustains the cosmos. Also known down the ages as, The Absolute, The Great Spirit, The Infinite, Universal Mind, Allah, Brahman, The Deity, etc.
Hauntings: Psychic visions of ghosts or earthbound spirit entities.
ITC (Instrumental Transcommunication): The receiving of spirit pictures and text via television, computer monitors, fax machines and other electronic devices.
Karma: The Spiritual Law of Cause and Effect governing health, death and rebirth.
Love: The prime energy and Spiritual Law of the Cosmos
Materialisation: Spirit people manifesting as solid persons.
Medium: Sensitives who have the clairvoyant ability to converse with spirit people from other dimensions.
Metaphysics: The study of the inner or deeper philosophical teachings of life.
Mind: The substance that causes thought.
Mystic: One who studies and has direct experiences of the spiritual nature of the cosmos.
Near-Death Experience (NDE): The astral body disengaging from the physical body when the latter has been pronounced clinically dead but later resuscitated (similar to an OBE).
Occult: The hidden and secret esoteric knowledge of the spiritual and psychic forces that control the cosmos. Occult science.
Out of Body Experience (OBE): The astral body disengaging from the physical body.
Philosophy: The love of and pursuit of wisdom and knowledge.
Psychic: The ability to sense beyond the normal five physical senses.
Psychometry: The ability of a sensitive person to hold or touch an object and see or feel impressions of the owner or circumstances relating to the object.
Regression: The act of reliving or experiencing past lives under hypnosis.
Reincarnation: The act of being born many times into a physical body. Also known as rebirth, metempsychosis and the plurality of lives.
Soul, The: The Overself. The Tiny atom of immortal and indestructible spiritual essence in all living things. That which survives the death of the physical body.
Spirit: The soul
Spiritual: Having the attributes of unconditional love and compassion for all living things. Also embodying kindness, consideration, humility etc.
Spiritualism: The opposite of materialism. The scientific philosophy of communicating with people who once lived on Earth but who are now living

in other dimensions.
Spirit Guides: Evolved spirit people who give of their time and love to encourage those of us on Earth to walk the spiritual pathway of life – often referred to as guardian angels.
Spirit, The: Of the soul.
Spirit Worlds: The name given to the afterlife frequencies. Also known as the Astral Worlds, The Happy Hunting Grounds, Heaven, Nirvana, Devachan and The Soul Worlds.
Theosophy: A system of philosophical and occult teachings based on Hinduism and Buddhism founded by Helena P. Blavatsky in 1875.
Thought Forms: 'Entities' created by thoughts. Usually resident in the astral planes.
Transfiguration: A spirit person superimposing themselves over the face of a sensitive person so that they can be recognised.
Truth: That which ***is***, and not based on opinions, beliefs, hearsay or myths.

Bibliography

The burning soul, the burden'd mind,
In books alone companions find.
Sarah Josepha Hale 1788 – 1879 (American writer)

Angels

Newcomb, Jacky. *I Can See Angels.* Hay House 2010
Virtue, Doreen Ph.D. *Messages From Your Angels.* Hay house 2002
Virtue, Doreen Ph.D. *The Angel Therapy Handbook.* Hay House 2011

Bullying

Field, Tim. *Bully in Sight (Workplace Bullying)* Success Unlimited 1996
Kinchin, David. *Post Traumatic Stress Disorder: The Invisible Injury.* Success Unlimited 2004
Lynn, Taylor. *Tame Your Terrible Office Tyrant.* Jossey-Bass 2009
Marr, Neil & Field, Tim. *Bullyside: death at playtime.* Success Unlimited 2001

Child Death

Byrne, Gwen. *Russell.* Janus Publishing Co. (London) 1994
Collins, Betty. *I'm Jane.* Regency Press Ltd. 1988
Murphy, Sarah. *Coping With Cot Death.* Sheldon Press 1990
Prentice, Margaret. *Richard, Spirit and I.* Lionheart Press 1999
(1 Sherwood, Letchworth, Hertfordshire, SG6 4SQ)

Child Abuse

Bass, Ellen & Davis Laura. *The Courage to Heal.* Harper Perennial 1994
Pelzer, Dave. *A Child Called 'It.'* Orion Books Ltd 2001
Pelzer, Dave. *The Lost Boy.* Orion Books Ltd 2000
Pelzer, Dave. *A Man Named Dave.* Orion Books Ltd 2001

Cosmic Consciousness

Bucke, Richard Maurice, M.D. *Cosmic Consciousness.* Citadel Press (New Jersey) 1989
Ramacharaka, Yogi. *Fourteen Lessons in Yogi Philosophy and Oriental Occultism.* Fowler & Co. 1983
White, John. *What is Enlightenment?* Jeremy P. Tarcher Inc. (Los Angeles) 1985

Death and Dying

Kubler-Ross, Elizabeth. *On Death and Dying.* Collier (New York) 1974
Rinpoche, Sogyal. *The Tibetan Book of Living and Dying.* Rider 1998

Down's Syndrome Children

Beck, Martha. *Expecting Adam.* Piatkus 2000
Mardell, Danny. *Danny's Challenge.* Short Books 2005
Merriman, Andrew. *A Minor Adjustment.* Pan Books 1999

Happiness

Dalai Lama (His Holiness the 14th) *The Art of Happiness.* Hodder & Stoughton 1999
Holden, Robert. *Hello Happiness.* Hodder & Stoughton 1999
Matthews, Andrew. *Being Happy!* Media Masters Pte. Ltd 1989

Healing

Angelo, Jack. *Spiritual Healing.* Element Books Ltd. 1998
Dong, Paul & Esser, Aristide H.,M.D. *Chi Gong – The Ancient Chinese Way to Health.* Paragon House (New York) 1990
Edwards, Harry. *A Guide to the Understanding and Practice of Spiritual Healing.* The Healer Publishing Co. Ltd 1974.
Fuller, John G. *ARIGO: Surgeon of the Rusty Knife.* Granada Publishing Ltd 1977
Green, Peter. *Heal My Son!* Van Duren Contract Publications Ltd 1977
Greenbank, Don. *A Healer's Pathway.* Regency Press Ltd 1992
Levine, Stephen. *Healing into Life and Death.* Gateway Books 1998
Meek, George W. *Healers and the Healing Process.* Quest Books (Illinois) 1979
Pearce, Ian. *The Gate of Healing.* Neville Spearman Ltd. 1983
Shine, Betty. *Mind to Mind.* Corgi Books 1990
Siegel, Bernie S., M.D. *Peace, Love & Healing (The path to self-healing)* Arrow Books 1991
Southwood, Malcolm S. *The Healing Experience.* Piatkus 1994
Turner, Gordon. *A Time to Heal.* Corgi Books 1975
Solomon, Grant. *Stephen Turoff: Psychic Surgeon.* Thorsons 1997

Health

Batmangheldidj, Dr F. *Your Body's Many Cries for Water.* Tagman Press 2000

Bishop, Beata. *A Time to Heal.* First Stone Publishing 2005
Carper, Jean. *Stop Ageing Now.* Thorsons 1996
Carper, Jean. *Miracle Cures.* Harper Collins 1998
Clark, Hulda Regehr, Ph.D., N.D. *The Cure for All Cancers.* ProMotion Publishing
Chopra, Deepak. *Ageless Body, Timeless Mind.* Rider 1993
Day, Phillip. *Health Wars.* Credence Publications 2002
Day, Phillip. *Cancer: Why We're Still Dying to Know the Truth.* Credence Publications 1999
Day, Phillip. *B17 Metabolic Therapy in the Prevention and Control of Cancer.* Credence Publications 2002
Day, Phillip. *Water – The Stuff of Life.* Credence Publications 2004
Epstein, Samuel S., M.D. *Unreasonable Risk – How to Avoid Cancer from Cosmetics and Personal Care Products.* Environmental Toxicology 2001. ISBN 0-9715186-0-2
Griffin, Joe & Tyrell, Ivan. *How to Lift Depression Fast.* Human Givens Publishing 2008
Hanson, Maurice. *E for Additives.* Thorsons 1985
Harvey, Graham. *We Want Real Food.* Constable & Robinson 2006
Holford, Patrick. *100% Health.* Piatkus 1999
Hull, Janet Starr. *SWEET POISON: How the World's Most Popular Artificial Sweetener is Harming Us.* Vision Paperbacks 2005
Kent, Howard. *Breath Better Feel Better.* Apple Press 1997
Kavounas, Alice. *Water – Pure Therapy.* Kyle Cathie Ltd 2000
McTaggart, Lynne. *What Doctors Don't Tell You.* Thorsons 1996
Melville, Dr Arabella & Johnson, Colin. *CURED TO DEATH: The Effects of Prescription Drugs.* Johnson Secker & Warburg Ltd. 1982
Sage, Dr J.S. *Live to be a 100 (And Enjoy It).* W.H. Allen & Co. Ltd 1975
Servan-Schreiber, Dr David. *Anticancer – A New Way of Life.* Penguin Books 2008 Theodosakis, Dr. Jason. *The Arthritis Cure (Osteoarthritis).* Century Books 1997

Health (Fluoride)

Bryson, Christopher. *The Fluoride Deception.* Severn Stories Press 2006
Groves, Barry. *Drinking Ourselves to Death.* Newleaf 2001
Connett, Paul PhD, Beck, James MD, PhD, Micklem, H. S., D Phil. *The Case Against Fluoride.* Chelsea Green Publishing Co. 2010

Life After Death

Alsop, Samuel. *Whispers of Immortality* (EVP) Regency Press 1989
Barbanell, Maurice. *This is Spiritualism.* Spiritualist Press 1975
Barbanell, Sylvia. *When Your Animal Dies.* Psychic Press Ltd 1940
Beard, Paul. *Living On.* George Allen & Unwin Ltd. 1980
Bentine, Michael. *The Door Marked Summer.* Granada Publishing 1981
Best, J.E. *Link and Communique.* Regency Press Ltd. 1997
Boddington, Harry. *The University of Spiritualism.* Spiritualist Press 1967
Borgia, Anthony. *Life in the World Unseen.* Corgi Books 1975
Brinkley, Dannion & Perry, Paul. *Saved by the Light.* Piatkus 1994
Brown, Rosemary. *Unfinished Symphonies (Voices from the Beyond).* Pan Books 1973
Brown, Sylvia. *Life on the Other Side.* Piatkus 2003
Browne, Sylvia. *All Pets go to Heaven. Piatkus 2009*
Chisholm, Judith. *Voices From Paradise* (EVP). Jon Carpenter Publishing 2000
Courteney, Hazel. *Divine Intervention.* Cima Books 1999
Cummins, Geraldine. *The Road to Immortality.* Ivor Nicholson & Watson Ltd.1933
Davies, Dr Brenda. *Journey of the Soul.* Hodder & Stoughton 2002
Delacour, Jean-Batiste. *Glimpses of the Beyond.* Dell Publishing (New York) 1975
Denis, Leon. *Here and Hereafter.* Rider and Son Ltd 1910
Devers, Edie, Ph.D. *After-Death Communications.* Robert Hale Ltd 1997
Dowding, Lord Hugh. *The Dark Star.* Museum Press Ltd 1951
Edward, John. *After Life.* Hay House 2004
Findlay, Arthur. *On the Edge of the Etheric.* Rider and Son Ltd 1931
Findlay, Arthur. *The Way of Life.* Psychic Press Ltd 1953
Findlay, Arthur. *Where Two Worlds Meet.* Psychic Press 1951
Fiore, Charles & Landsburg, Alan. *Death Encounters.* Bantam Books 1979
Fontana, David. *Is There An Afterlife.* O Books 2006
Forman, Joan. *The Golden Shore.* Futura Publications 1989
Foy, Robin P. *In Pursuit of Physical Mediumship.* Janus Publishing Co. 1996
Fry, Colin. *Secrets From the Afterlife.* Rider 2008
Fry, Colin. *The Afterlife.* Random House 2008
Fuller, John G. *The Ghost of 29 Megacycles.* Grafton Books 1987
Hamilton-Parker, Craig. *What to Do When You Are Dead.* Sterling Publishing 2001
Harris, Louie. *They Walked Among Us.* Psychic Press 1980
Harrison, Tom. *Visits by our Friends from the Other Side.* Saturday Night

Press 1989 ISBN: 0-9514534-08
Heathcote-James, Emma. *They Walk Among Us.* Metro Books 2004
Jacobson, Nils O. M.D. *Life Without Death?* Dell Publishing (New York) 1974
Johnson, Raynor C. *Nurslings of Immortality.* Hodder & Stoughton 1957
Kubis, Dr Pat & Macy, Mark. *Conversations Beyond the Light* (ITC). Griffin Publishing & Continuing Life Research 1995
Kubler-Ross. *The Wheel of Life.* Bantam Books 1999
Lawson, Lee. *Visitations From the Afterlife.* Harper Collins 2000
Lodge, Sir Oliver. *Why I Believe in Personal Immortality.* Cassell & Co Ltd 1928
Macdonald, Allan, M.S.F. *A Path Prepared [Isa Northage]* (Materialisations: self-published – no publication date).
Macy, Mark. *Miracles in the Storm* (ITC). NAL/Penguin Putnam 2001
Meek, George W. *After We Die What Then.* Ariel Press (Ohio) 1987
Meek, George W. *Enjoy Your Own Funeral.* Galde Press (Lakeville U.S.A.) 1999
Meek, George & Harris, Bertha. *Séance to Science.* Regency Press 1973
O'Brien, Stephen. *Visions of Another World.* Aquarian Press 1989
Parker-Wakefield, Maurice. *The Facts About Orthodox Religions and Spiritualism Explained.* Regency Press Ltd 1995
Permutt, Cyril. *Photographing the Spirit World.* Aquarian Press 1988
Pike, Bishop James A. *The Other Side.* Sphere Books Ltd 1975
Randall, Neville. *Life after Death.* Corgi Books 1980
Remmers, J. H. *The Great Reality.* Spiritualist Press 1967
Richelieu, Peter. *A Soul's Journey.* Thorson 1975
Roberts, Estelle. *Fifty Years a Medium.* Corgi Books 1975
Rogo, D. Scott, & Bayless, Raymond. *Phone Calls from the Dead* (EVP). New English Library 1980
Rogo, D.Scott. *Life After Death.* Aquarian Press 1986
Russell, Edward W. *Prospects of Eternity (Debunking Death).* Neville Spearman 1982
Sheridan, Kim. *Animals in the Afterlife.* Hay House 2003
Shine, Betty. *Mind to Mind.* Corgi Books 1990
Smedley, Jenny. *Animals Have Souls Too.* Hay House 2009
Smith, Gordon. *Spirit Messenger.* Hay House 2003
Smith, Gordon. *Stories From the Other Side.* Hay House 2006
Solomon, Grant & Jane. *The Scole Experiment – Scientific Evidence for Life After Death.* Piatkus 2000
Twigg, Ena. *Ena Twigg: Medium.* W. H. Allen & Co. Ltd (Star Books) 1974
Williams, Gary. *A Life After Death.* Robert Hale Ltd 1989

Meditation and Chakras

Fontana, Dr. David. *The Meditator's Handbook.* Fontana 2002
Fontana, Dr. David. *Meditation – An Introductory Guide to Relaxation for Mind and Body.* Element Books 1999
Leshan, Lawrence. *How to Meditate.* Thorsons 1995
Mercier, Patricia. *The Chakra Bible.* Octopus Publishing (Godsfield) 2009
Mercier, Patricia. *Chakras (Balance Your Energy Flow for Health and Harmony).* Goldfield Press 2000
Sharamon, Shalila & Baginski, Bodo J. *The Chakra Handbook.* Lotus Light Publications 1999
Vinod, Dr Samprasad. *9 Secrets of Successful Meditation.* Watkins Publishing 2002
Wills, Pauline. *Chakra Workbook.* Journey Editions 2002

Near-Death Experiences (NDEs)

Atwater, Phyllis M. H. *Coming Back to Life.* Ballantine Books 1992
Atwater, Phyllis M. H. *The Complete Idiots Guide to Near-Death Experiences.* Macmillan (Alpha Group) N.Y. 1999
Atwater, Phyllis M. H. *The New Children and Near-Death Experiences.* Bear & Co. 2003
Atwater, Phyllis M. H. *The Big Book of Near-Death Experiences.* Hampton Roads Publishing 2007
Eadie, Betty J. *Embraced by the Light.* Bantam Books 1997
Moody, Raymond A. Jr., M.D. *Life After Life.* Corgi Books 1976
Moody, Raymond A. Jr., M.D. *Reflections on Life After Life.* Bantam Books 1978
Moody, Raymond A. Jr., M.D. *The Light Beyond.* Pan Books 1988
Moody, Raymond A. Jr., M.D. *Glimpses of Eternity.* Rider 2010
Osis, Karlis. *Deathbed Observations by Physicians and Nurses.* Parapsychology Foundation Inc. 1961
Sabom, Michael B. *Recollections of Death: A Medical Investigation of the Near-Death Experience.* Corgi Books 1982

Out of the Body Experiences (OBEs) and Astral Projection

Crookall, Robert, B.Sc., D.Sc., Ph.D. *The Study and Practise of Astral Projection.* Aquarian Press.1961
Fox, Oliver. *Astral Projection.* University Books 1962
Frost, Gavin & Yvonne. *Astral Travel.* Granada Publishing Ltd 1982
Martin, Anthony. *Understanding Astral Projection.* Aquarian Press 1990
Monroe, Robert A. *Journeys Out of the Body.* Corgi Books 1974

Muldoon, Sylvan & Carrington, Hereward. *The Projection of the Astral Body.* Rider 1974
Muldoon, Sylvan & Carrington Hereward. *The Phenomena of Astral Projection.* Rider 1989
Shirley, Ralph. *The Mystery of the Human Double.* Rider 1972

Reincarnation

Bowman, Carol. *Children's Past Lives.* Bantam Books (New York) 1998
Cerminara, Gina. *Many Mansions.* Neville Spearman 1983
Cockell, Jenny. *Yesterday's Children.* Piatkus 2001
Cockell, Jenny. *Past Lives, Future Lives.* Piatkus Books 1996
Fenwick, Peter & Elizabeth. *Past Lives.* The Berkley Publishing Group 1999
Fisher, Joe. *The Case for Reincarnation.* Diamond Books 1993
Grant, Joan & Kelsey, Denys. *Many Lifetimes.* Corgi Books 1976
Guirdham, Arthur. *The Cathars & Reincarnation.* C.W. Daniel Co. Ltd 1990
Hall, Judy. *Way of Reincarnation.* Thorsons 2001
Iverson, Jeffrey. *More Lives Than One.* Pan Books 1977
Leek, Sybil. *Reincarnation, the Second Chance.* Bantam Books 1975
Leininger, Bruce & Andrea. *Soul Survivor – The Reincarnation of a World War 2 Fighter Pilot.* Hay House 2009
Moss, Peter & Keeton, Joe. *Encounters With the Past.* Penguin Books 1981
Muller, Dr. Karl E. *Reincarnation – Based on Facts.* Psychic Press Ltd 1970
Rocha, Adriana & Jorde, Kristi. *A Child of Eternity.* Piatkus 1995
Ryall, Edward. *Second Time Round.* Neville Spearman 1974
Steiger, Brad. *You Will Live Again.* Dell Books 1978
Stemman, Roy. *Reincarnation: True Stories of Past Lives.* Piatkus 1997
Stevenson, Ian, M.D. *Twenty Cases Suggestive of Reincarnation.* University Press 1974
Stevenson, Ian, M.D. *Children Who Remember Previous Lives.* University Press 1987
Wambach, Helen, Ph.D. *Life Before Life.* Bantam Books (New York) 1979
Wambach, Helen, Ph.D. *Reliving Past Lives.* Arrow Books Ltd 1980
Weiss, Dr Brian. *Many Lives Many Masters.* Piatkus Books 1996
Weiss, Dr Brian. *Same Soul, Many Bodies.* Piatkus 2010
Whitton, Dr. Joel L., Ph.D. & Fisher, Joe. *Life Between Life.* Grafton Books 1988

General Reading

Capra, Fritjof. *The Tao of Physics: An Exploration of the Parallels Between Modern Physics and Eastern Mysticism.* Shambhala Publications, Inc. 1999

Emoto, Masaru. *The Hidden Messages in Water.* Beyond Words Publishing, Inc. 2004
Emoto, Masaru. *The True Power of Water.* Beyond Words Publishing, Inc. 2005
Esther de Boer. *The Mary Magdalene Cover-Up.* T & T Clark (Continuum) 2006
Evans-Wentz. *The Tibetan Book of the Dead.* Oxford University Press 1970
Faber-Kaiser. *Jesus Died in Kashmir.* Abacus Books 1976
Feeley, Michael & Sarah. *Beyond the Illusion – A Time of Awakening.* Sazmick Books 2011
Findlay, Arthur. *The Unfolding Universe.* Psychic Press 1973
Findlay, Arthur. *The Rock of Truth.* Rider & Co. 1933
Findlay, Arthur. *The Curse of Ignorance* (Two Volumes) Psychic Press Ltd 1948
Freke, Timothy & Gandy, Peter. *The Jesus Mysteries.* Thorsons 2000
Gaines, Ray. *Start Your Own Business.* Matador 2009
Good, Timothy. *Beyond Top Secret.* Sidgwick & Jackson Ltd 1987
Hassnain, Professor Fida. *A Search for the Historical Jesus.* Gateway Books 1994
Heinemann, Klaus & Ledwith Miceal. *The Orb Project.* Simon & Schuster 2007
Meyer, Marvin. *The Secret Gospels of Jesus.* Darton, Longman & Todd Ltd 2006
McQuitty, James. *Religion: Man's Insult to God.* Tarpon House Publishing 1999
Millman, Dan. *Way of the Peaceful Warrior.* H.J. Kramer Inc. (U.S.A.) 1984
Paine, Thomas. *The Age of Reason.* Prometheus Books 1984
Tompkins, Peter & Bird, Christopher. *The Secret Life of Plants.* Book Club Associates 1975
Trine, Ralph Waldo. *In Tune with the Infinite.* Bell & Hyman Ltd 1979
Wickland, Carl A., MD. *Thirty Years Among the Dead.* Spiritualist Press 1968
Whitman, John. *The Psychic Power of Plants.* Star Books 1975
Wood, David R. *Genisis – The First Book of Revelations.* The Baton Press 1985

Spiritual Philosophy

Besant, Annie. *The Ancient Wisdom.* The Theosophical Publishing House 1972
Brunton, Dr Paul. *What is Karma?* Larson Publications 1998

Brunton, Dr Paul. *The Wisdom of the Overself.* Samuel Weiser, Inc. 1994
Brunton, Dr Paul. *The Hidden Teaching Beyond Yoga.* Samuel Weiser 1991
Brunton, Dr Paul. *Discover Yourself.* Samuel Weiser 1983
Brunton, Dr Paul. *The Secret Path.* Rider 1977
Brunton, Dr Paul. *Quest of the Overself.* Century Hutchinson Ltd 1986
Brunton, Dr Paul. *The Notebooks of Paul Brunton* (various: Volumes 1 – 16) Larson Publications
The Paul Brunton Philosophic Foundation (PBPF) www.paulbrunton.org
Chopra, Deepak. *The Seven Spiritual Laws of Success.* Amber-Allen Publishing 1994
Dyer, Dr Wayne W. *Change Your Thoughts Change Your Life.* Hay House 2009
Humphreys, Christmas. *Karma and Rebirth.* Curzon Press 1994
Rama, Swami. *Living With the Himalayan Masters.* The Himalayan Institute Press 1999
Ramacharaka, Yogi. *Advanced Course in Yogi Philosophy and Oriental Occultism.* Fowler 1984
Yogananda, Paramahansa. *Autobiography of a Yogi.* Rider 1987

Those of us who refuse to read material that we think we might not agree with, are no better off than those who can't read at all.
T. K. Kennett

Useful Contact Details

Alcohol Problems:

Alcoholics Anonymous: Helpline 0845 769 7555

Al Anon (Family groups – self help fellowship for those who live with people who have a drink problem): Helpline 020 7403 0888
www.al.anonuk.org.uk

Drinkline: 0800 917 8282 [24 hrs]

National Association for Children of Alcoholics:
Helpline 0800 358 3456 E: helpline@nacoa.org.uk

The Linwood Group (Alcohol & Drug Treatment Centre):
0800 066 4173 www.thelinwoodgroup.co.uk

Alternative Health:

British Homeopathic Association
27A Devonshire Street
London
W1N 1RJ
020 7935 2163 (see area websites)

British Complementary Medicine Association
St Charles Hospital
Exmoor Street
London
W10 6DZ
0845 345 5977 (see area websites)

Bereavement:

Cruse Bereavement Care: 0870 167 1677
www.crusebereavementcare.org.uk

Child Death Helpline: 0800 282 986

Child Bereavement Charity (CBC): 01494 568900
www.childbereavement.org.uk

The Compassionate Friends (Support for bereaved parents by bereaved parents): Helpline 0845 123 2304

Cot Death Helpline: 020 7235 1721 [24 hrs]

Bereavement Advice Centre: Helpline: 0800 634 9494
www.bereavementadvice.org

www.bereavementinfo.com

Bullying:

School Bullying Helpline Website: www.pupiline.net

Kidscape (Helpline for parents of bullied children): 020 7730 3300
www.kidscape.org.uk

Childline: 0800 1111 [24 hrs] www.childline.org.uk

Workplace Bullying and School Bullying: www.bullyonline.org

Carers:

Helpline (Advice and information): 0808 808 7777

Child Abuse:

NSPCC (Child protection Helpline): 0800 800 5000 [24 hrs]
E: **help@nspcc.org.uk** www.nspcc.org.uk

ChildLine: 0800 1111 [24 hrs]

Crime:

Victim Support (for victims of crime): 0845 30 30 900

Cruelty to Animals:

RSPCA (National Cruelty Line): 08705 555 999 [24 hrs]
www.four-paws.org.uk

Debt Problems:

National Debtline: 0808 808 4000
www.nationaldebtline.co.uk

Consumer Credit Counselling Service: 0800 138 111 www.cccs.co.uk

PayPlan: 0800 280 2816 www.payplan.com

Citizens Advice Bureau: www.adviceguide.org.uk

Depression (see also Suicide):

The Human Givens Institute
Chalvington
East Sussex
BN27 3TD
01323 811662
www.hgi.org.uk E: hgi@humangivens.com

Domestic Violence:

Women's Aid Helpline: 08457 023 468 [24 hrs]
www.womensaid.org.uk E: info@womensaid.org.uk

Refuge (for women experiencing domestic violence): 0808 808 9999 [24 hrs]
www.refuge.org.uk E: info@refuge.org.uk

National Domestic Violence Helpline: 0808 2000 247 [24 hrs]

Respect: 0808 802 4040 E: info@respect.uk.net

Men Suffering Domestic Violence Helpline: 0808 801 0327
E: info@mensadvice.org.uk

Men's Advice Line and Enquiries (MALE): 01752 213535
www.ahimsa.org.uk E: enquiries@ahimsa.org.uk

Drug Problems:

National Drugs Helpline: 0800 776 600 [24hrs]

Narcotics Anonymous (UKNA): 0300 999 1212

Release (advice and help relating to drug abuse): 0845 450 0215 [24hrs]
E: ask@release.org.uk

Turning Point (advice and help relating to drug abuse): 0808 149 6345 [24hrs]

Elderly People:

Age Concern: 0800 009 966 www.ageuk.org.uk

Elder Abuse: 020 8765 7000 E: enquiries@elderabuse.org.uk

Seniorline: 0800 800 6565 [24hrs]

Gambling:

Gamblers Anonymous: 020 7384 3040

GamCare: Helpline 0845 6000 0133 E: info@gamcare.org.uk

Handicapped Children:

Down's Syndrome Association: 0845 230 0372 www.downs-syndrome.org.uk

Healing:

The National Federation of Spiritual Healers
Old Manor Farm Studios
Church Street
Sunbury - on -Thames
TW16 6RG
01932 783164 www.nfsh.org.uk

National Federation of Reiki Practitioners: 01264 791441

The Harry Edwards Spiritual Healing Sanctuary:
Burrows Lea
Hook Lane
Shere,
Guilford,
Surrey
GU5 9QG
01483 202054 www.sanctuary-burrowslea.org.uk E: info@burrowslea.org.uk

Meditation:

Brama Kumaris World Spiritual University
Global Co-operation House
65 Pound Lane
London
NW10 2HH
020 8727 3350 www.bkwsu.com

Brama Kumaris World Spiritual University
Global Retreat Centre
Nuneham Park
Nuneham Courtenay
Oxford
OX44 9PG
01865 343 551 www.bkwsu.com

The London Buddhist Centre
51 Roman Road
Bethnal Green
London
E2 0HU
020 8981 1225 www.lbc.org.uk E: info@lbc.org.uk

Meditation Centre & Japanese Garden
Buddha Maitreya (Koji Takeuchi)
'Pureland'
North Clifton
Nr. Newark
Nottingham
NG23 7AT
01777 228567 www.buddhamaitreya.co.uk

Mediums (booking, seminars, training courses, workshops, etc.):

The Spiritualist Association of Great Britain (SAGB)
11 Belgrave Road
London
SW1V 1RB
020 7931 6488 www.spiritualistassocoation.org.uk

The College of Psychic Studies
16 Queensbury Place
London
SW7 2EB
020 7589 3292   www.psychic-studies.org.uk

The Spiritualist National Union (SNU)
Redwoods
Stansted
Essex
CM24 8UD
01279 816 363   www. Snu.org.uk

Missing People:

National Missing Persons Helpline: 0500 700 700 [24hrs]

Rape and Sexual Abuse:

Rape Crisis Centre: 0808 802 9999

Sleep:

Sleep Problems: www.sleepnet.com

Smoking:

NHS Quit Smoking Helpline: 0800 169 0169   www.smokefree.nhs.uk

Quitline: 0800 002 200

Stillbirth:

Stillbirth and Neonatal Death Society (SANDS) Helpline: 020 7436 5881

Suicide (see also Depression):

Calm (Campaign Against Living Miserably) Helpline: 0800 58 58 58 (5pm – 3am 7 days) E: thehelpline@thecalmzone.net

PAPYRUS (Young suicide prevention charity): HopeLine UK: 0800 068 4141
www.papyrus-uk.org   E: admin@papyrus-uk.org

SOBS (Survivors of Bereavement by Suicide): 0844 561 6855 (9am – 9pm)
E: sobs.admin@care4free.net

Samaritans (Chronic depression, suicidal emotions, etc.): 08457 90 90 90 (24Hrs)
www.samaritans.org

Seniors' Activities

U3A (University of the Third Age)
The Old Municipal Buildings
19 East Street
Bromley
Kent
BR1 1QE
020 8466 6139 www.u3a.org.uk E: national.office@u3a.org.uk

Yoga (training and area classes, etc):

British Wheel of Yoga
25 Jermyn Street
Sleaford
Lincolnshire
NG34 7RU
01529 306851 www.bwy.org.uk E: office@bwy.org.uk

NB. All information correct at time of publication.

Index

Note: Page references to figures and illustrations are given in italics. Glossary entries are given in bold.

Index

Index

Index

Index

Index

Index

Index

Index

Index

Index

Index

Index

Index